Edward G. Bisone
Selected Works

Edward G. Bisone
Selected Works

A collection of the artist's paintings and drawings
as photographed by Leonard W. Kagelmacher

Published by
Buffalo Arts Publishing

Second Edition

Front cover: *North Light*, 2005, 26 x 20 inches
Back cover: *The Committee*, 1992, 27 x 21 inches

Buffalo Arts Publishing
Tonawanda, New York

ISBN 978-0-692-43404-8

Contents

Front cover: *North Light*, 2005, 26 x 20 inches
Back cover: *The Committee*, 1992, 27 x 21 inches

To those who seek to
understand life's mysteries
through pen and brush

Foreword

I don't recall the moment I first met Edward G. Bisone. I do know that he was one of the first artists to walk through the door of my gallery some thirty years ago, looking for a place to exhibit his work. At that time, there were not many opportunities for area artists, which is why Art Dialogue Gallery came into being. Eddie, as he is best known to his friends, is a major part of the gallery's success.

While Eddie resided for ten years in California, we corresponded regularly, and he often sent art works for me to display. When he returned to Western New York, our bond strengthened. Friend and mentor, he has become a major part of my life. I think the qualities I most admire in Eddie are his intellect and his sense of humor. We have shared secrets, laughed at each other's jokes and stories, have broken bread together and have compared notes on every subject from local politics to the most recent "topic of the day". Knowing Eddie has made my own art better. We often critiqued each other's work, but I know I was the one who benefitted most from our discussions, as I learned more about creating my art work by studying his.

This book reflects a small part of the gift of creativity given by this artist. Fortunately, Eddie documented many of the works he created; unfortunately, he has painted over some of the works represented here. I think this is because he tends to be his own worst critic. Although works were sometimes photographed, thereby preserving the image, he might later find that he was unhappy with the work and would gesso over it, preparing it for his next inspired creation.

A unique feature of this book is the text and poetry that accompany many of the images, transforming the book from a documented study of Bisone's work, to a resource giving the reader a more in-depth understanding of this brilliant artist.

I will always be grateful for having Eddie as an inspiration, a teacher and, most importantly, a friend. There is no other single person I have known who has influenced the direction of my own art work more than Edward G. Bisone.

Donald J. Siuta, Director
Art Dialogue Gallery
Buffalo, New York

Preface

Note concerning this publication: The present soft cover edition contains the same material, with minor formatting changes, as the collector's (first) edition published in February 2011. That volume was limited to 100 signed hard cover copies that quickly sold out. This second edition is in response to those who have expressed an interest in seeing the book and the many Bisone pieces presented in it, but did not have the opportunity to either view or purchase the first book.

LK

June, 2015

These pages contain 204 photographs of art works by Edward G. Bisone, a contemporary expressionist artist from Buffalo, NY. Over the past year, it has been my privilege and joy to study and photograph 775 paintings, drawings, and collages by Bisone, produced from 1964 to the present, to scan over 300 slides of his work, and to dialog with the artist himself. This activity and this book are components of a larger project to ensure that the collective works of Edward G. Bisone are recorded and made accessible to future generations.

I am not an art critic, and have not studied art formally. I do, however, know when a work of art speaks to me in a profound way. And that has happened on more than one occasion in the presence of Bisone's paintings. While I was, and continue to be, captivated by his work, it was the artist himself who inspired me to assemble this book.

My wife, Donna, and I met Bisone only a few years ago, when I decided to test the local art exhibition waters with my photographs. We learned then that Bisone was a volunteer docent nearly every Friday and Saturday at the Art Dialogue Gallery where I entered my first show. A slight, unassuming man, Edward Bisone had a way of making visitors, both newcomers and repeat customers of the gallery, feel quite at home. Local artists and collectors, and just friends of the gallery would come to view the exhibited art, of course; but just as likely they came to be engaged in stimulating conversation with Bisone on all sorts of subjects, some of it even about art!

Time and space have limited the number of images included in the book to a quarter of those I was able to photograph and scan, comprising, I hope, a representative cross-section of the artist's larger body of work. I've organized the works into chapters, representing categories of Bisone's art. The verbiage is scant, with brief introductory statements before chapters and selected paintings, as well as snippets of Don Scheller's poetry sprinkled among the images. This is by design, as I believe Bisone's paintings speak eloquently for themselves. In the end, the artist's paintings will stand in relation to each viewer's particular predilections.

Edward G. Bisone has exhibited internationally, but Western New York is where he is best known. My fervent hope is that this book will make Bisone's art more widely recognized and as appreciated by that wider audience as it is by his many local friends and fellow art lovers.

I'm grateful to Donald J. Siuta, director of the Art Dialogue Gallery in Buffalo, and founder of the Western New York Artists Group, for putting me in contact with collectors of Bisone's paintings and drawings, for making his gallery facilities available to me to photograph works brought in for that purpose, and for writing the Foreword for this book.

The Schellers have supported this effort in many ways. I thank Donald Scheller, Buffalo poet, artist and teacher, who generously provided writings for use in conjunction with selected images, as well as a personal essay on the artist, entitled "Eddie". Bonnie Scheller provided valuable assistance in proof reading the manuscript, for which I am most grateful. I would also like to express my gratitude to Dr. Jack Cichon for his encouragement along the way.

Many thanks go to the staff at the Burchfield-Penney Art Center for allowing me to review the hundreds of slides in their archives of Bisone's art. Several works included in this volume are from scans of those slides. Michael J. Beam, of the Castellani Art Museum at Niagara University, generously allowed me to use, in its entirety, the introduction to Bisone (titled here "About the Artist") that he wrote for a solo exhibition of the artist's paintings at the Castellani in 2005.

Collectors who have kindly permitted me to photograph their Bisone pieces include Len Biszkont and Dianne Hull, Sandra Clark, Mr. & Mrs. Mark A. Fennie, William Laurie, Claire Marrone, Gerald C. Mead Jr., Kenneth E. Peterson and Joy Stanli Pepper, Bonnie and Donald Scheller, Robert J. Seivert, Donald J. Siuta and Dr. John "Jack" Cichon, Michael Wood, and others who wish to remain anonymous.

Donna, affectionately dubbed "the Baroness" by Bisone, has been her usual encouraging self. Without my wife's patient assistance throughout this endeavor, and her numerous helpful suggestions, this work could not have been completed.

And lastly, I shall forever be grateful to the artist himself, Edward G. Bisone, for being my friend and consenting to this book.

Len Kagelmacher
February, 2011

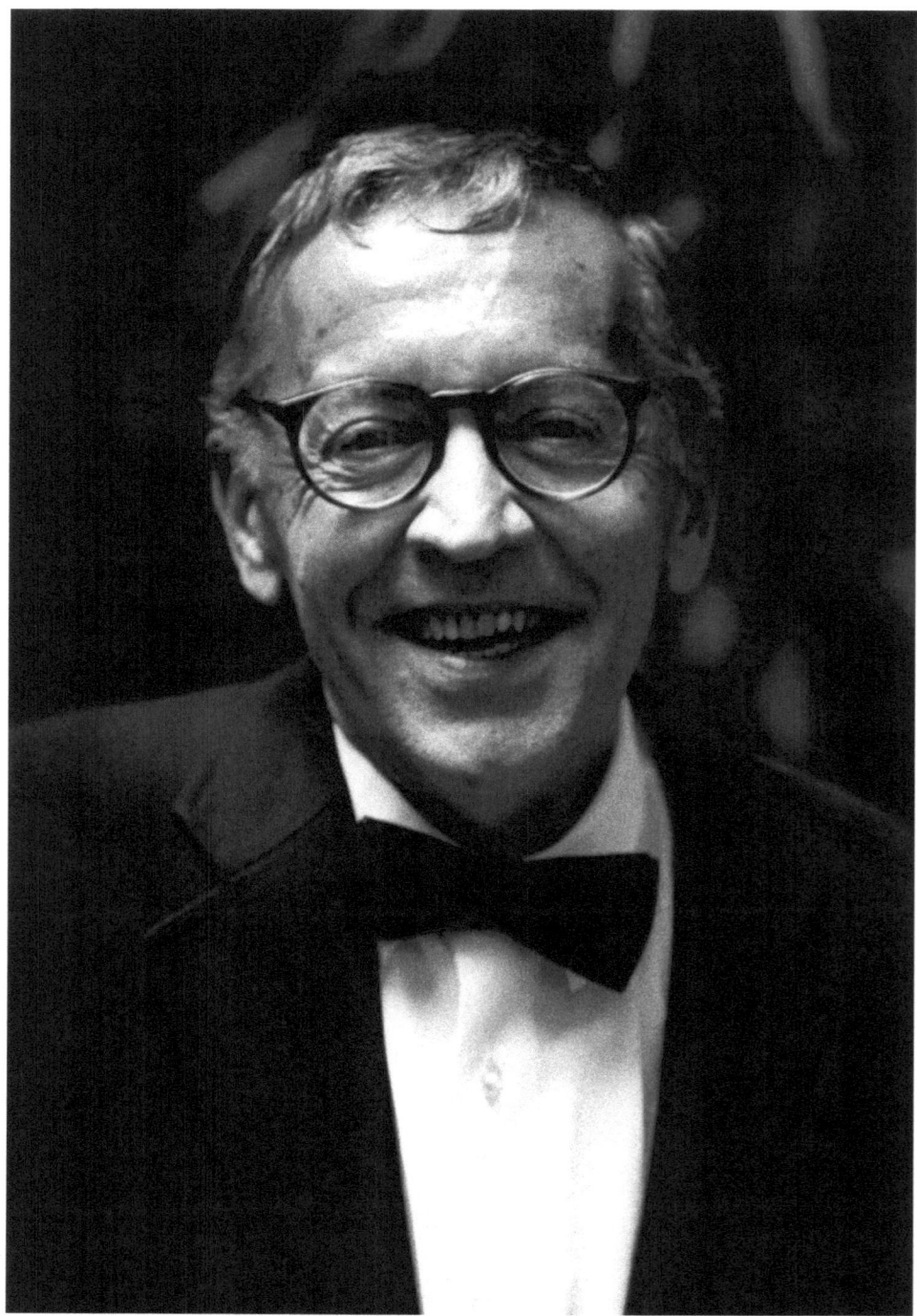

(ca1995, from the archives at the Burchfield Penney Art Center, Buffalo, NY)

Edward G. Bisone

About the Artist

Artist Statement: The two words that probably describe my interest in creating visual images during the last decade are "process" and "experimentation." Prior to that, my artwork was influenced by the Sturm und Drang movement of the Expressionists. I am also interested in the naiveté of the children's and outsider art.

The initial working of a piece is very often automatic. As the work progresses, more conscious attempts to externalize a feeling or an idea intrude. The process involves adding, subtracting, and altering elements, all in the name of "the search." The final result is sometimes totally unrelated to the original concept.

In Edward Bisone's commanding and poignant work, the paintings take on a life of their own, flowing in opaque and translucent washes of brown, white, red, and yellow. The end result is a shroud through which organically-derived shapes such as flowers, human faces, and amoeba-like characters come to life. These images float across the surface of the paper, at times pushed by brilliant fields of color, drawing the viewer into the picture. The use of abstract forms in these compositions owes much to the Surrealist language of Wassily Kandinsky, Joan Miro, Max Ernst, and Andre Masson. Edward Bisone is also greatly influenced by the Post Impressionists and Abstract Expressionists, identifying, in particular, with the work of Paul Cezanne and Richard Diebenkorn. Bisone's aversion to precision and mechanical aesthetics becomes apparent in his colored shapes and lines, arranged in vibrant, biomorphic compositions. The shapes suggest drama and movement. The intense, vivid colors create a sense of space, while the lines give the works an energy and visual tempo.

Bisone's work is a lyrical, symbolic reflection of his life journey. He describes his work as "a cerebral exploration of pictorial space." Adamantly disconnecting his present artwork from commentary on the values of the current zeitgeist, he concerns himself more with the "holistic spirituality of the metamorphosis and fragility time plays on life." In his words, the creation of art work is "a result of a necessity to create - plain and simple." Bisone works on approximately ten pieces simultaneously. Through strong sales and a committed regional collector base, Bisone never keeps a large inventory. Once a work leaves the "coop," as Bisone calls it, he is relieved of the responsibility for its development, akin to an offspring leaving the nest.

In the last decade, Bisone has developed an interest in spirituality, reflecting his idea that "art is influenced by something unexplainable. The more scientists and mathematicians discover, the more questions that arise - for example, the mystery of creation." Once in the home of one of his patrons, the work takes on its own life force. When he finds himself in that home and looking intently at the work he created, Bisone is always enlightened and surprised at its evolution.

In the end, Bisone finds that "the picture does all the work. Each artwork is a pause in time - a snapshot in the journey of life." He refers often to one of his favorite motivational quotes from Marcel Duchamp: "Artists rarely know what they are doing." Bisone follows this mantra to explore and experiment with a freedom and confidence not many artists achieve in a lifetime.

Michael J. Beam,
Curator of Exhibitions & Collections
Castellani Art Museum
Niagara University, NY

Note on the media used by Bisone in producing his paintings and drawings: Bisone's early works were frequently oil on canvas; e.g., *Buffalo City Scape*, page 3, or collage, as seen in *The Day He Died* on page 4. Others were charcoal drawings, as exemplified by *They Also Serve* and *Remembrances* on page 5. The artist's later works were predominantly mixed media or acrylic on paper, with some limited collage work.

Edward G. Bisone
Selected Works

"Eddie"

[**Author's note:** *I asked Don Scheller to write something about Bisone, reflecting the intellectual relationship between two artists who have known one another for many years. This is Scheller's contribution.* -LK]

Eddie Bisone - a little about art, based on conversations with him over the years.

We've talked for hours about art, what it may be, why we create, where it comes from, and the only thing we can say, with any certainty, is we do and don't know what it is, where it comes from or why we do what we do but because we can, we produce it.

Sometimes Eddie begins a piece only knowing he wants to use yellow and blue in it. Sometimes it's a vague notion, a word, the play of shadow or reflections on a wall, or a lost memory briefly resurfacing to tease before leaving again.

Sometimes we're in control of where the line goes, or think we are. Sometimes the important thing is to know when to relinquish control to let the line go where it will. Equally important is knowing when to stop, to walk away, because sometimes the piece is finished before we think it is.

Sometimes creating helps us to throw off, or sublimate the adult part of us, our too thinking and over thinking so much in life so we can return to the child in us, fascinated with the simplest, most ordinary objects around us. It simplifies vision, removes clutter and makes the work stronger. It's the "I never thought of looking at and seeing a bird, a flower, a wall, a person, like that before." It's so simple, yet it isn't. Eddie does this again and again in his art.

Sometimes a question has him begin, or a fascination with the materials or with process itself. Sometimes he knows a piece is good and lets it remain as is, finished. If not, perhaps it can be reworked, added to, subtracted from, saved. If not, nothing is so precious it can't be gessoed over and begun anew. I've been fortunate, have been able to see his pieces change from day to day until he feels they are finally finished.

Endings and beginnings are pretty much the same. The purpose of beginning presupposes an end, just as ending means you can begin anew. Sometimes we know more about beginning and ending than everything that occurs in between.

It's that mystery, the question of how and why, that keeps us searching and creating. And if the question is never answered, we keep creating because it amuses us, fascinates us, teases us, and we find it so fulfilling and worthwhile.

One quality in particular I admire in Eddie is, in our many conversations, in spite of our both knowing many long and art esoteric words, so much is very simply expressed with never a need to impress. This carries into his art as well, and is one of its greatest strengths, its vision, simplicity and clarity.

Don Scheller
October 16, 2010

1. From the Early Years

For the artist whose career spans several decades, it's no surprise that his earliest work is lost or forgotten. In Bisone's case, many of his pieces from the 1950's and 60's were simply painted over, to reuse material from art that no longer held interest for him. Others were sold or given away, but eventually lost in time.

We've attempted to find and photograph as many of Edward Bisone's early work, as possible. The oil painting on the facing page, the earliest thus photographed, depicts a mid-60's scene recognized by any Buffalo native, showing the twin statues atop the Liberty Bank building in the upper right, among other locally familiar landmarks.

does world exist
outside of my mind? It's gone
when I close my eyes

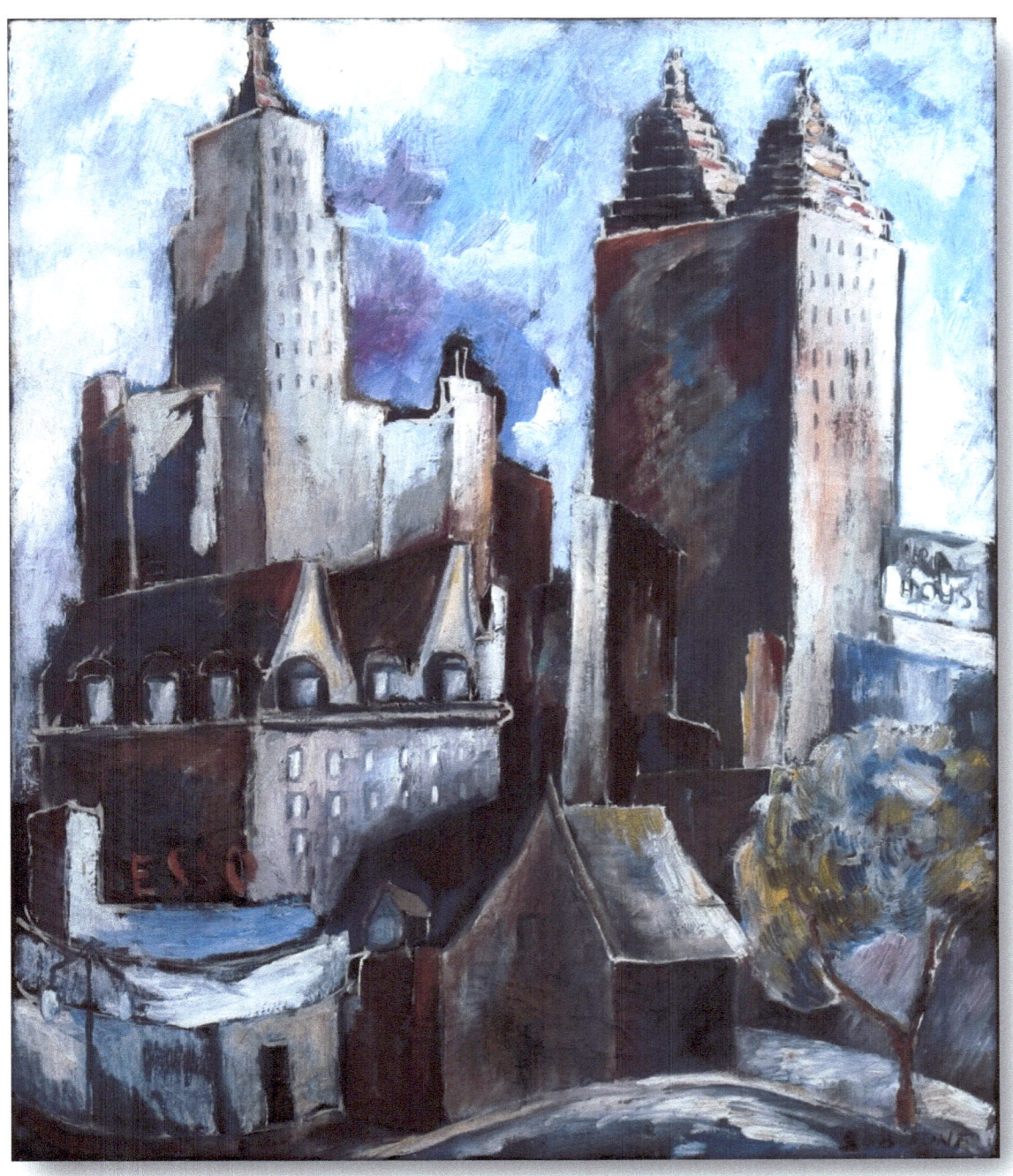

Buffalo City Scape, ca1964, 42 x 36 inches

the beginning of
     the end or the end of the
          beginning; which is...?

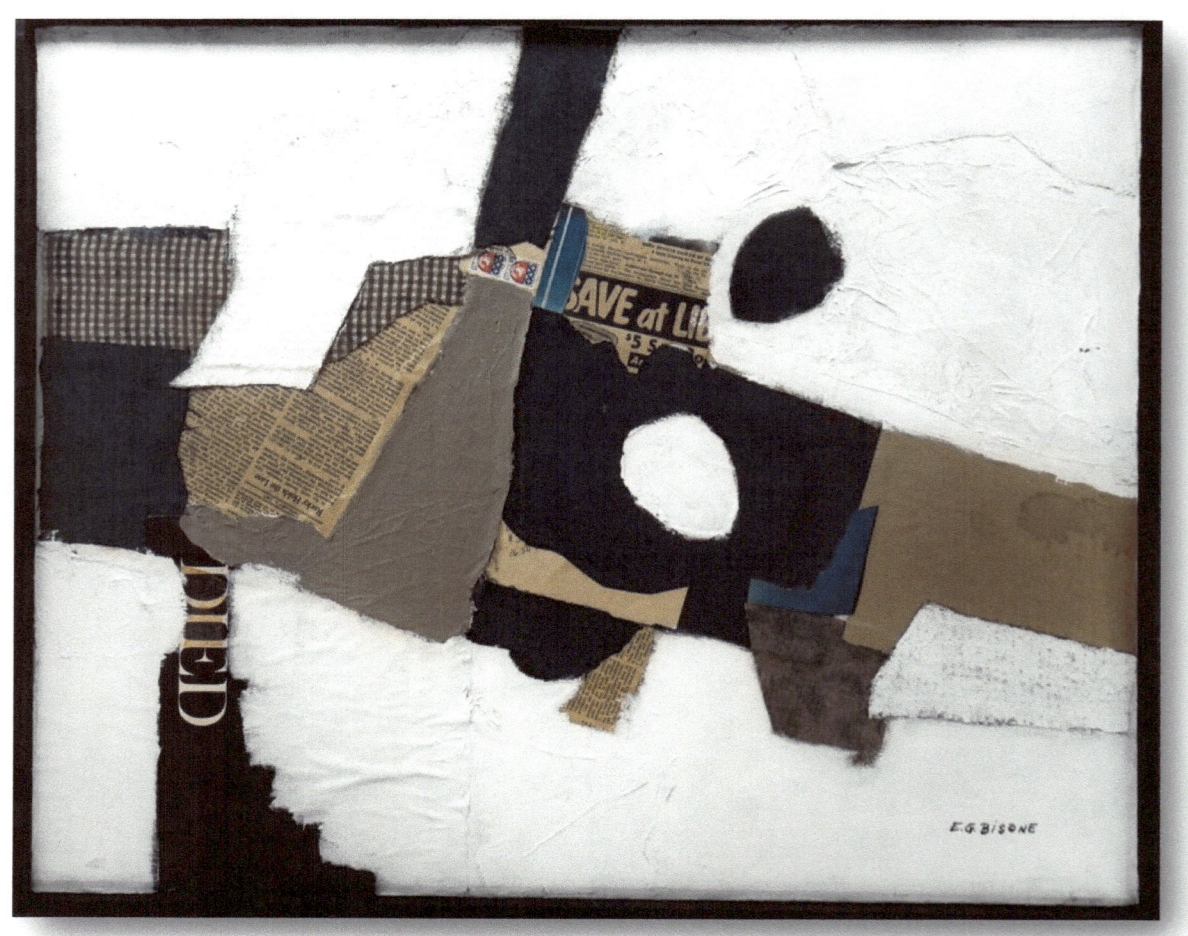

The Day He Died, 1969, 27.25 x 30 inches

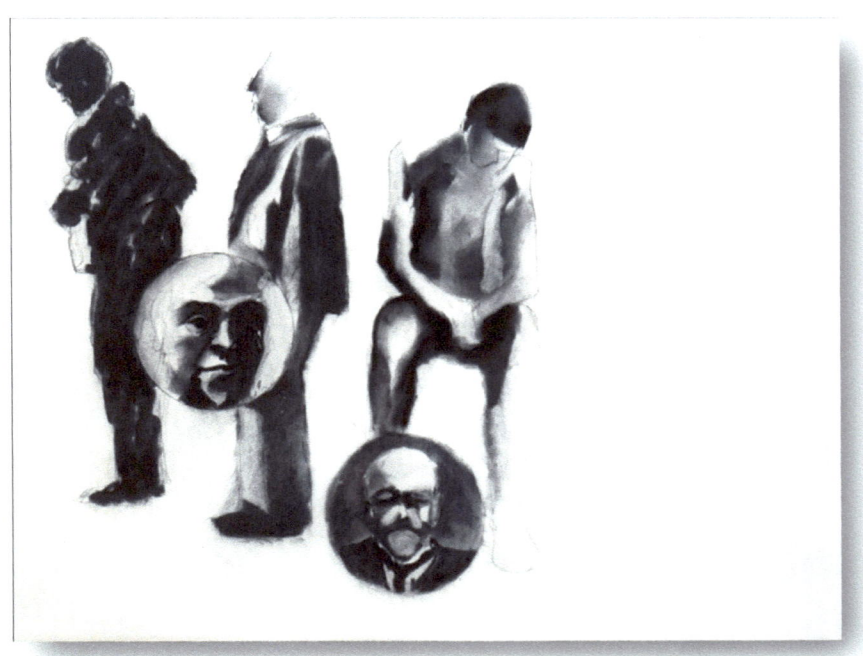

They Also Serve, ca1970, 24 x 32 inches

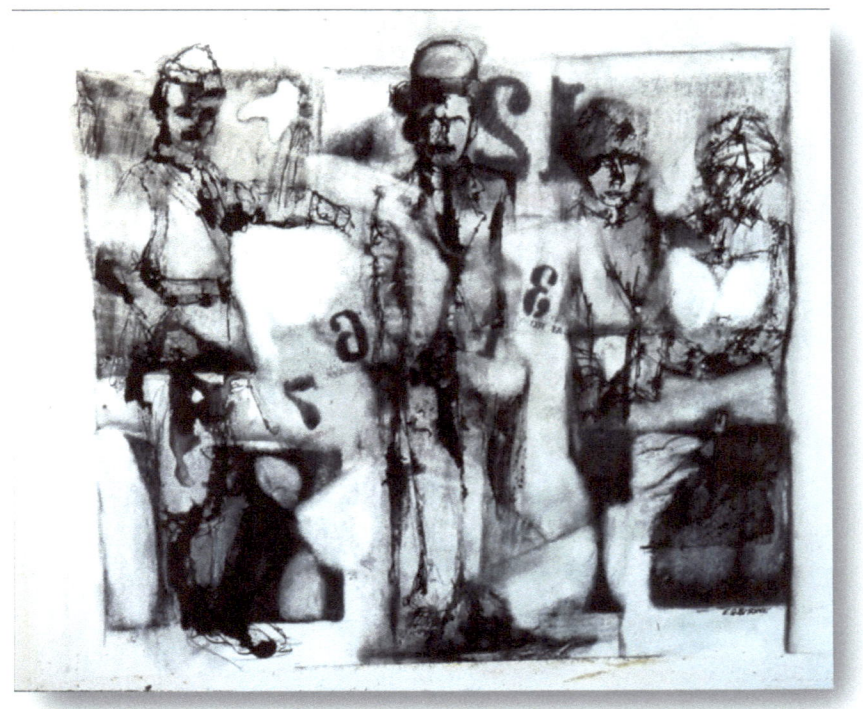

Remembrances, 1984, 24 x 30 inches

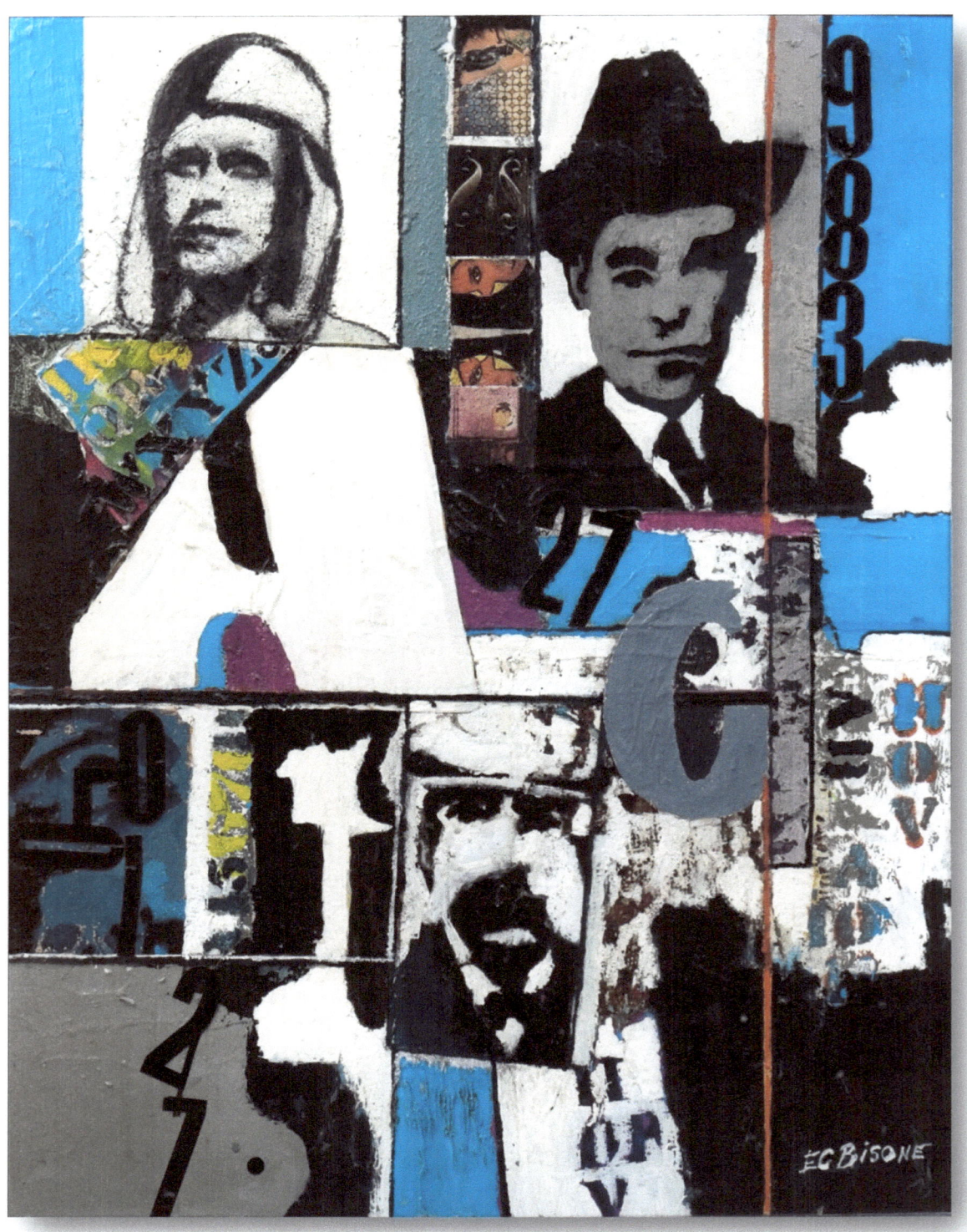

The Immigrants, 1979, 36 x 28 inches

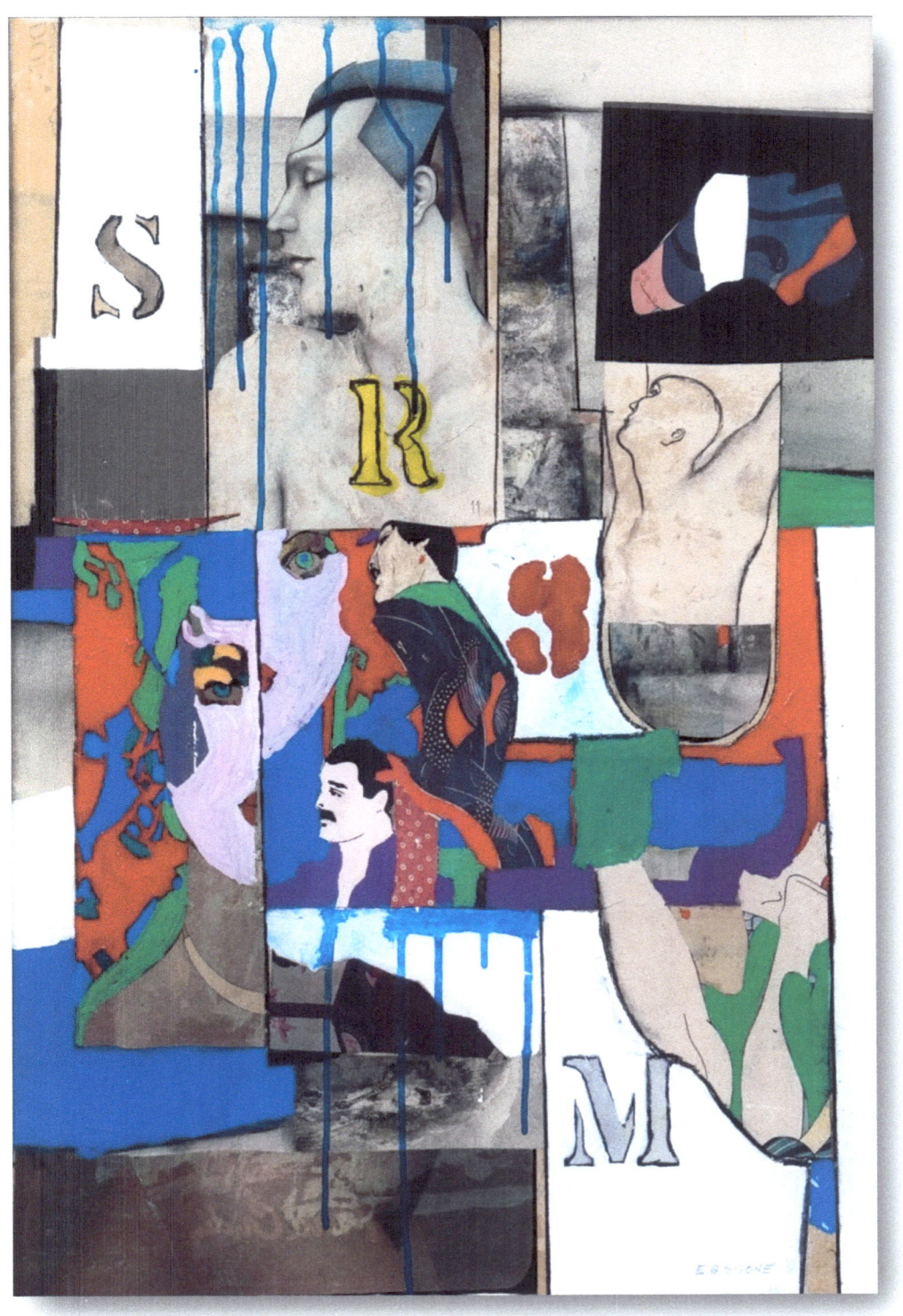

Go-Go Again Gaugin, 1979, 36 x 24 inches

2. Alienation

At the end of the day, aren't we all, as the artist states, "...sentenced to solitary confinement for life"? We may relate and participate in social life, – often to great enjoyment, but aren't we ultimately left alone to confront our own personal existential angst?

"In Custody" was painted in 1981, and featured on the cover of *The Witness Magazine* in 1982. The image, as shown on the following page, was scanned from a slide maintained in a collection of Bisone slides at the Burchfield-Penney Art Center.

to see beyond

what is easily seen, then

to see within

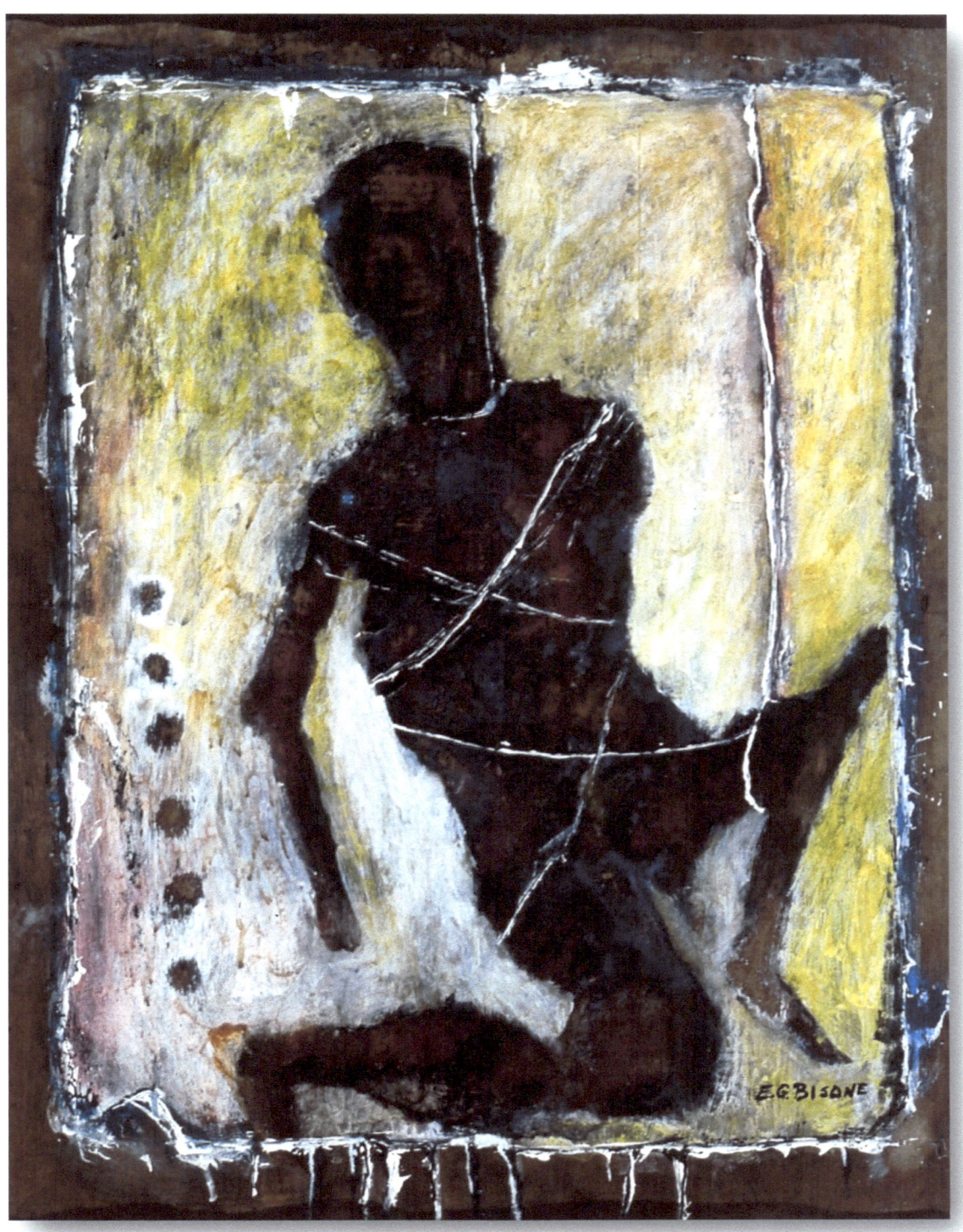

In Custody, 1981, 30 x 22 inches

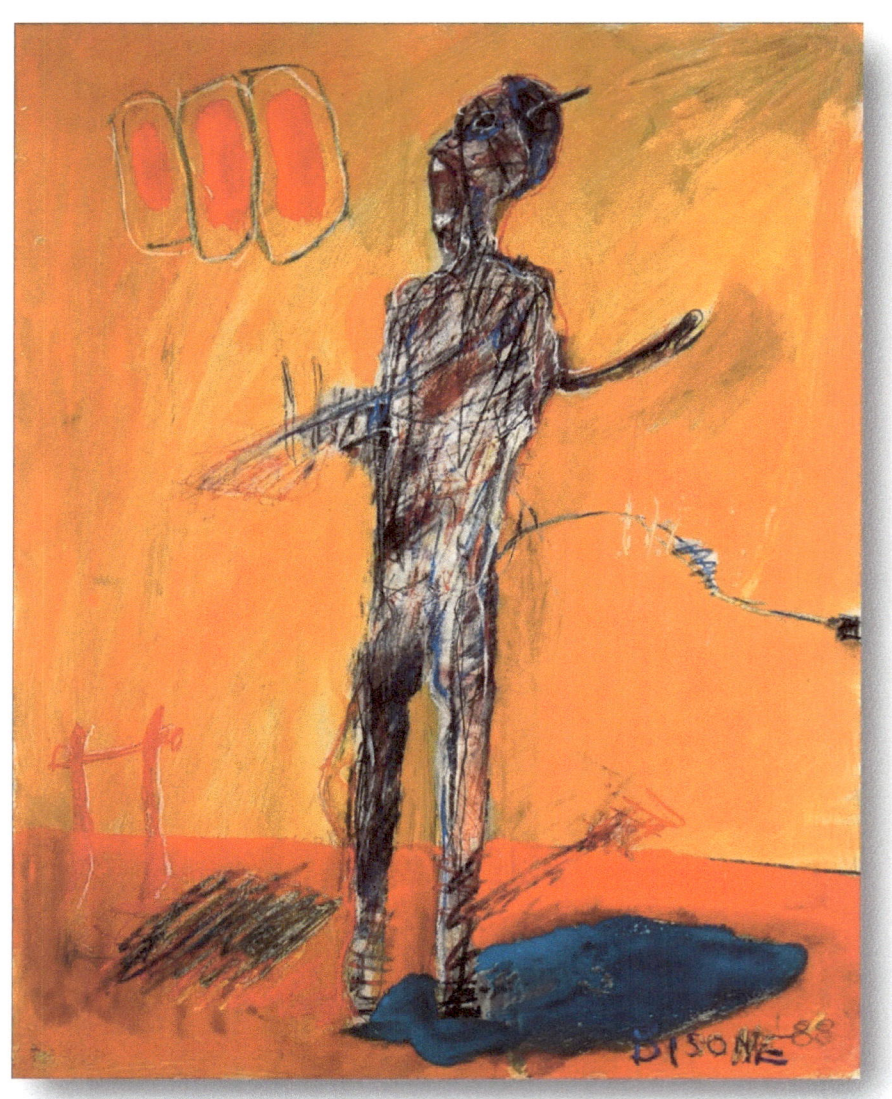

Demagogue, 1988, 27.75 x 22 inches

what comes from within,

what comes from without? can you

tell the difference?

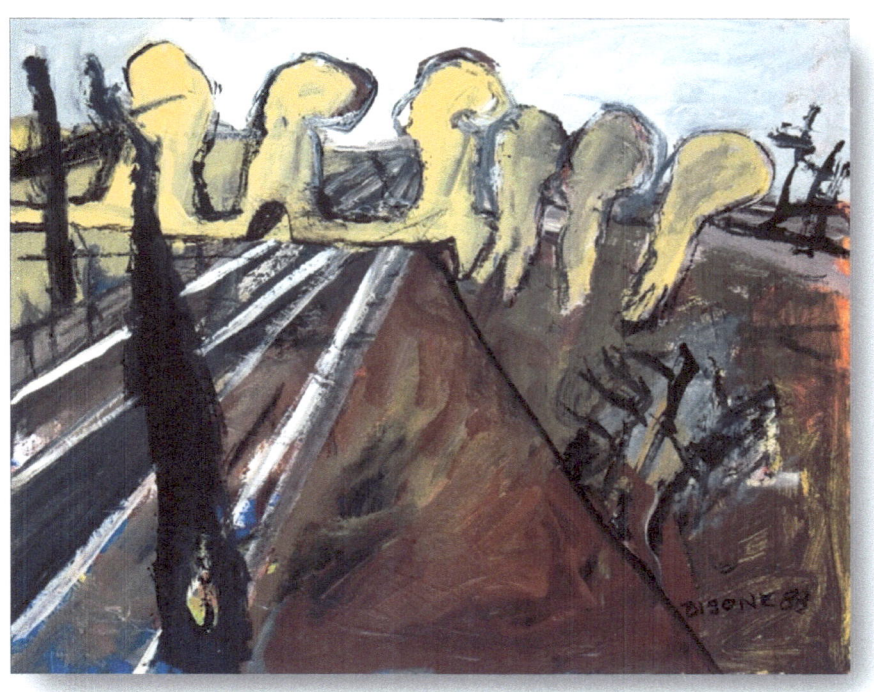

No Man's Land I, 1988, 22 x 28 inches

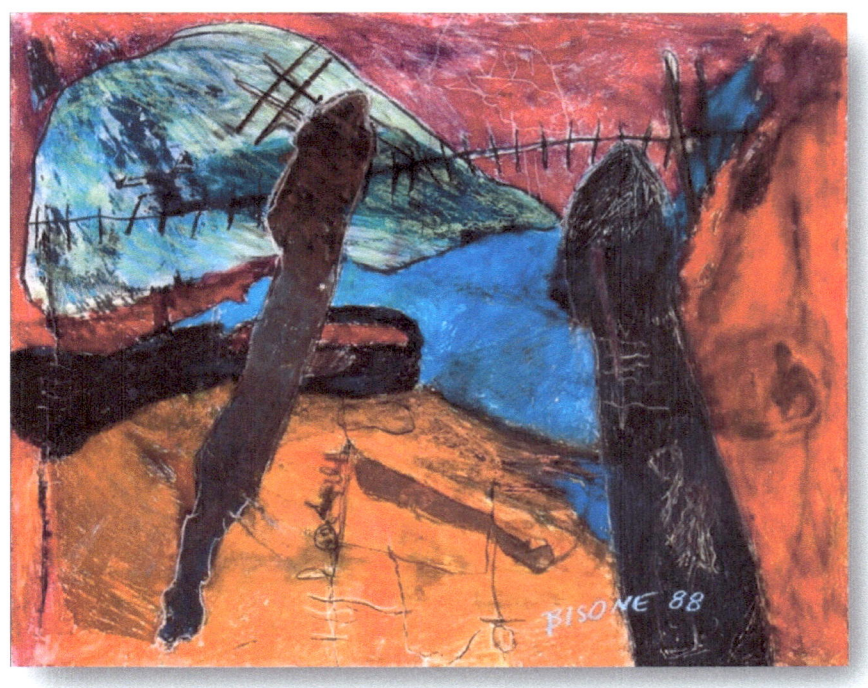

No Man's Land II, 1988, 22 x 28 inches

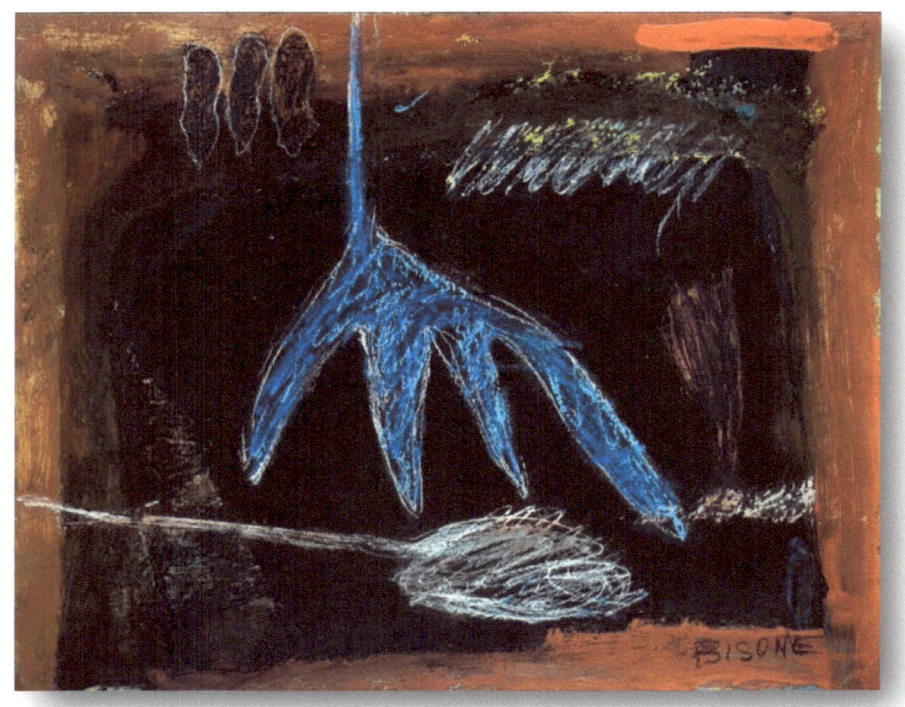

No Man's Land III, 1988, 22 x 27.75 inches

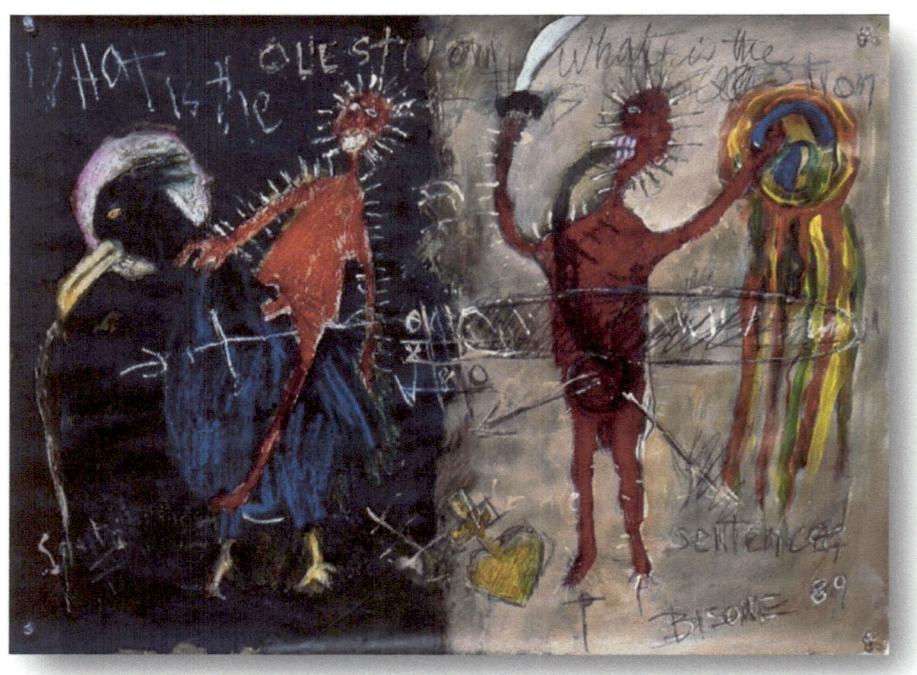

Nightmare, 1989, 22 x 28 inches

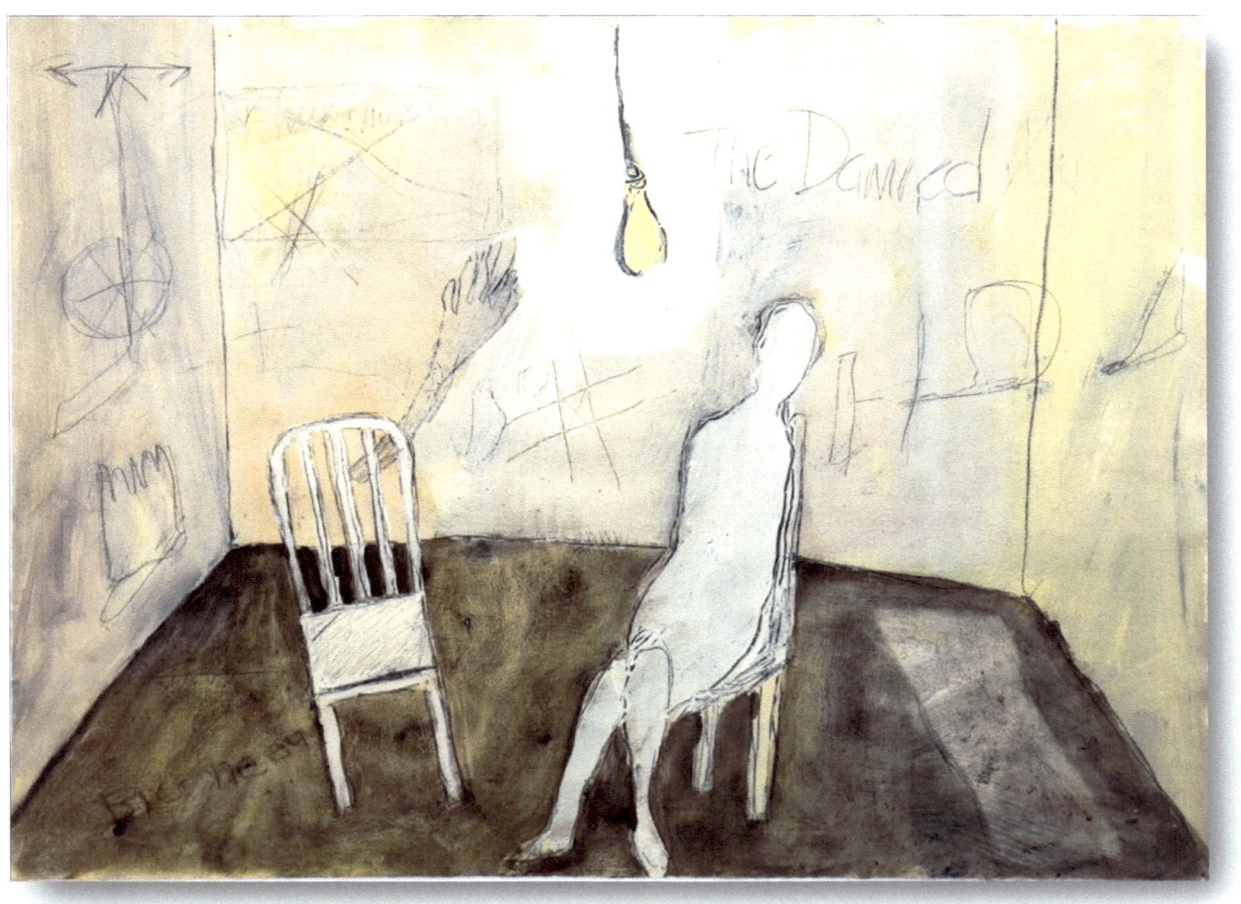

The Damned, 1989, 22 x 30 inches

most limits are

limiting only if you

don't go beyond them

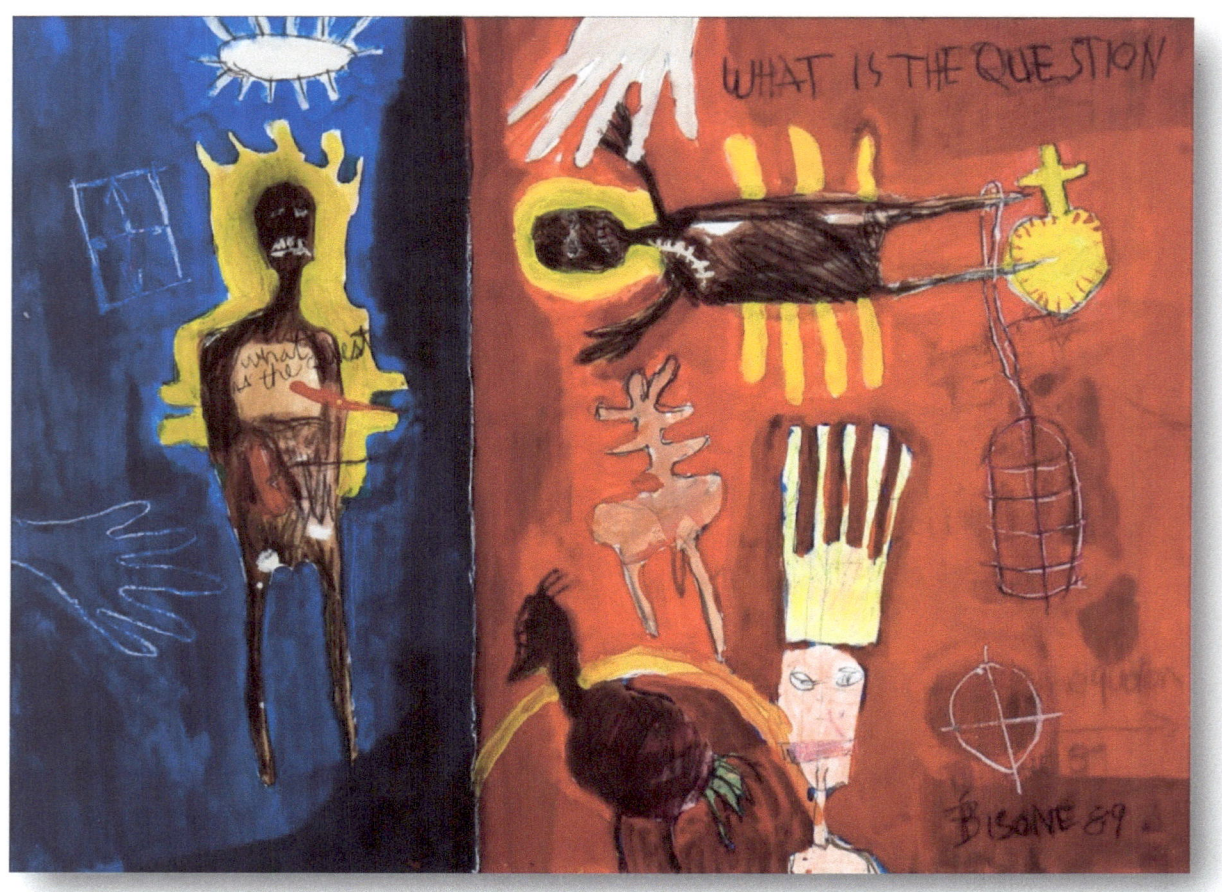

What is the Question Series I, 1989, 22 x 30 inches

some questions are asked
not for answers but to
excite the mind

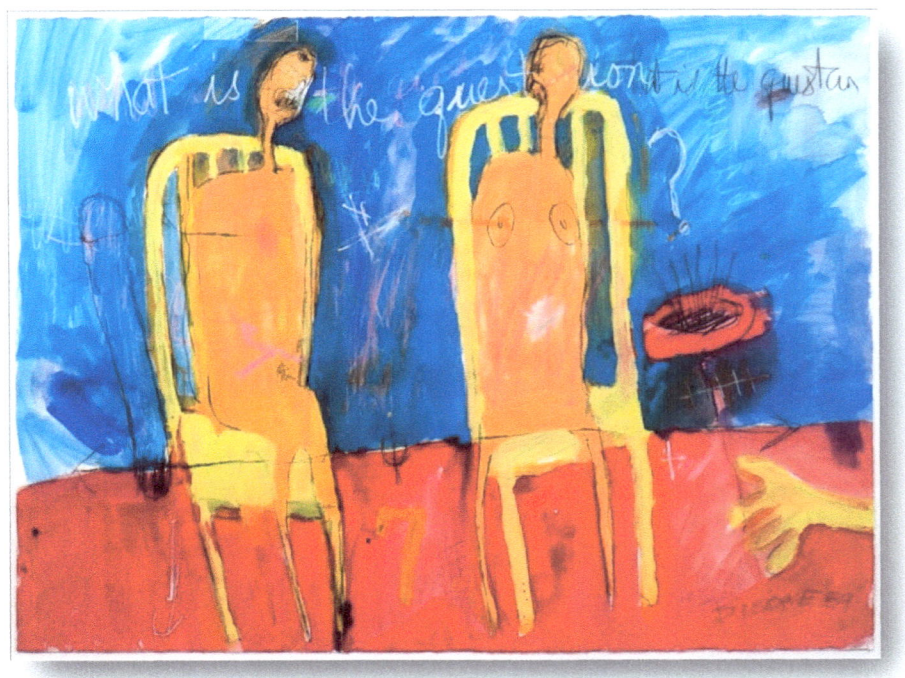

What is the Question Series II, 1989, 23 x 30.5 inches

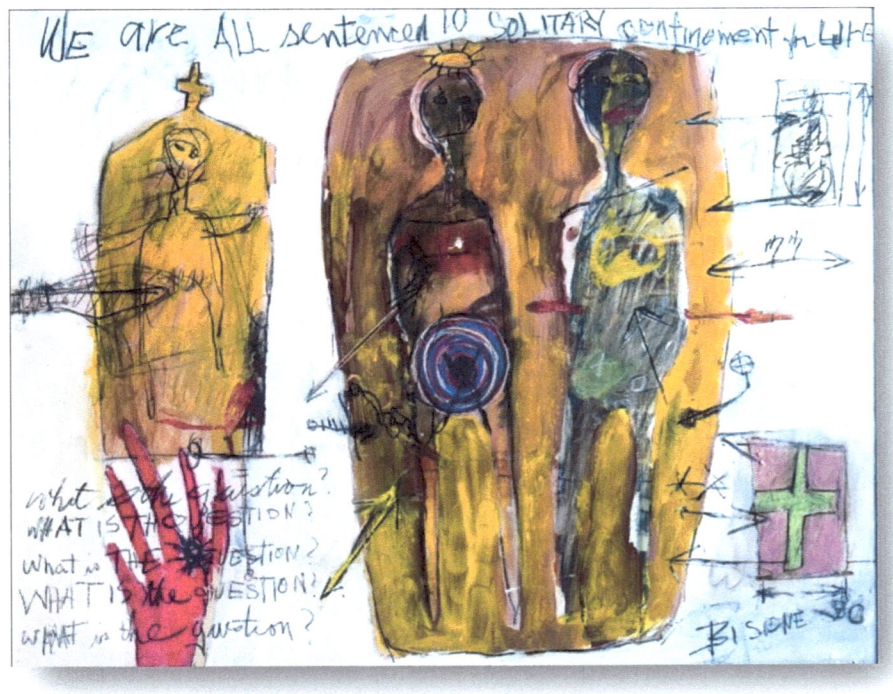

Confinement Series I, 1990, 22 x 30 inches

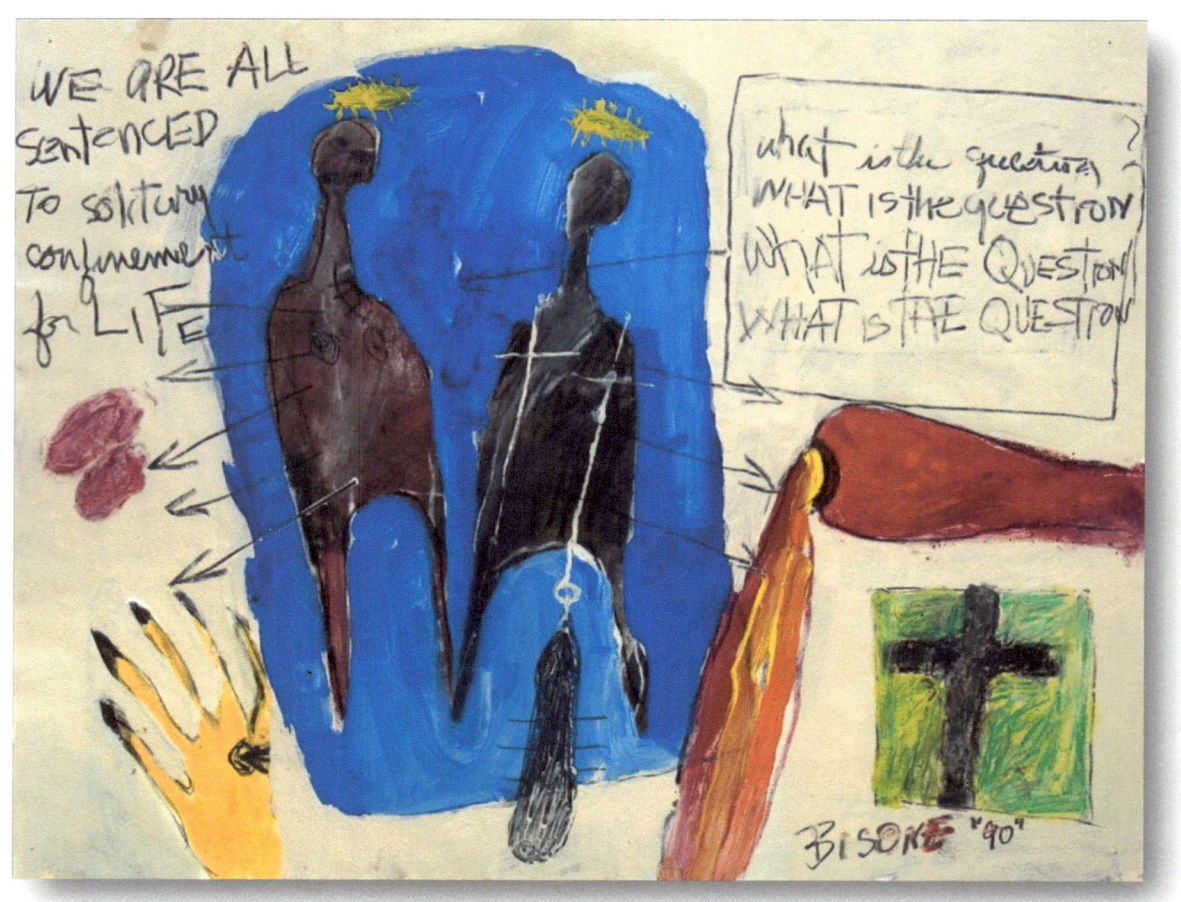

Confinement Series II, 1990, 19.5 x 25.25 inches

always the questions
and questioning the questions,
were answers given?

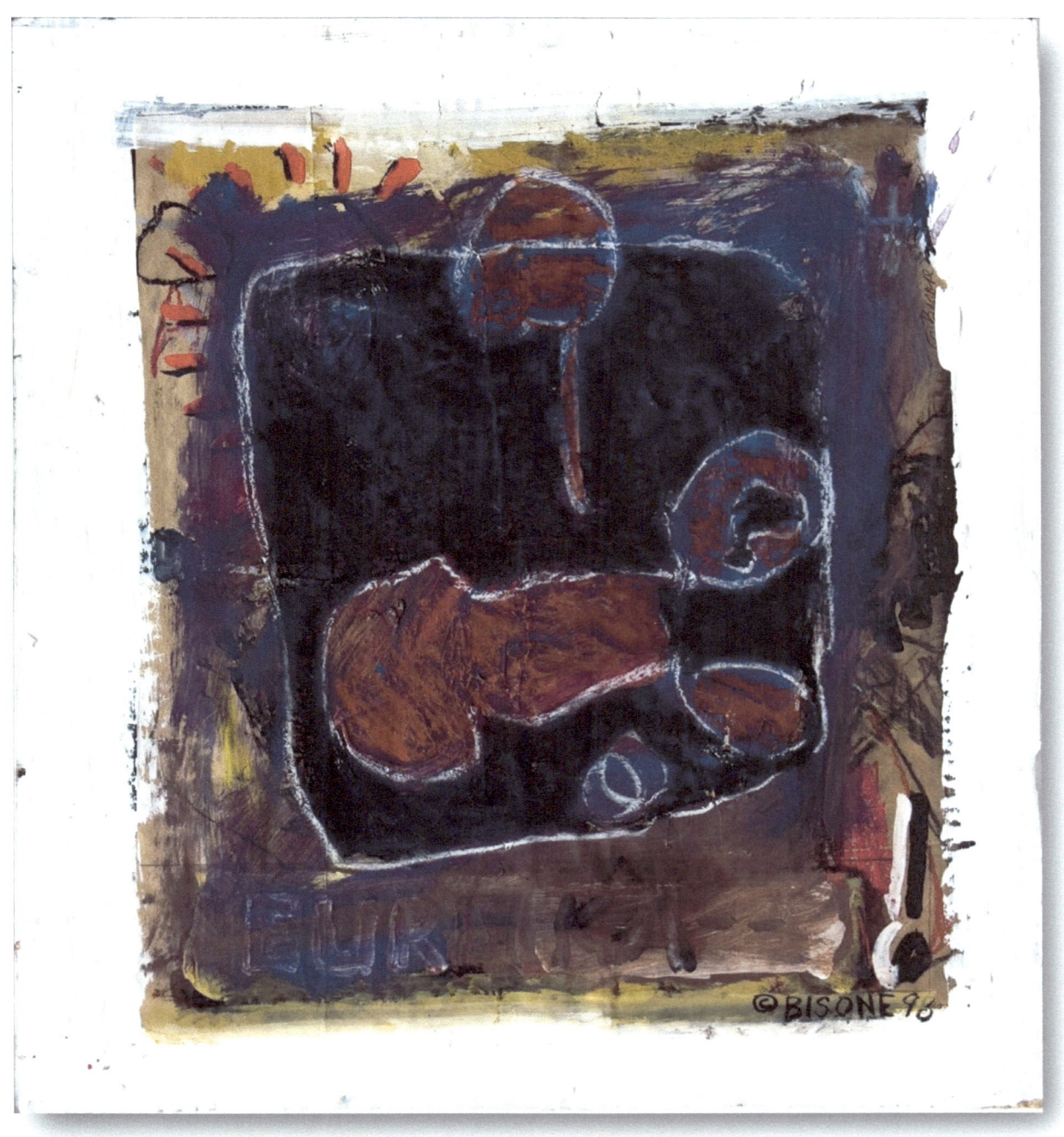

Imprisoned Boxer, 1998, 18.5 x 20 inches

3. Perilous Journey

The wagon wheels and stick figures of Bisone's 1998 Perilous Journey series are reminders of the Kindertransport that carried 10,000 Jewish children from Germany, Austria, Czechoslovakia, and Poland to Great Britain, in pursuit of their freedom in 1939. There's sadness in these paintings.

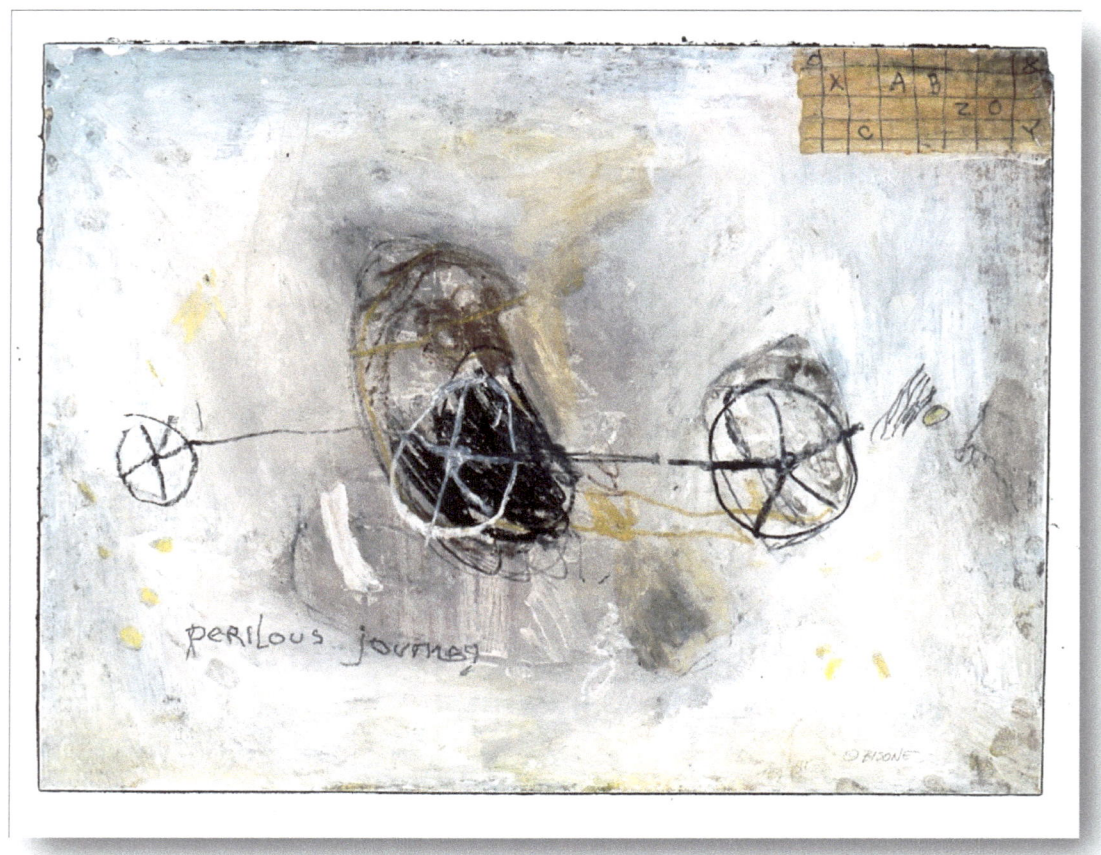

Perilous Journey #4, 1998, 19 x 25 inches

once conscious of,

how do we return to not

being conscious of?

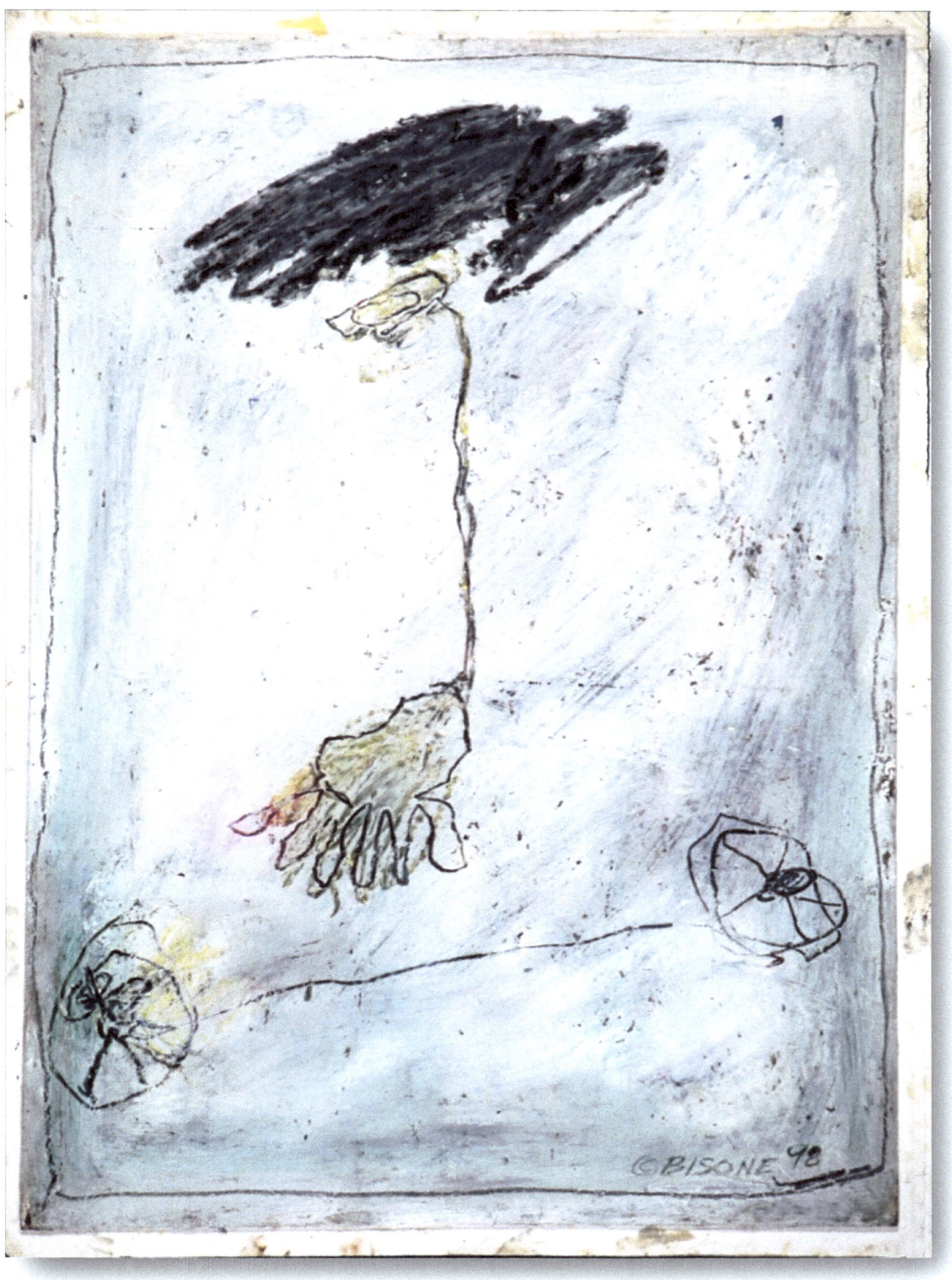

Perilous Journey #6, 1998, 14.5 x 10.75 inches

Edward G. Bisone

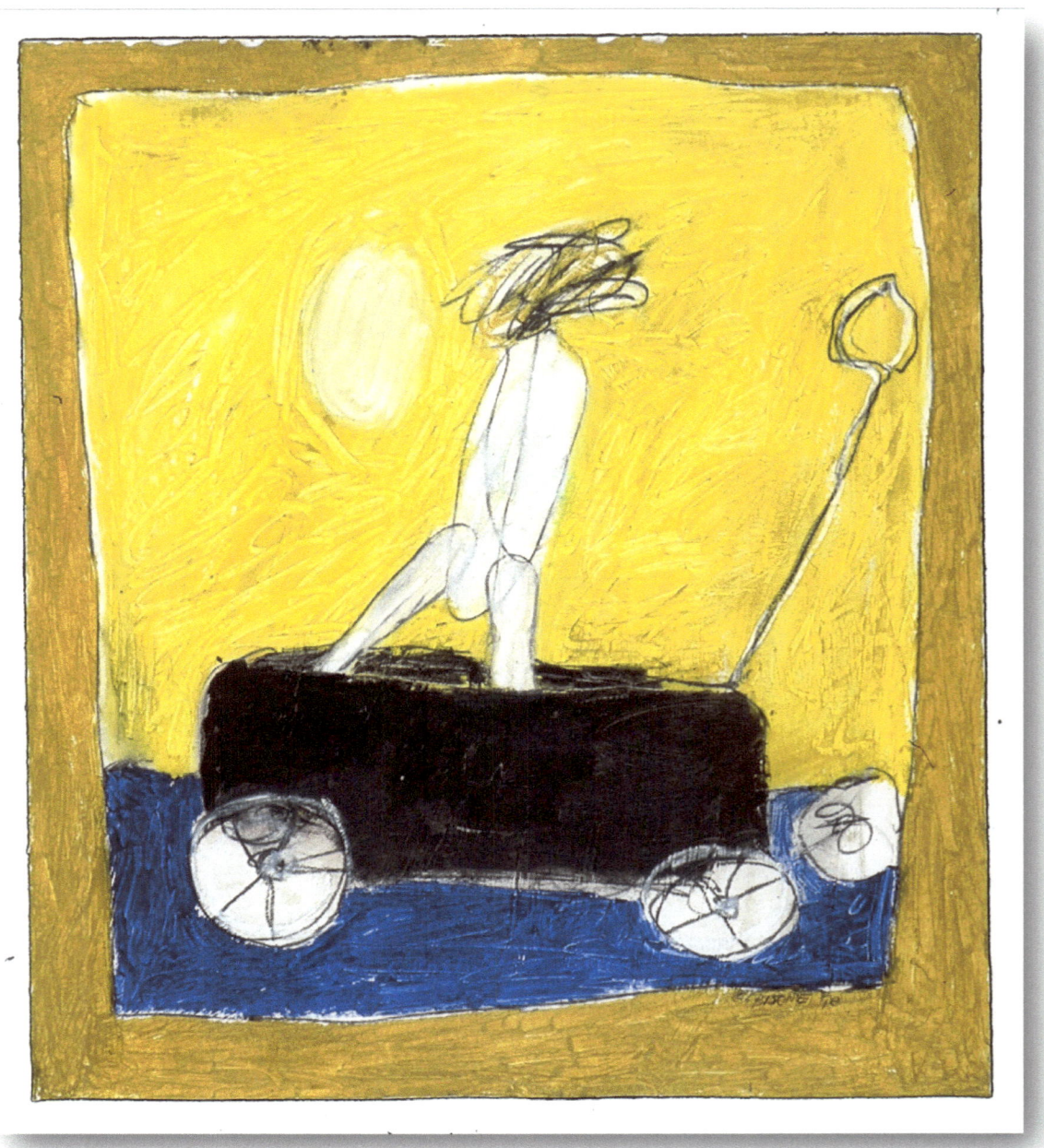

Perilous Journey #10, 1998, 18 x 14 inches

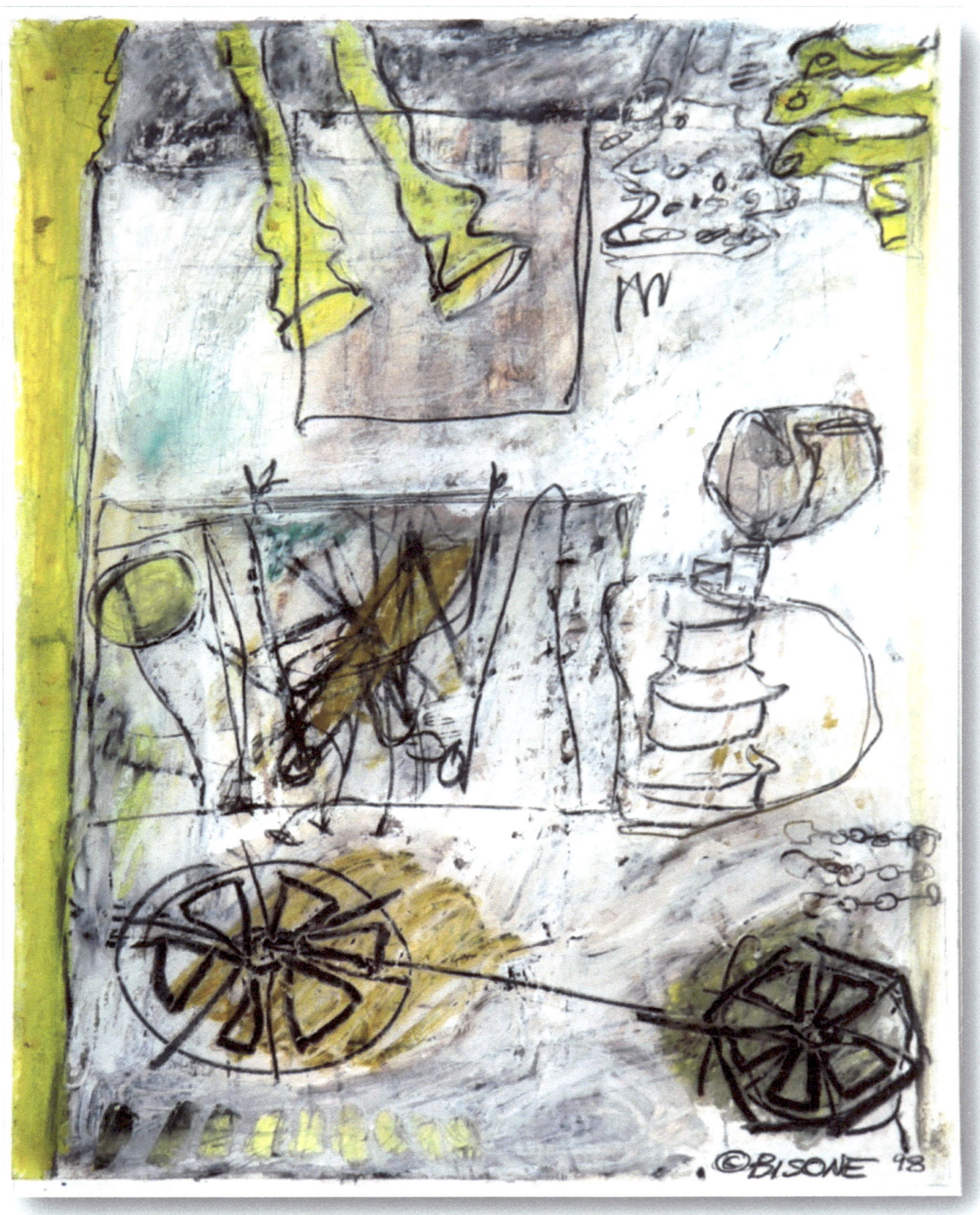

Perilous Journey (a), 1998, 11 x 8.75 inches

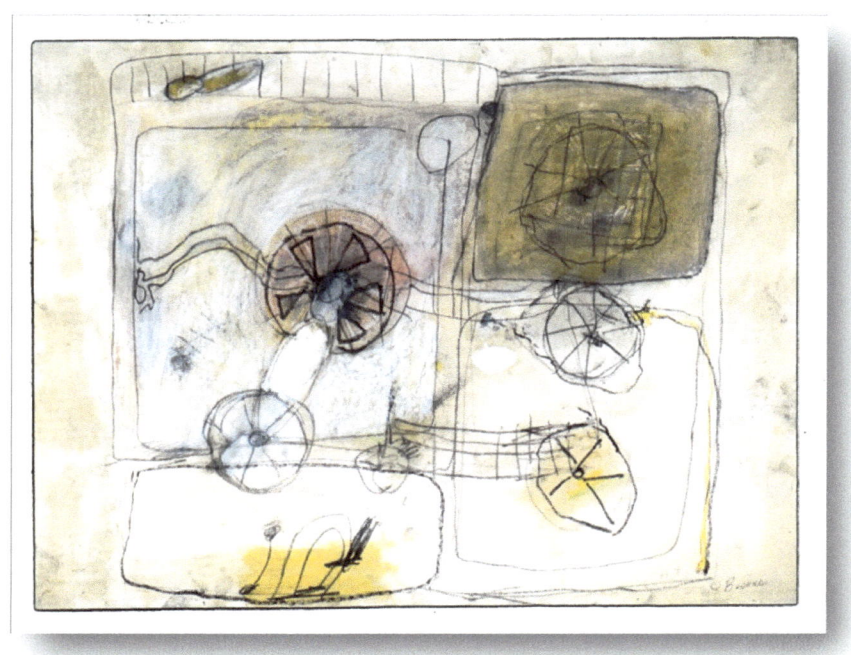

Perilous Journey #5, 1998, 18 x 24 inches

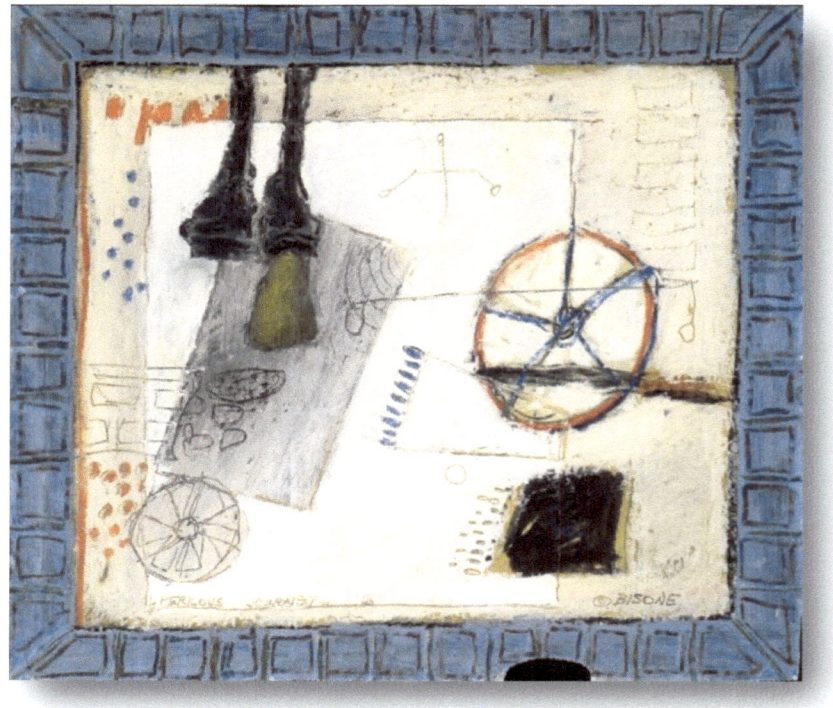

Perilous Journey #8, 1998, 16 x 18.5 inches

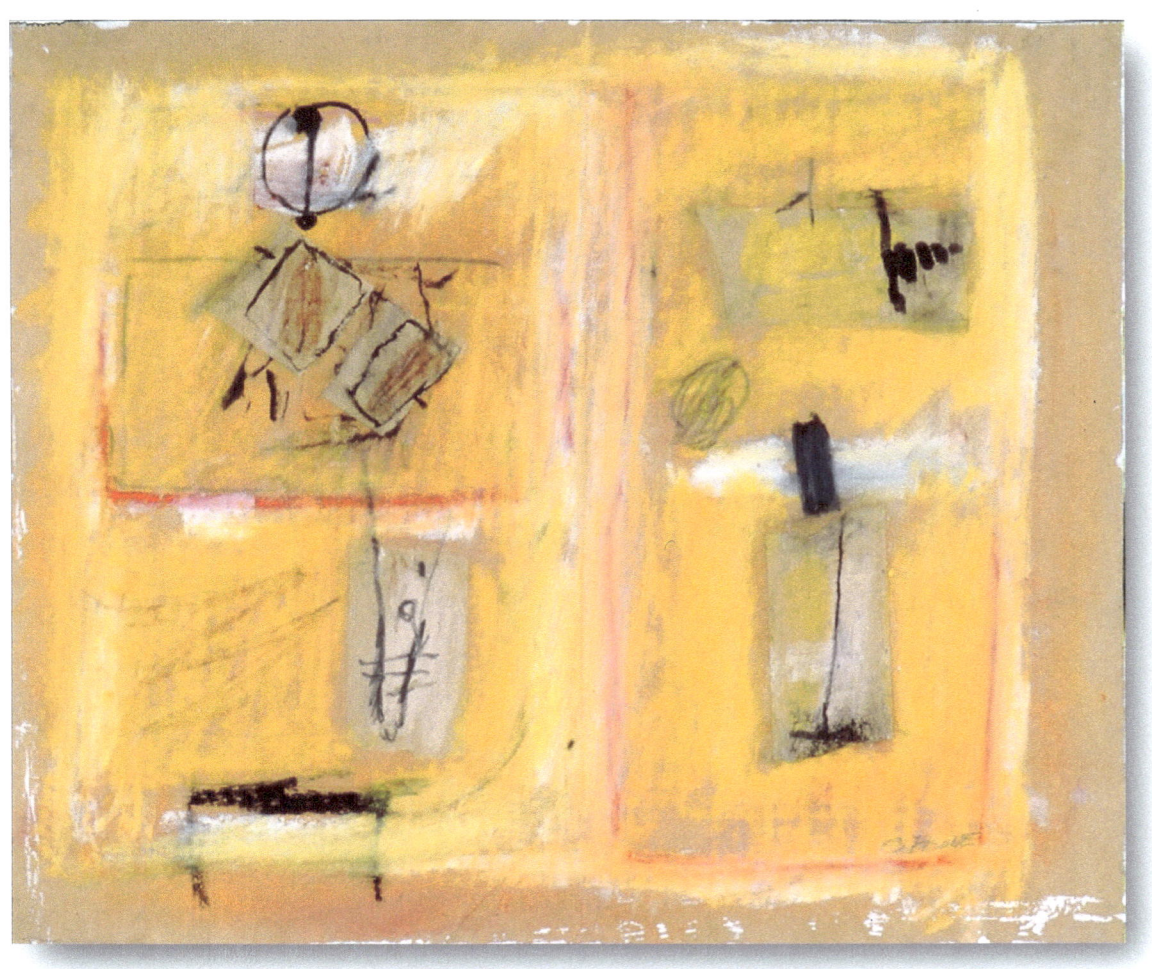

Perilous Journey #9, 1998, 16 x 18.75 inches

to see more
        than is shown, learn to see
                both through and beyond

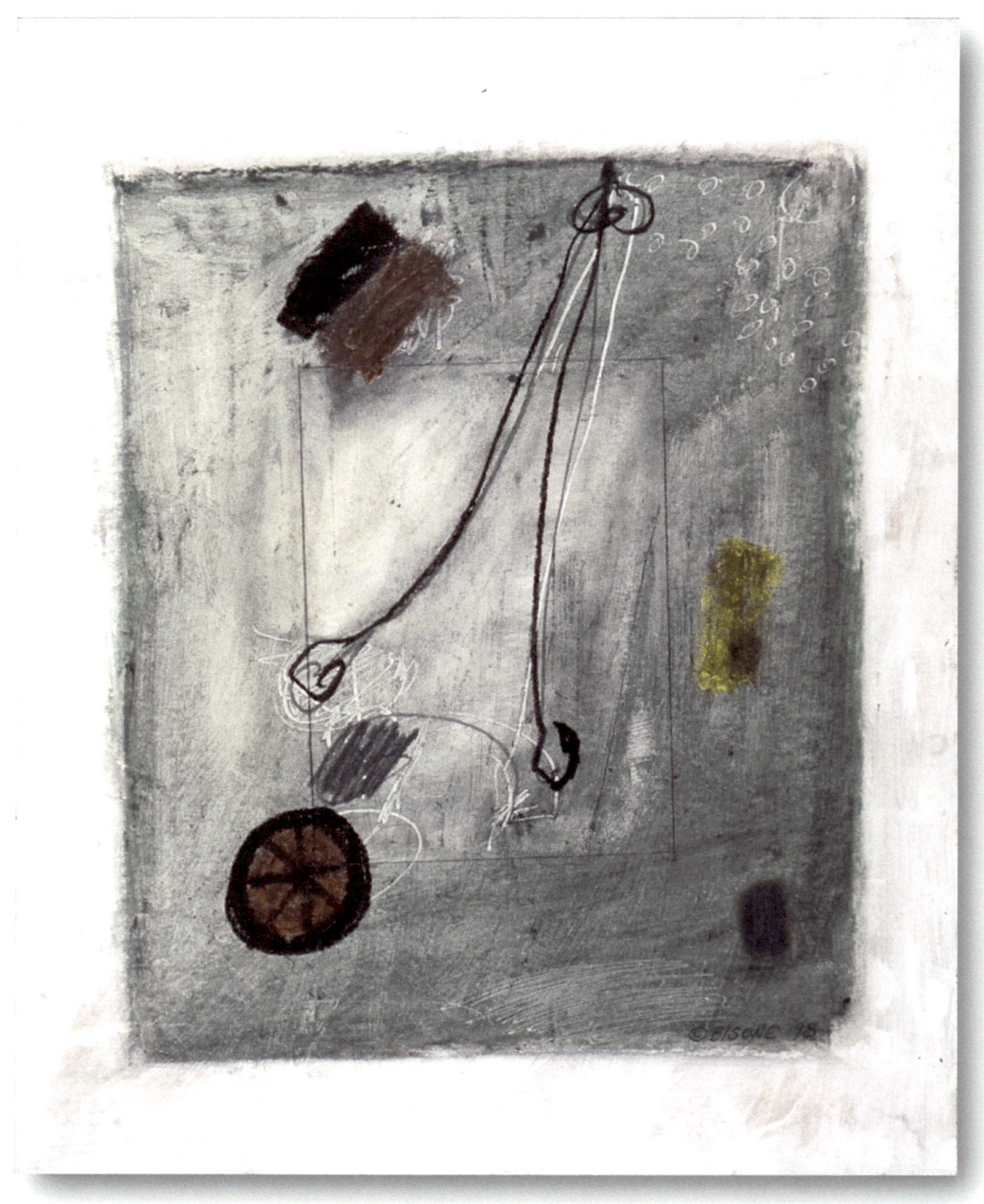

Perilous Journey (b), 1998, 24.75 x 20 inches

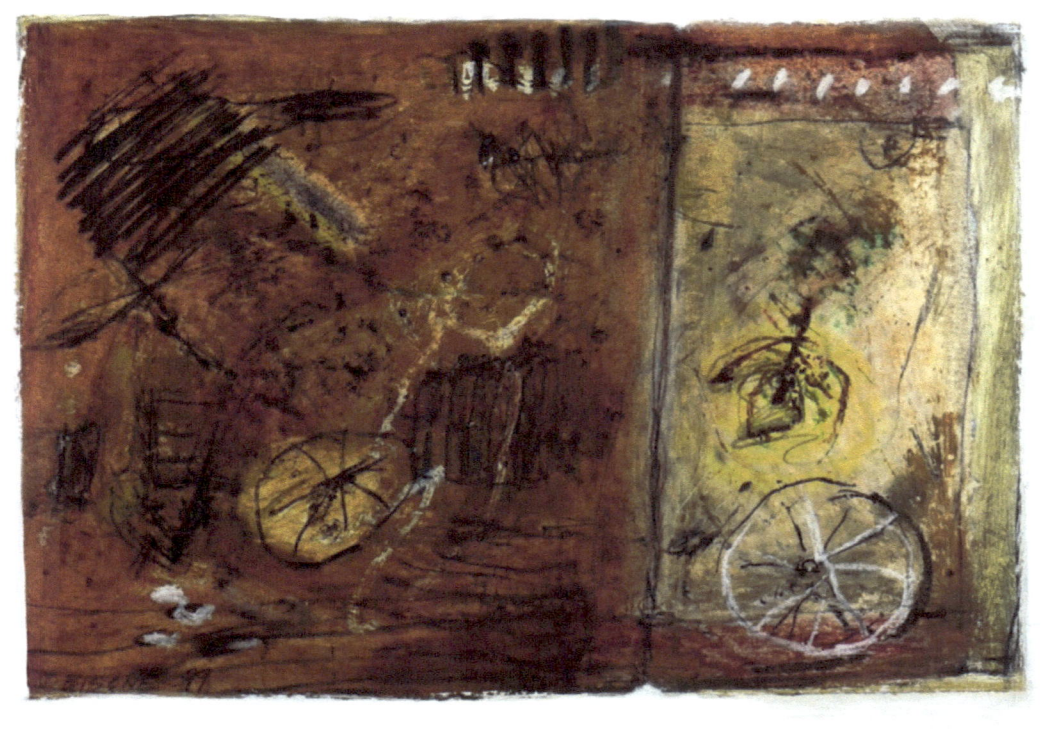

Perilous Journey Part II, 1999, 10 x 14 inches

making sense of...
        isn't always possible
                when creating art

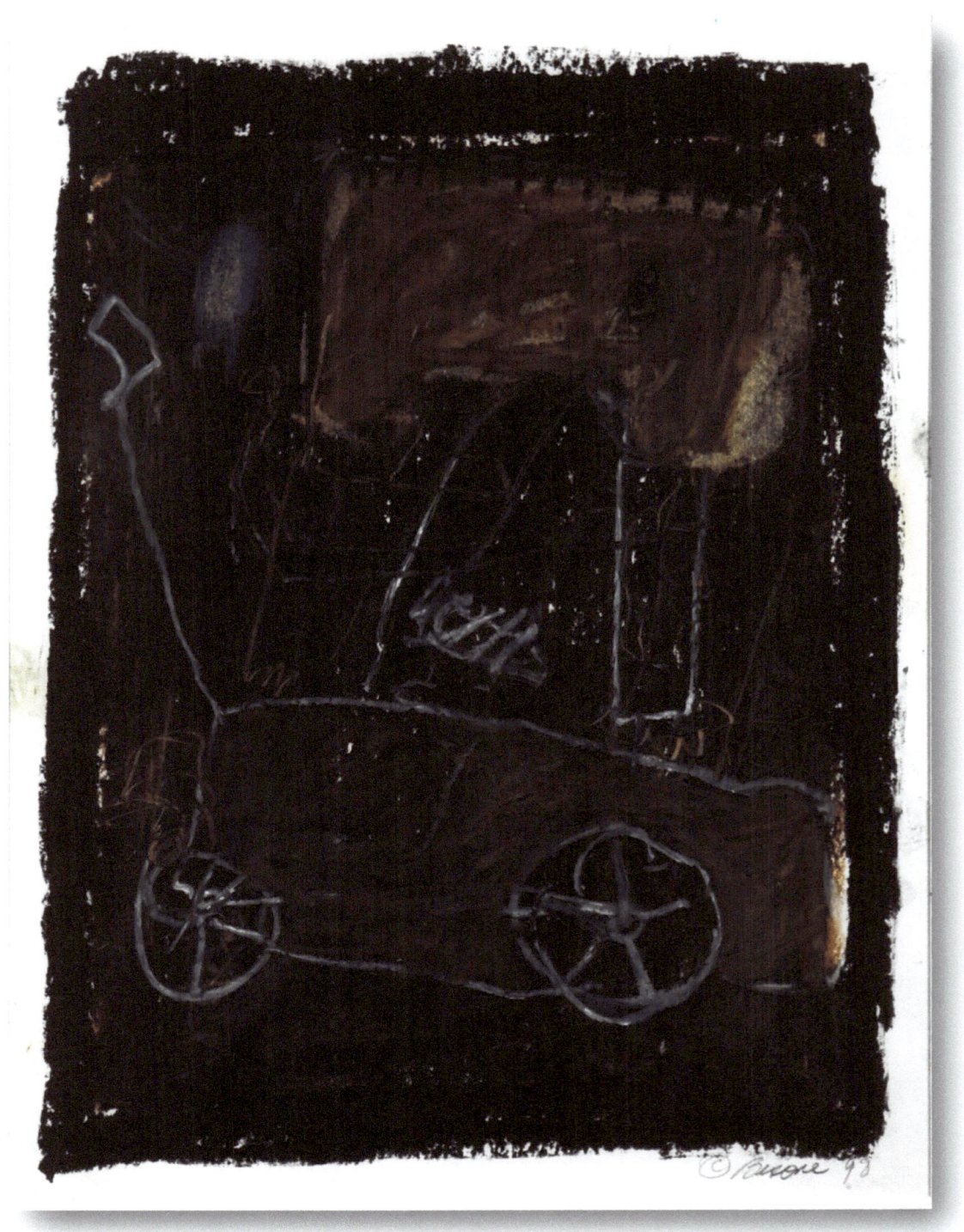

Perilous Journey #7, 1998, 13.5 x 10 inches

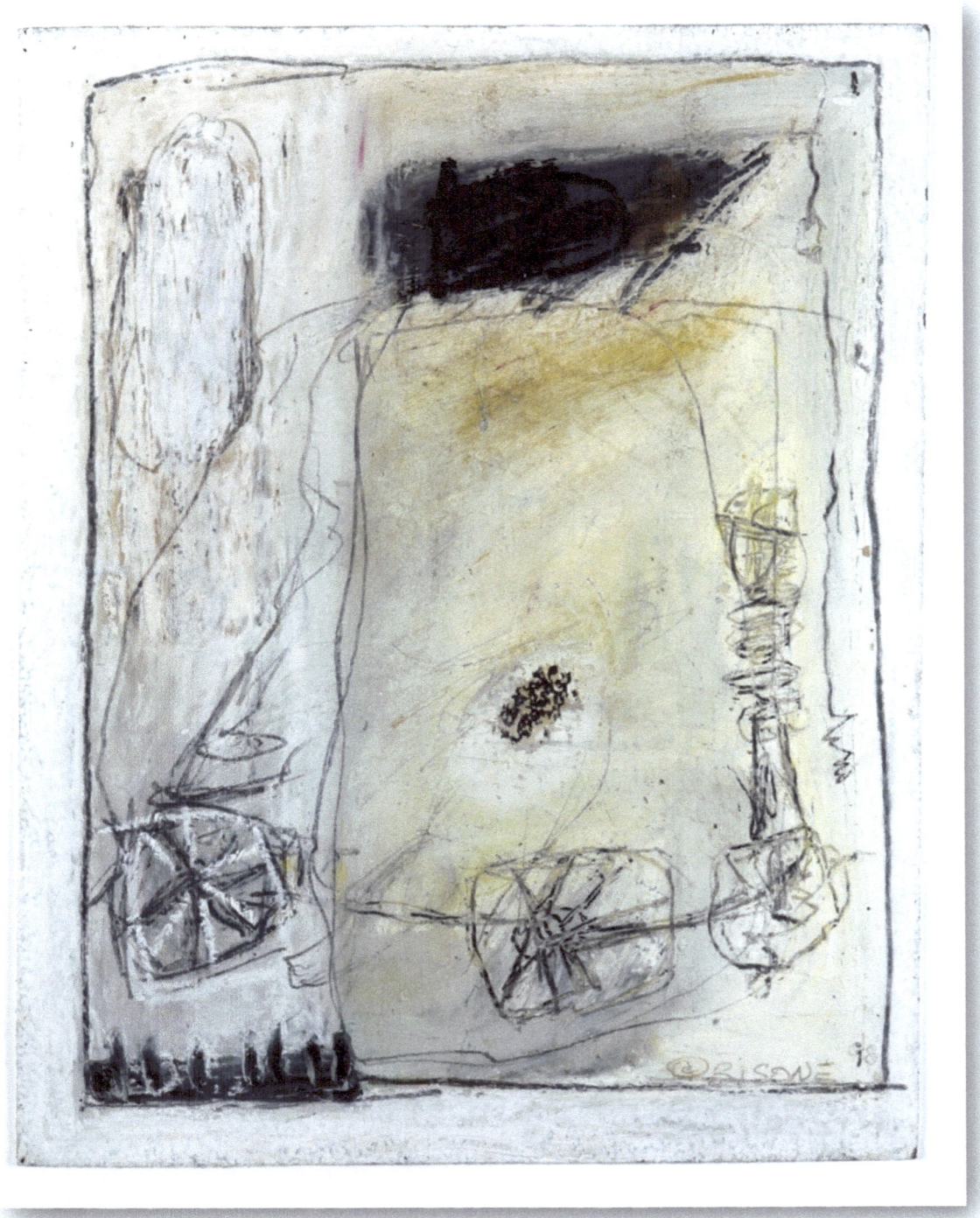

Perilous Journey #24, 1998, 10 x 7.5 inches

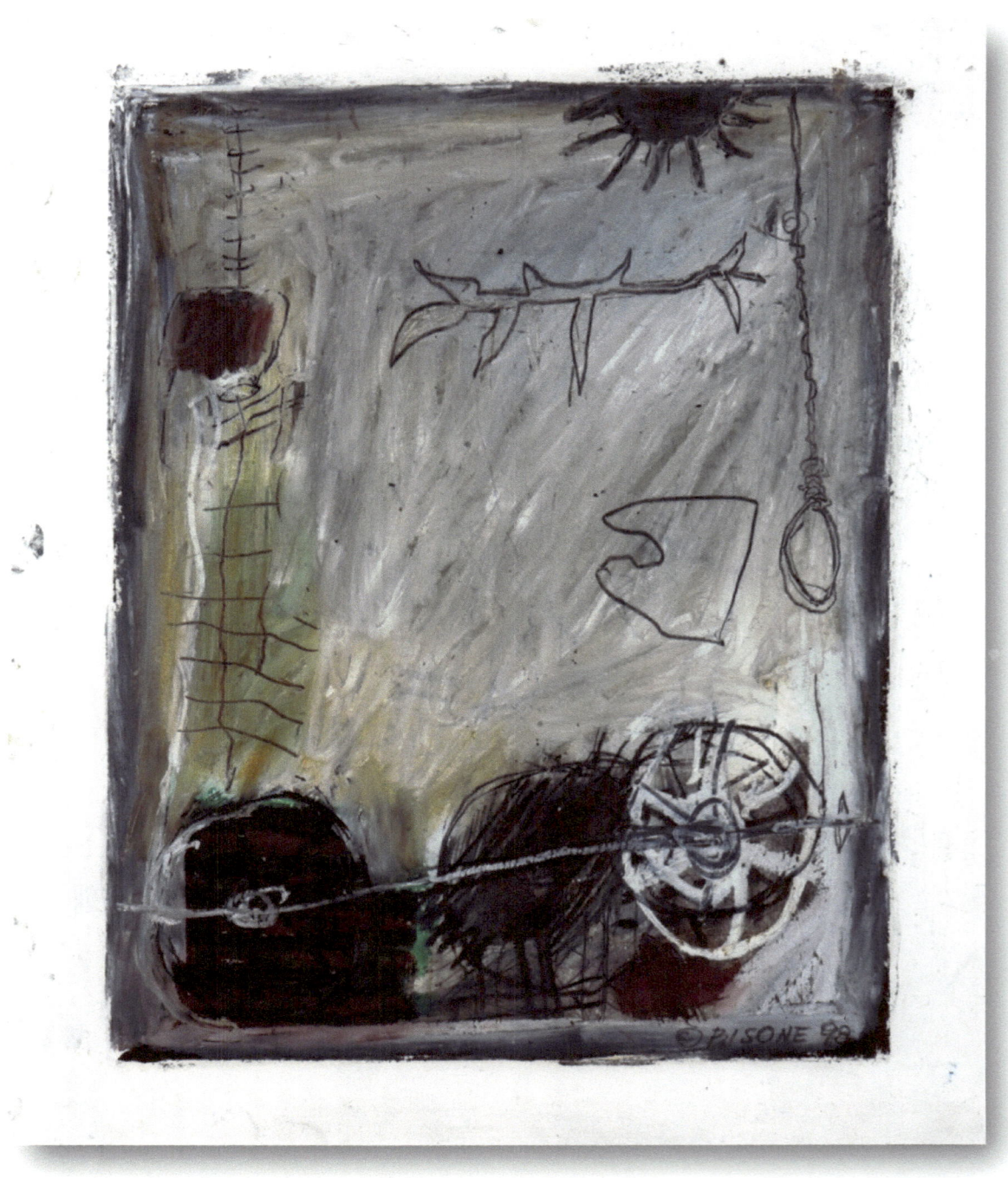

Perilous Journey #26, 1998, 12.75 x 10.75 inches

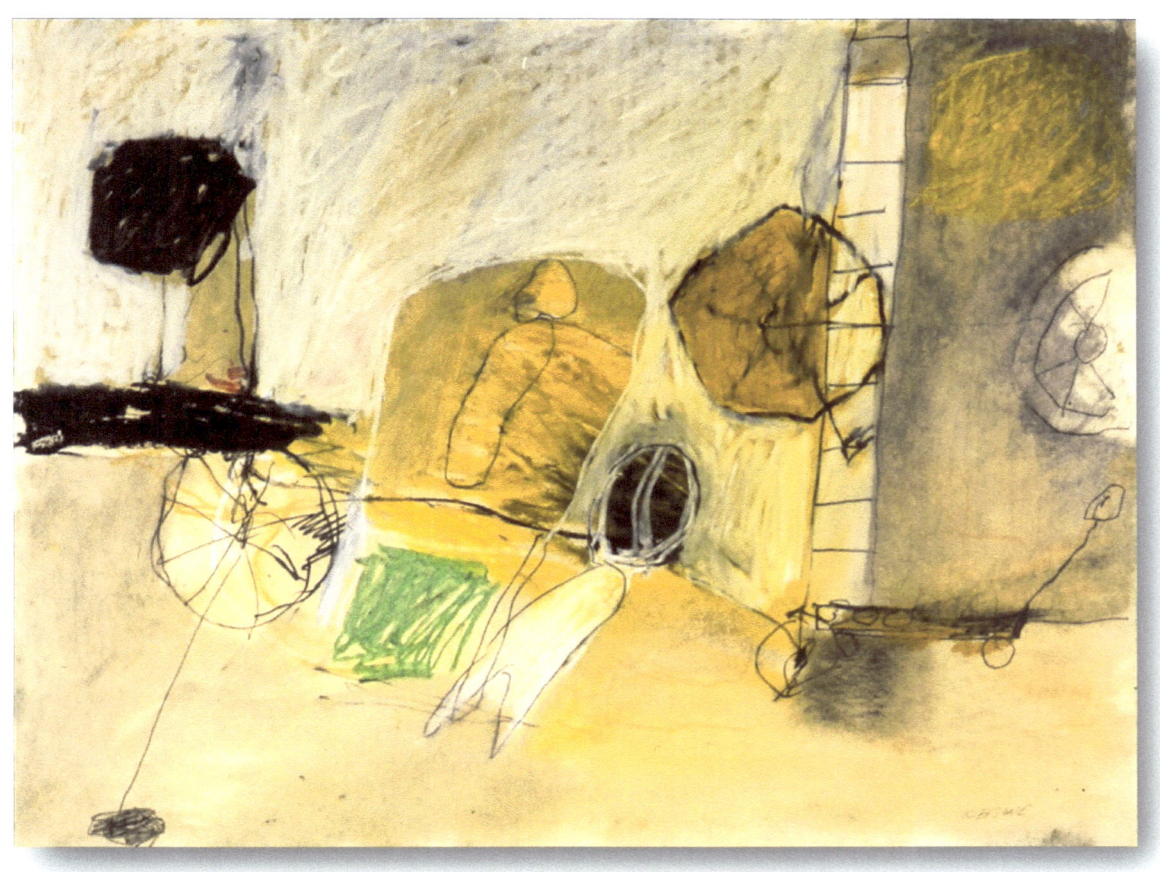

Perilous Journey (c), 1998, 17 x 24 inches

4. Before I Get to Cordoba

(Song of the Rider)

-Federico Garcia Lorca (1898-1936)

Córdoba.
Far away, and lonely.

Full moon, black pony,
olives against my saddle.
Though I know all the roadways
I'll never get to Córdoba.

Through the breezes, through the valley,
red moon, black pony.
Death is looking at me
from the towers of Córdoba.

Ay, how long the road is!
Ay, my brave pony!
Ay, death is waiting for me,
before I get to Córdoba.

Córdoba.
Far away, and lonely.

The following images represent an homage to Garcia Lorca, the Spanish poet and dramatist who was executed by Nationalists at the beginning of the Spanish Civil War. Garcia Lorca's themes of alienation and isolation resonate in Bisone's work.

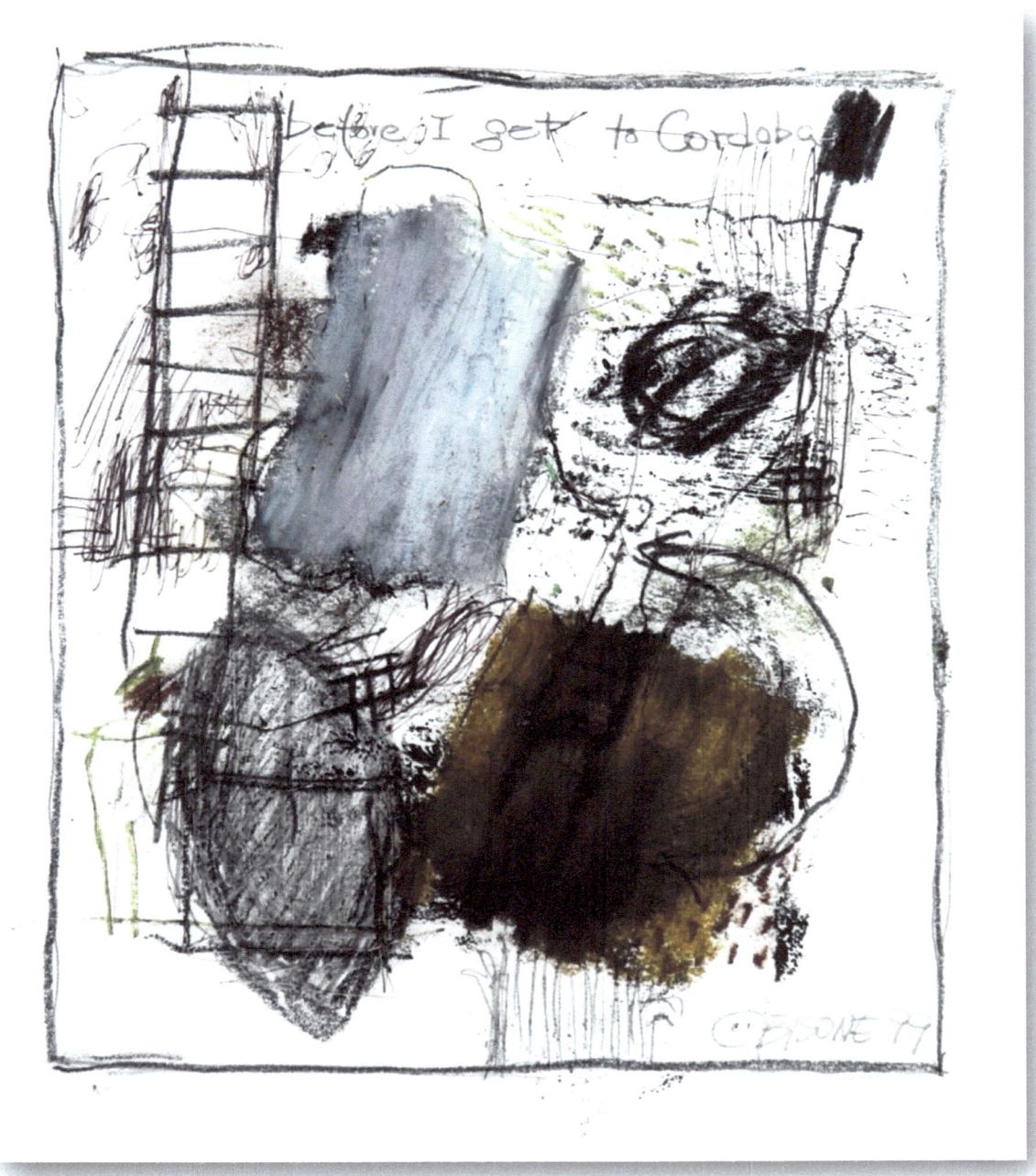

Before I Get to Cordoba, 1999, 11 x 9.75 inches

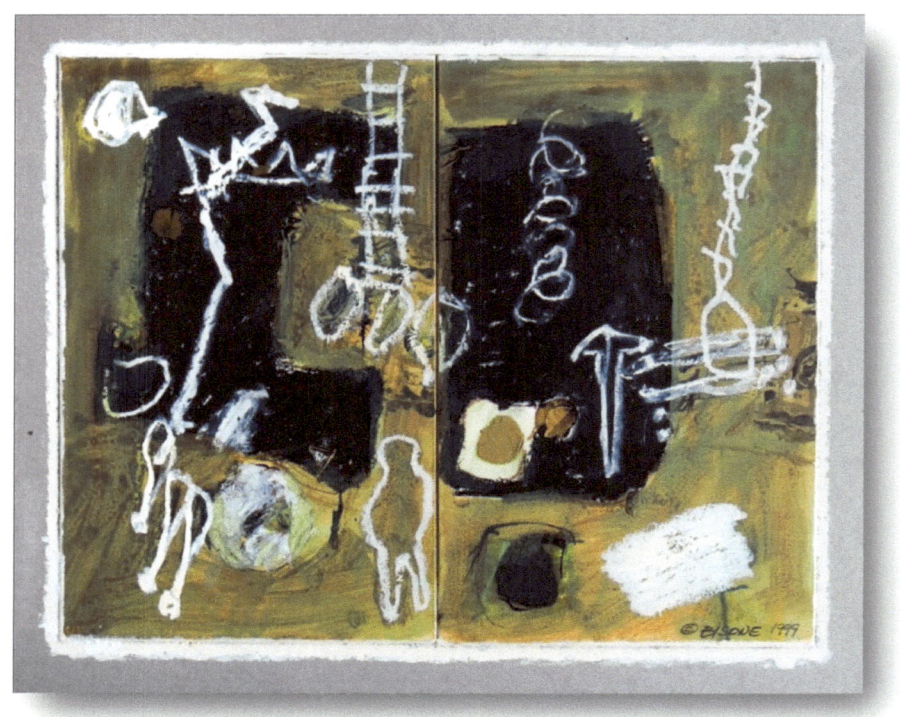

Before I Get to Cordoba II, 1999, 16 x 20 inches

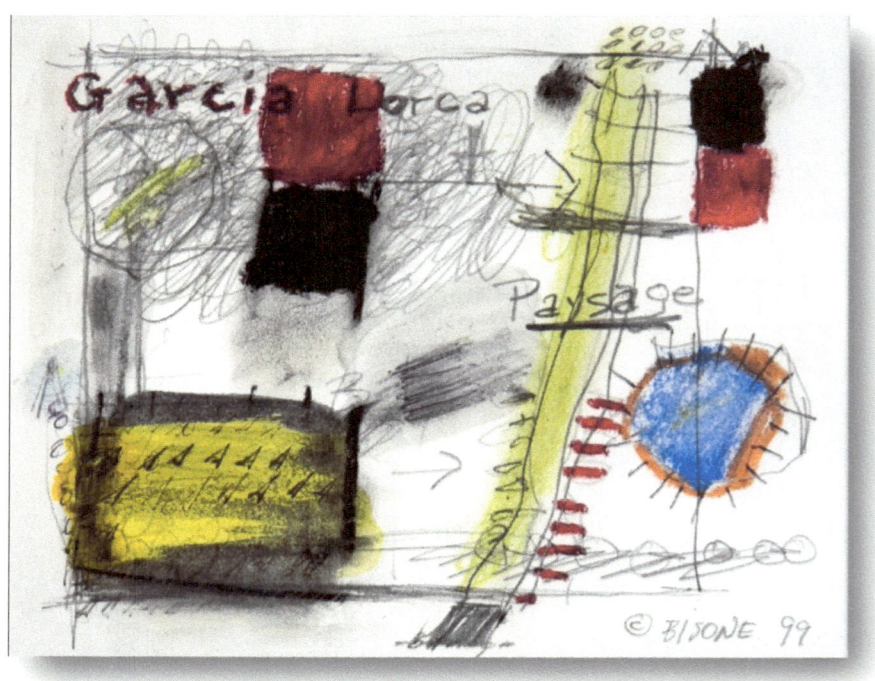

Garcia Lorca, 1999, 6 x 7.75 inches

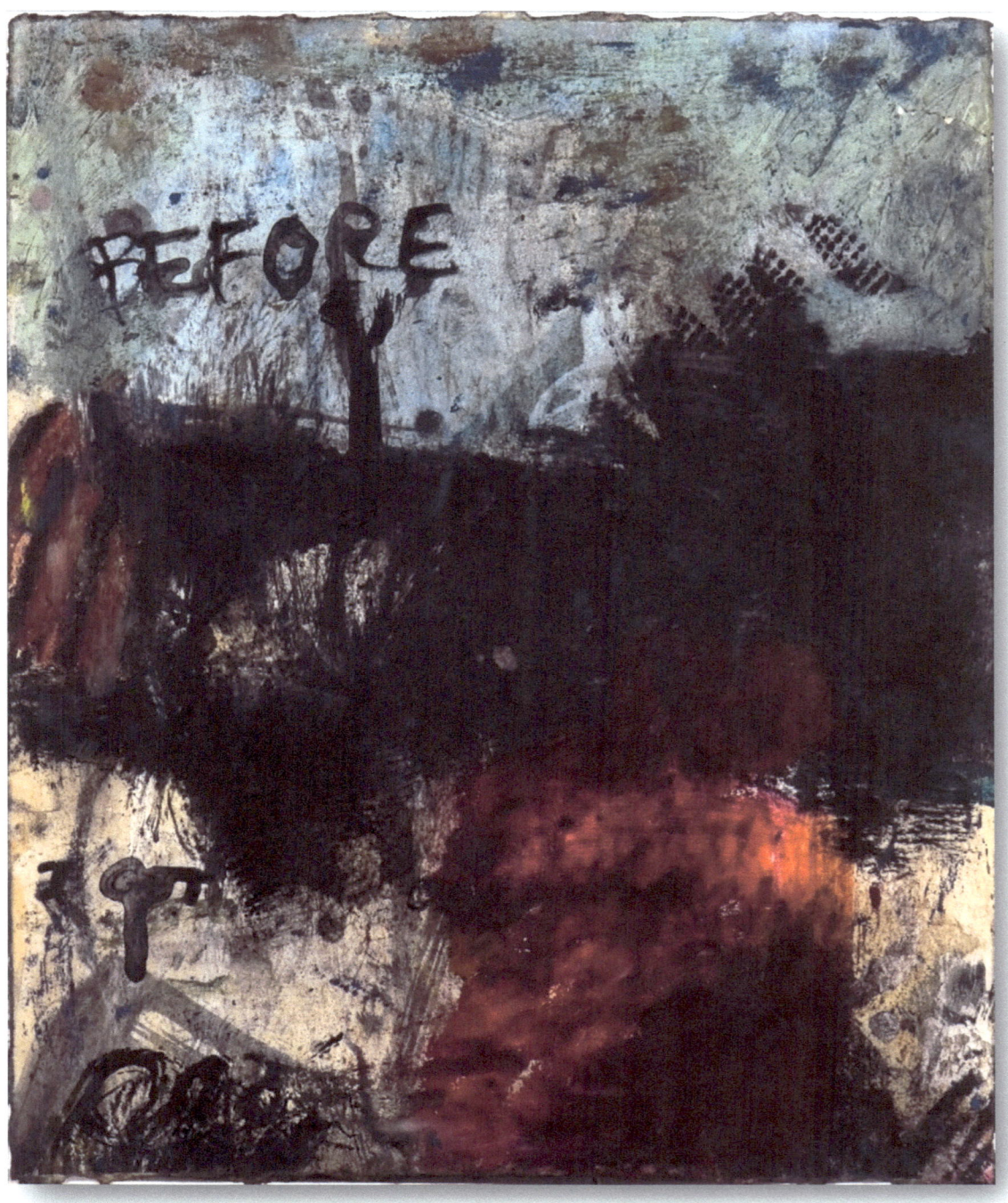

Before, 2000, 9 x 7 inches

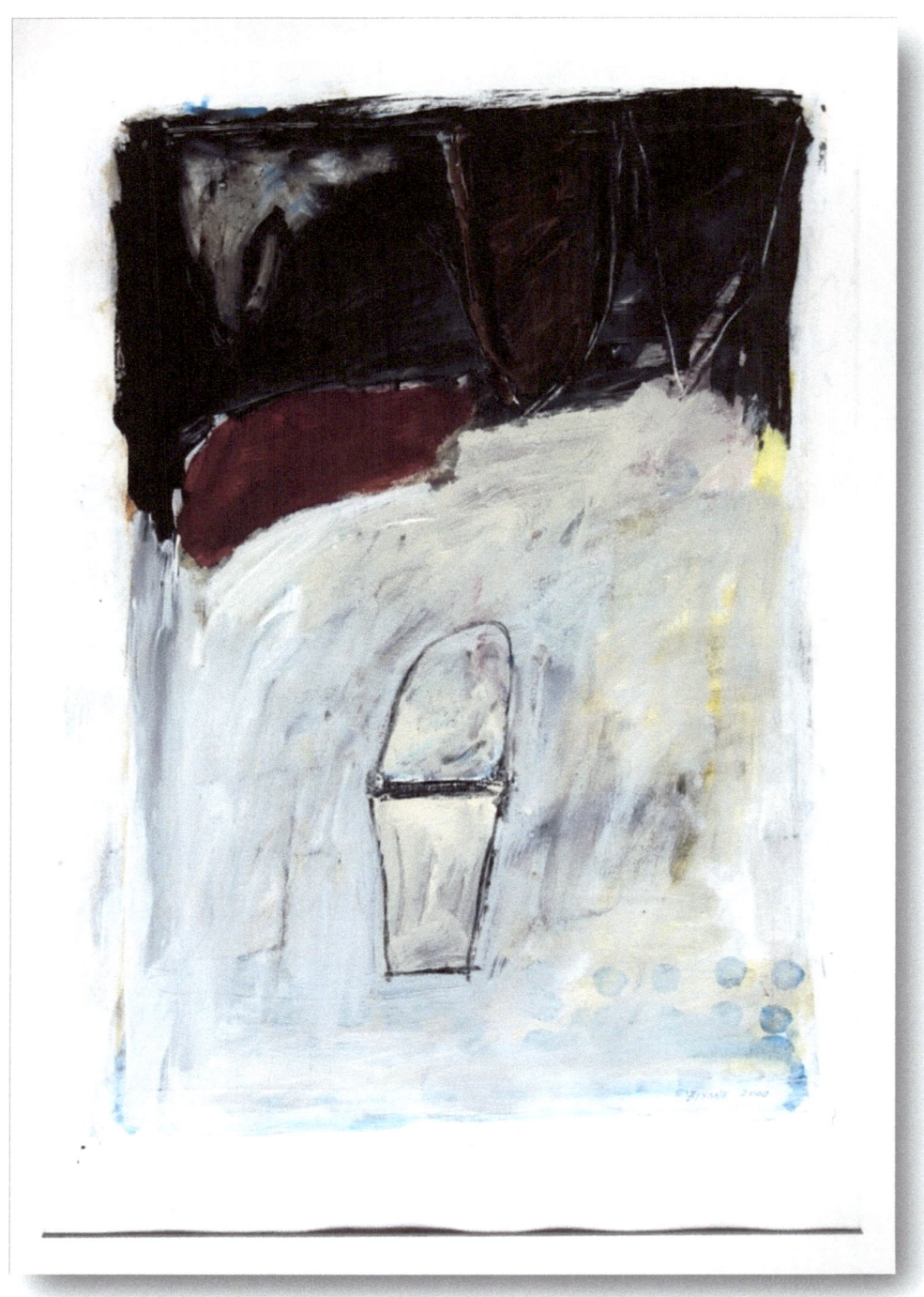

Remembrance of Garcia Lorca, 2000, 24 x 18 inches

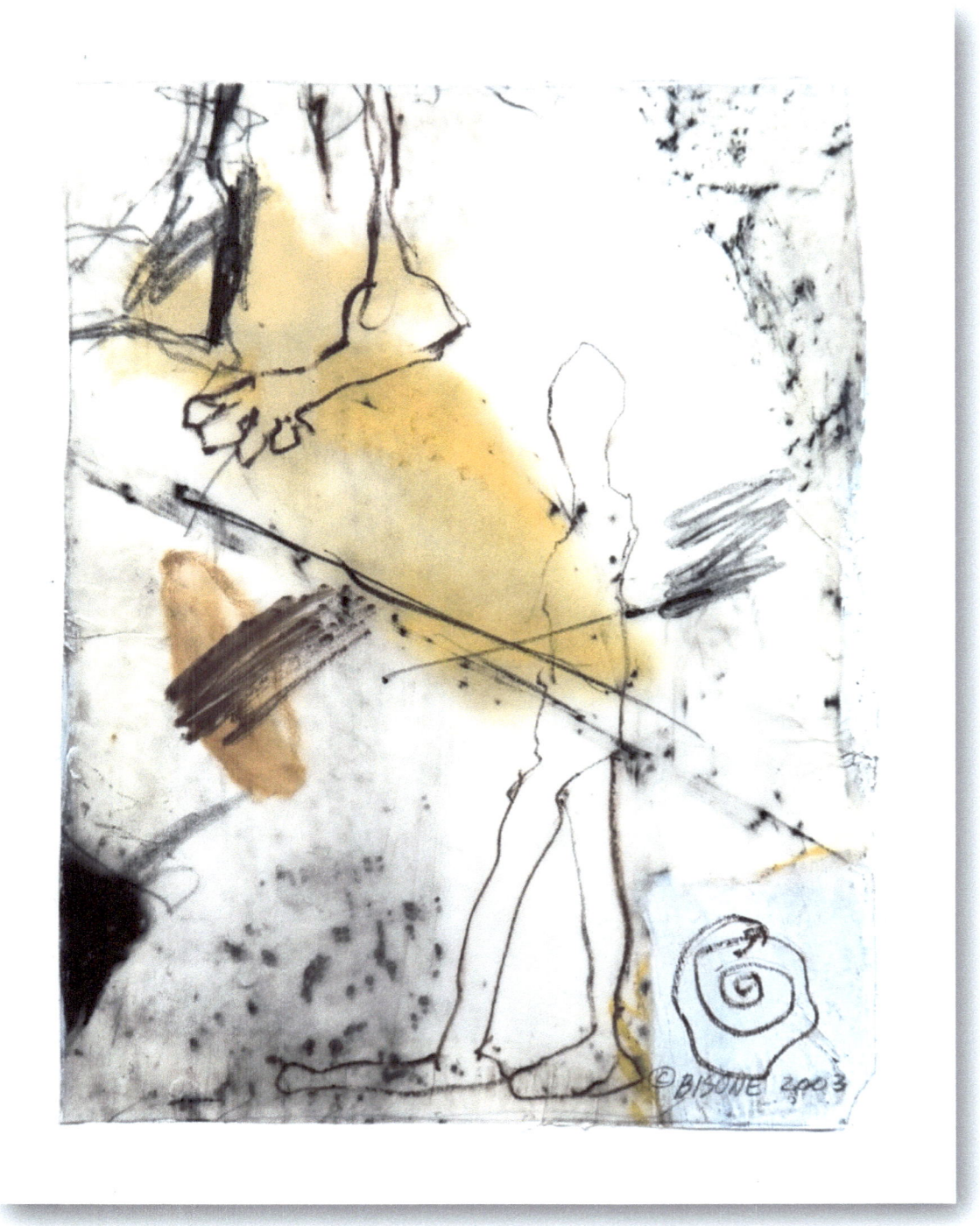

Before I Get to Cordoba XV, 2003, 26 x 20 inches

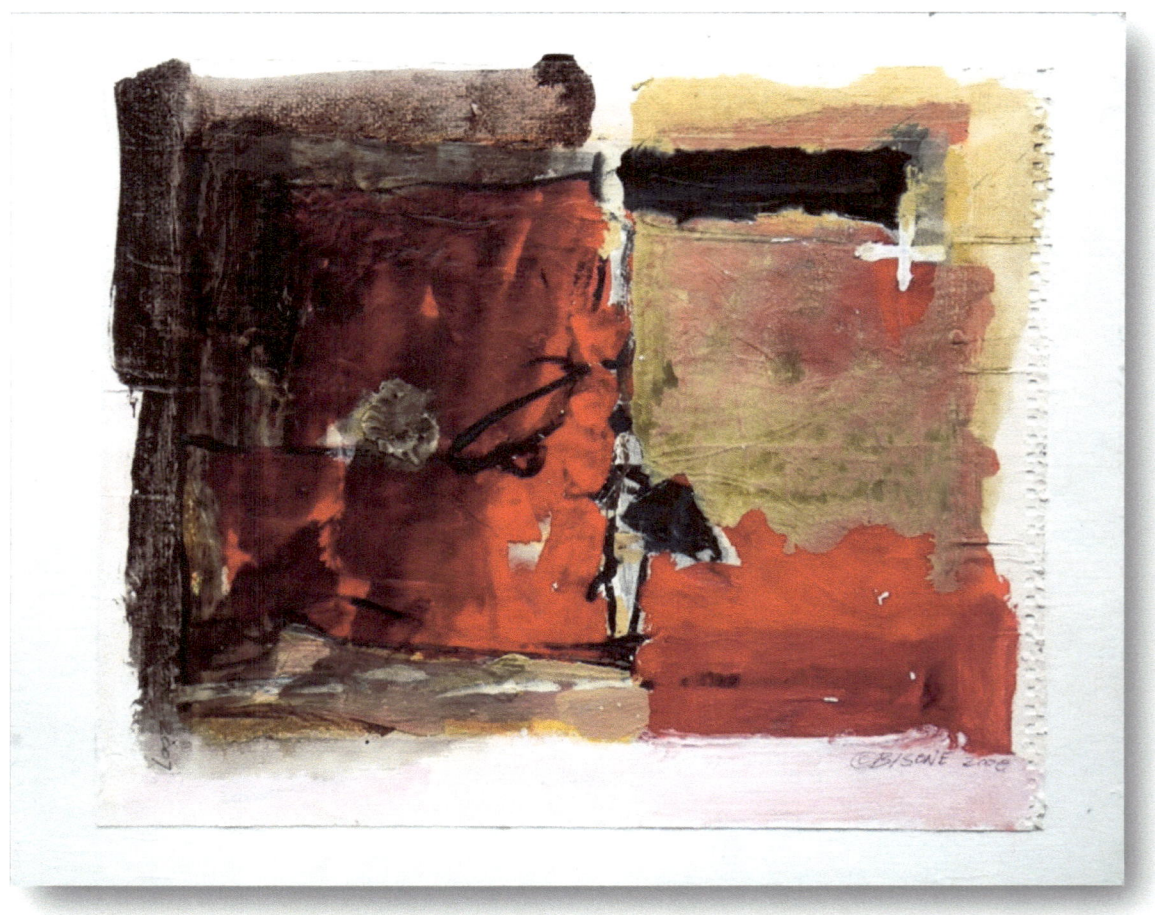

Federico Garcia Lorca #1, 2008, 16 x 20 inches

the evidence of
what was often lingers if
you know where to look

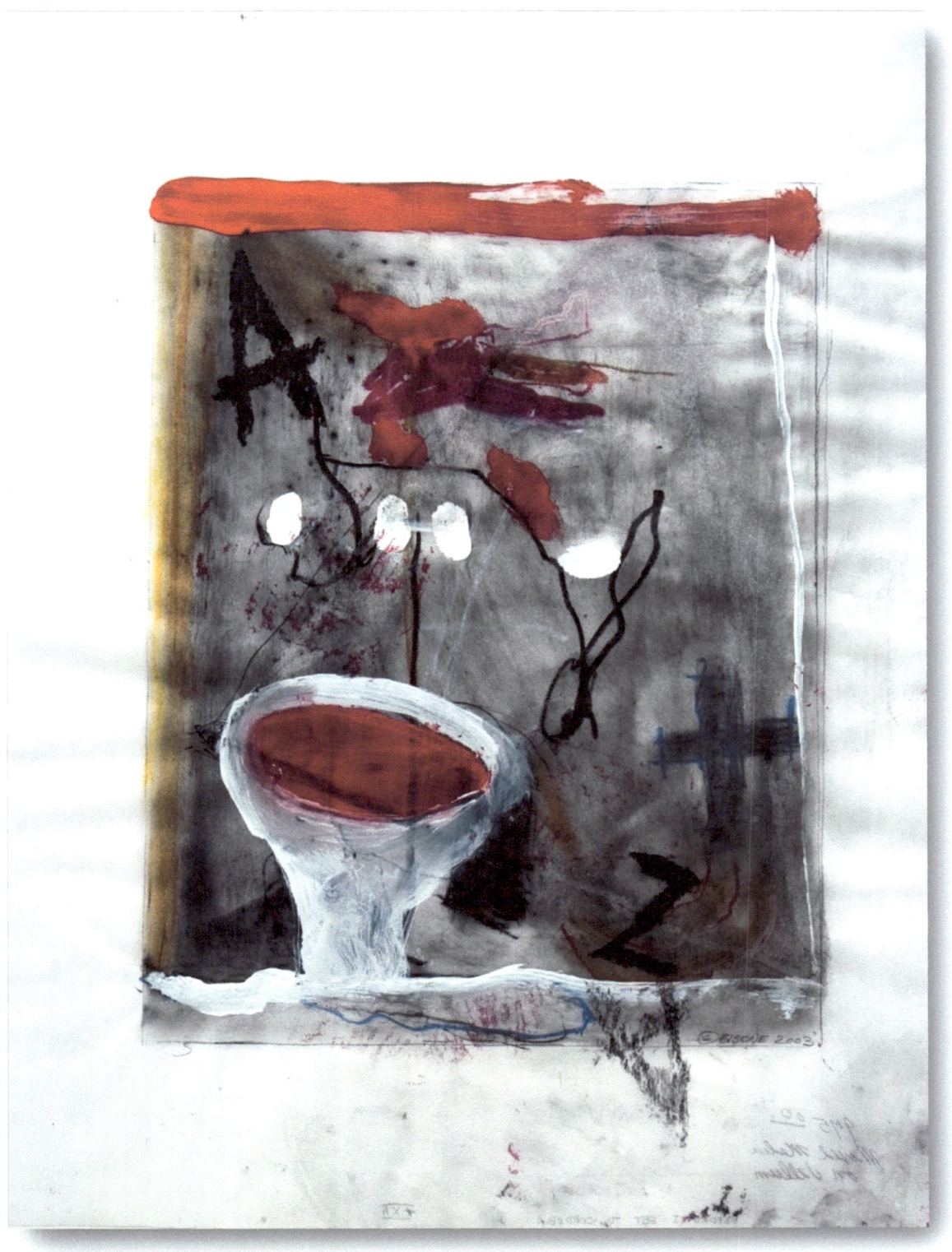

Before I Get to Cordoba, 2003, 25 x 19 inches

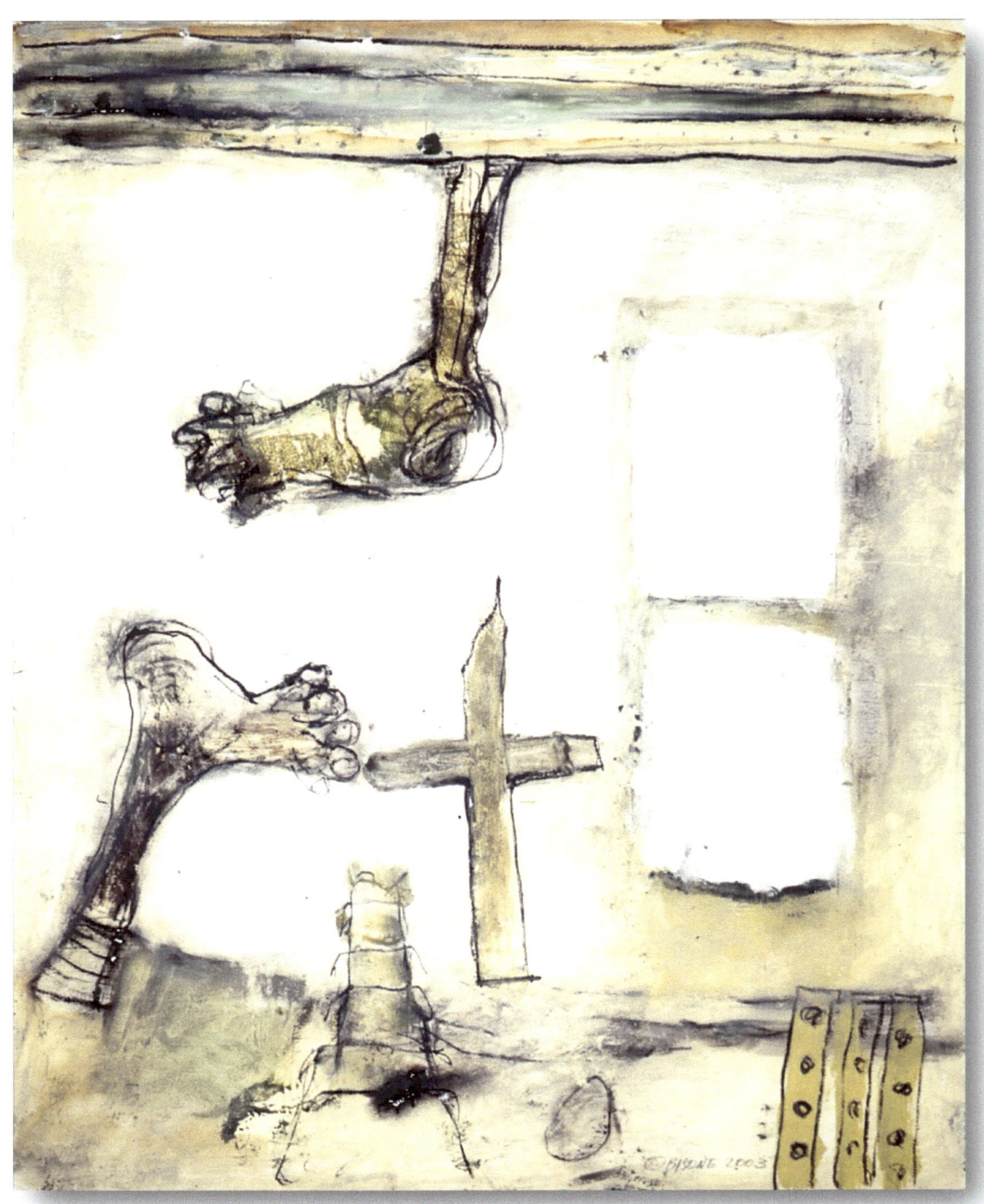

Before I Get to Cordoba VI, 2003, 24 x 18 inches

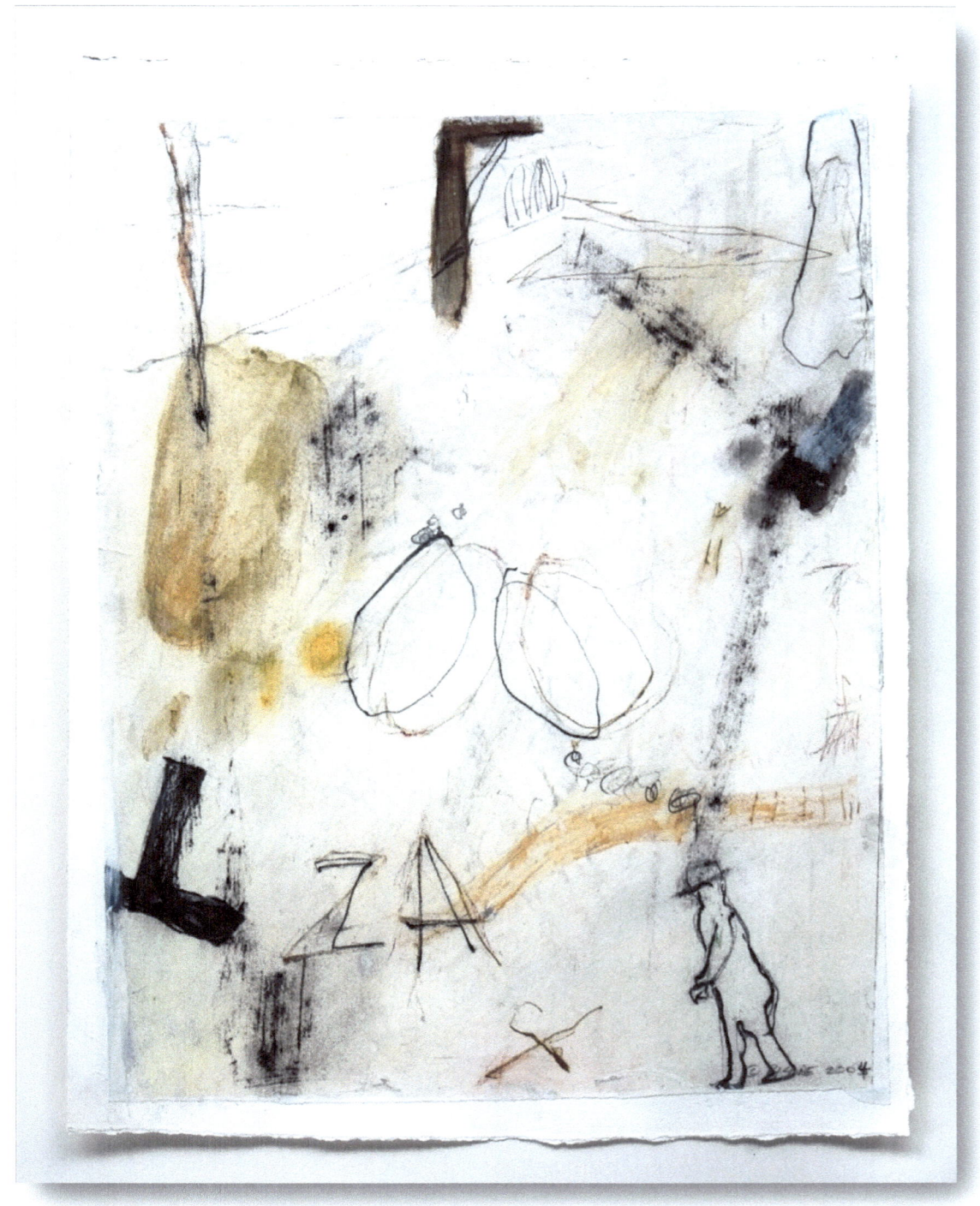

Before I Get to Cordoba, 2004, 26 x 20 inches

5. Cards of Identity

Bisone painted this series in 2006. It depicts nondescript, nearly featureless faces of individuals as they might pose for identification photos, lit from various angles, but always facing the camera. Can ID cards really identify a person? The artist's answer seems obvious. A person's identity isn't readily defined nor easily captured, regardless of the angle. Each of the dozen paintings shown here presents a man or a woman in four straight-on poses, with hats, without hats, with glasses, without glasses, eyes shut, eyes open, and some without facial features entirely. What can we learn from someone's appearance? ...Certainly not their identity.

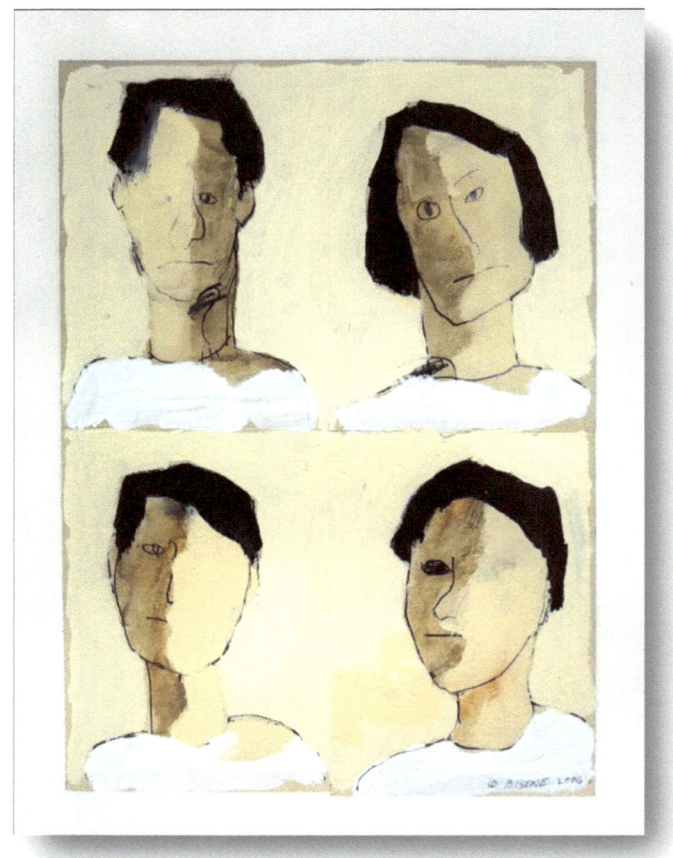

Cards of Identity VII, 2006, 28 x 22 inches

what I see and

what I sense, how different

are they? what is real?

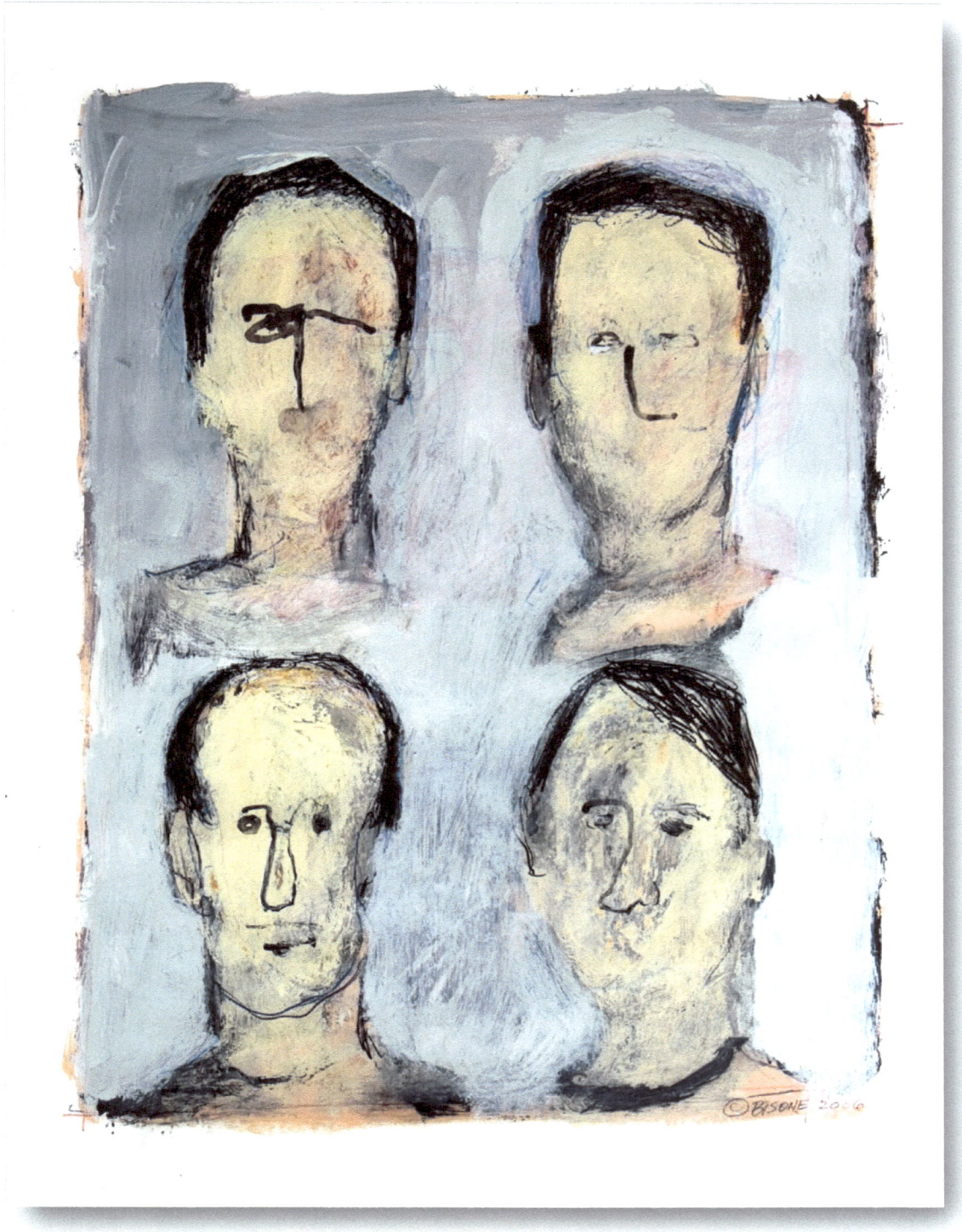

Cards of Identity IV, 2006, 28 x 22 inches

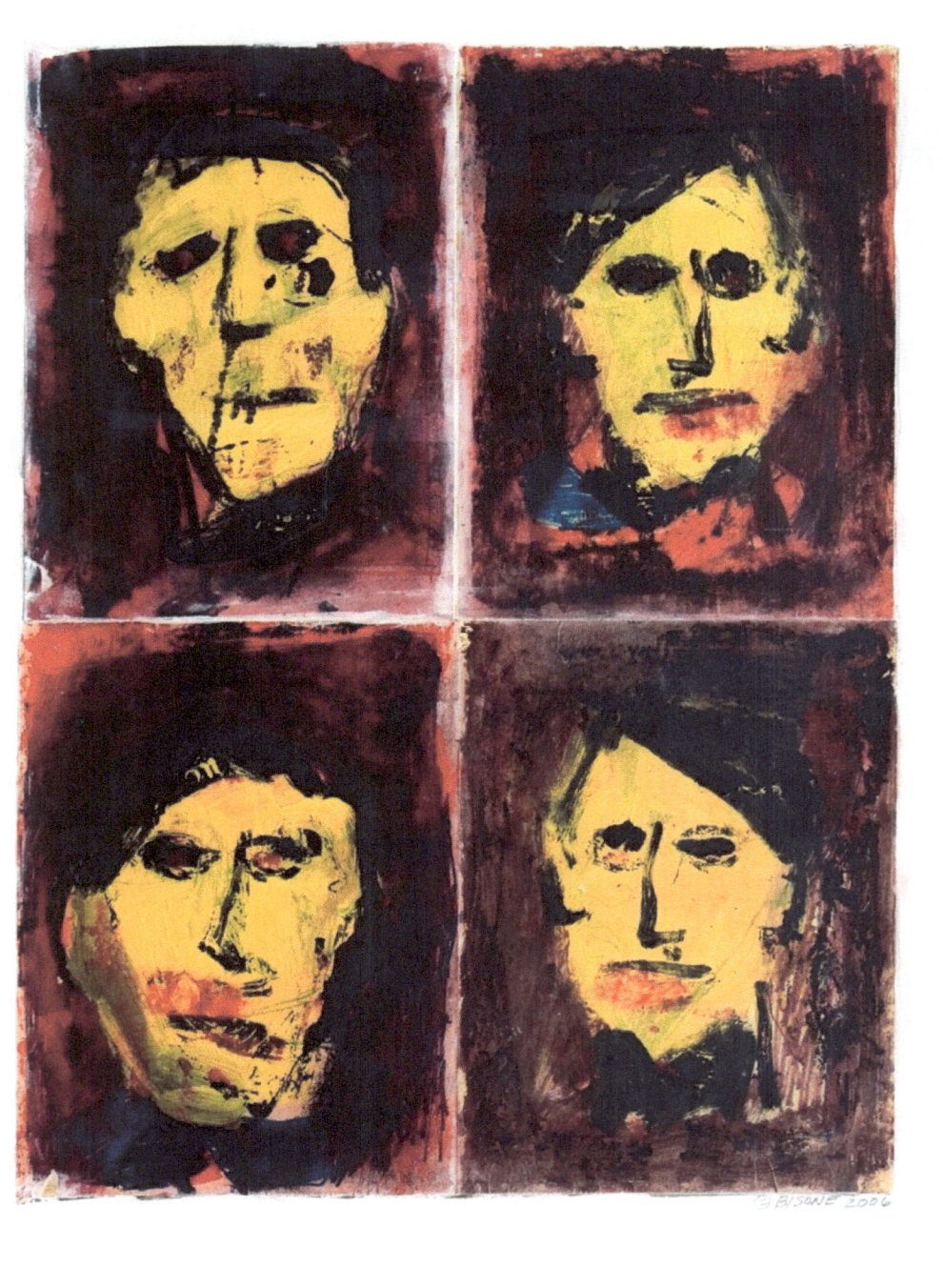

Cards of Identity IXa, 2006, 28 x 22 inches

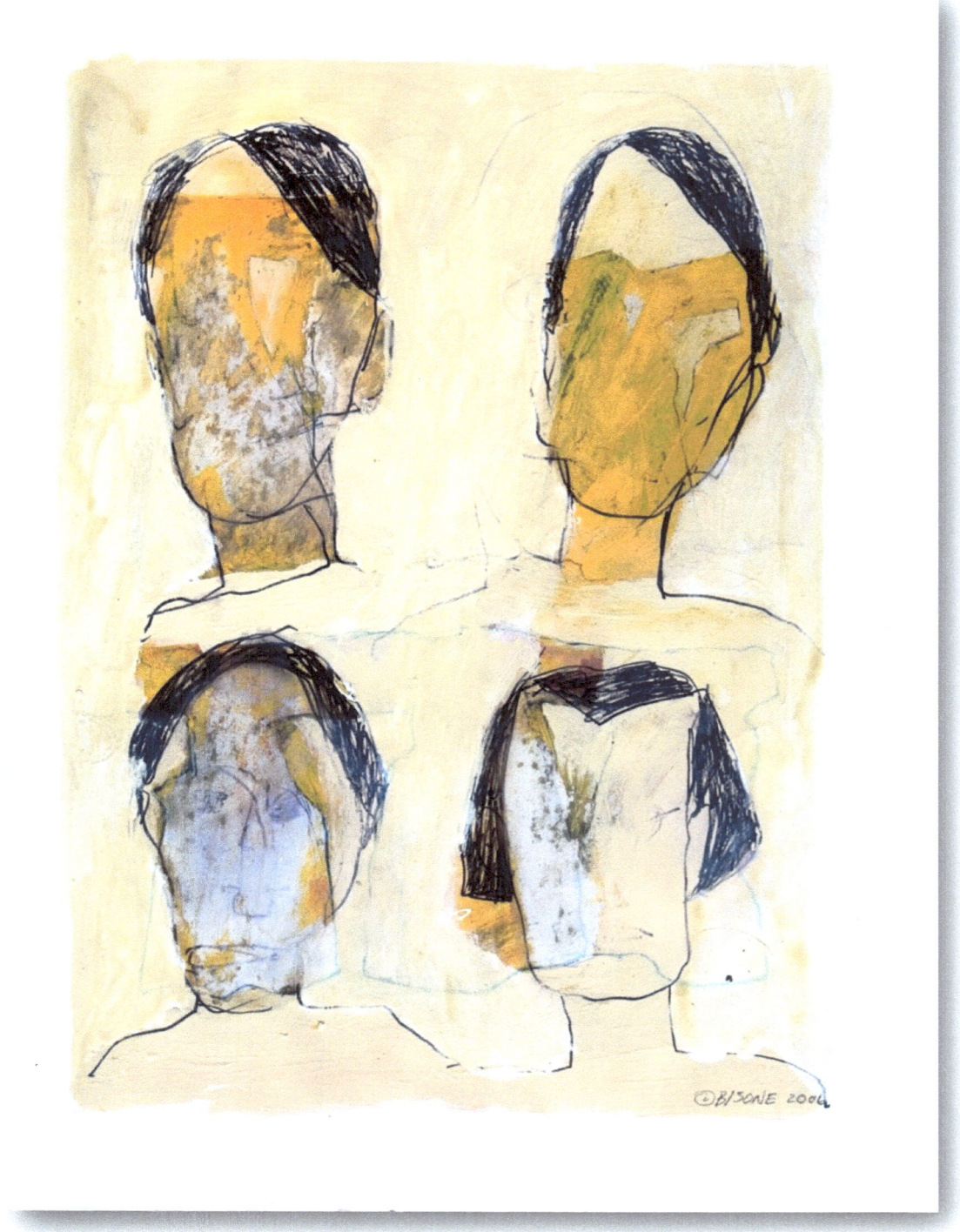

Cards of Identity IXb, 2006, 28 x 22 inches

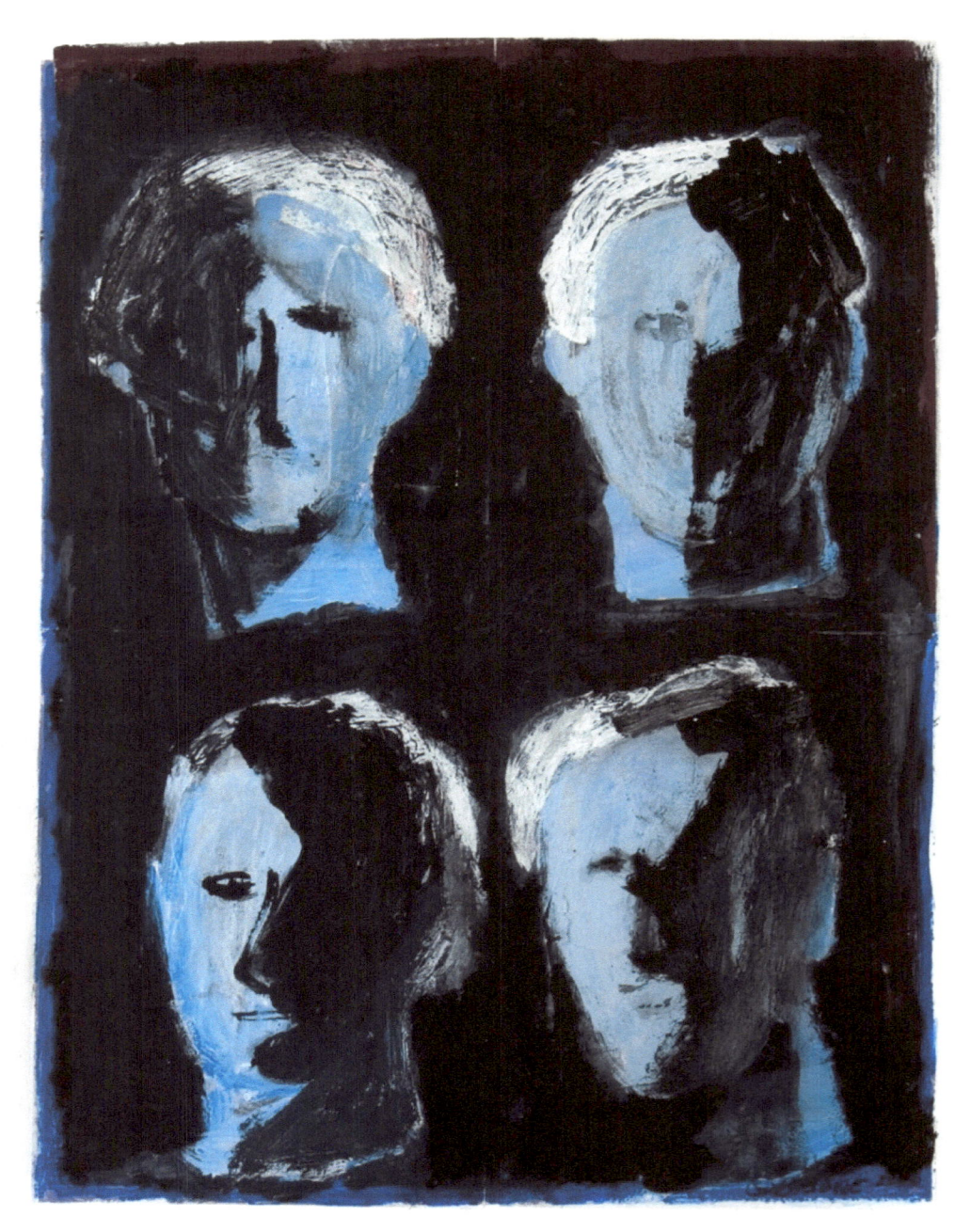

Cards of Identity Va, 2006, 28 x 22 inches

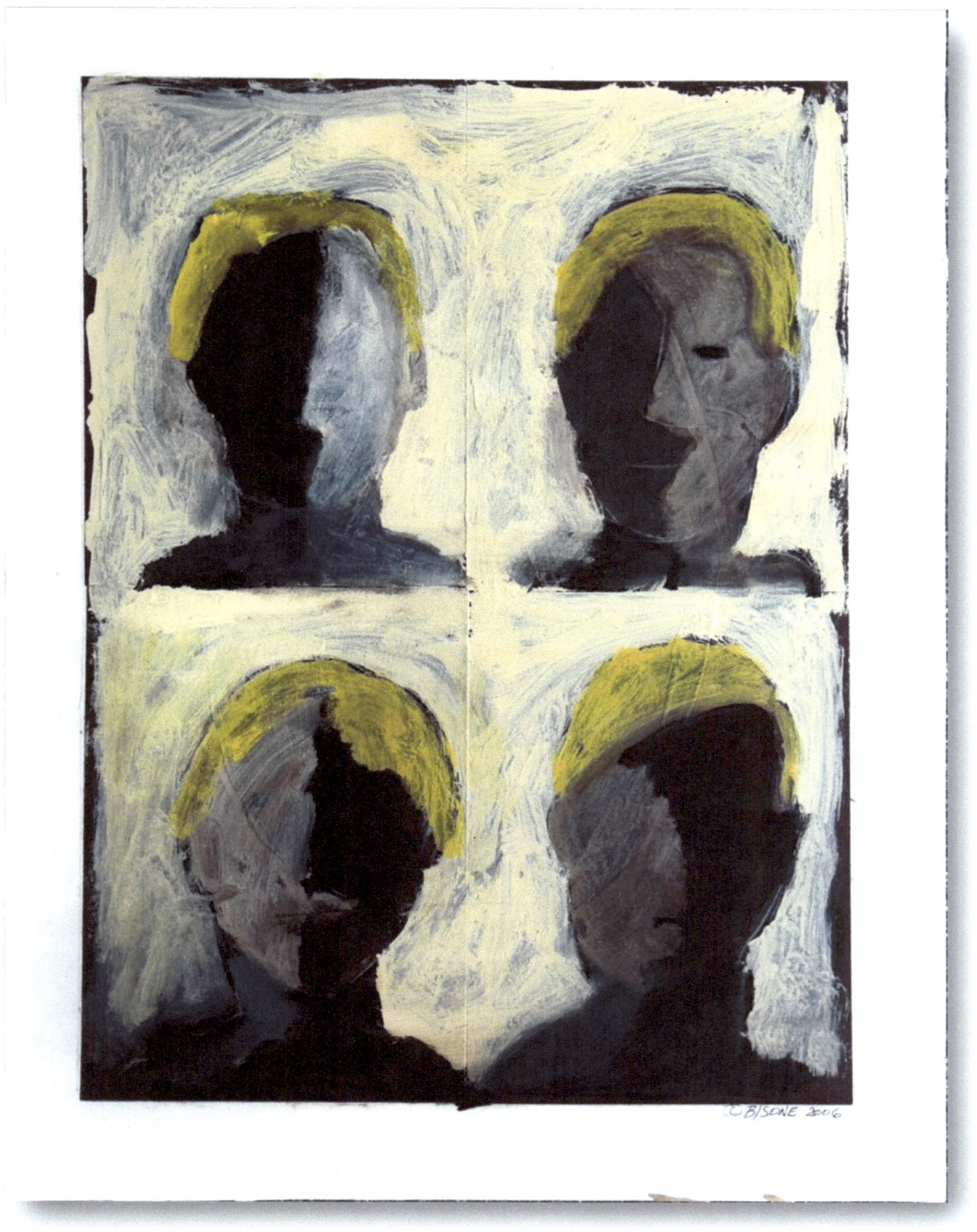

Cards of Identity VIII, 2006, 28 x 22 inches

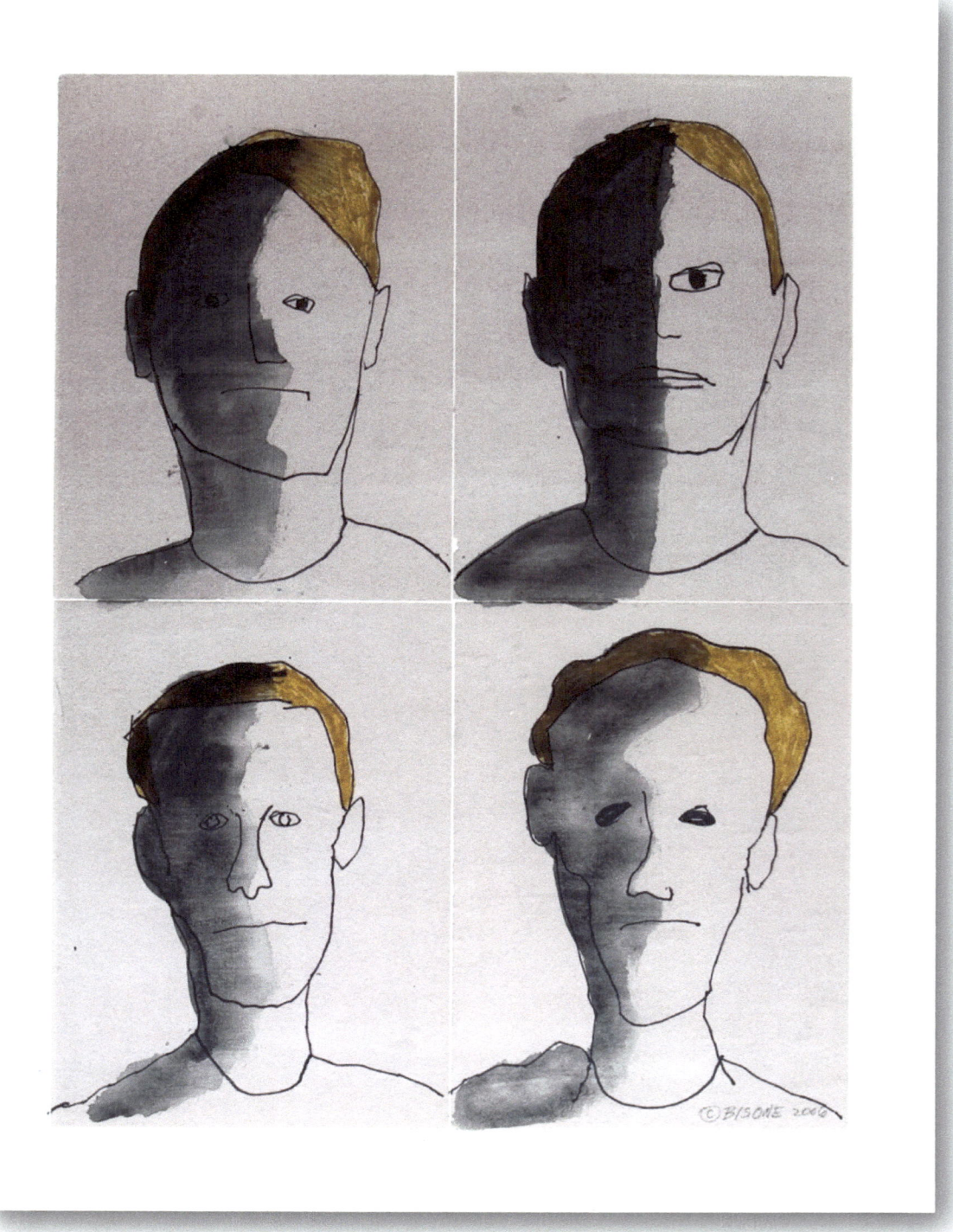

Cards of Identity Xa, 2006, 28 x 22 inches

sometimes we're faceless

by our own design, and shown

as such in paintings

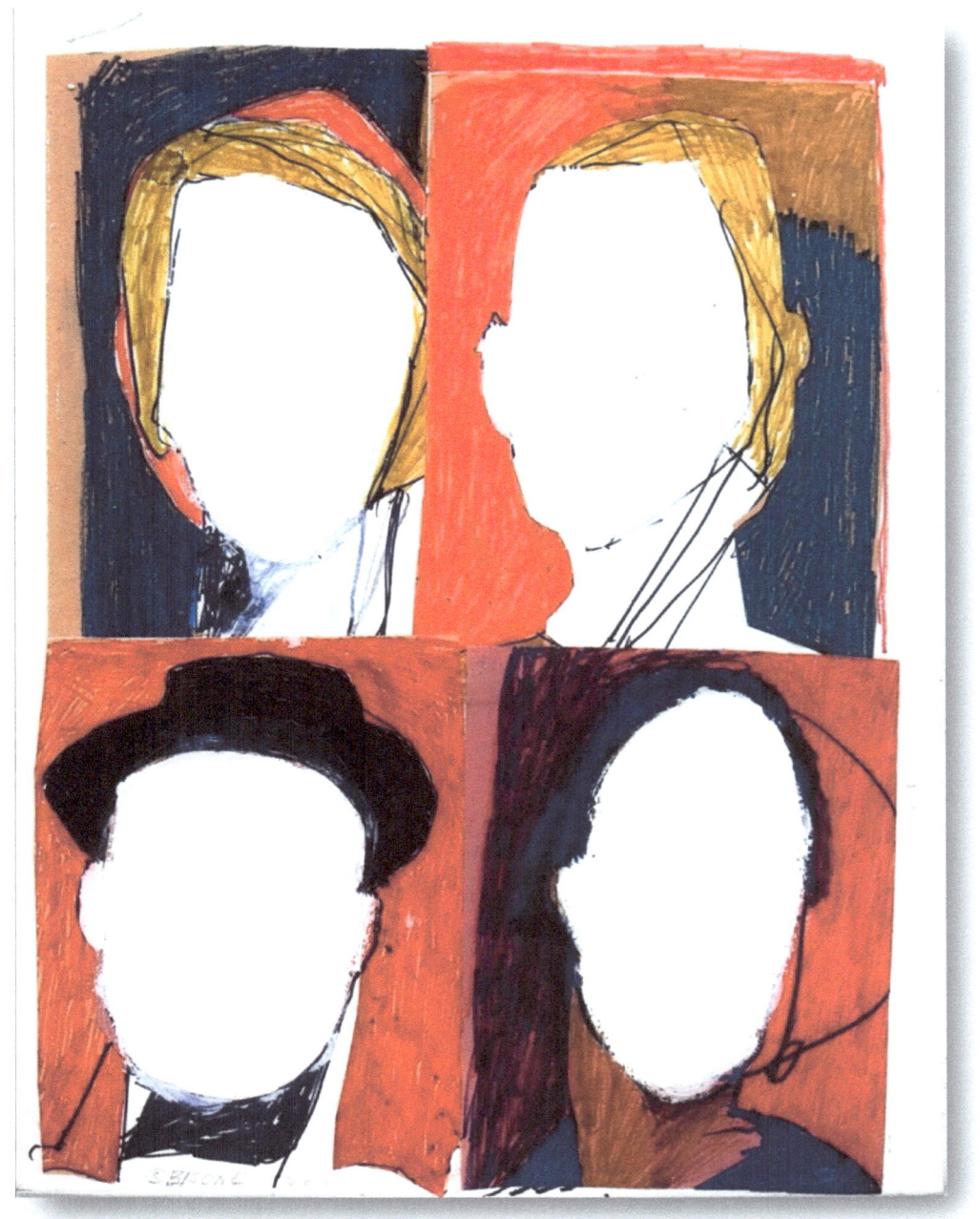

Cards of Identity Xb, 2006, 28 x 22 inches

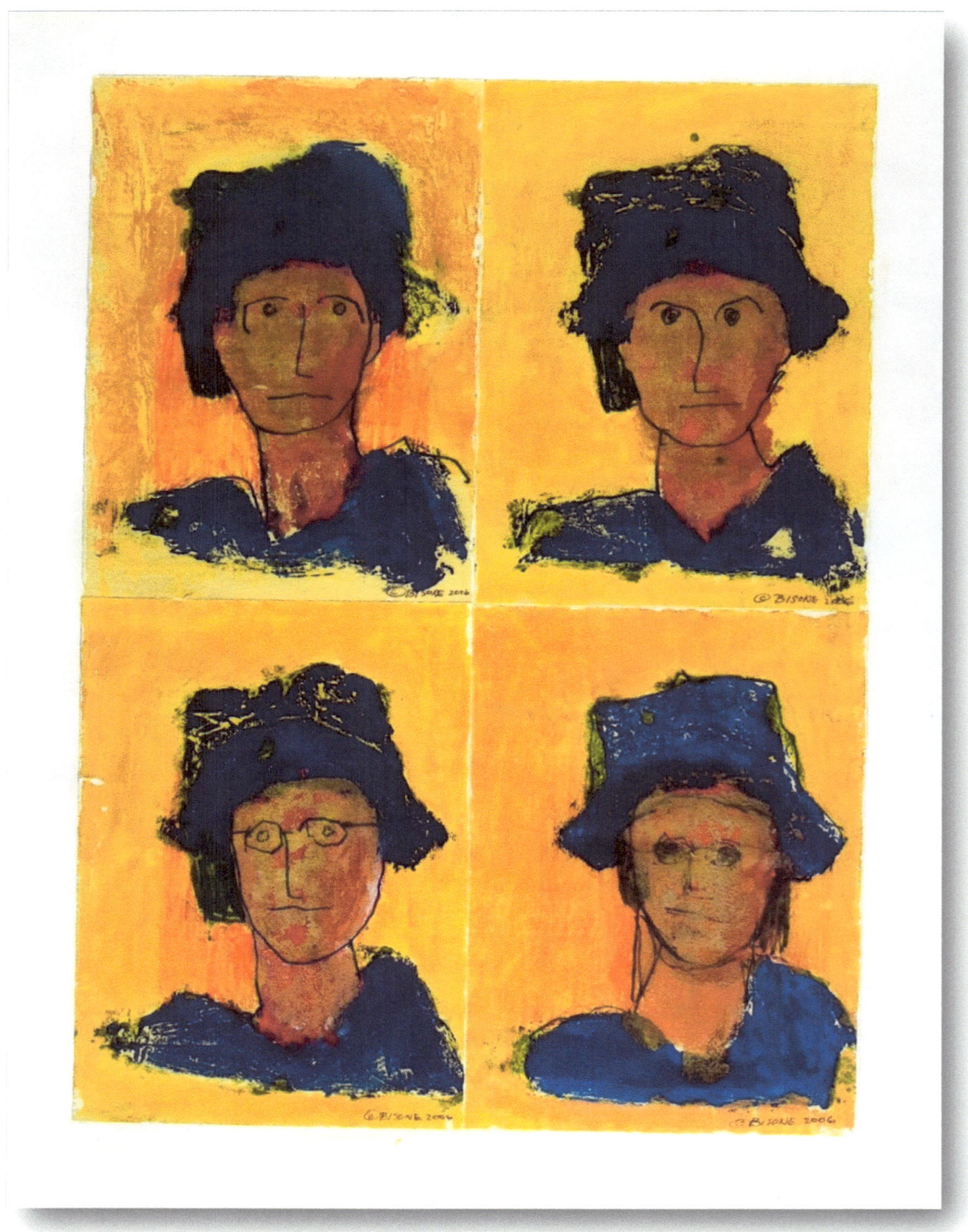

Four Cloche Hats, 2006, 28 x 22 inches

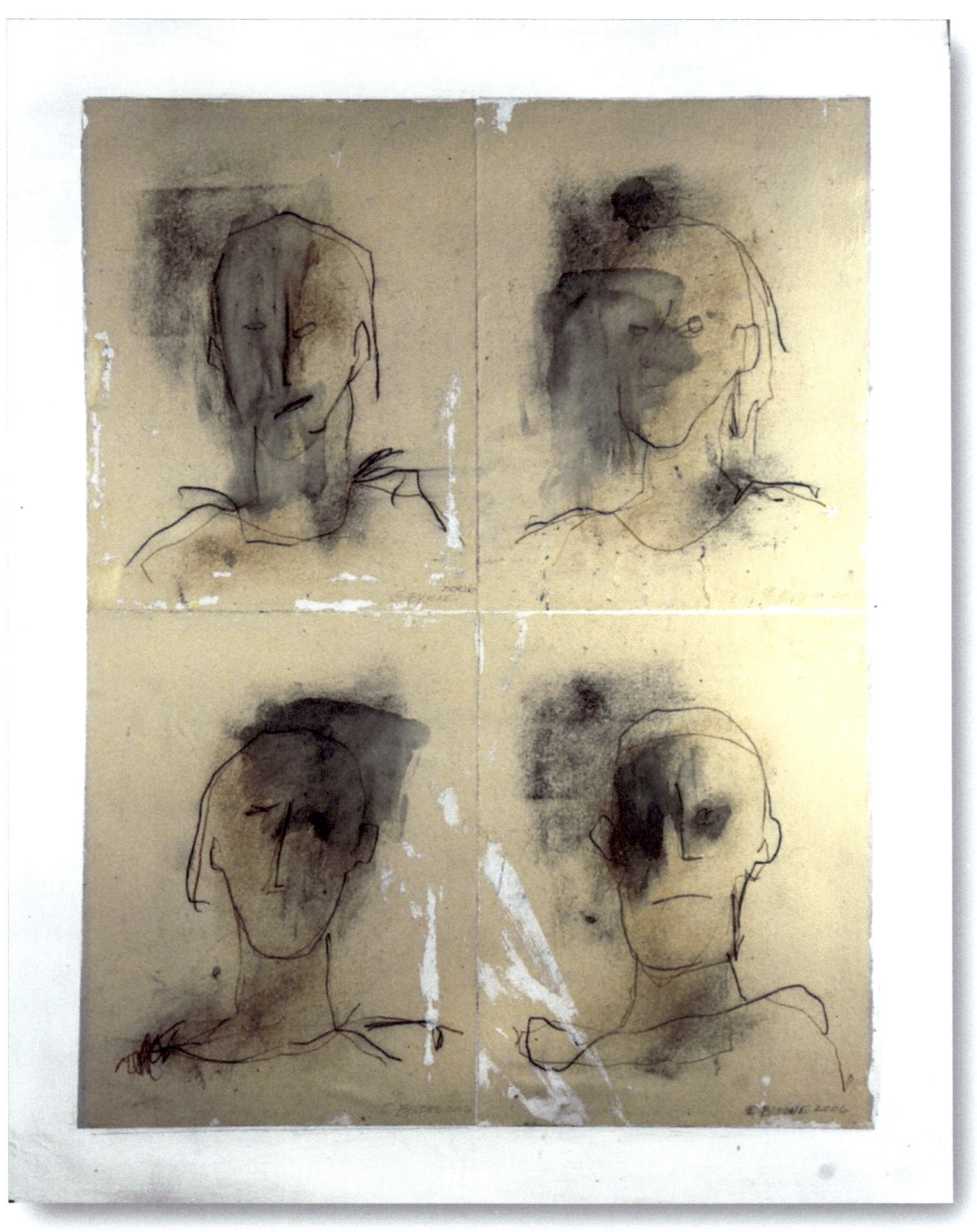

Four Faces, 2006, 28 x 22 inches

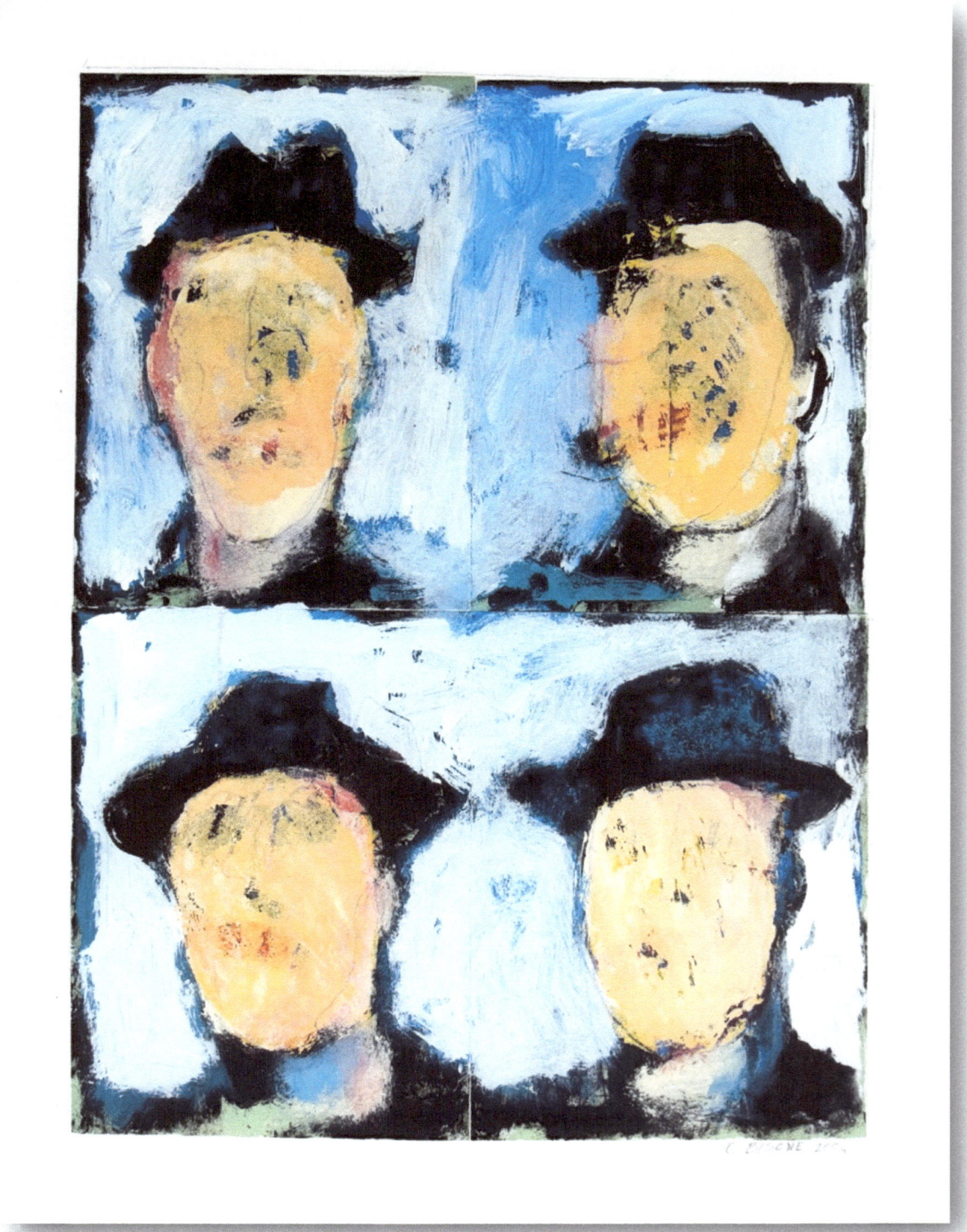

Stolen Identities, 2006, 28 x 22 inches

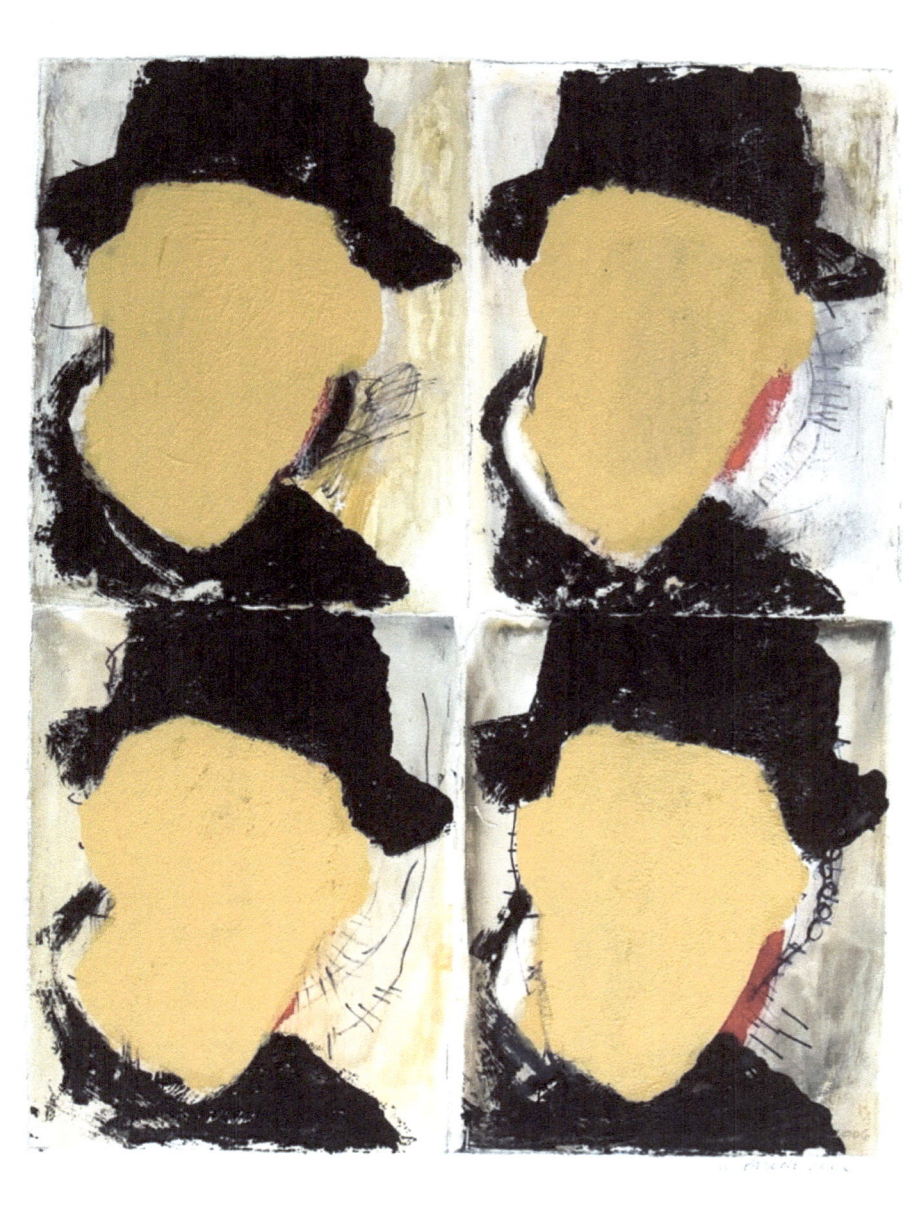

Stolen Identities II, 2006, 28 x 22 inches

6. Cedar Tavern

Cedar Tavern, located in New York City, was the hangout of the Abstract Expressionists in the 1940's, and later the beat poets, Allen Ginsburg and Jack Kerouac. The following five paintings were created by Bisone in 2008-9.

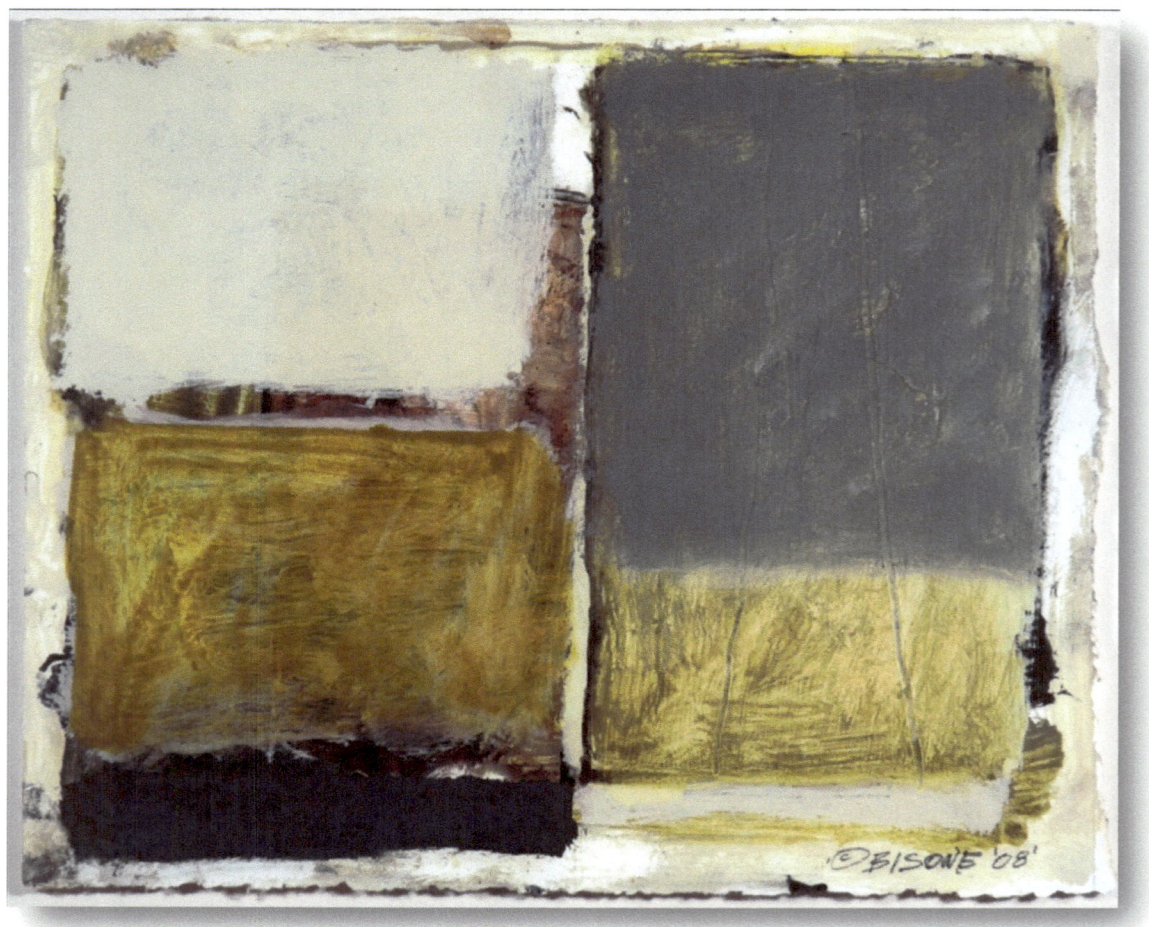

Cedar Tavern Series #7, 2008, 11.5 x 14 inches

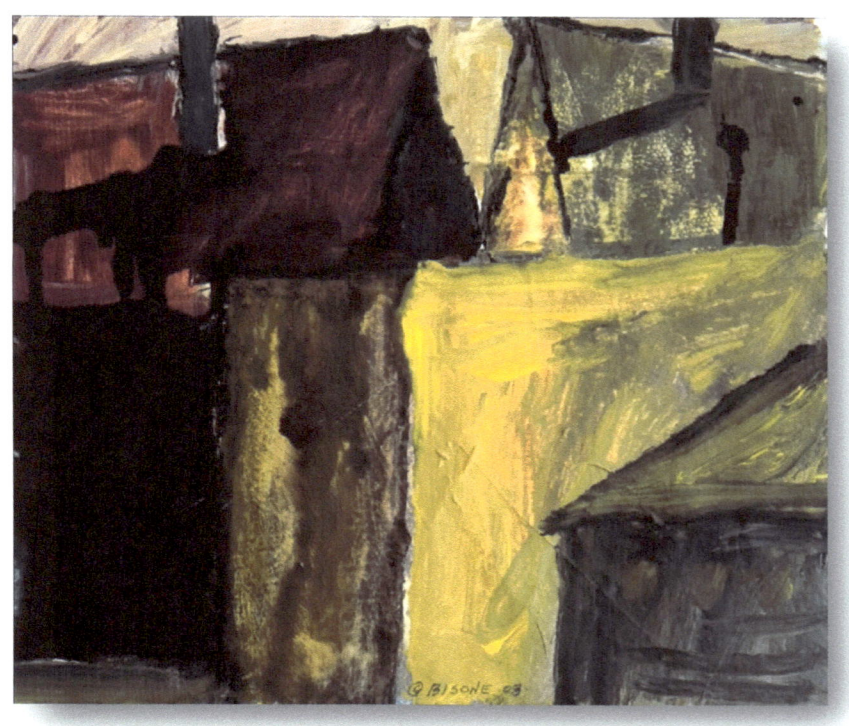

Cedar Tavern Series XIV, 2008, 9.75 x 11 inches

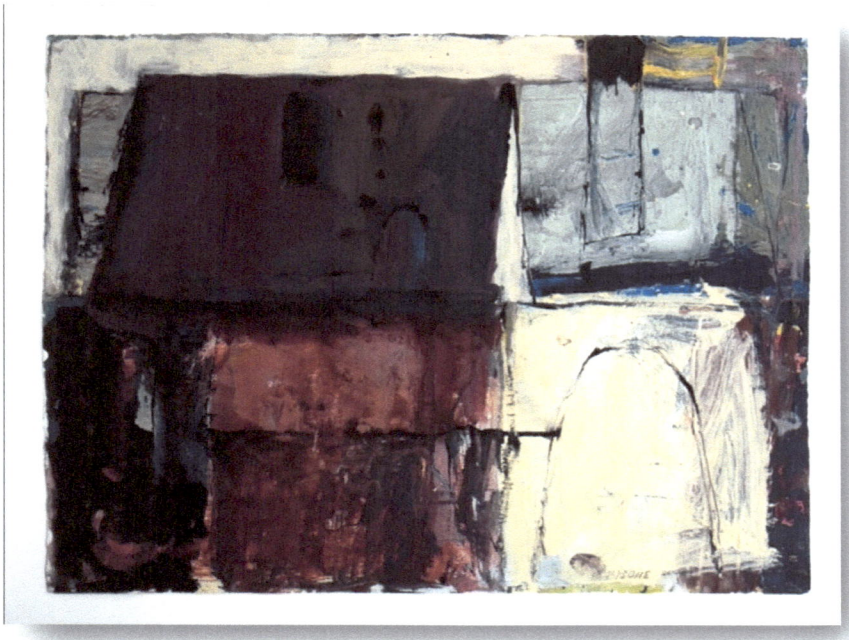

Cedar Tavern Series, 2008-9, 12 x 16 inches

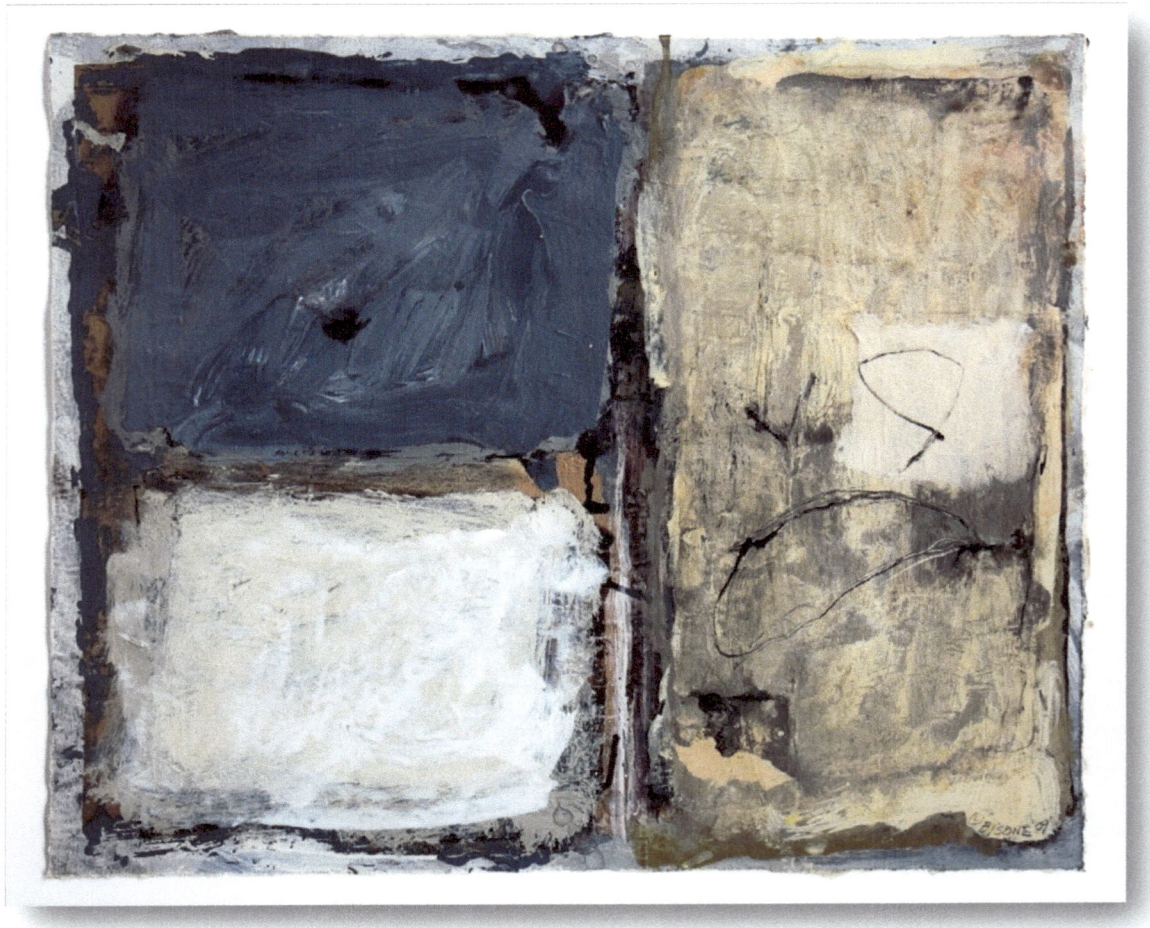

Cedar Tavern Series #1, 2008-9, 12 x 14 inches

somewhere, between seen
     and related, the mind
          creates new meaning

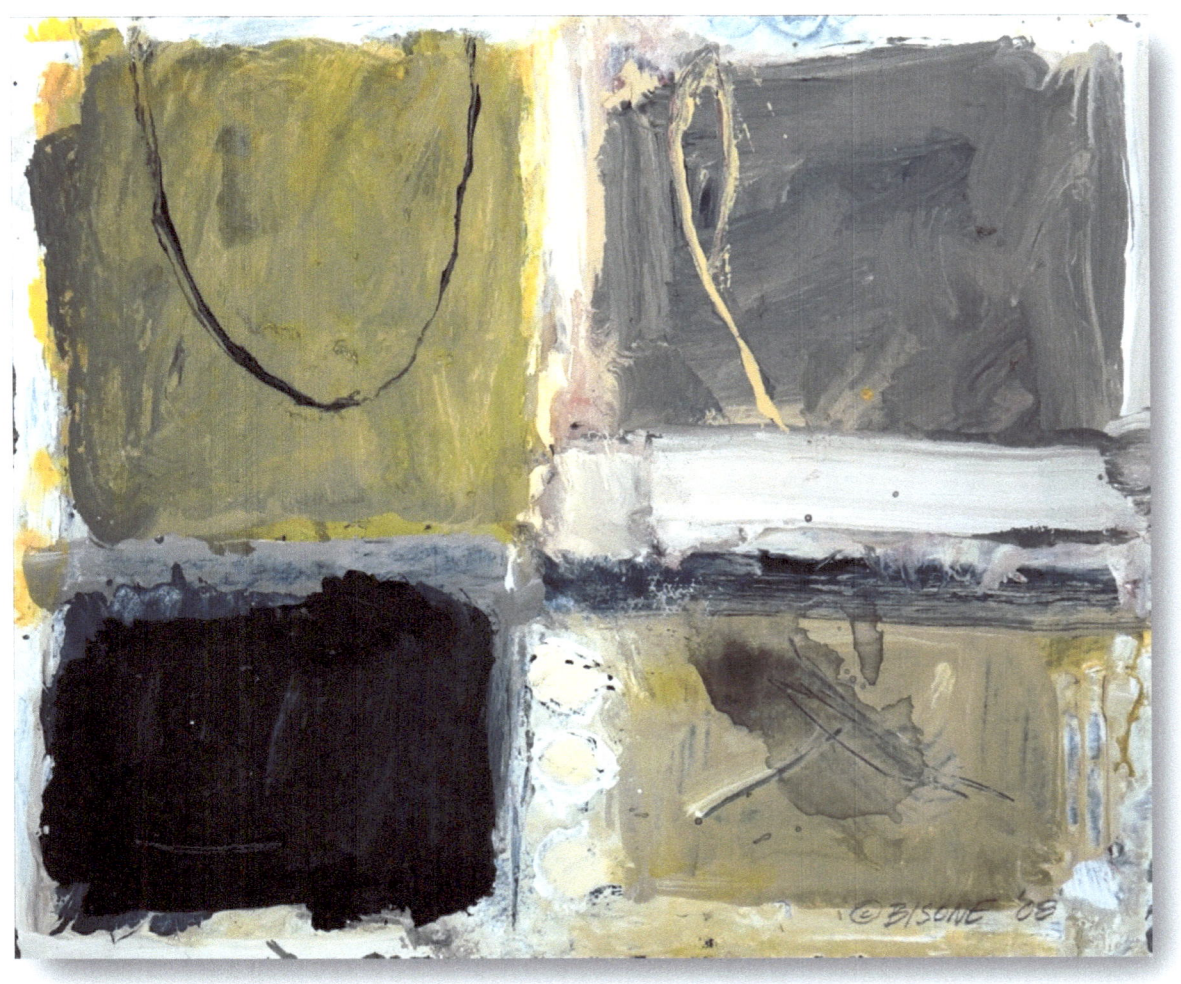

Cedar Tavern Series IV, 2008, 11.5 x 13.75 inches

7. Seated Figures

Painted from 1994 through 2009, these images depict men and women sitting without expression, with mostly featureless faces. These passive figures appear to be waiting – for what?

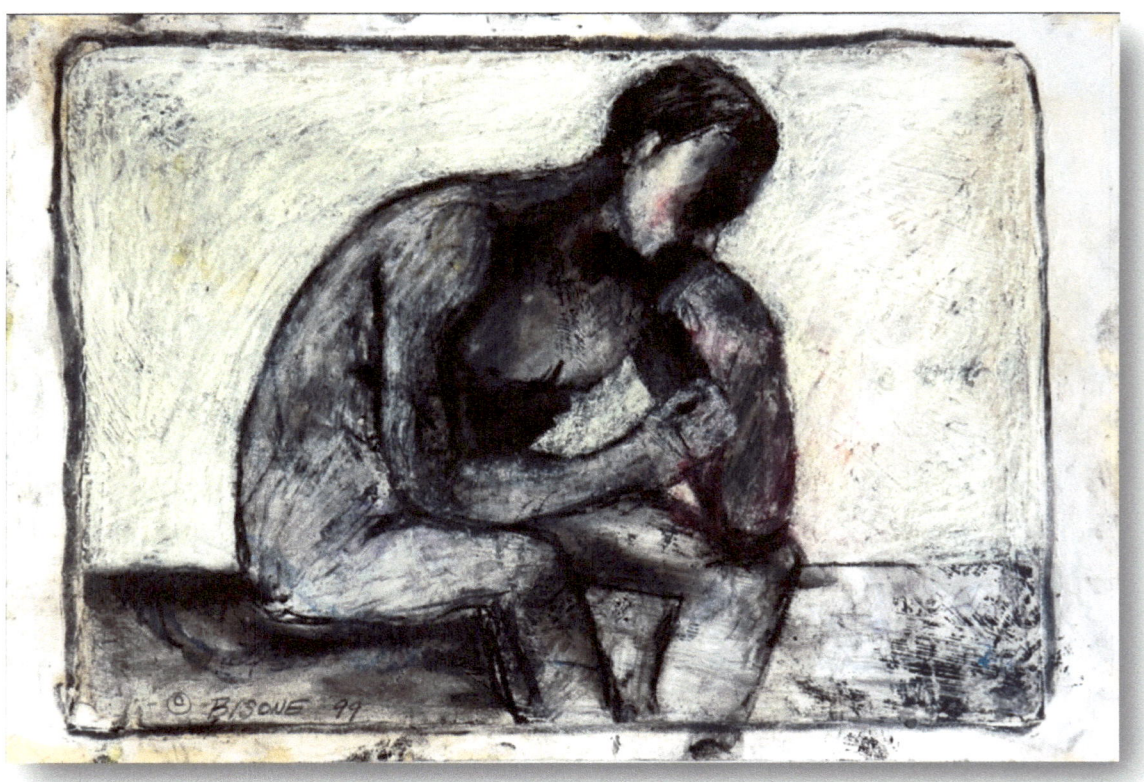

Time Out, 1999, 9.75 x 12.25 inches

at the edge of mind,
or the edge of the room, the same
living on the edge

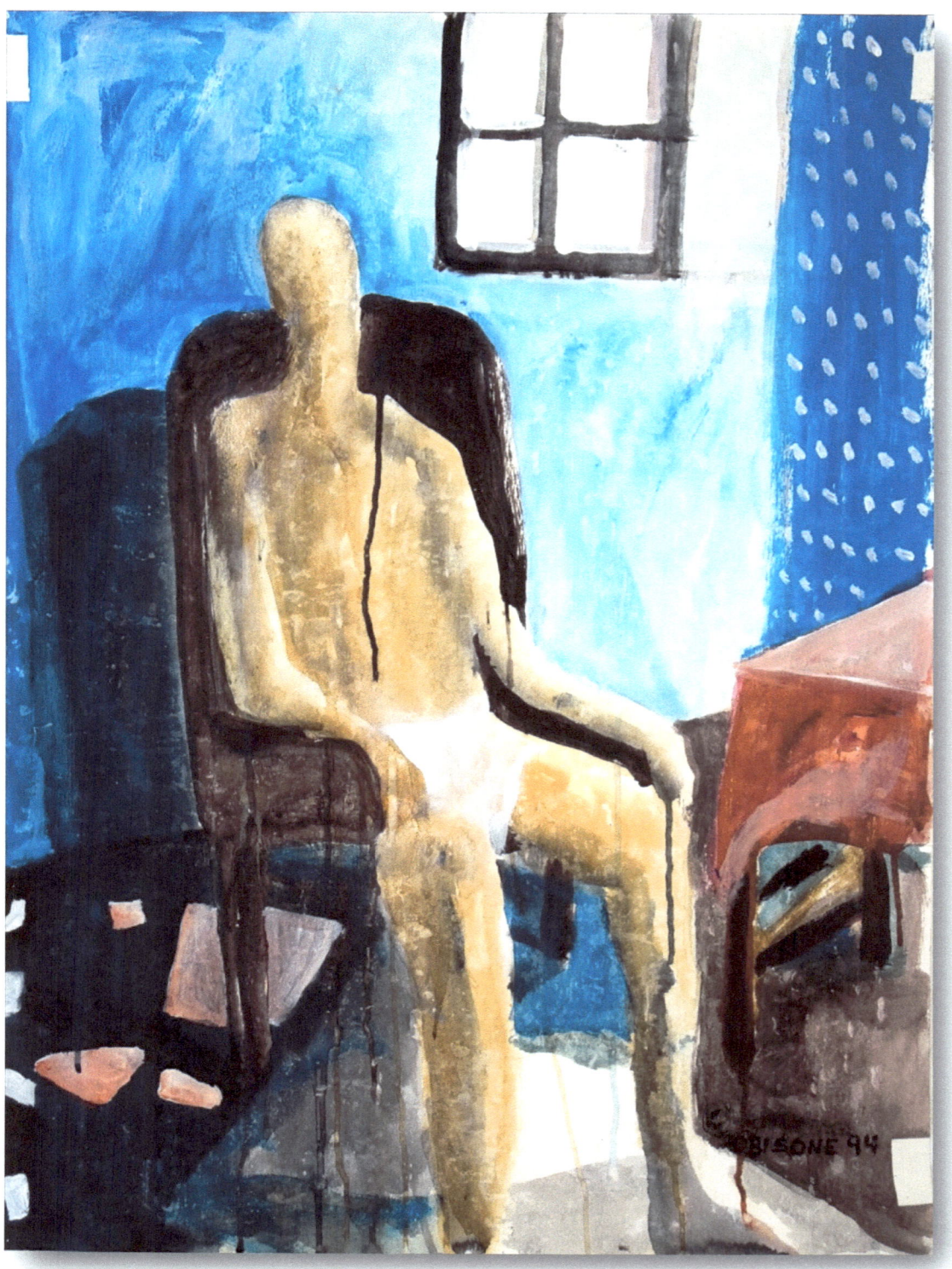

Figure in Easy Chair, 1994, 29.75 x 22 inches

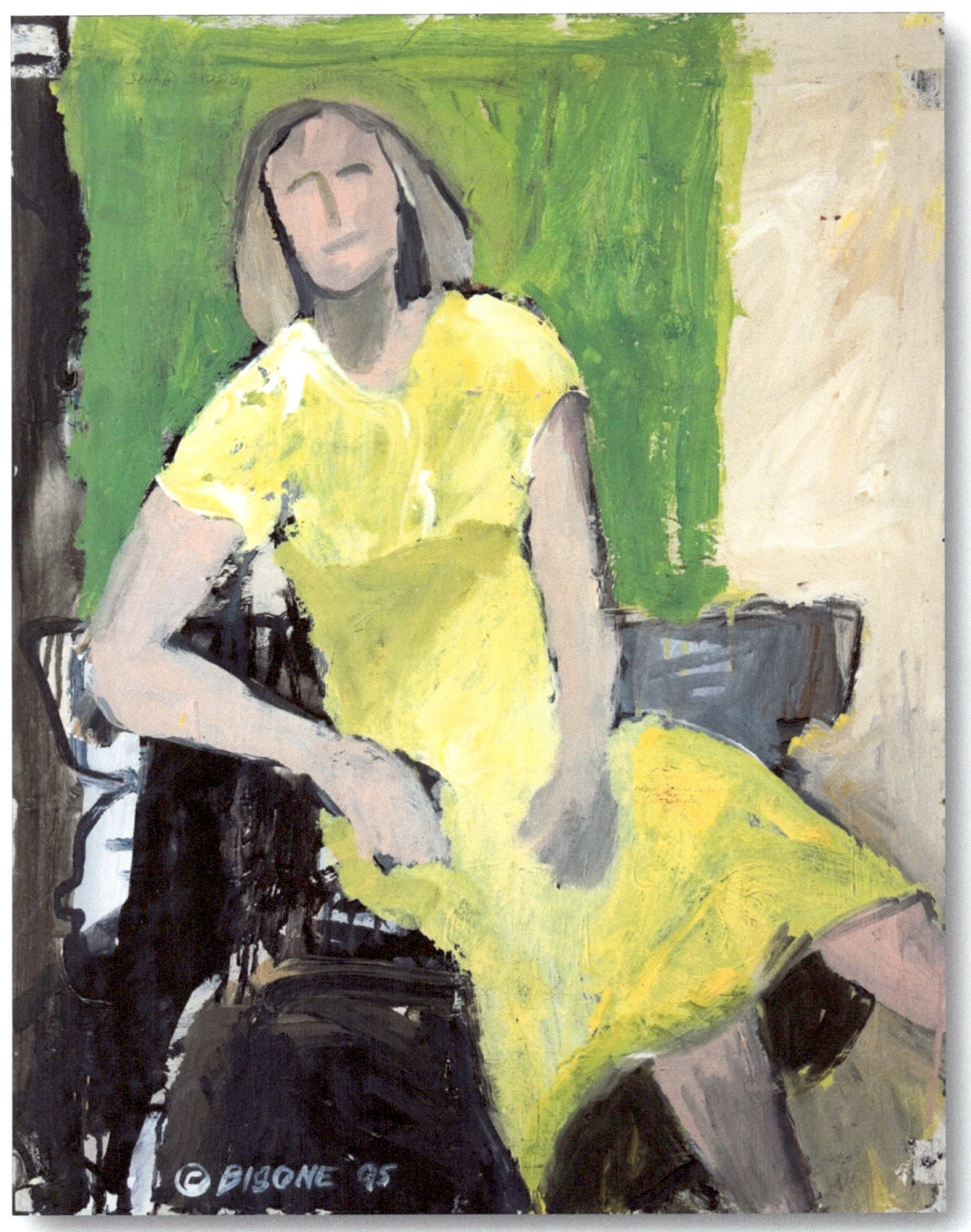

Girl with Yellow Dress, 1995, 26 x 20 inches

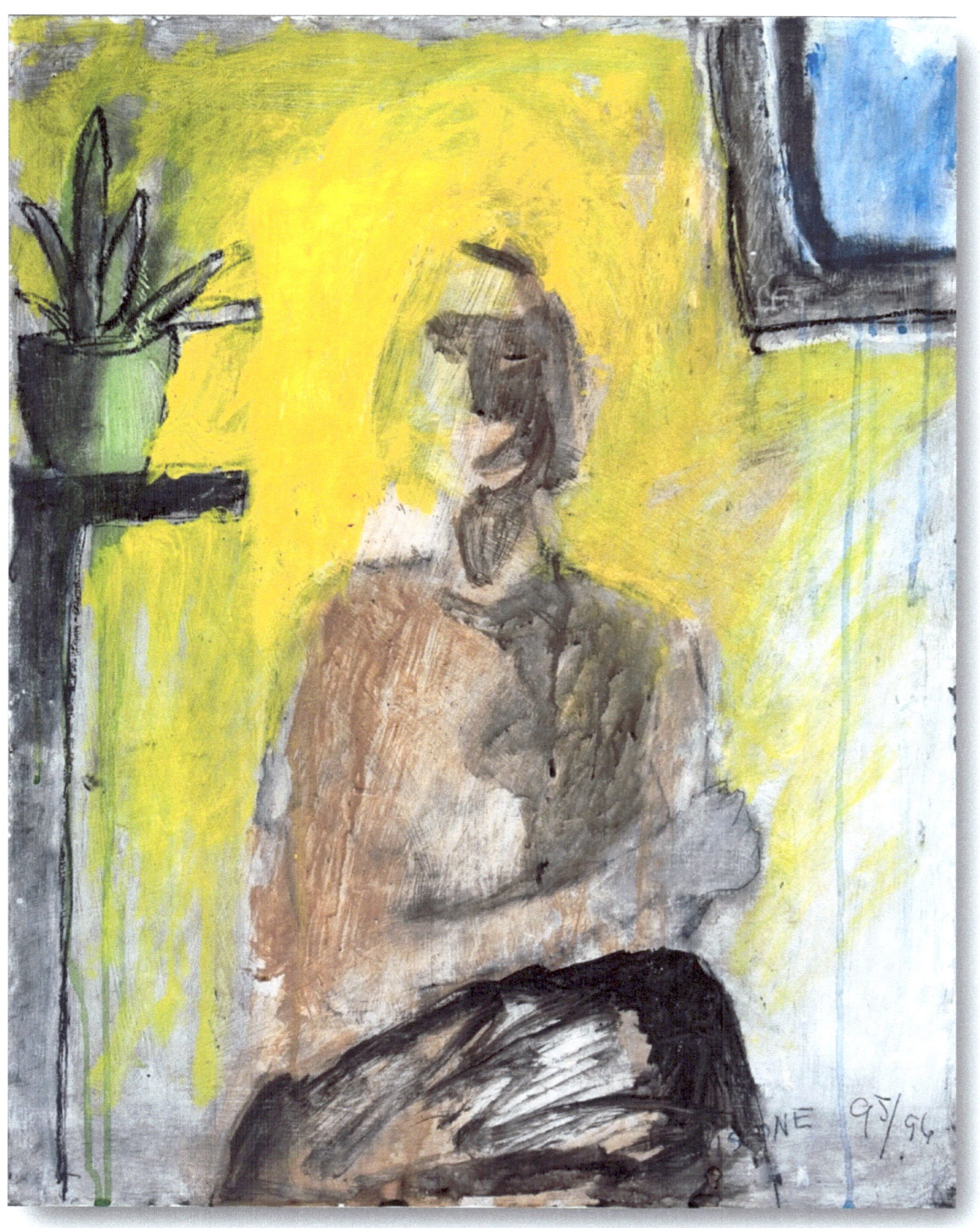

Keep the Aspidistra Flying, 1995-96, 25 x 19 inches

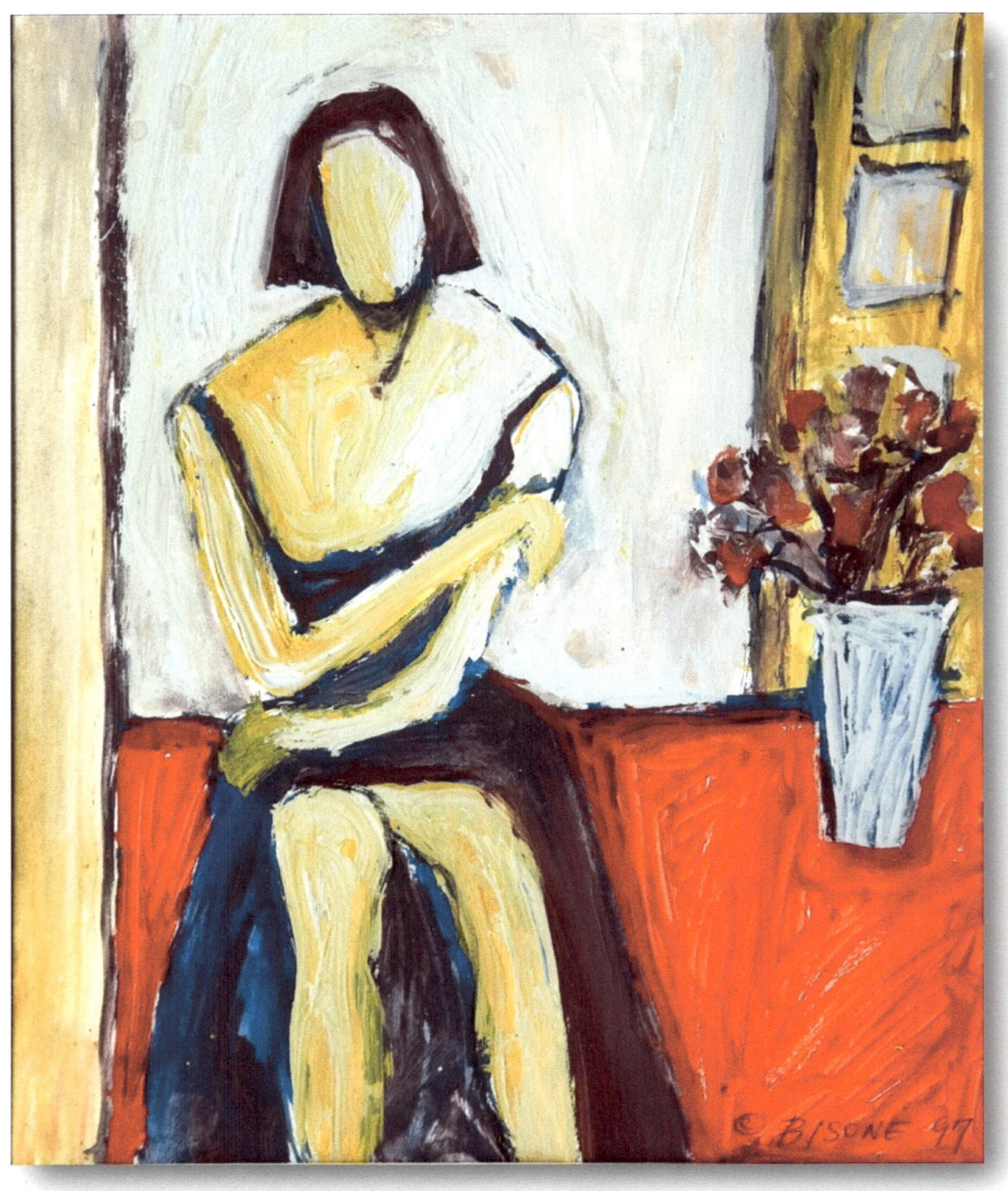

Seated Figure with Red Flowers, 1997, 12 x 10 inches

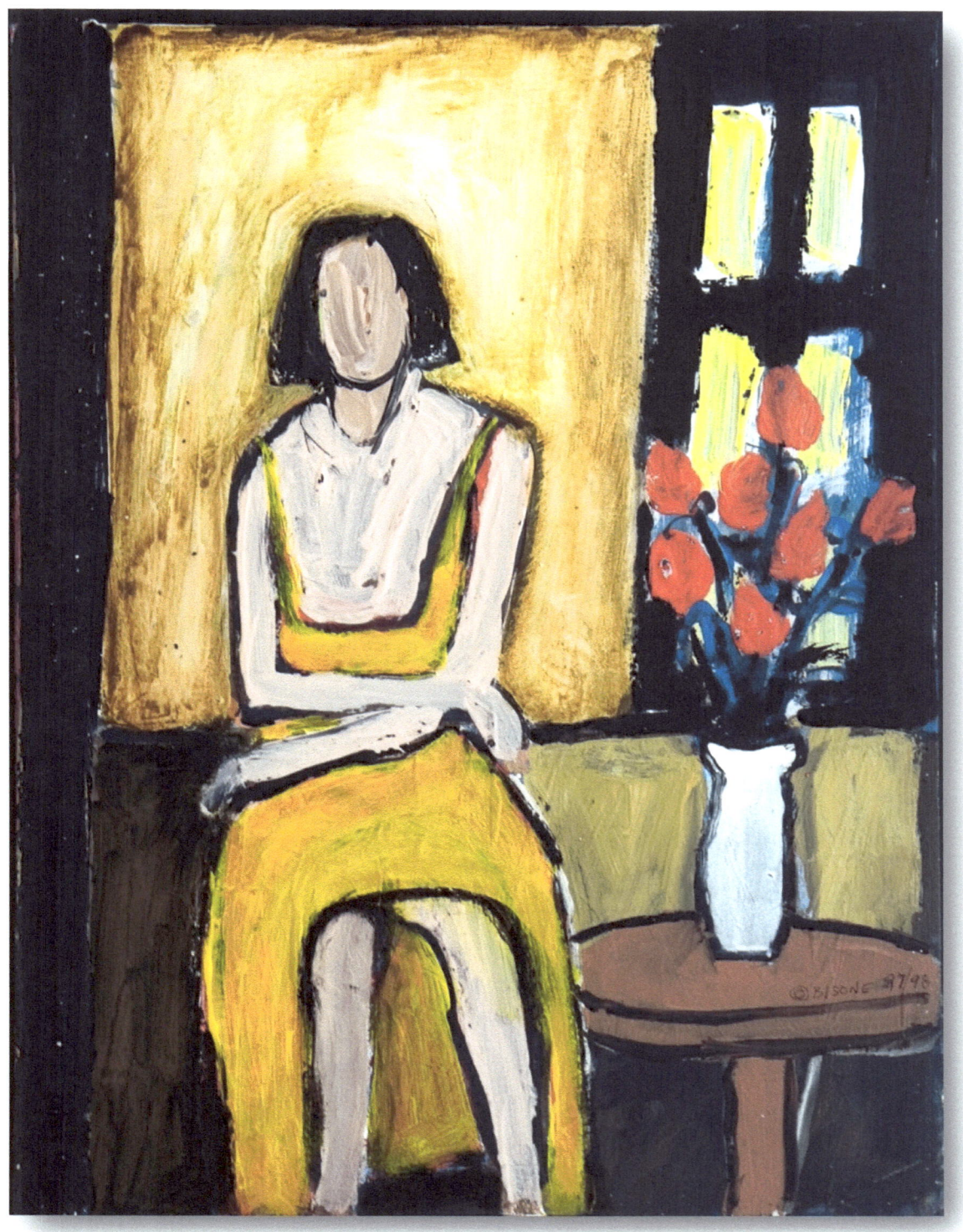

Yellow Dress Red Flowers, 1997-98, 16 x 12.25 inches

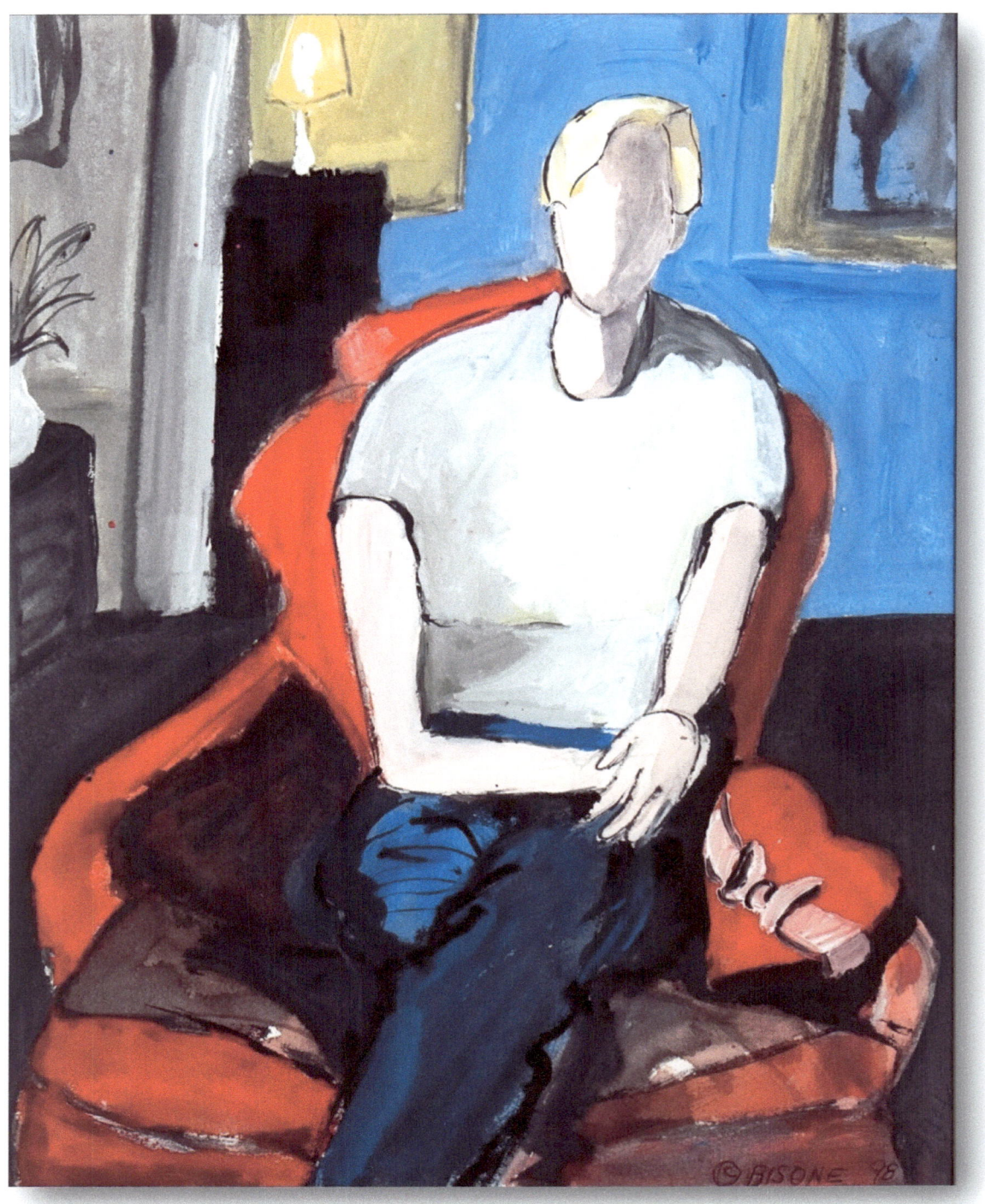

Untitled, 1998, 16.25 x 13 inches

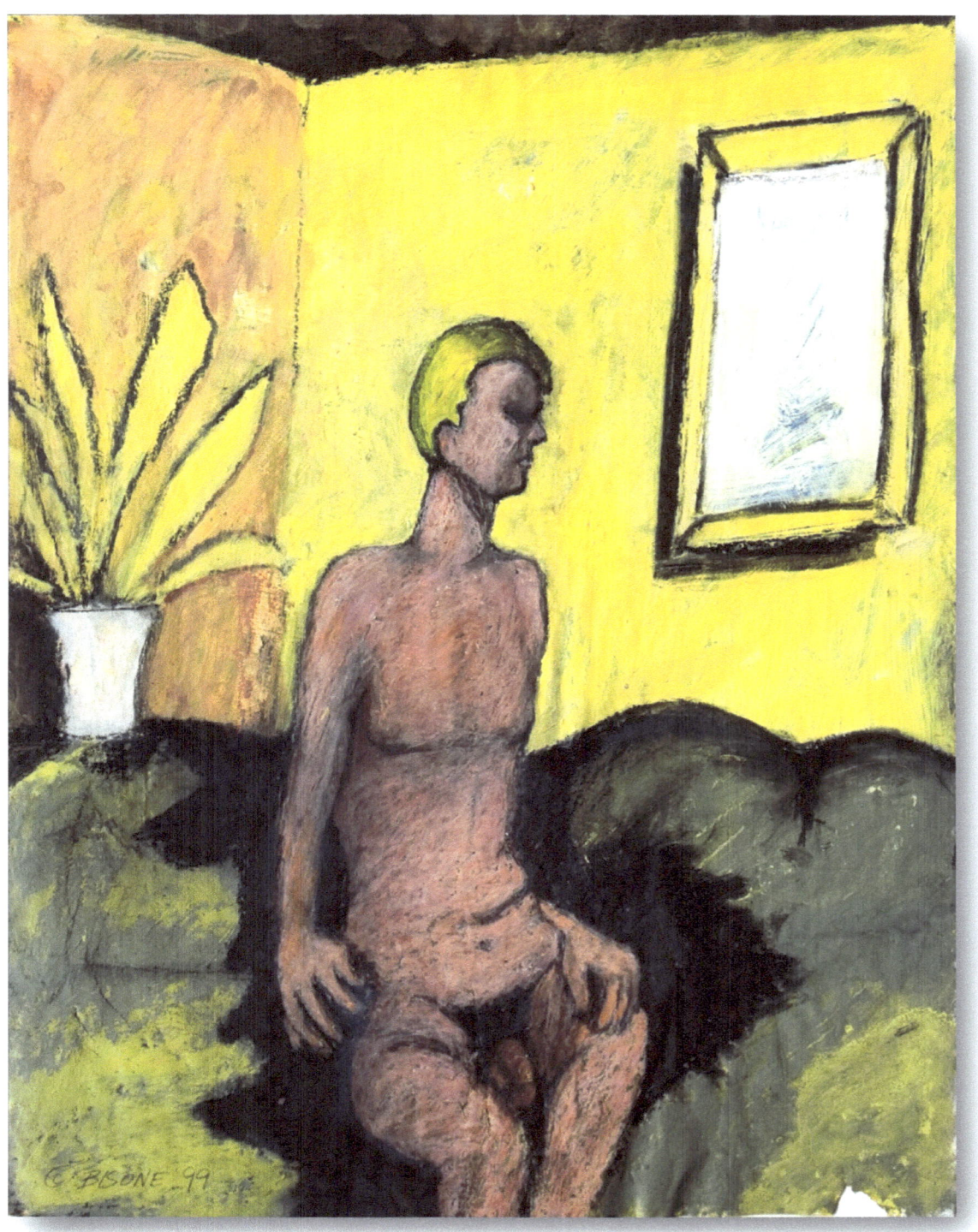

Green Couch, 1999, 24 x 18.75 inches

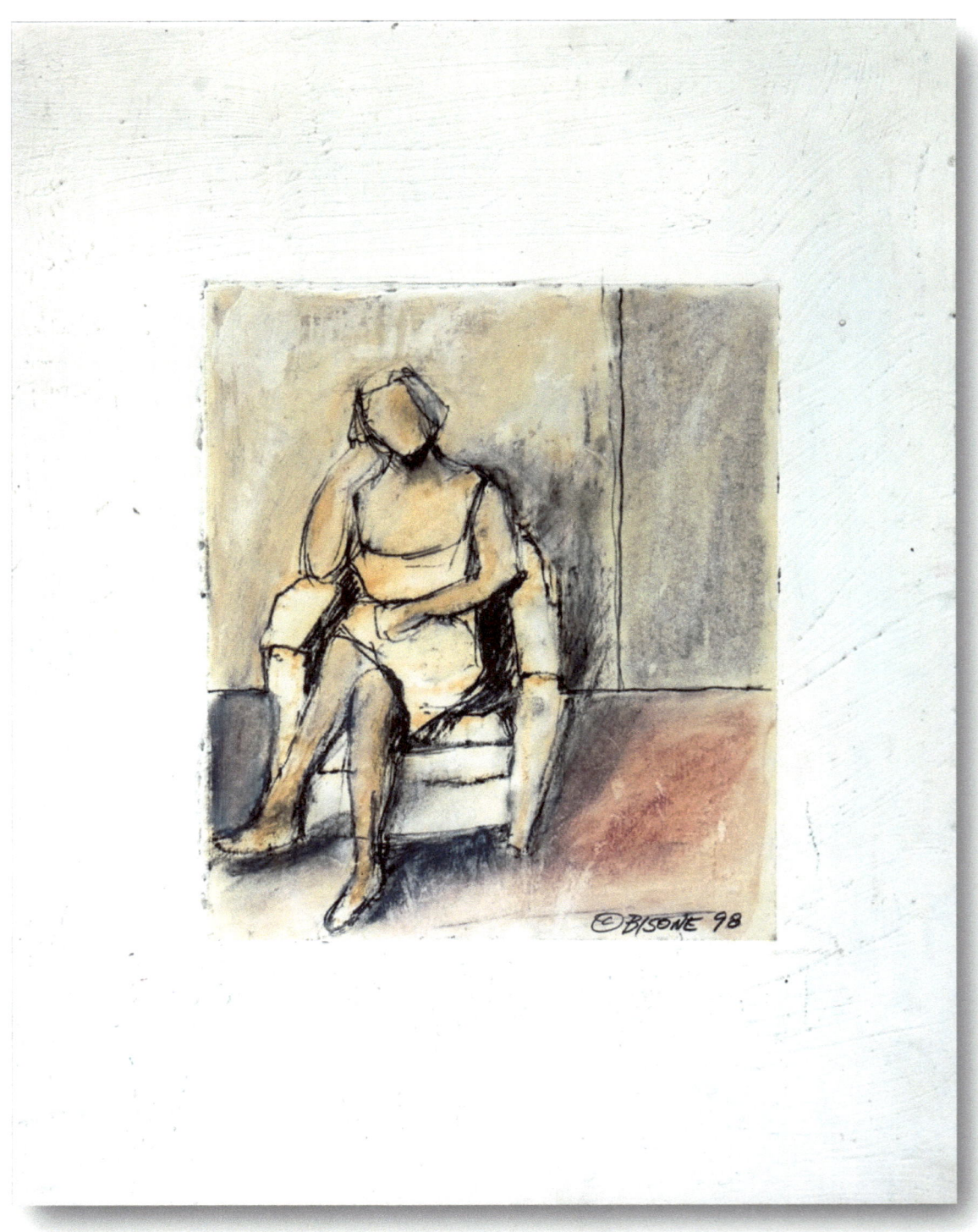

Seated Woman, 1998, 14 x 11 inches

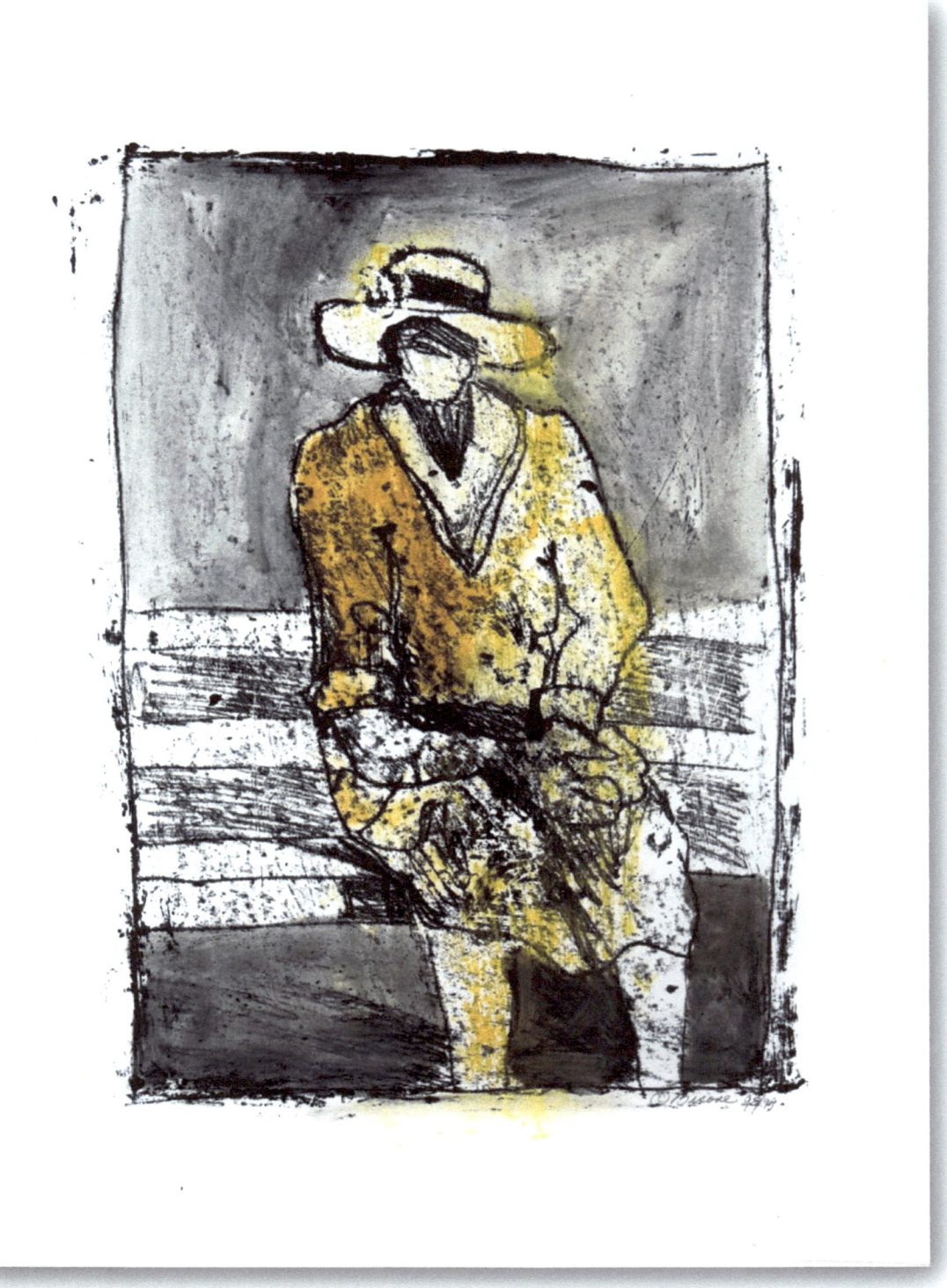

Seated Female Figure with Hat, 1998-99, 24 x 18 inches

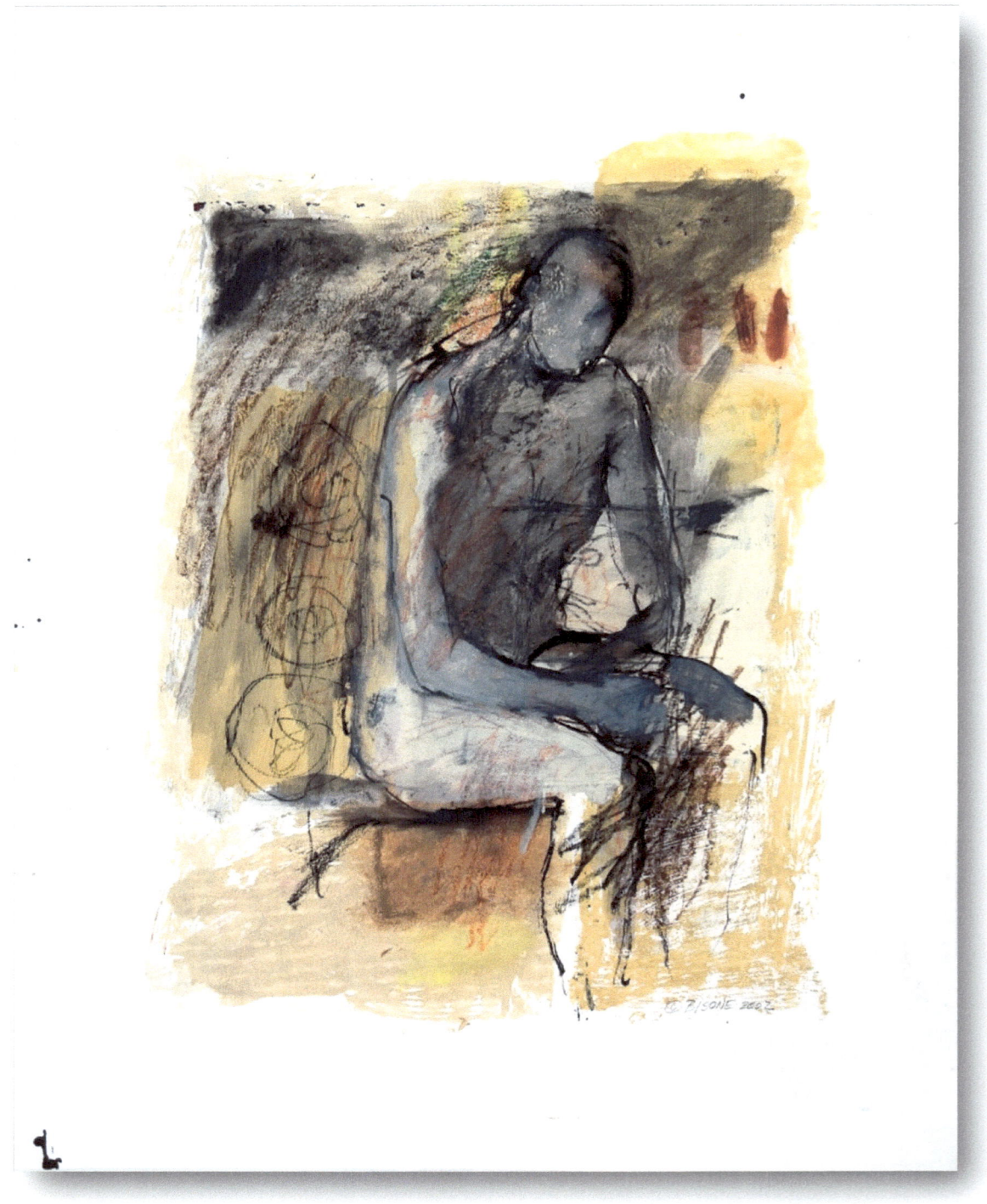

Sitting Down, 2002, 23.75 x 19 inches

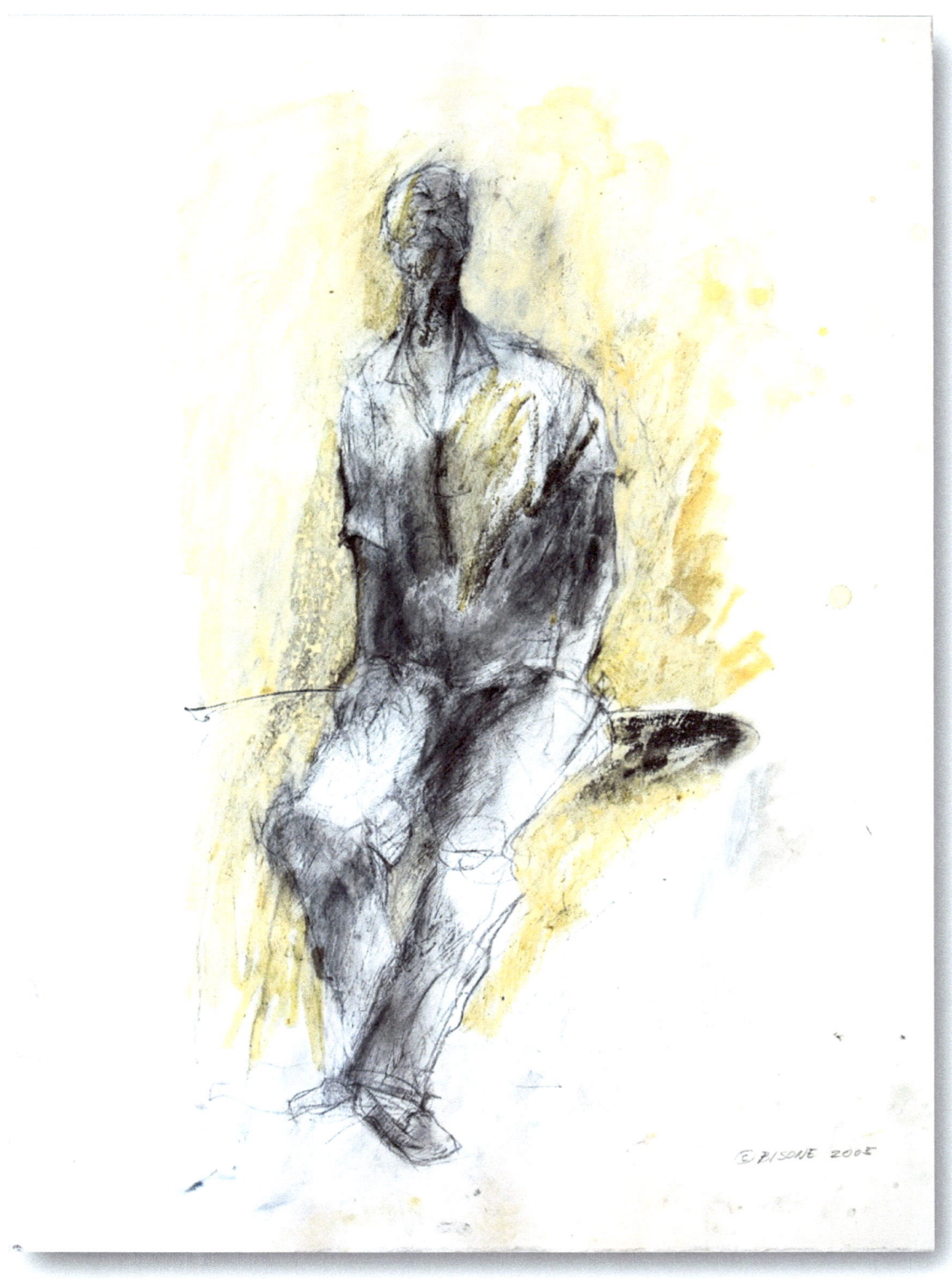

Untitled, 2005, 27 x 20 inches

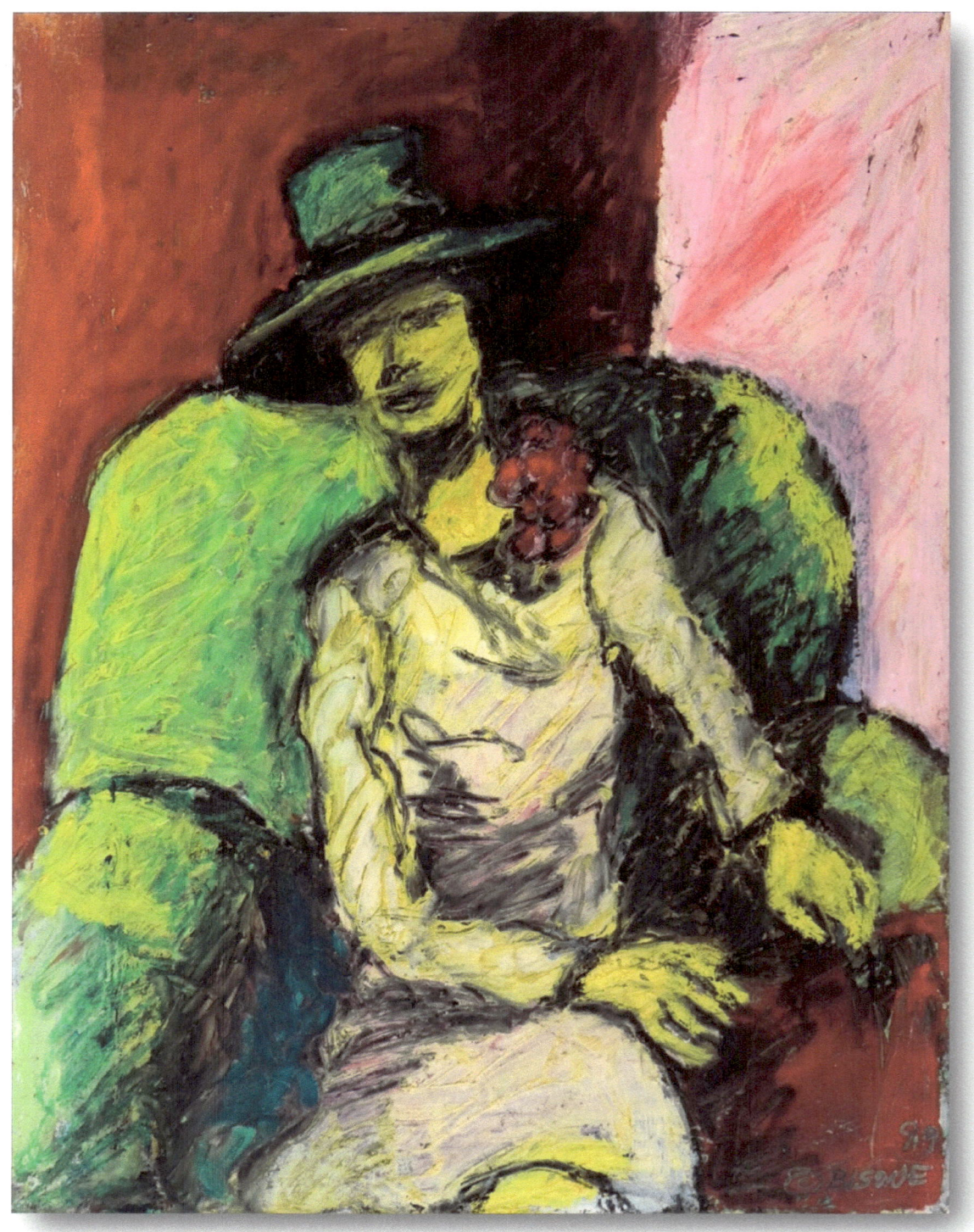

Green Hat with Corsage, 1999, 13 x 10 inches

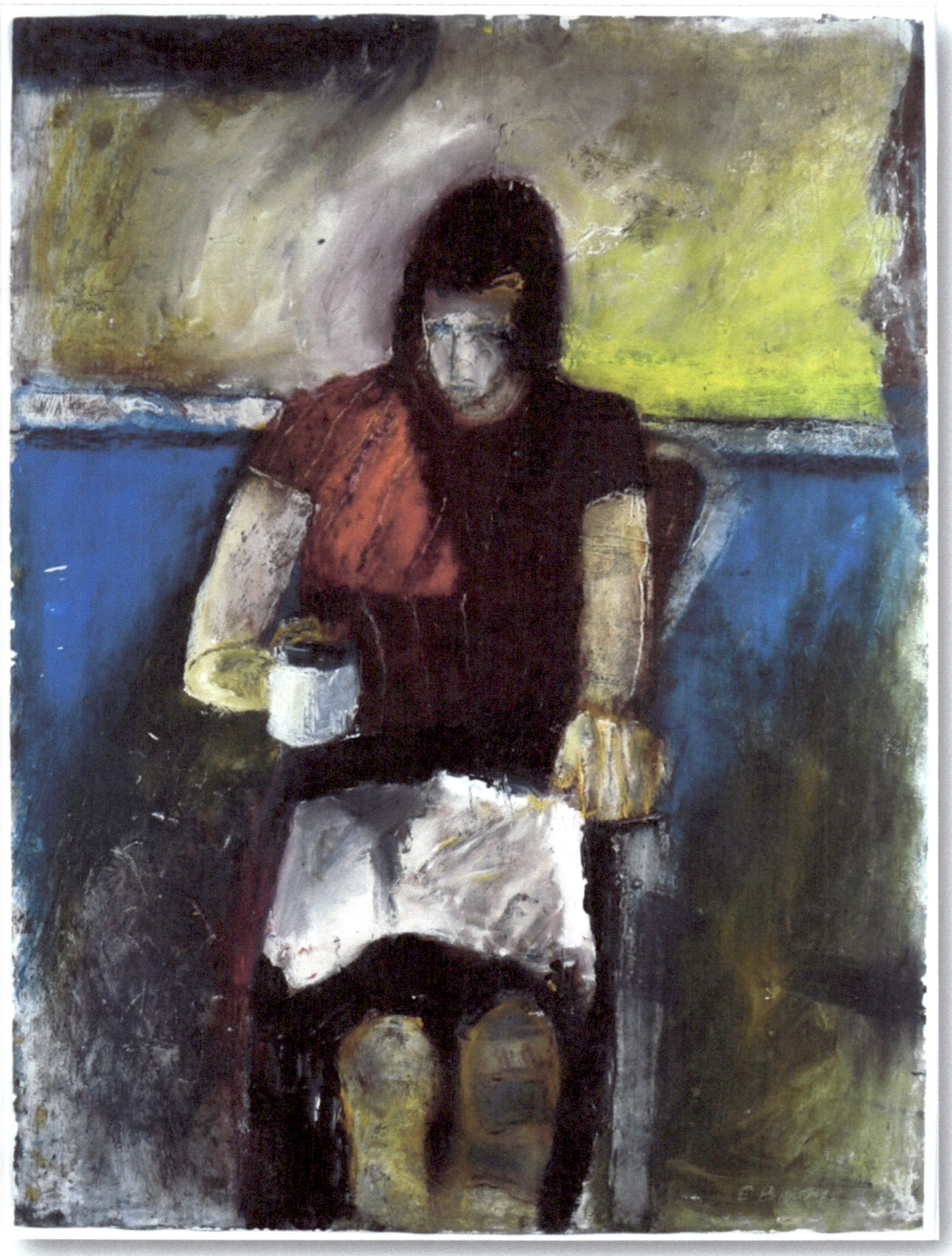

Seated Lady (Homage to Richard Diebenkorn), 2000, 24 x 18 inches

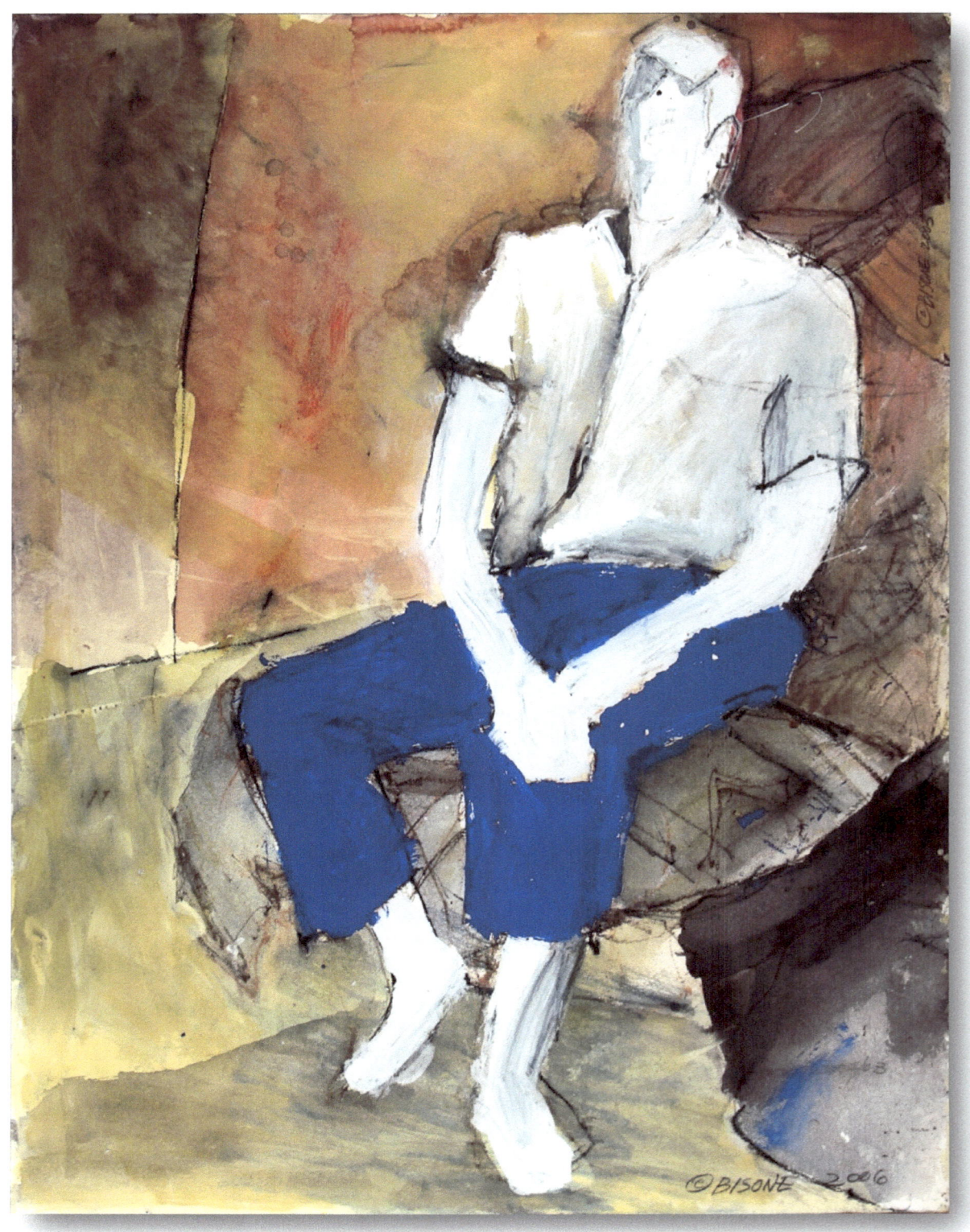

Blue Trousers, 2006, 22 x 17 inches

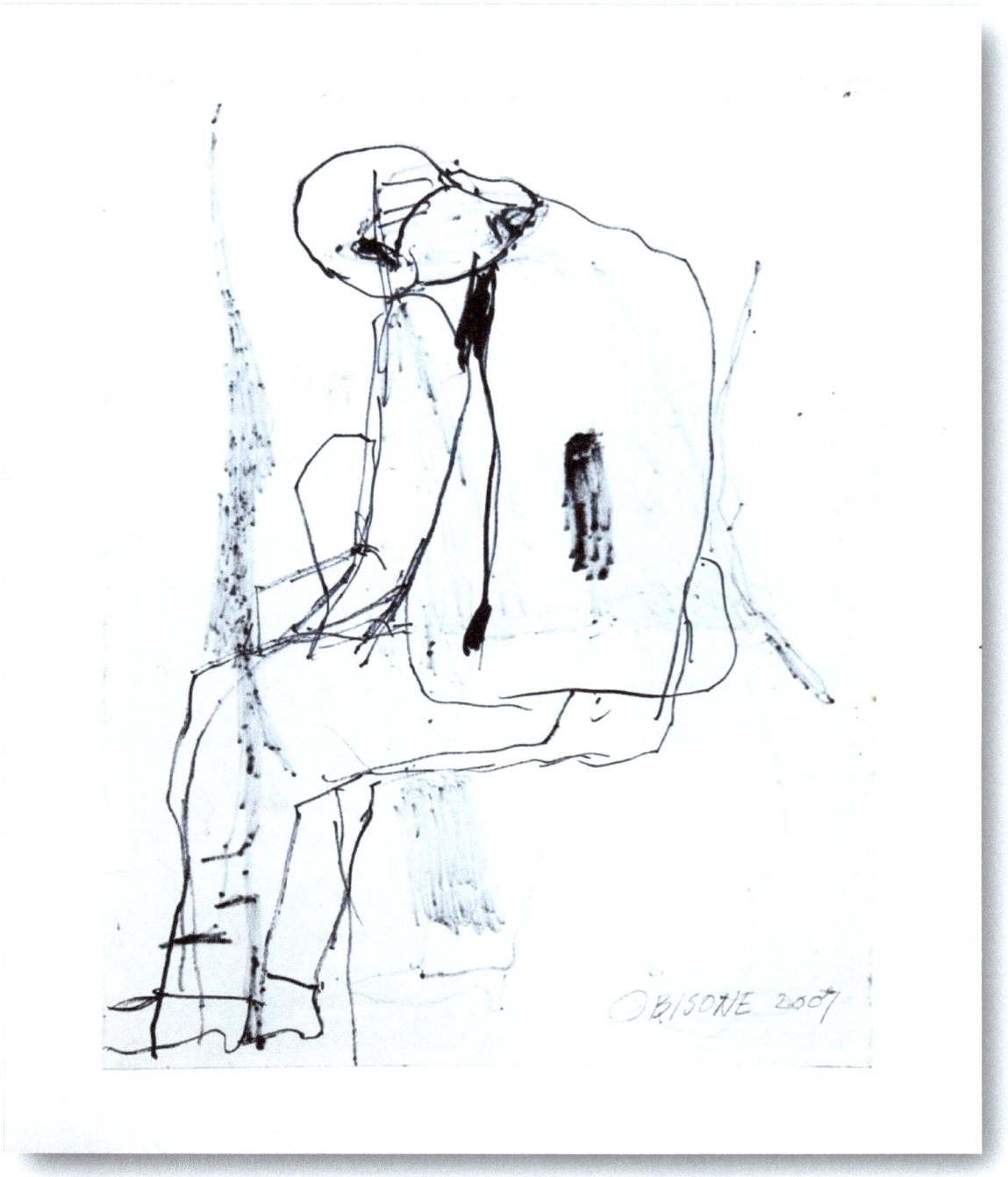

Drawing, 2007, 14 x 11 inches

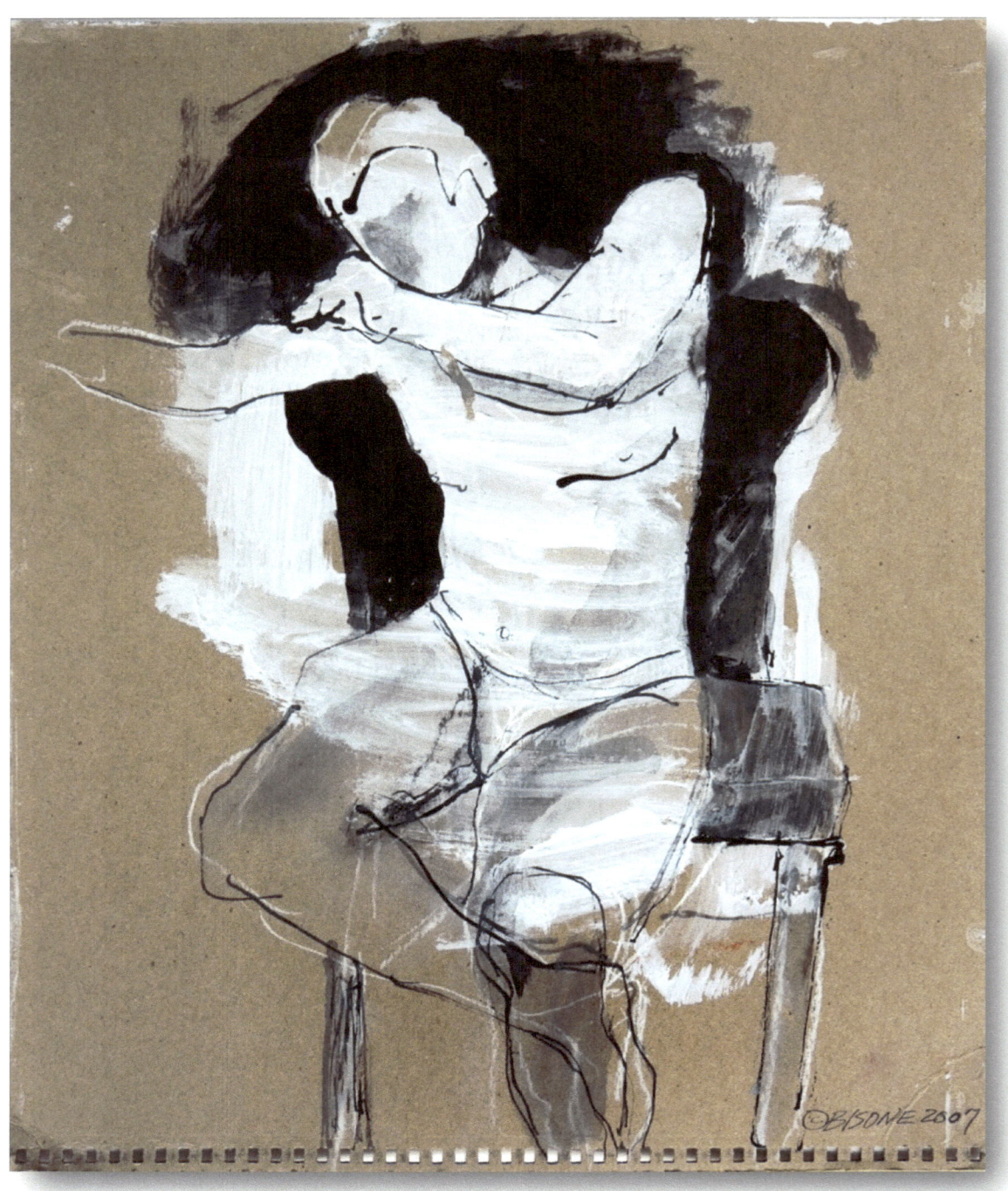

Young Man Resting, 2007, 18 x 15 inches

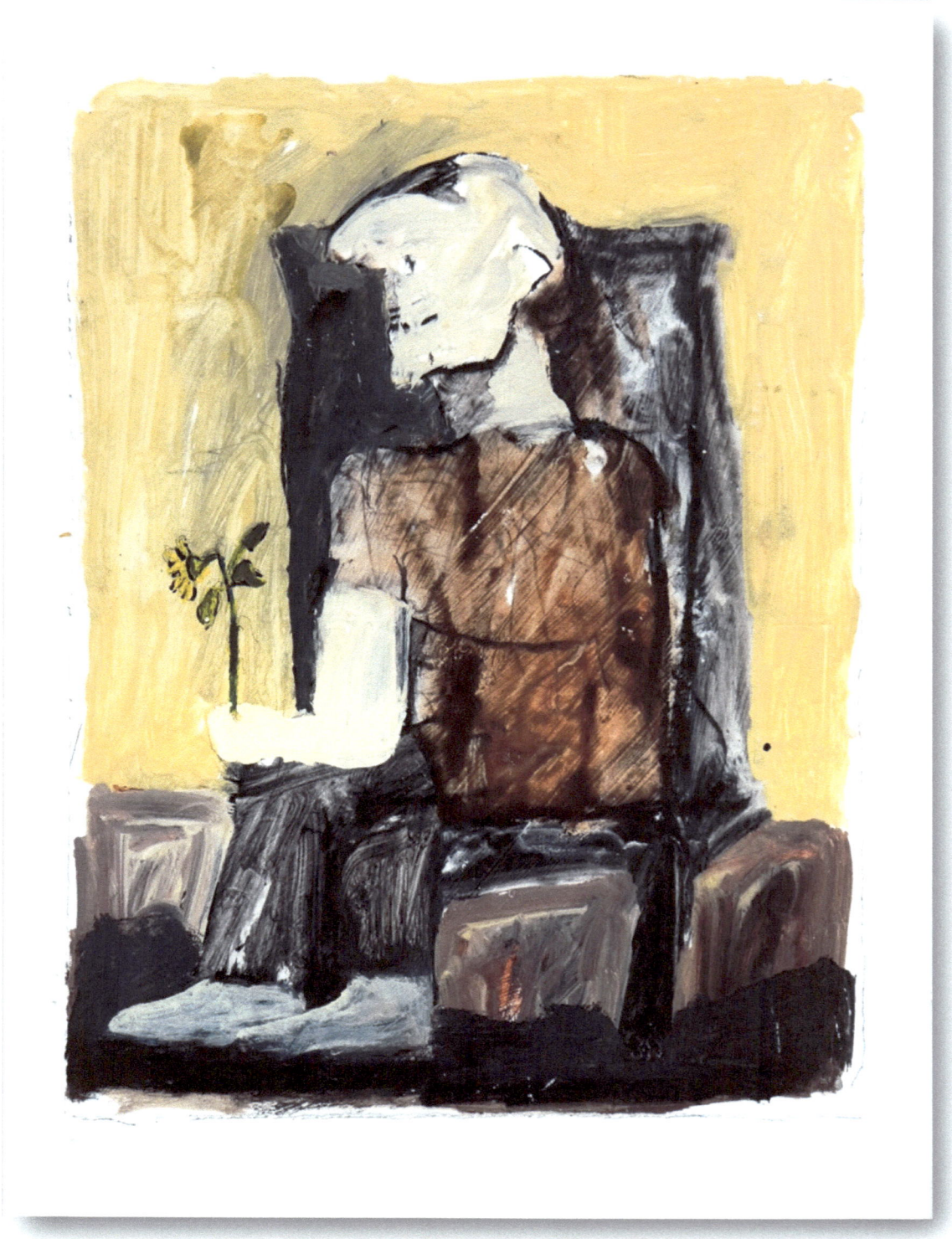

Broken Blossoms, 2007, 27 x 20 inches

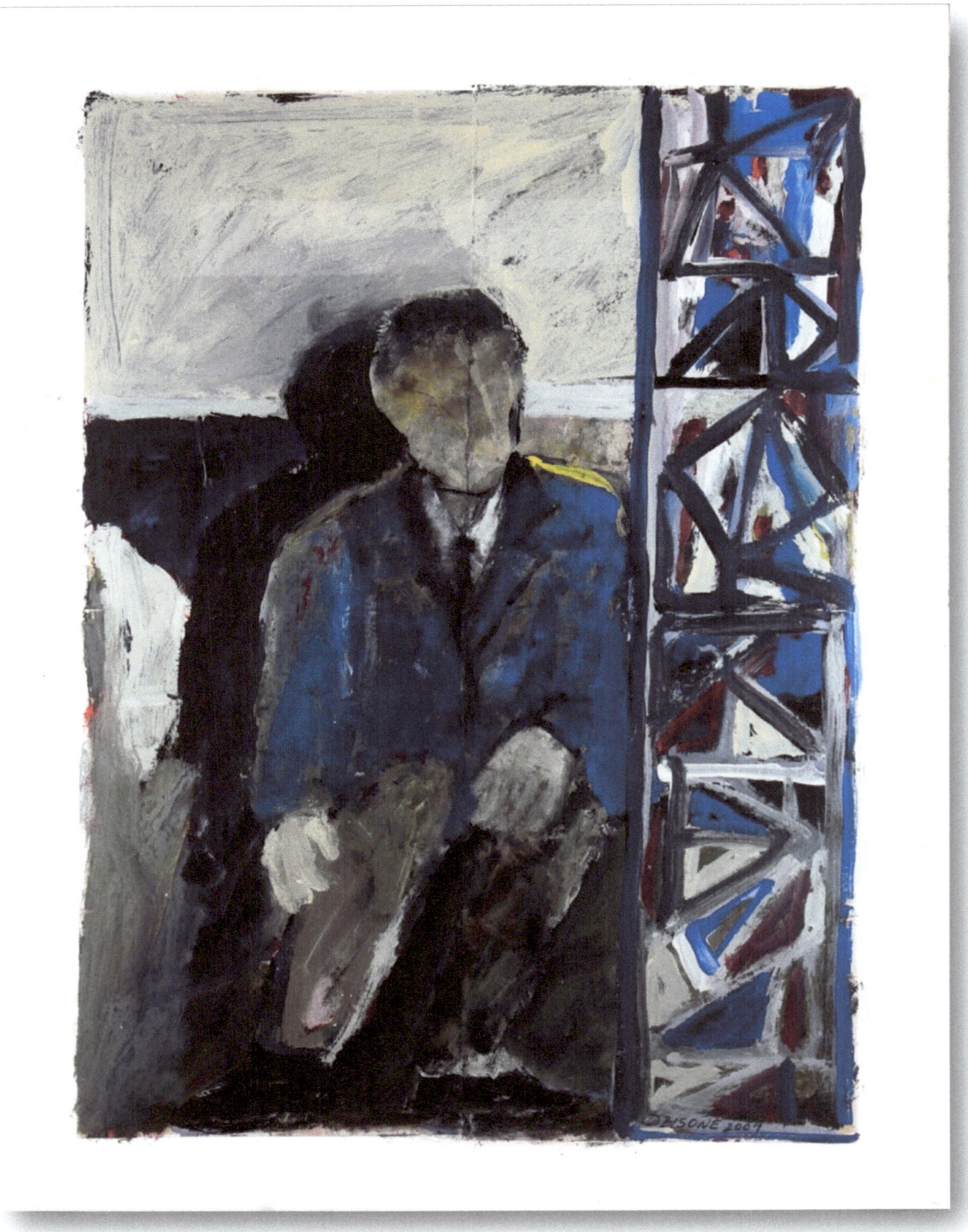

Waiting for ..., 2007, 28 x 22 inches

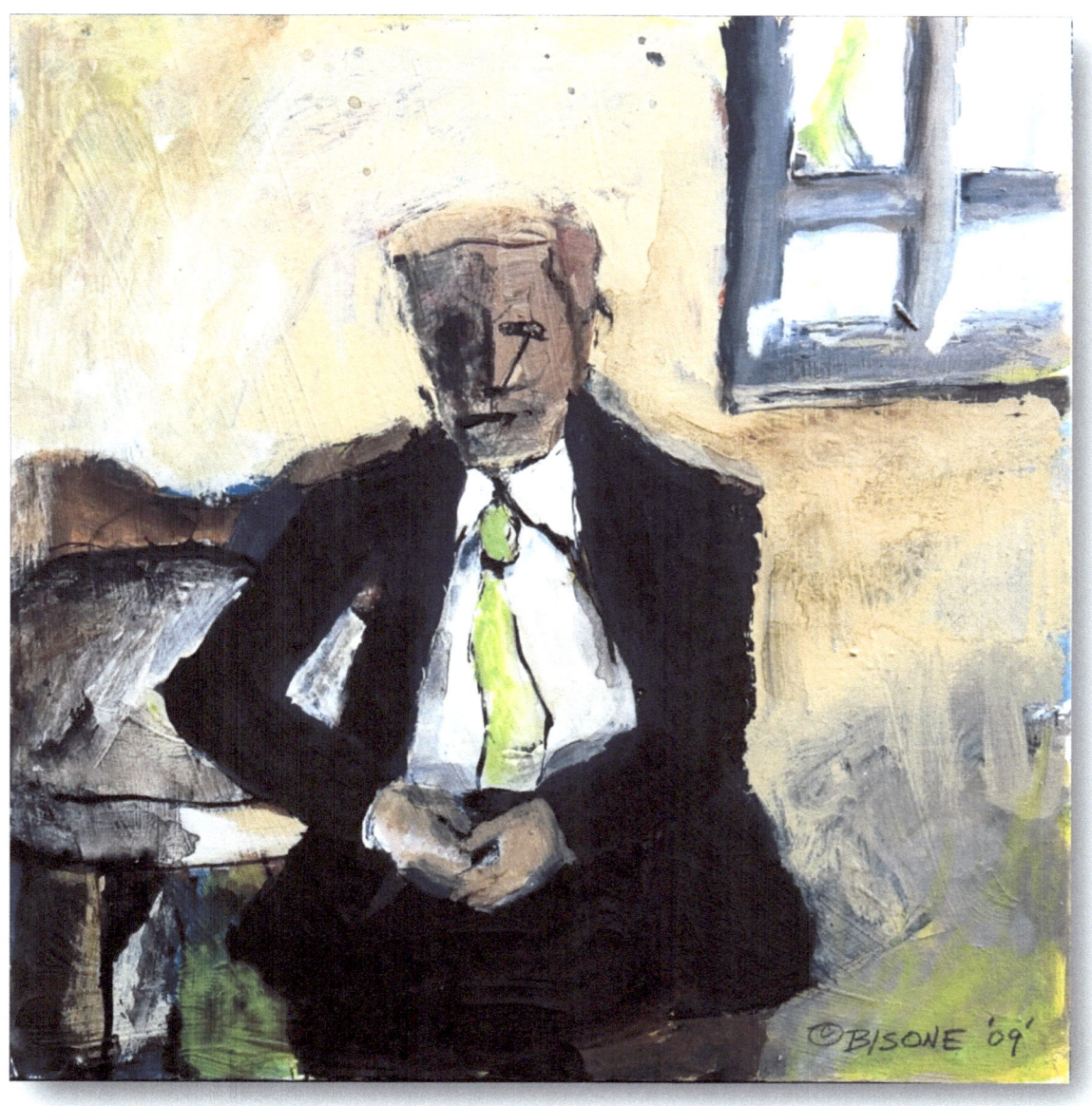

Waiting, 2009, 15 x 14.5 inches

8. Houses

Houses, painted in 2008-9 in the warmest yellows, browns, and greens, invite the viewer. Emotion exudes. The homes beckon, but something, - or some one -, is missing. Ghostly, haunting, shapes are found near several of the buildings. Smokestacks exhale vestiges of life.

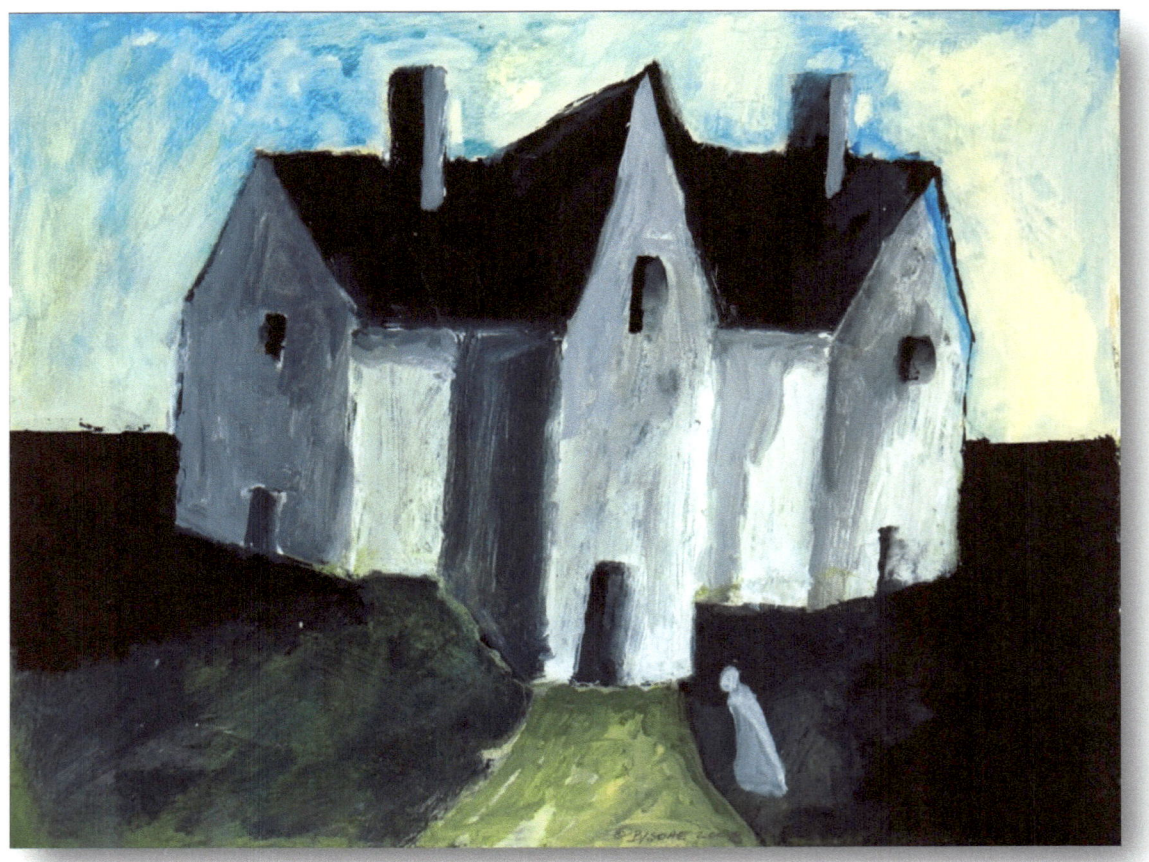

Evening Song, 2008, 13 x 17 inches

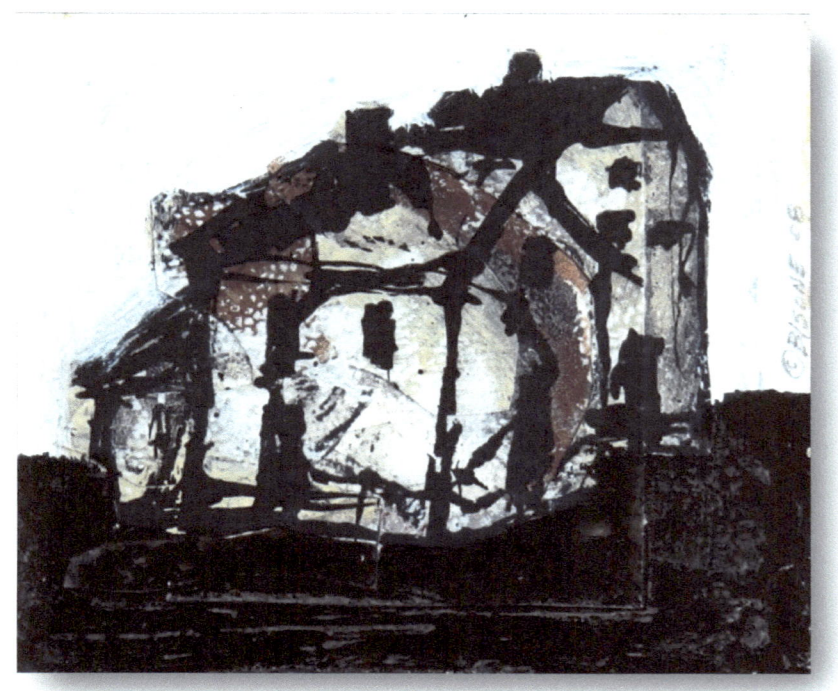

Untitled, 2008, 6.75 x 7.5 inches

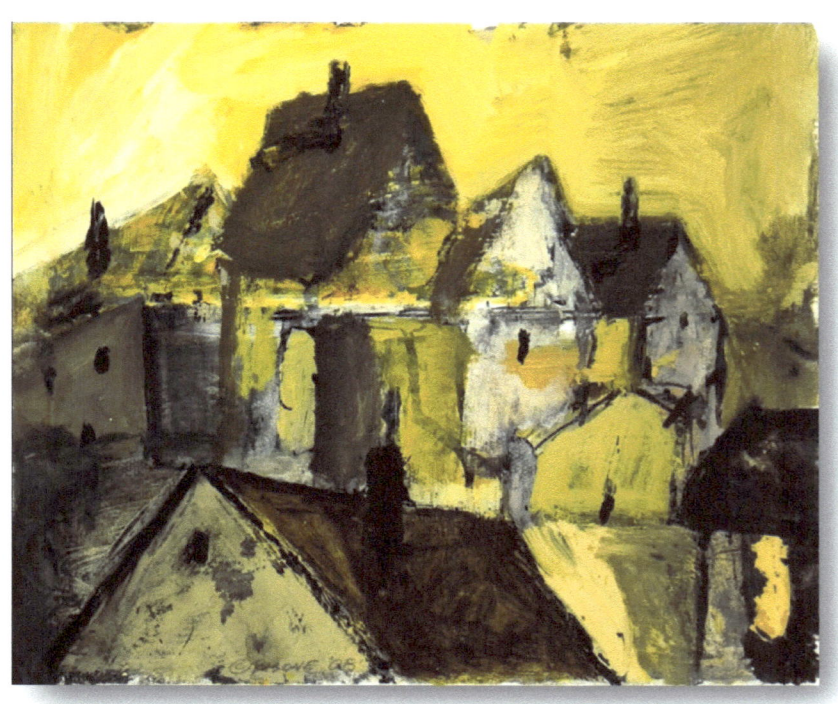

A Dickensian Town, 2008, 11 x 13.25 inches

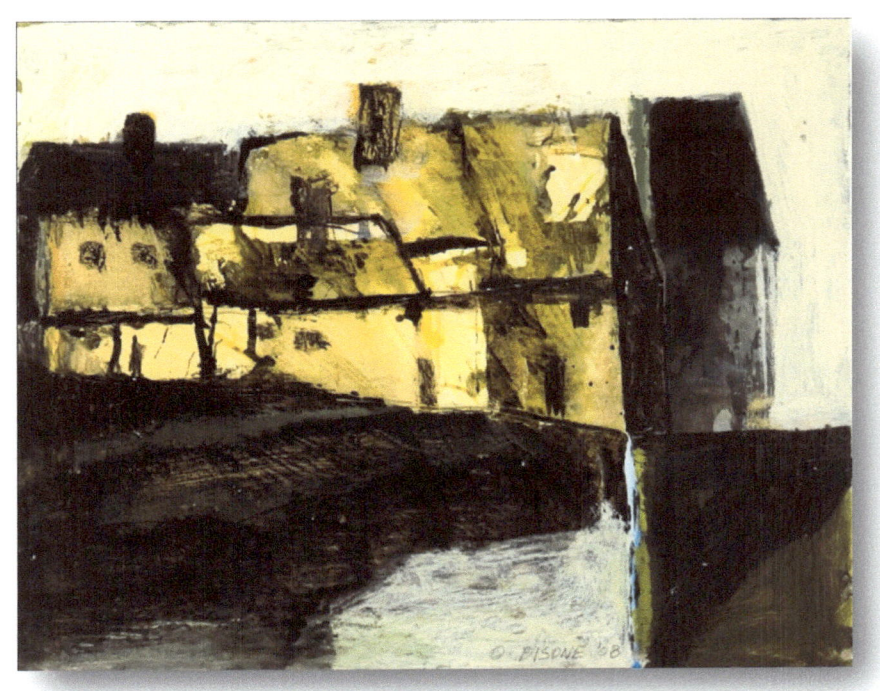

Chimney Pots, 2008, 11 x 14 inches

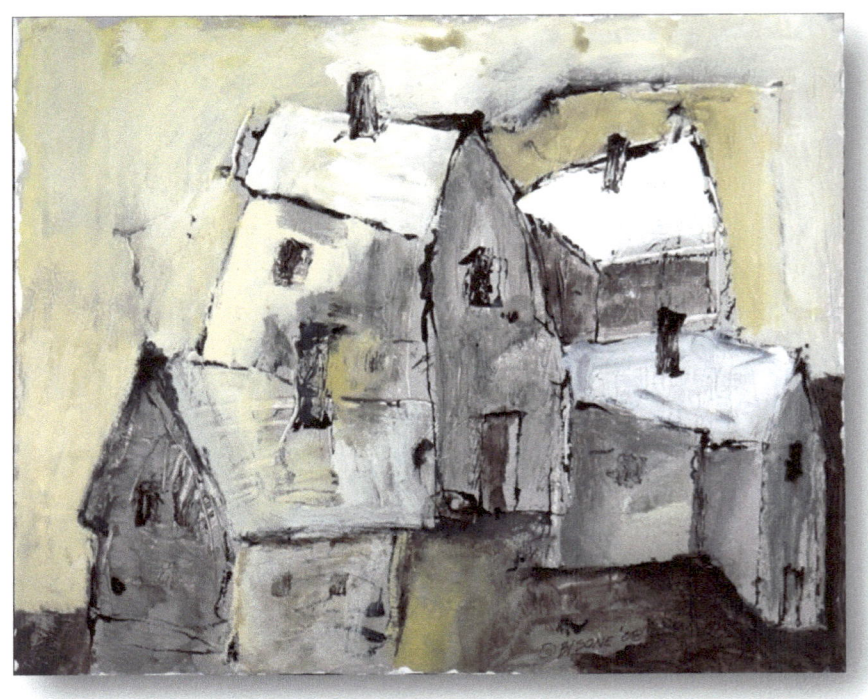

Hillside Houses, 2008 16 x 20 inches

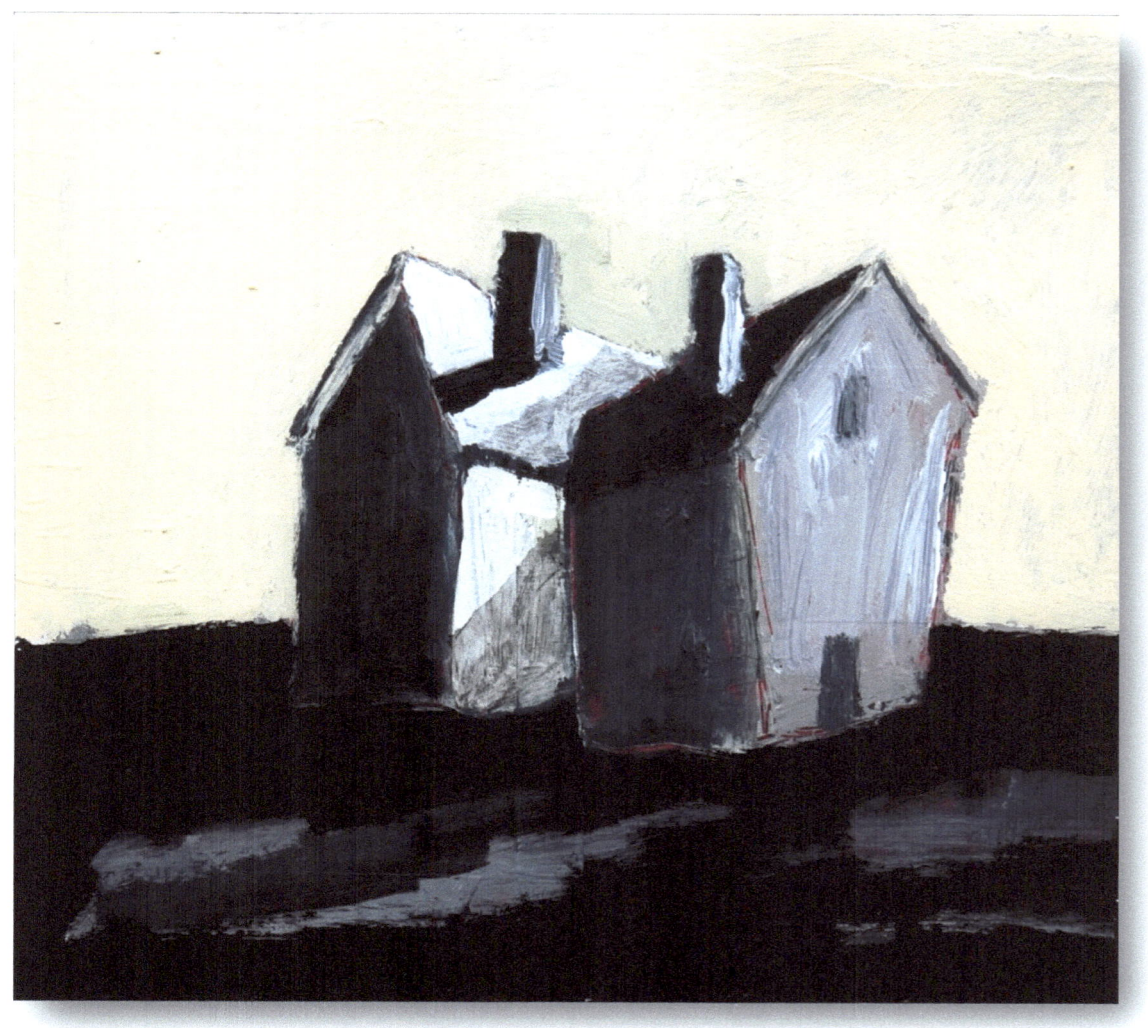

Houses in Sunlight & Shadow, 2008, 15.5 x 17 inches

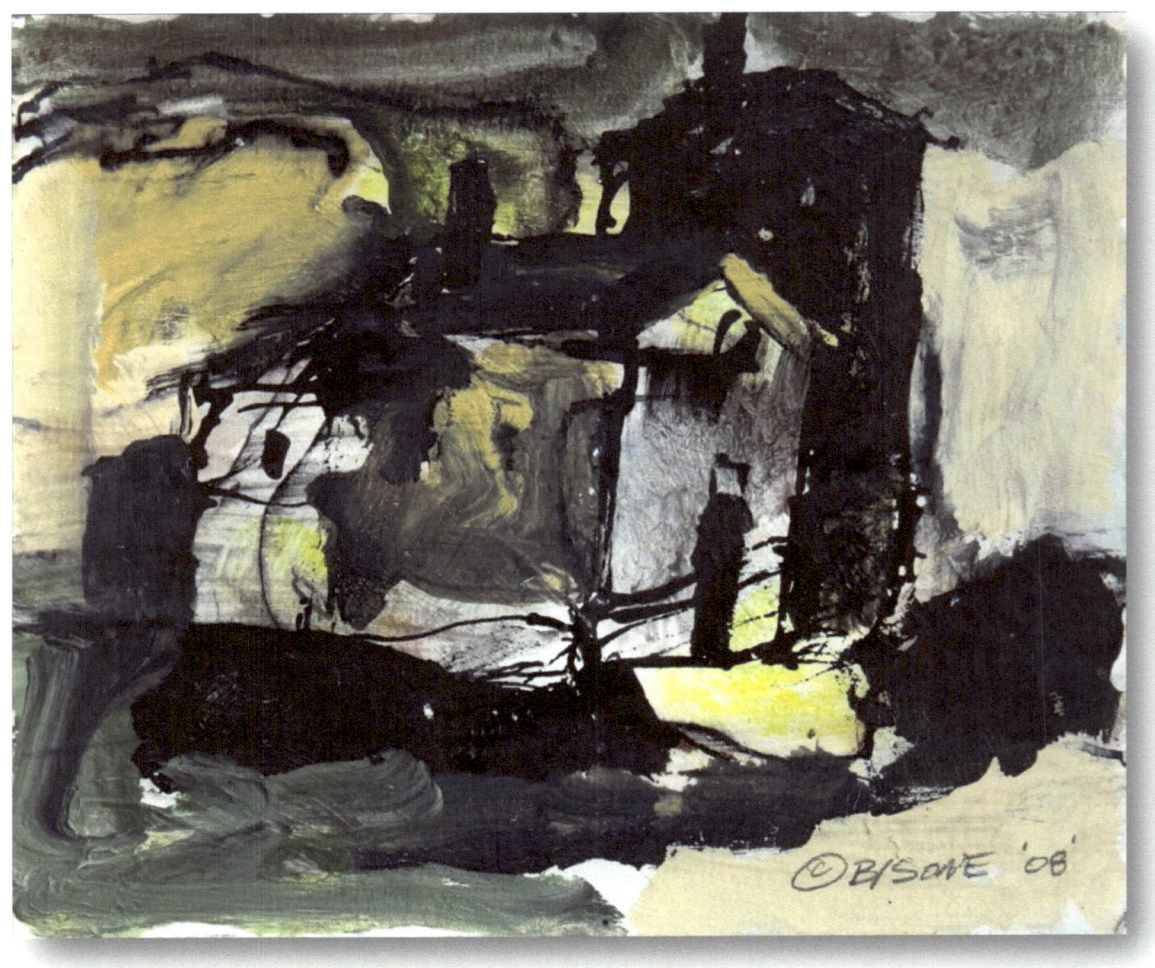

Industry, 2008, 8 x 9 inches

the whirlpool of art
       where to reach the center
              is to disappear

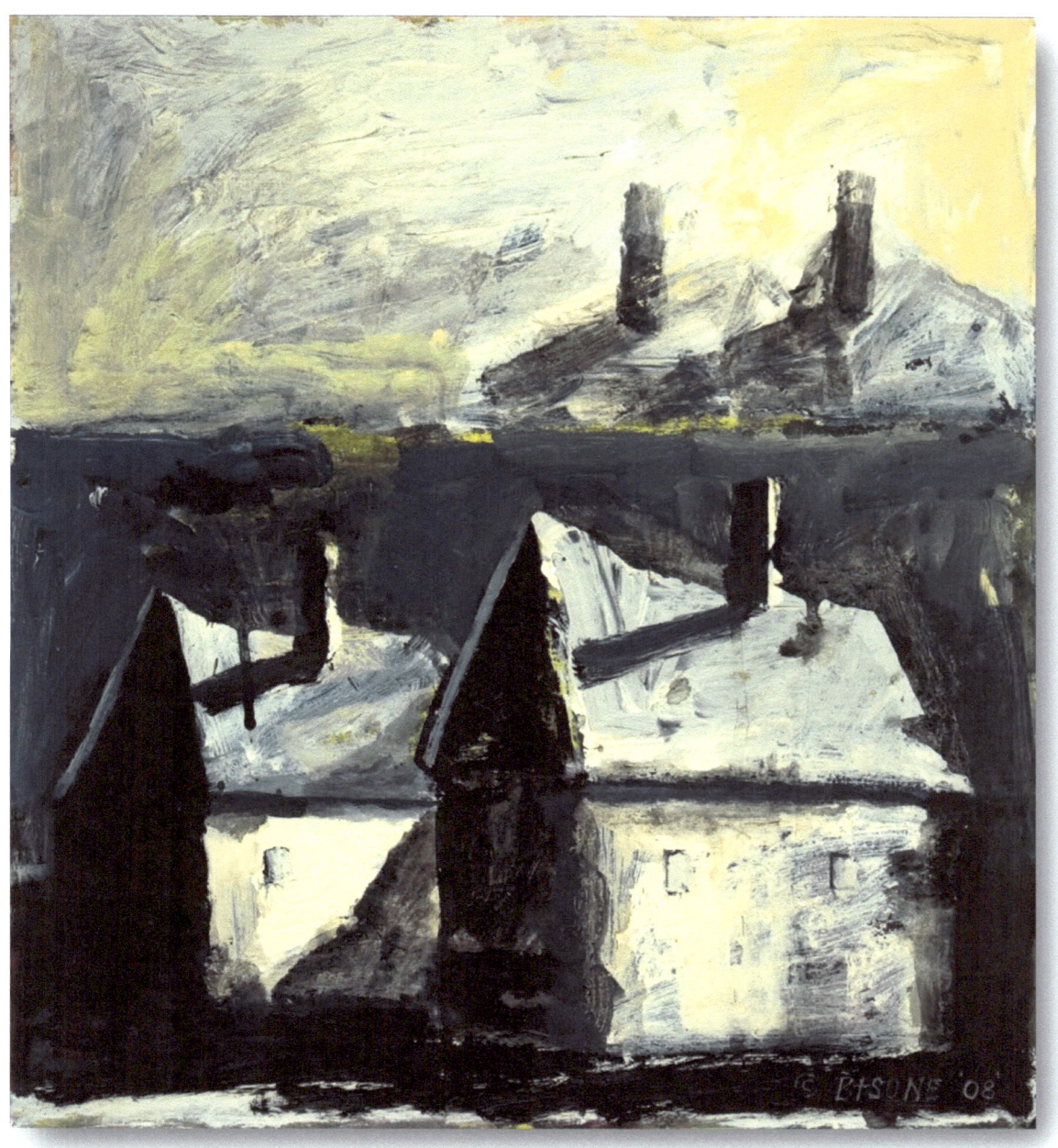

Smokestacks and Chimneys, 2008, 22 x 20 inches

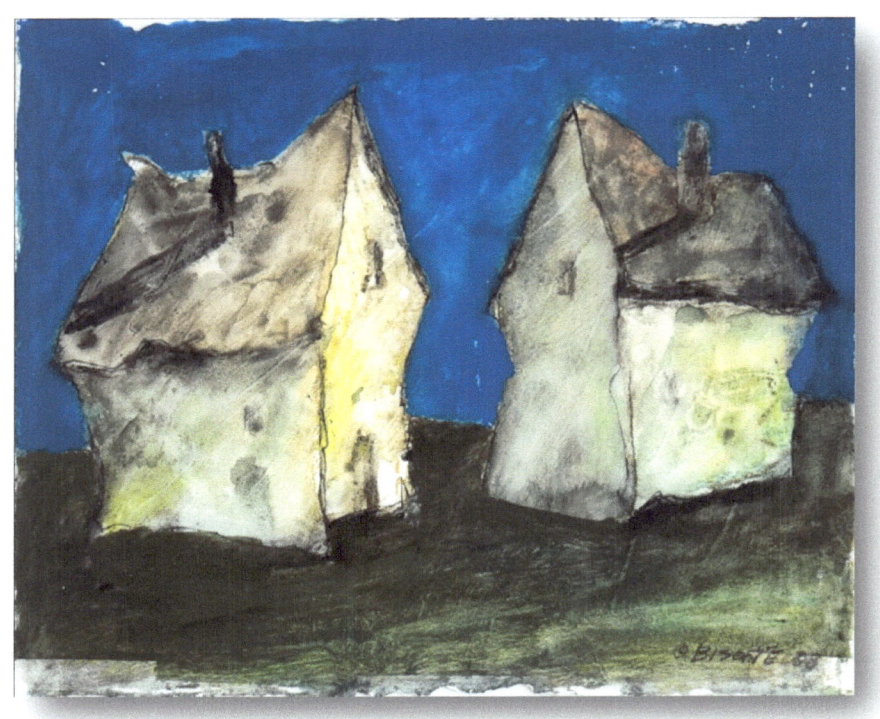

Neighbors #I, 2008, 11 x 13.5 inches

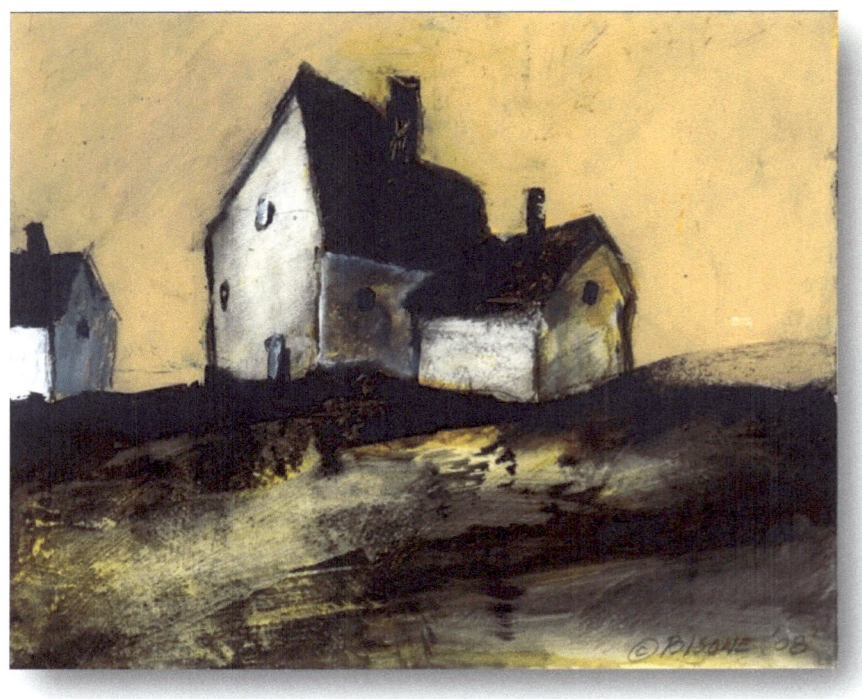

White House Series II, 2008, 6.75 x 8.5 inches

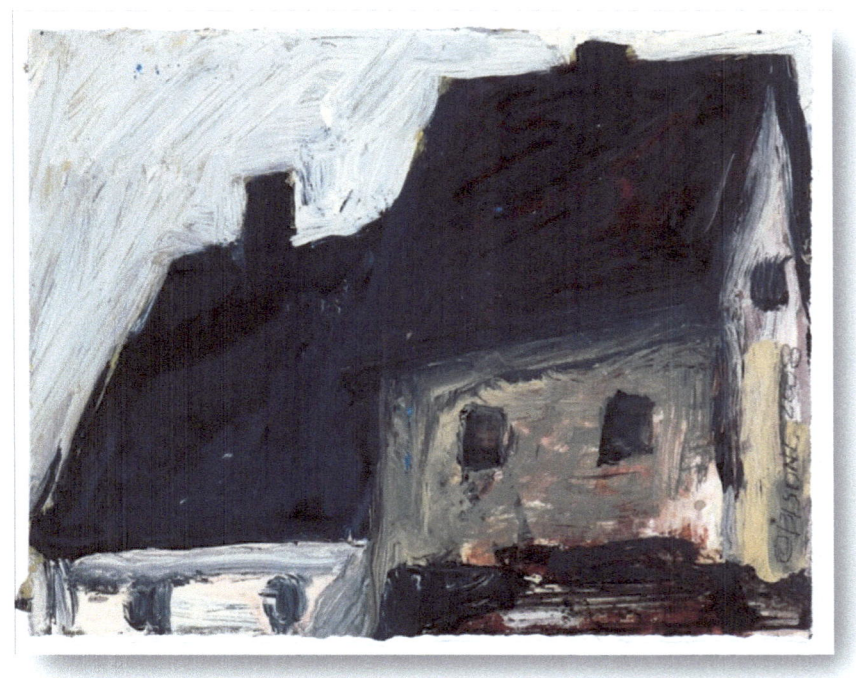

Rooftops, 2008, 15 x 17 inches

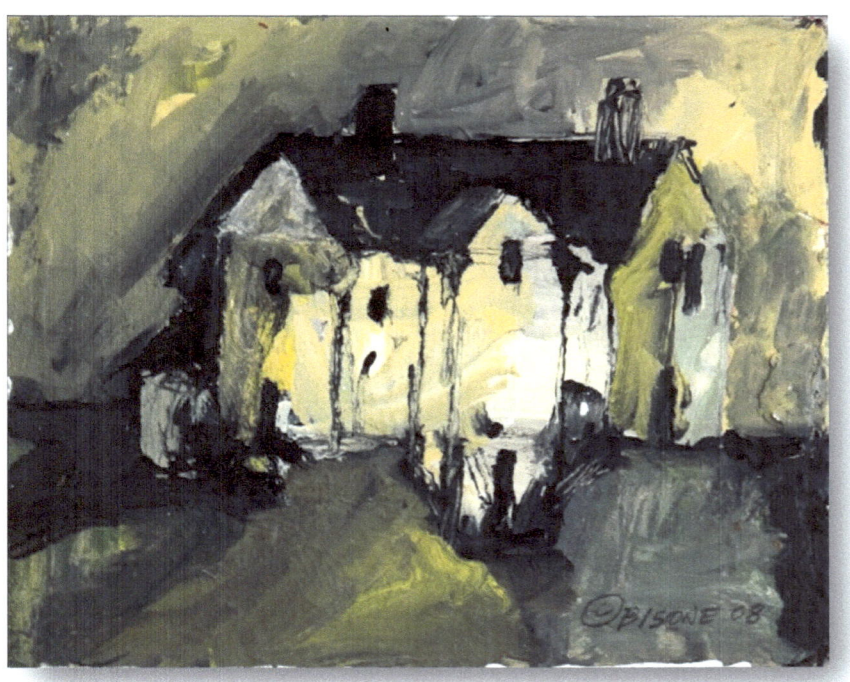

The Chateau, 2008, 8 x 10 inches

Edward G. Bisone

sometimes what we see
      is only part of what's there
            but we don't know this

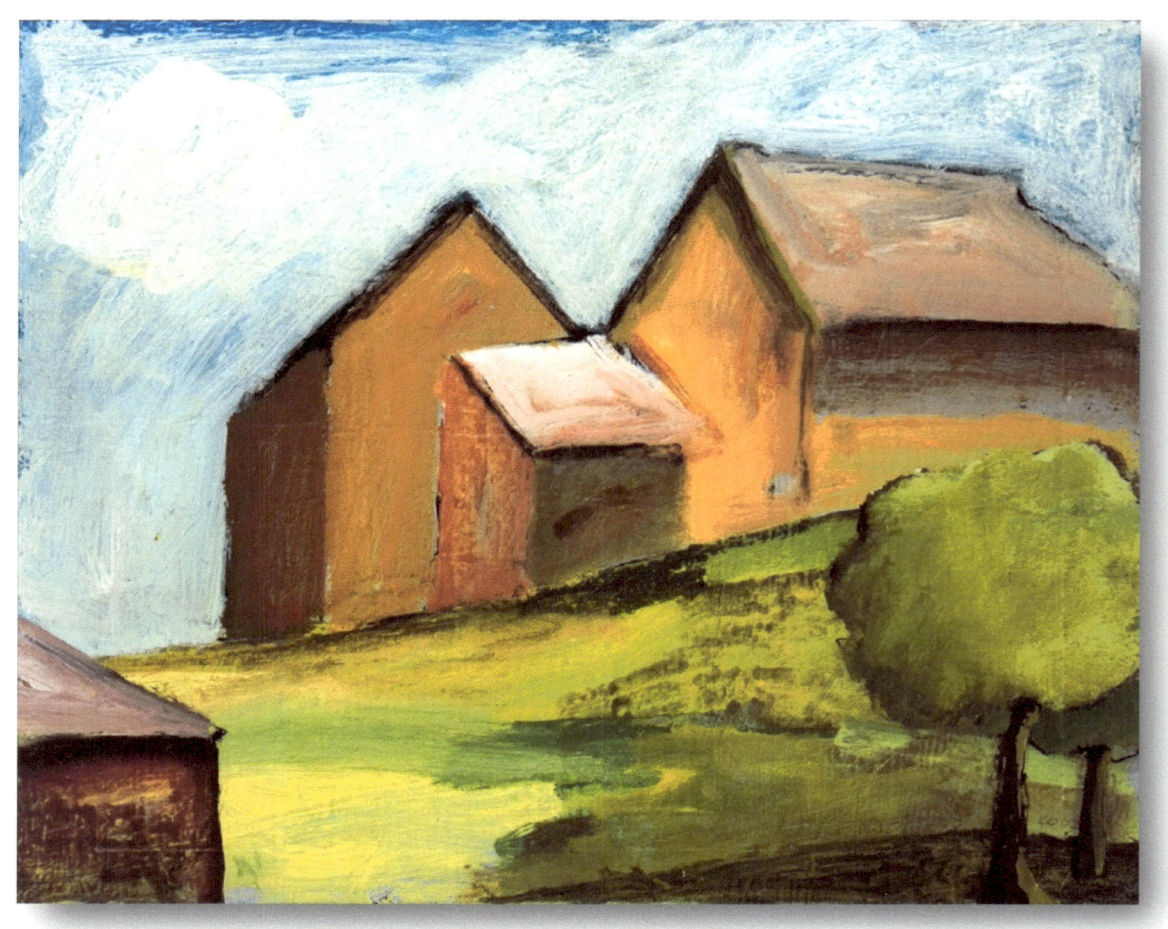

The Country Side, 2008, 16 x 20 inches

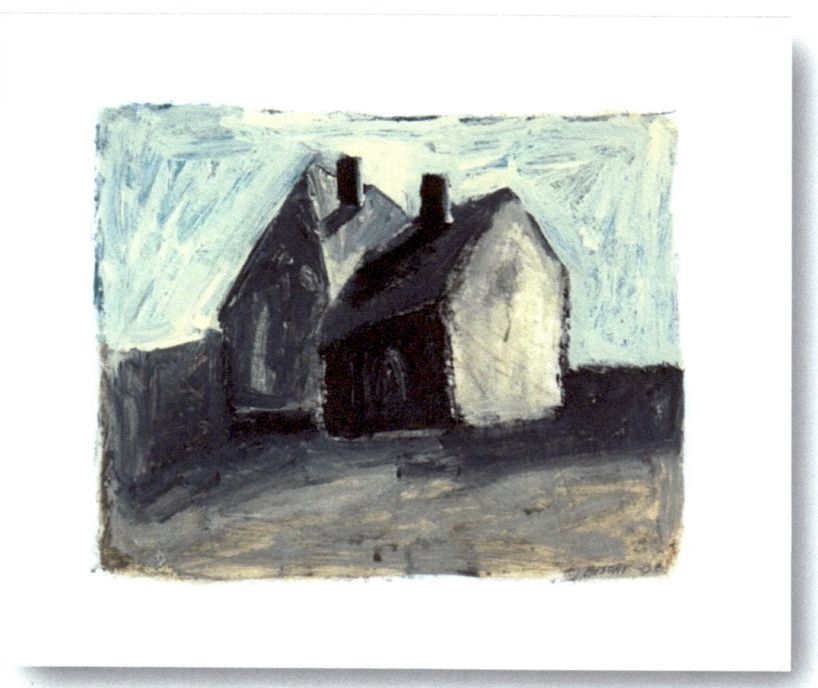

Two Houses, 2008, 16.75 x 20 inches

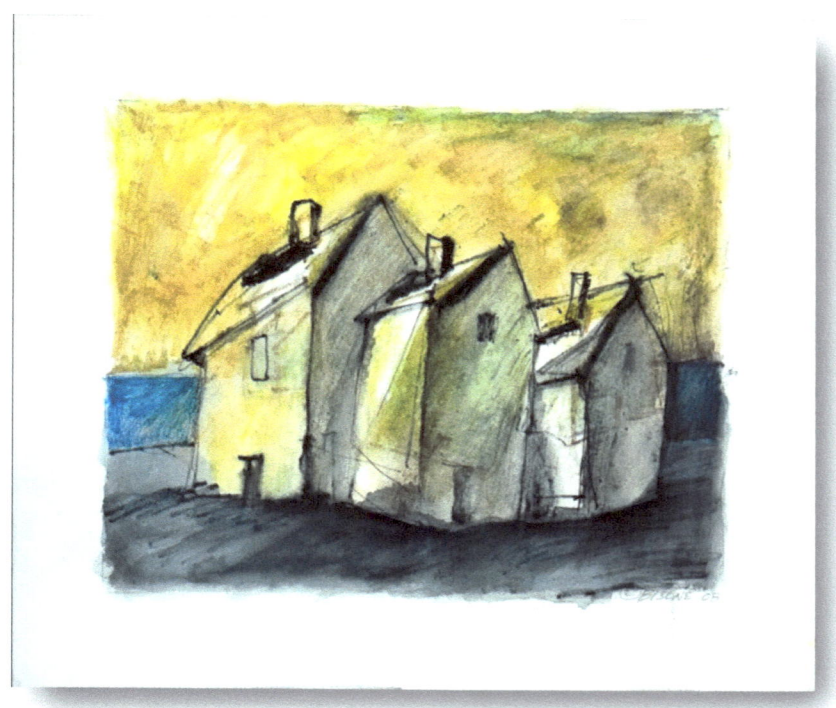

Yellow Sky, 2008, 15 x 17.75 inches

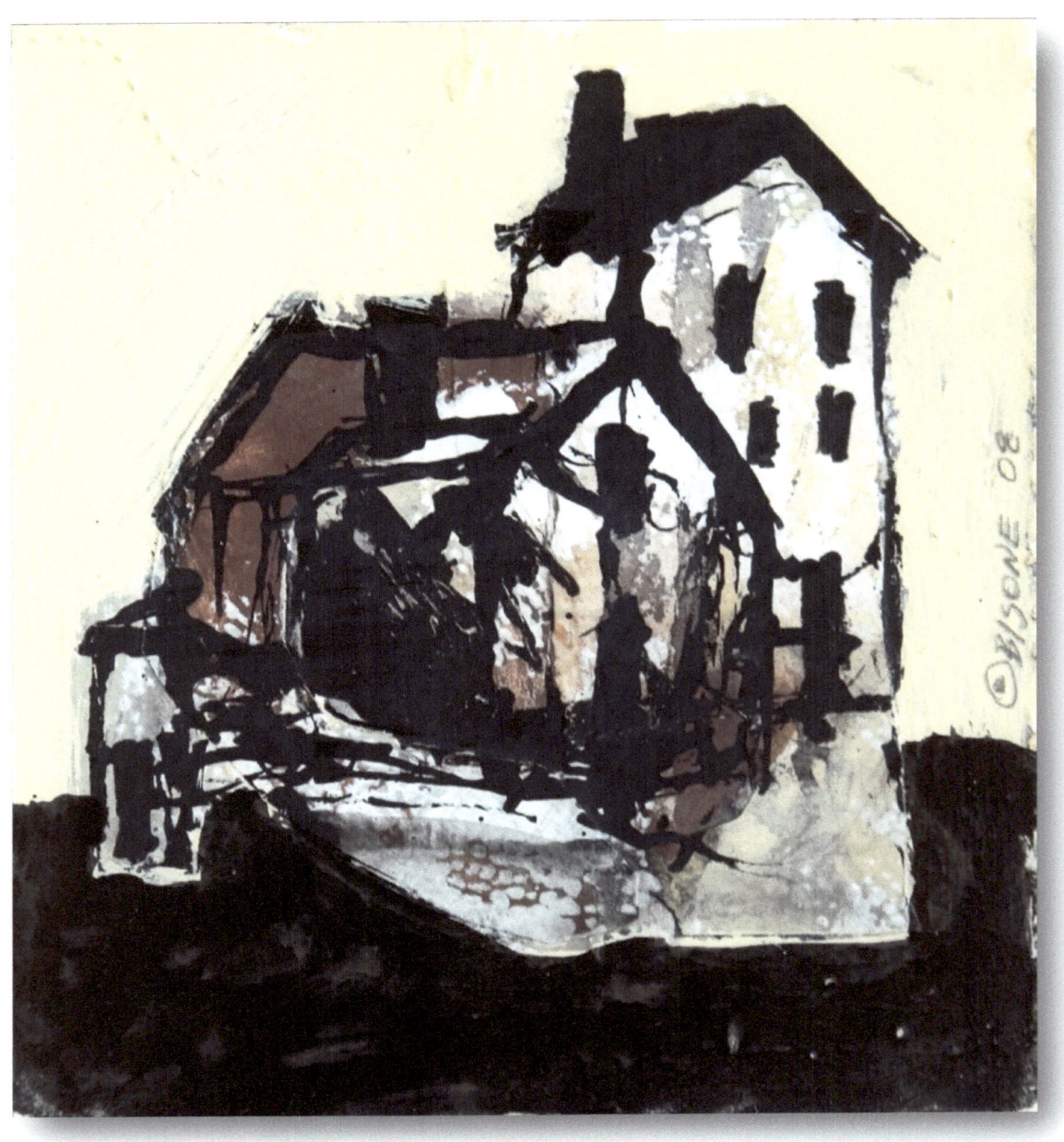

Untitled, 2008, 6 x 6.5 inches

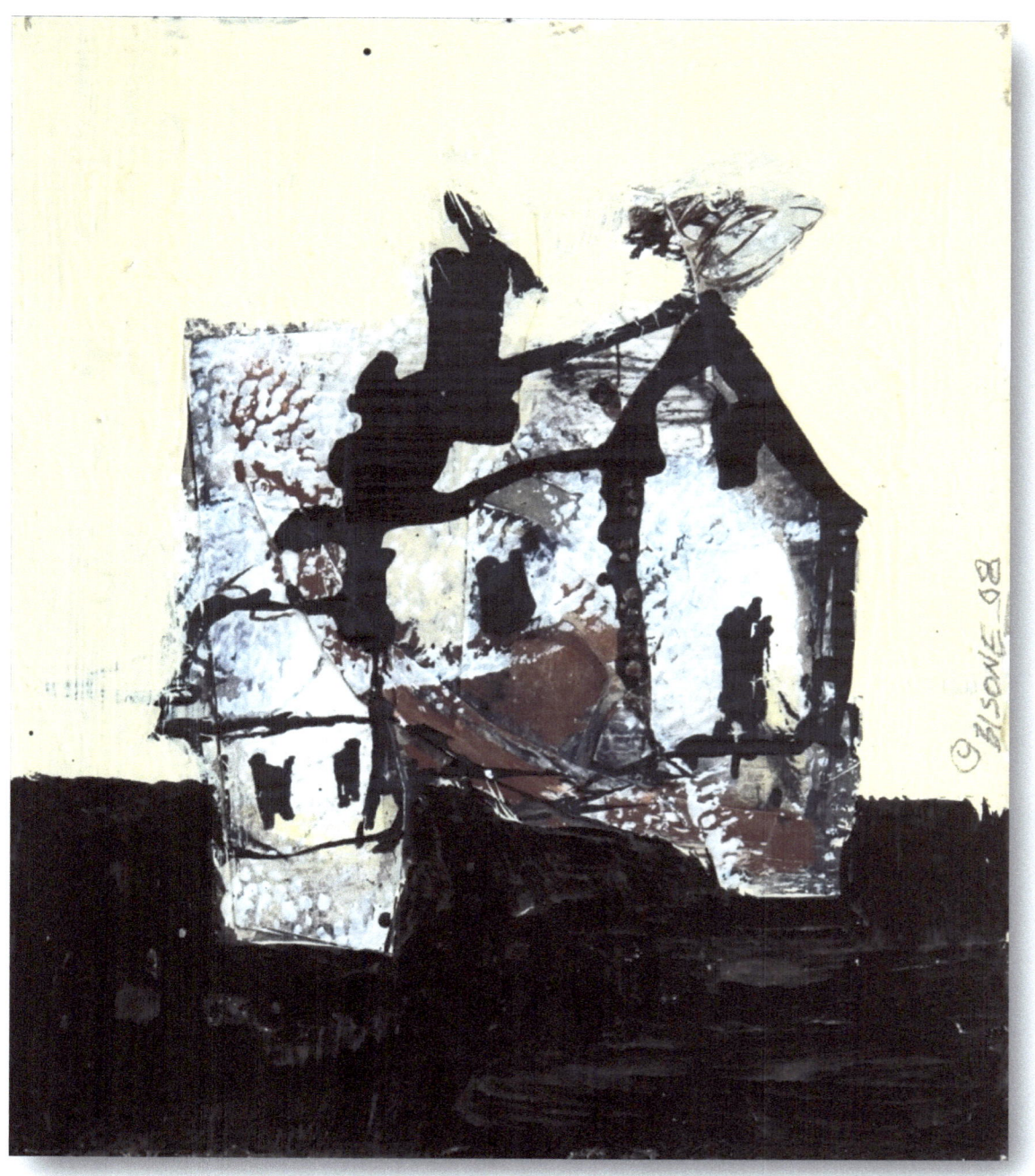

Untitled, 2008, 7.5 x 6.5 inches

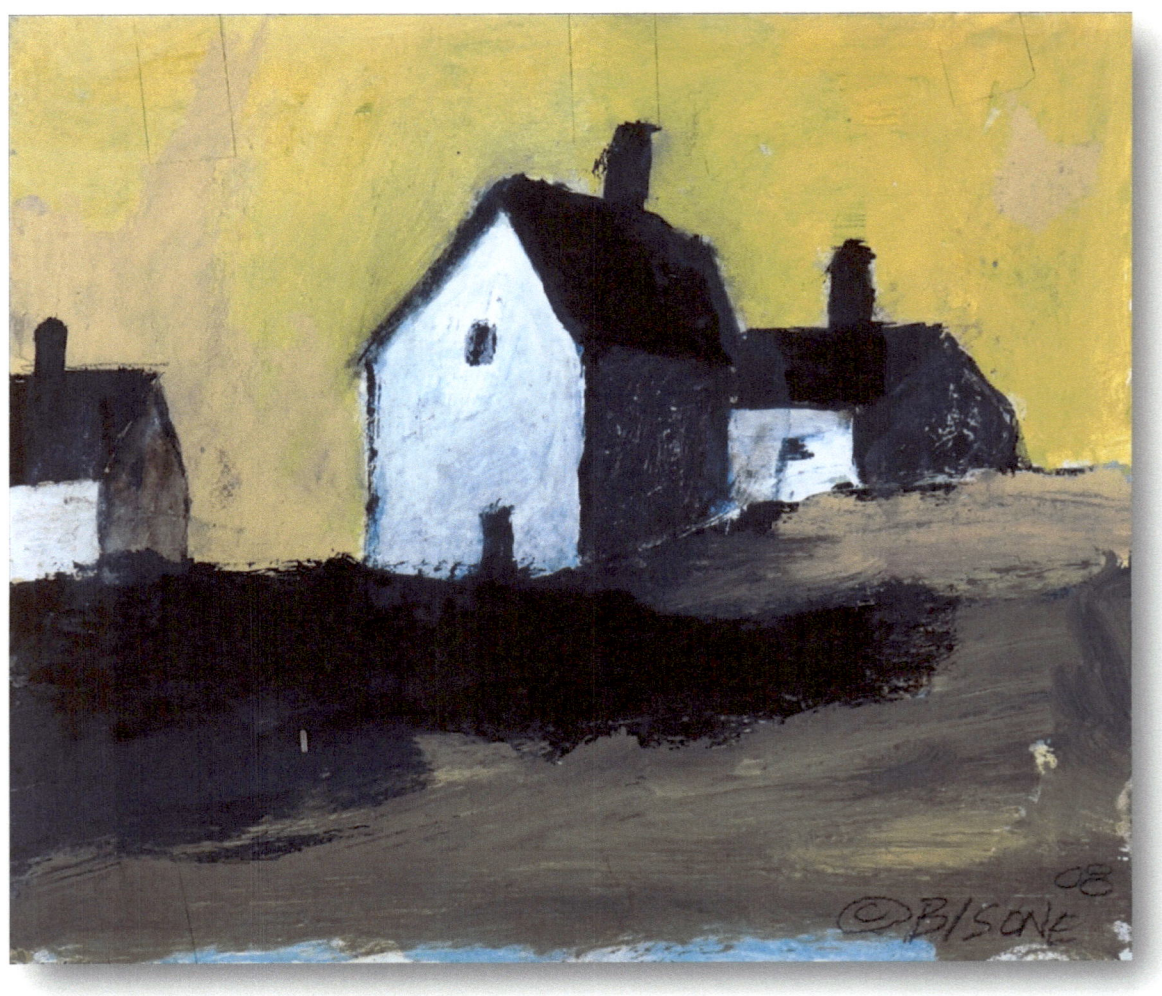

Untitled, 2008, 8.5 x 10 inches

do titles tell us
  what's there or what to look for?
    what does untitled mean?

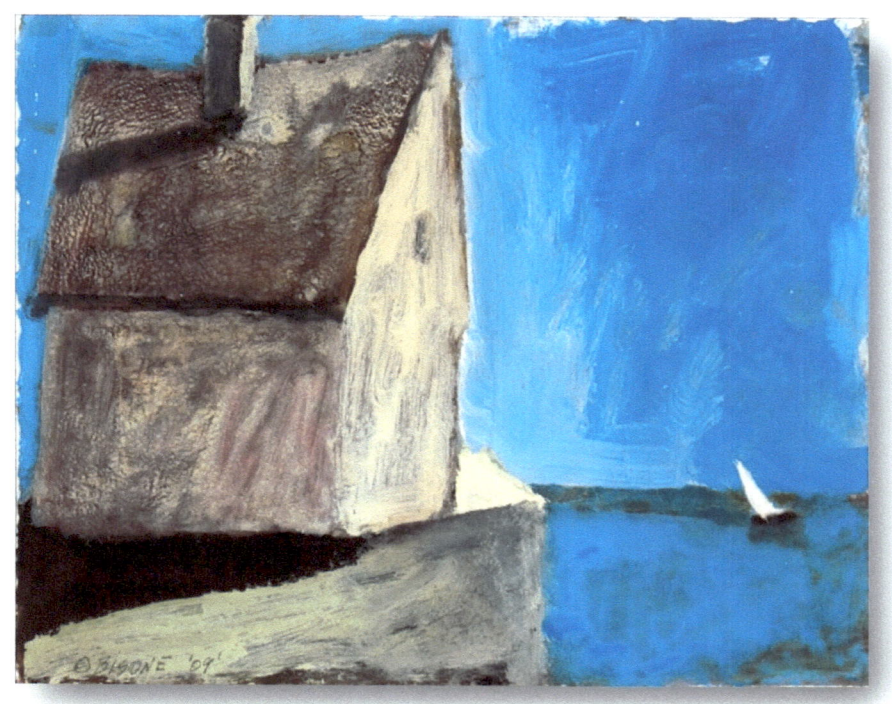

House of Cliffs, 2009, 10.75 x 13.5 inches

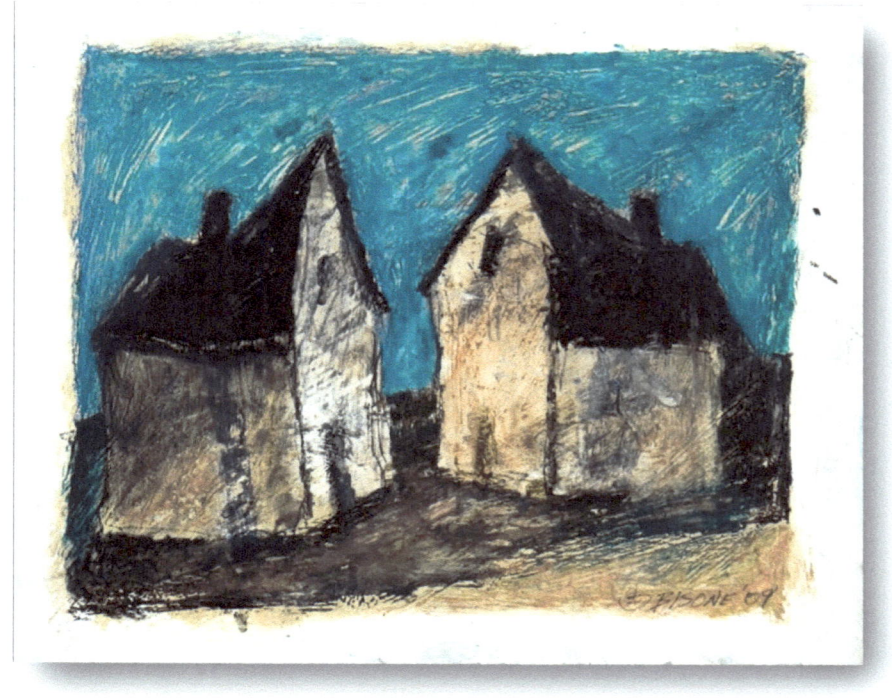

Neighbors #II, 2009, 11 x 14 inches

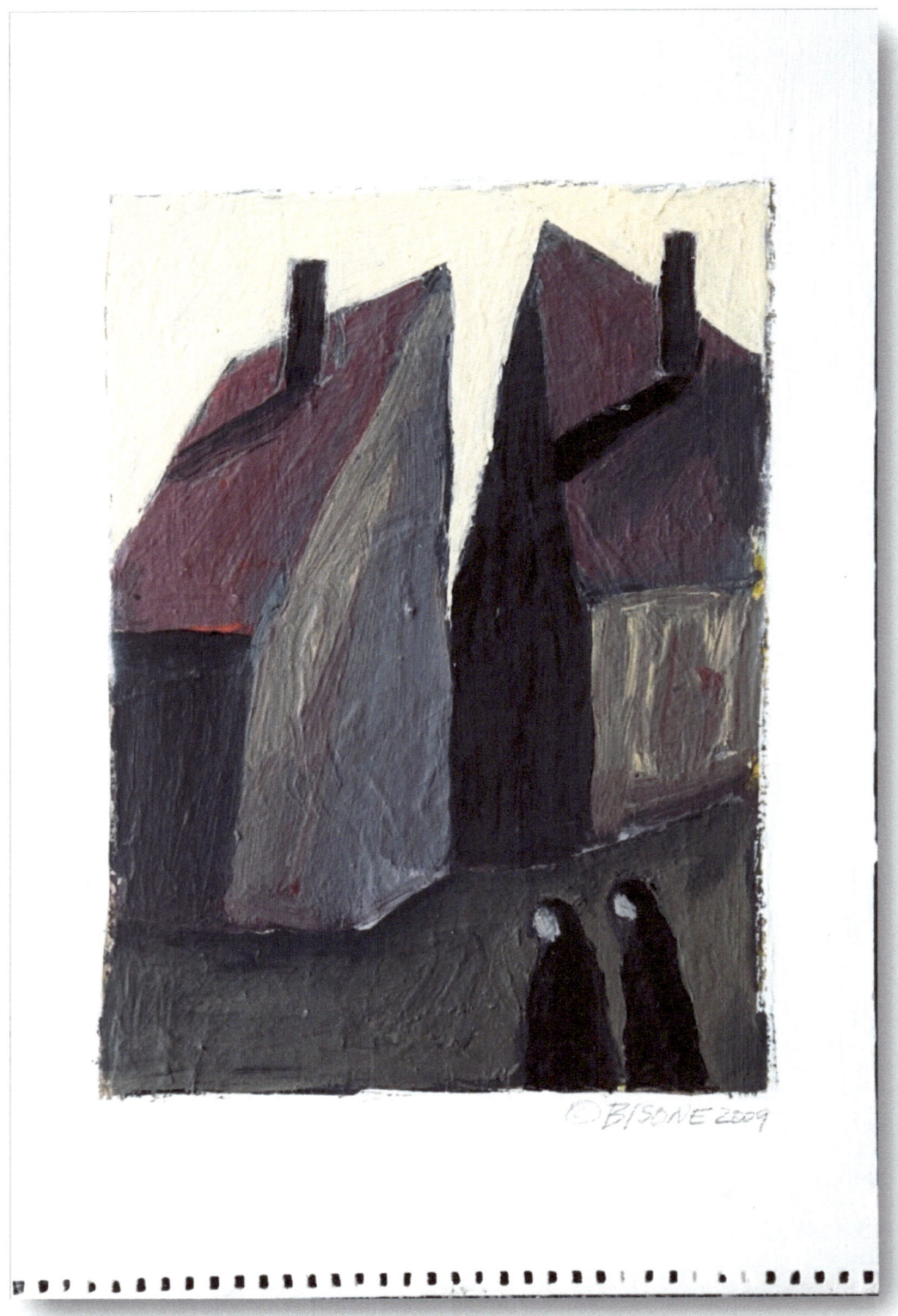

The Penitents, 2009, 18 x 12 inches

9. Hats

Hats seem to be of particular interest to Bisone, as evidenced not only by these figures, but also by the titles he's given the paintings. It's as though the artist is trying the hats on for size and look.

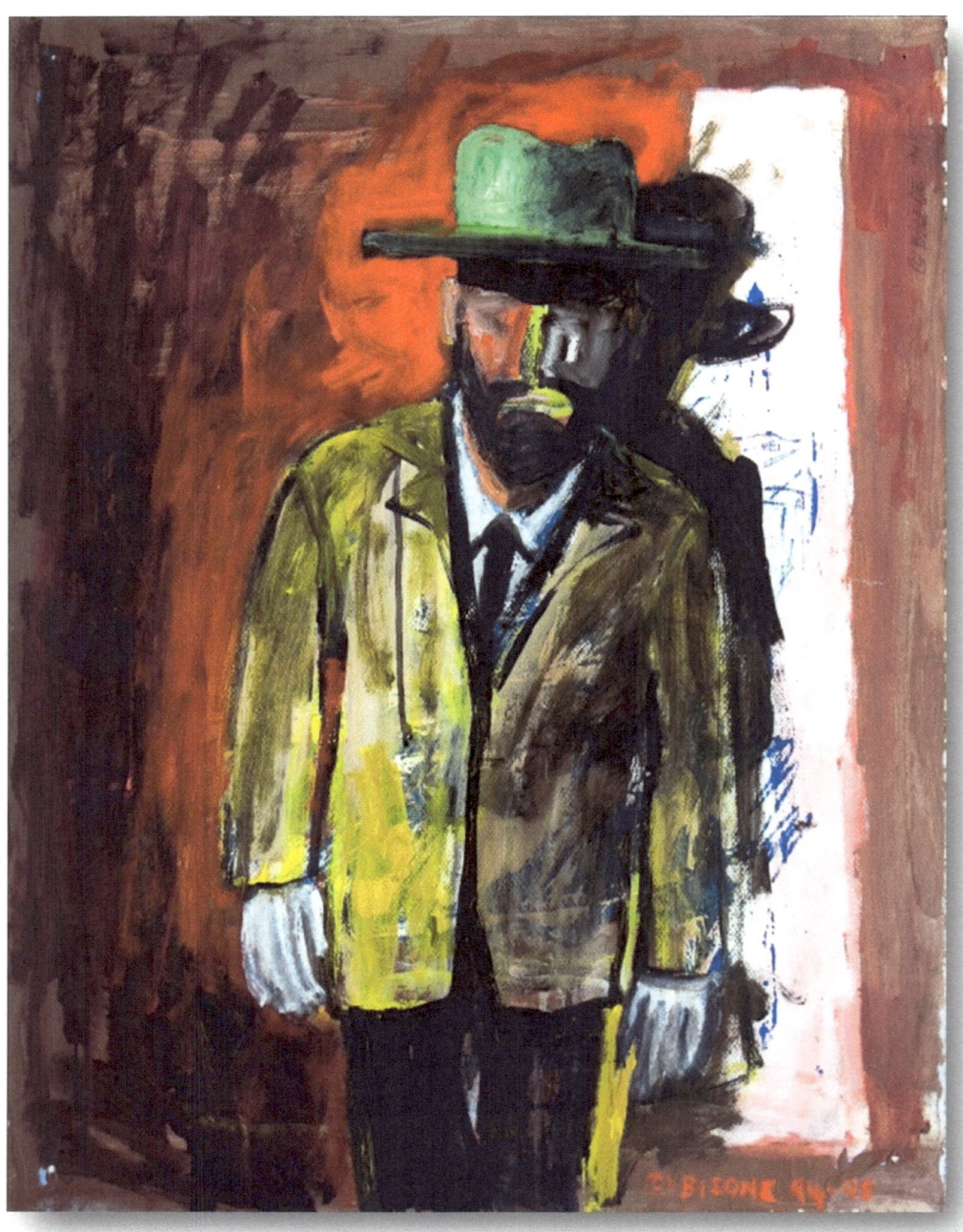

Green Hat, 1994-95, 18 x 14 inches

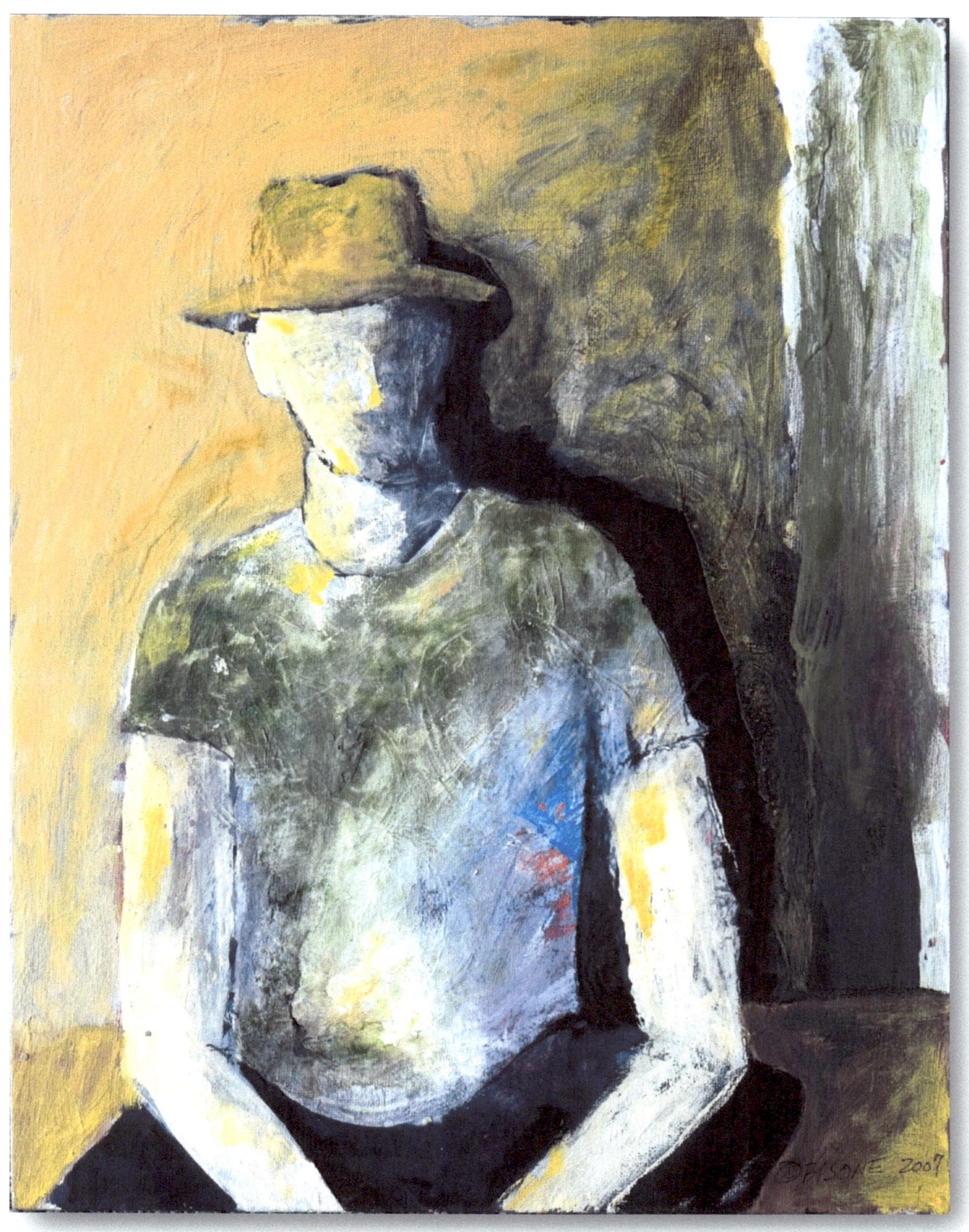

Brown Hat, 2007, 18 x 14 inches

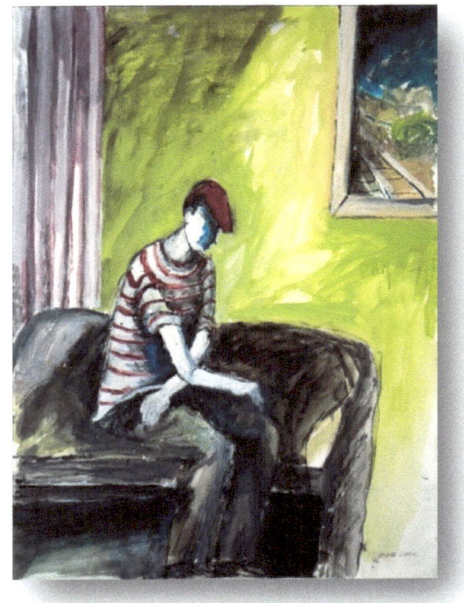

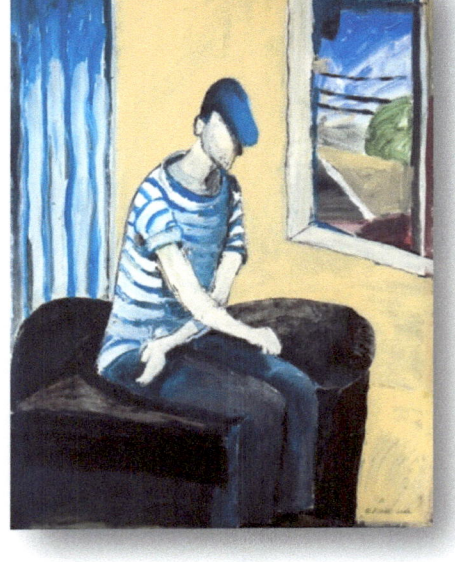

Red Cap, 2002, 30 x 22 inches

Scene Through a Window, 2002, 30 x 22 inches

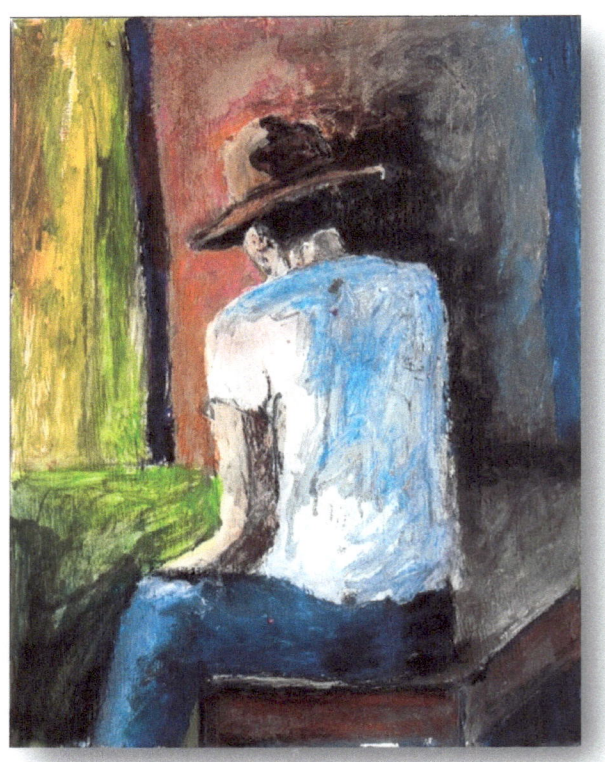

Pensive Figure with Hat, 2004, 15.5 x 12 inches

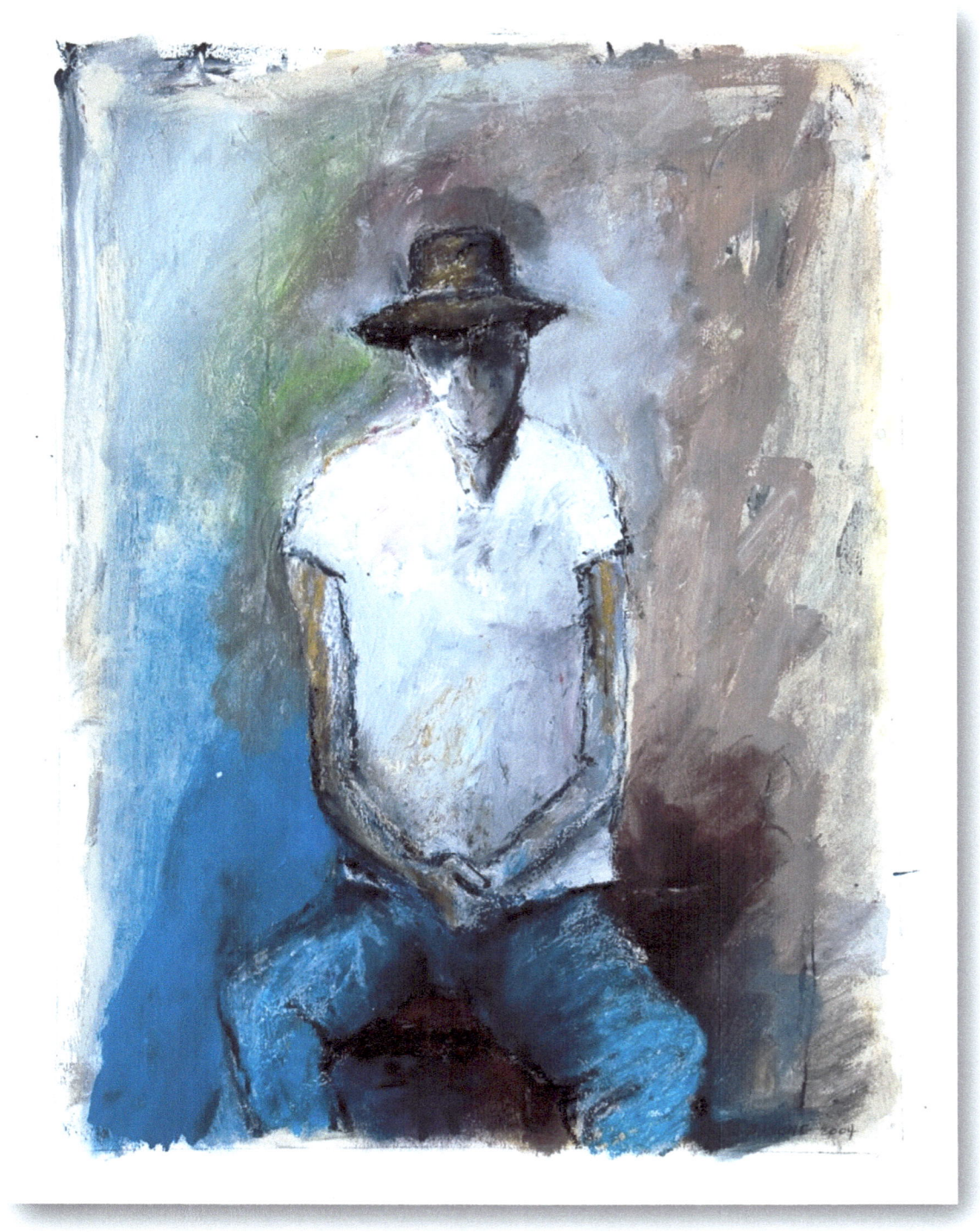

Man Wearing a Brown Hat, 2004, 25 x 20 inches

the best work speaks twice;

what you first see and hear

and then what comes next

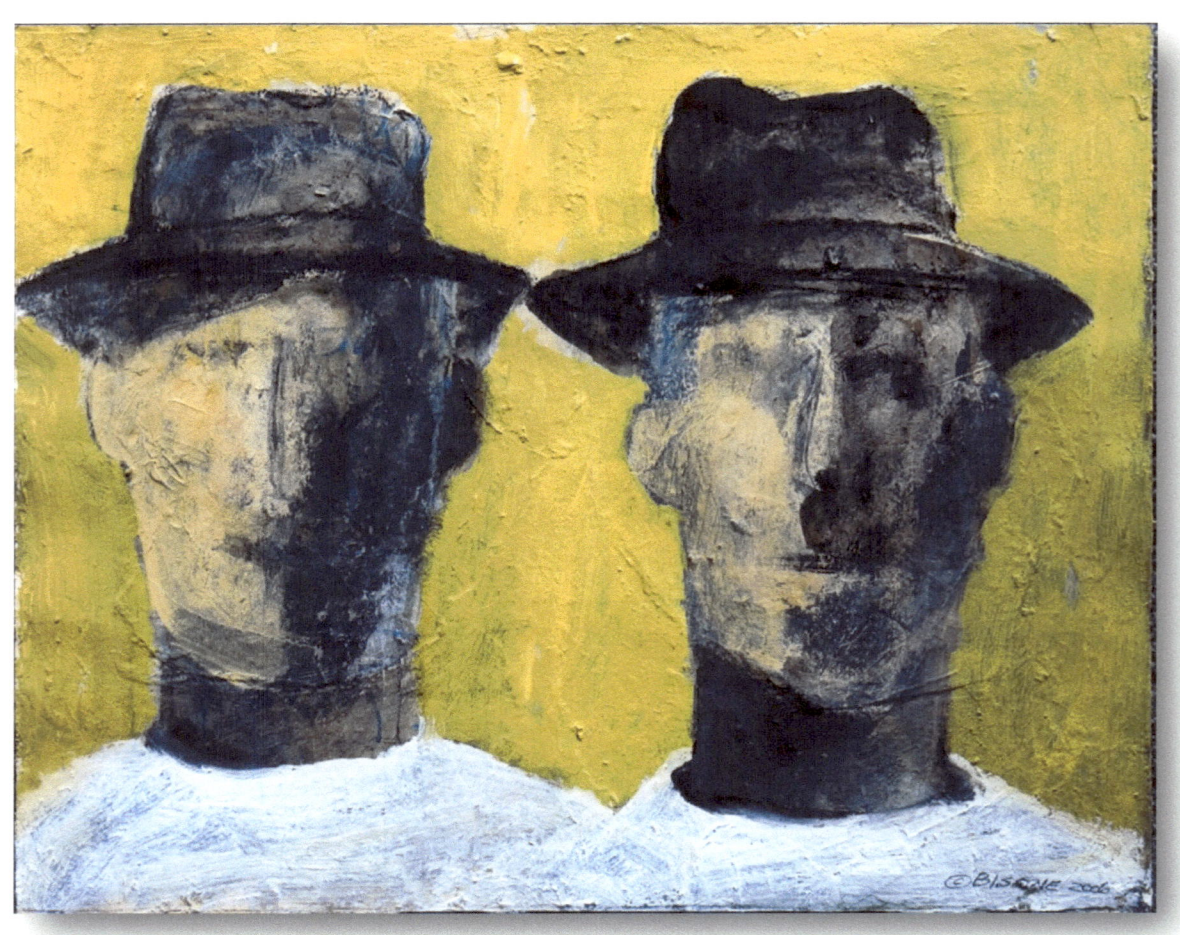

The Pork Pie Twins, 2006, 16 x 20 inches

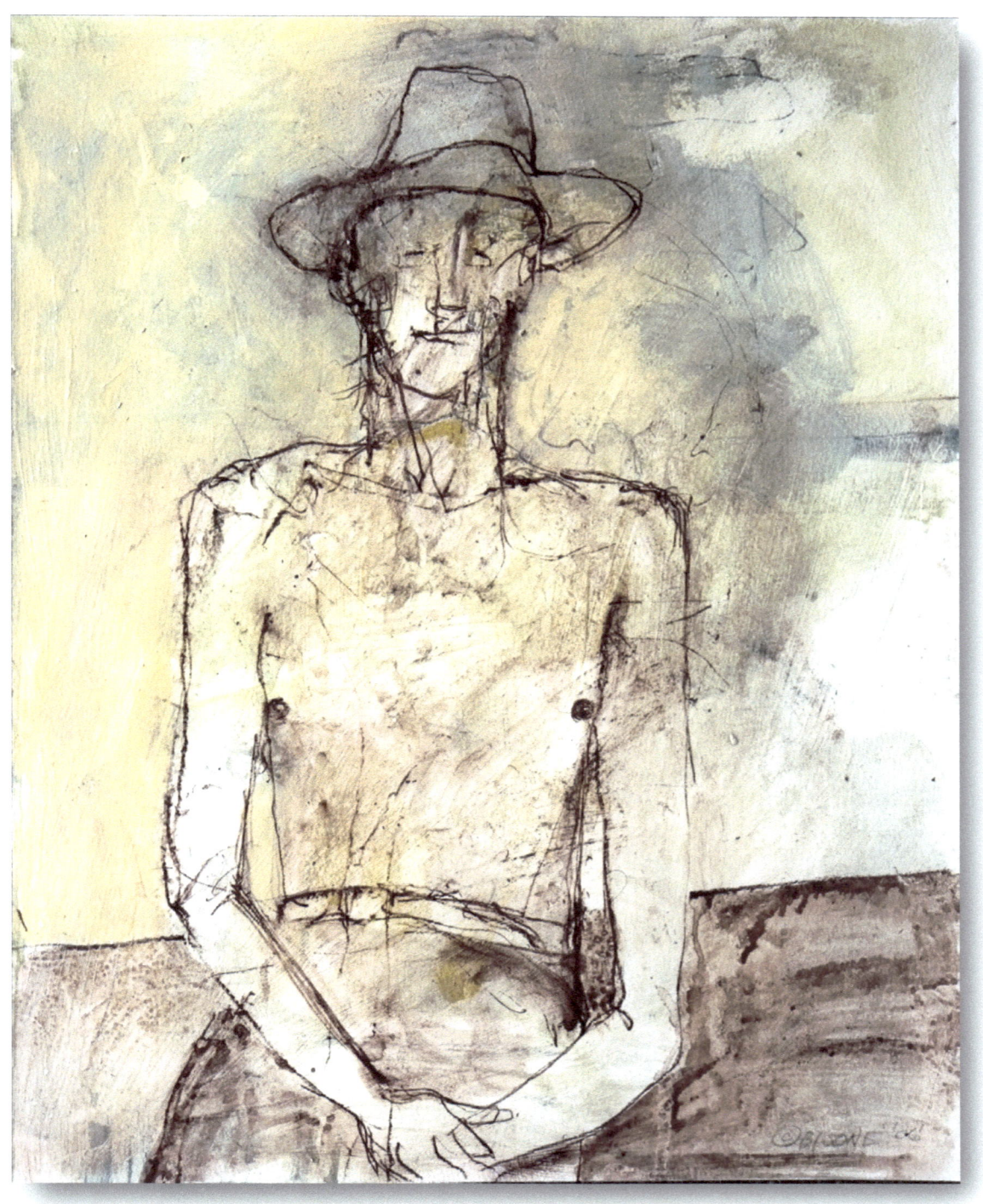

Resting Man with Hat, 2006, 20 x 16 inches

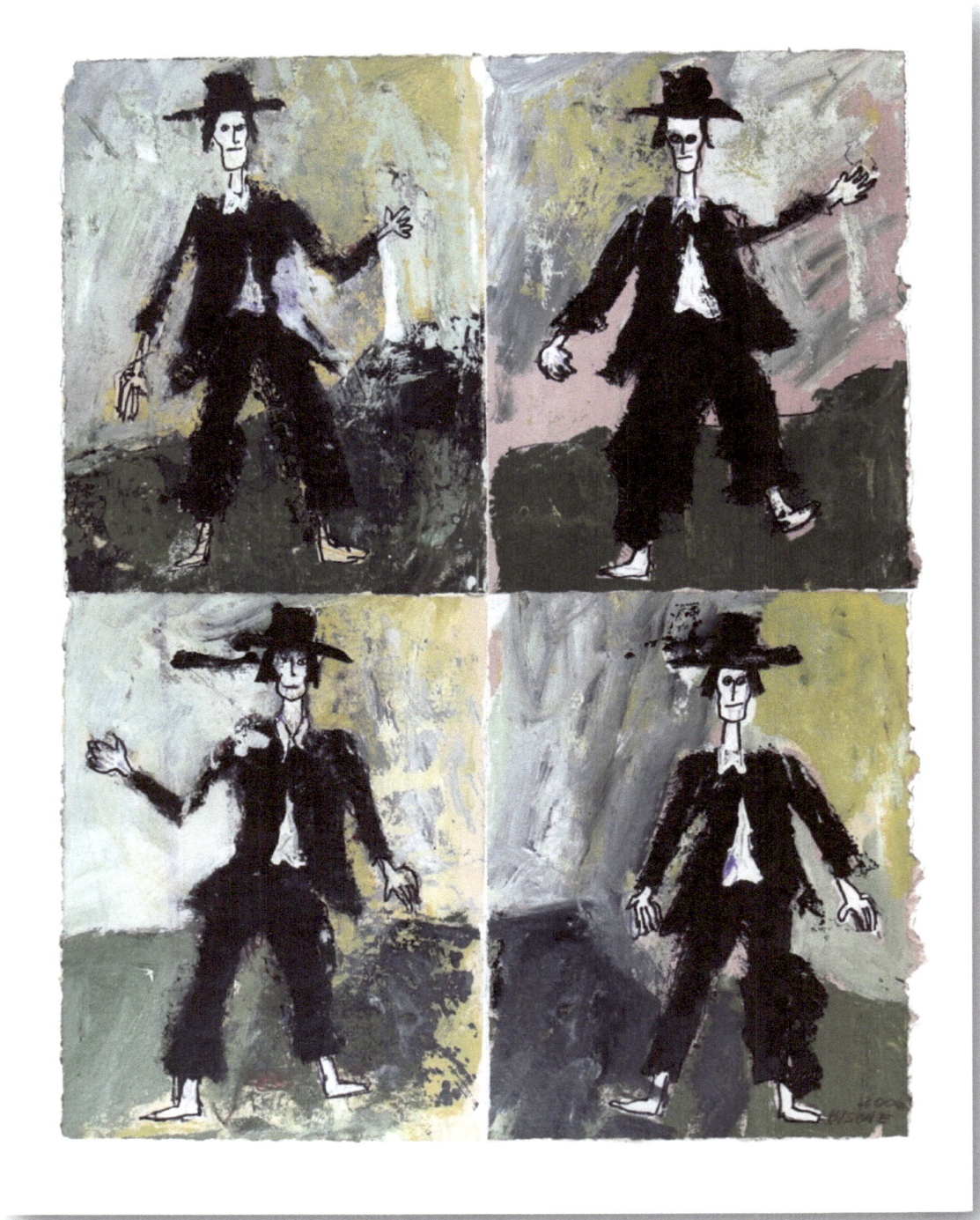

4 Existential Men, 2006, 24.25 x 19.25 inches

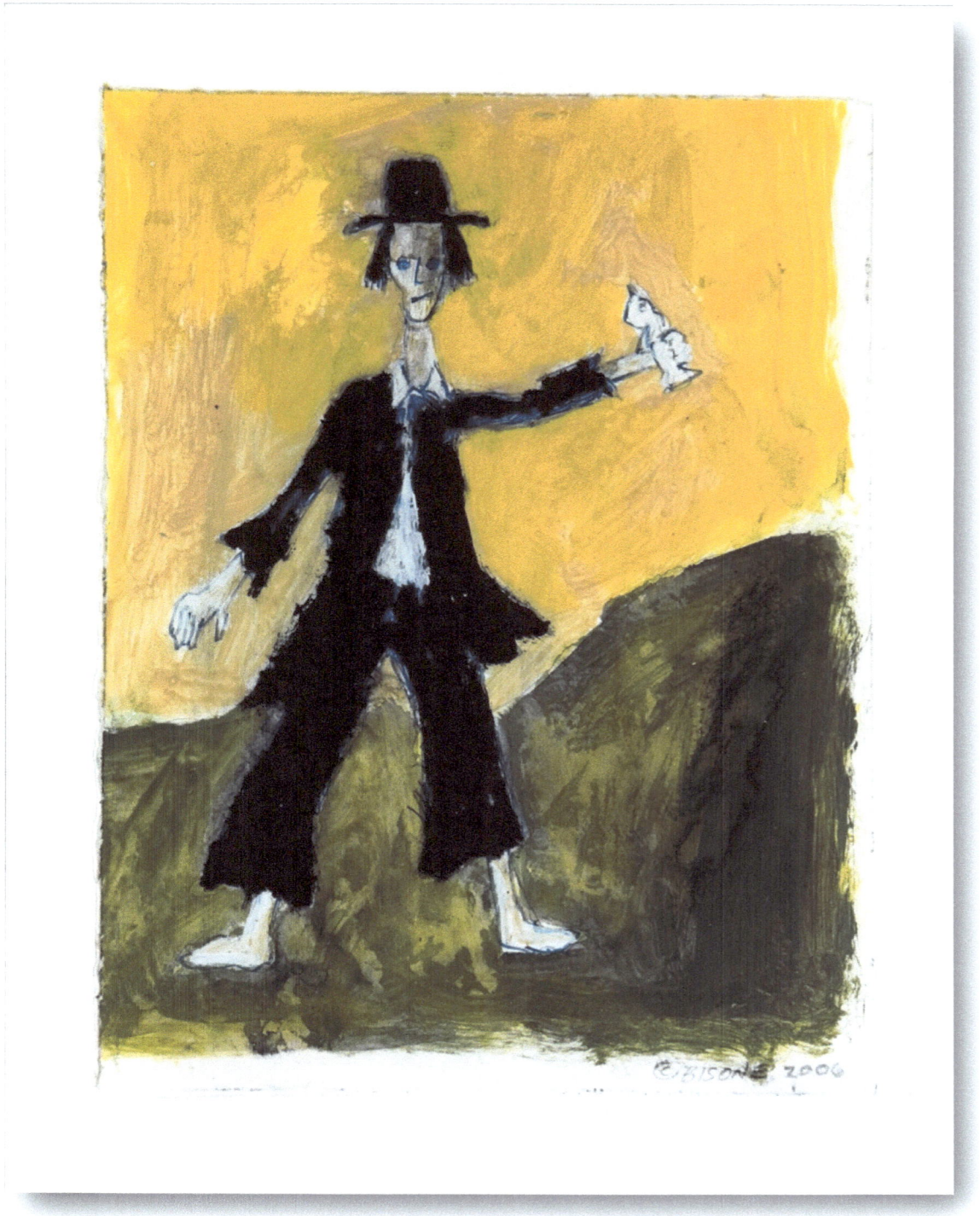

A Bird in the Hand, 2006, 15.5 x 12.25 inches

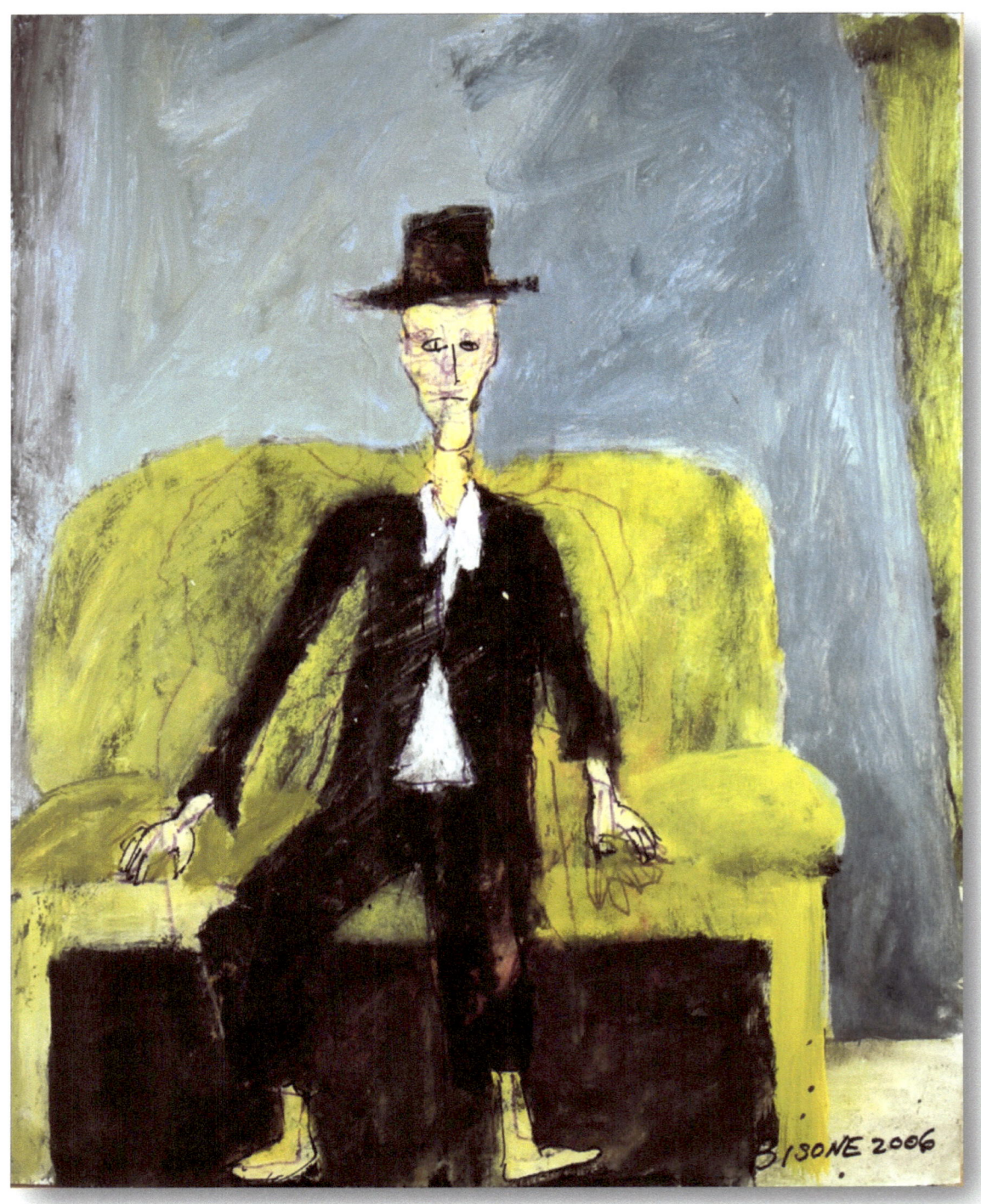

Existential Man with Hat, 2006, 20 x 16 inches

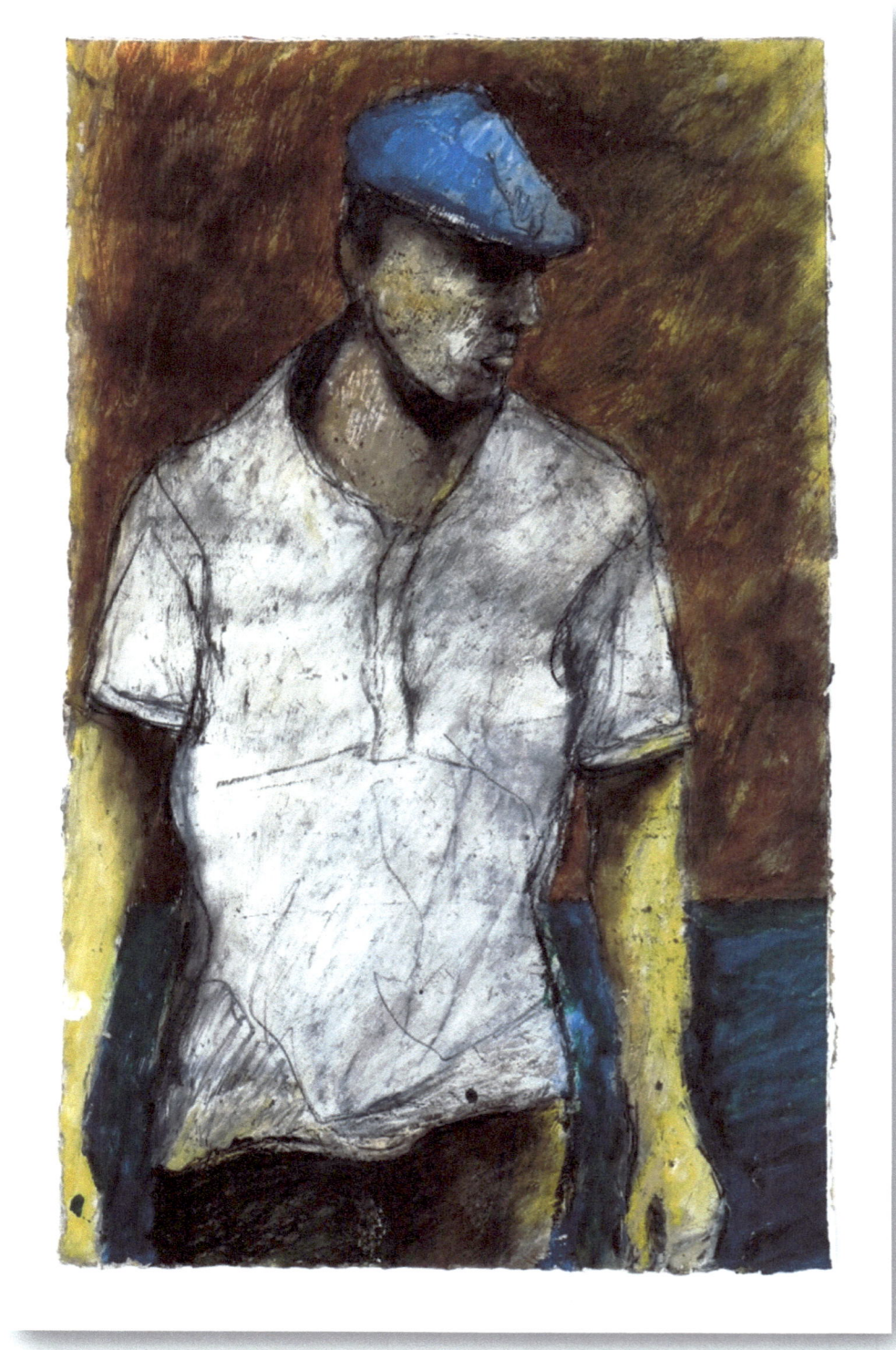

Man in Blue Cap, 2000, 20 x 13 inches

10. Abstracts

These paintings are an exploration of, and experimentation with, the materials at hand: papers, boards, acrylics; sometimes envelopes, sticks, or puzzle pieces are added. Emotions and ideas are expressed in strokes, lines, and circles of color and black & white that speak individually to the viewer, who finds meaning often at variance to the artist's intended message (if there is such). Elements of a work are components of the evolutionary process that created it.

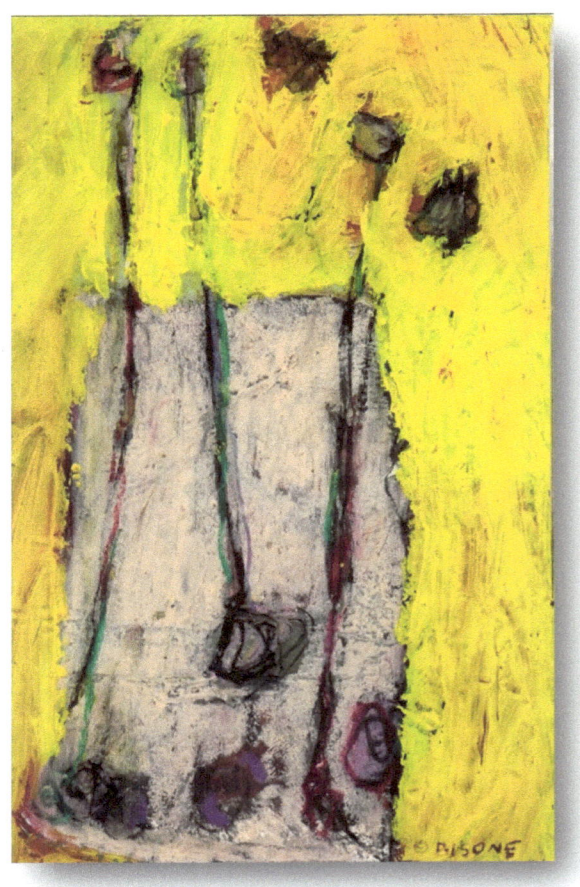

Blooming, 2000, 9.5 x 6 inches

the move of image
in the mind as focused gaze
becomes unfocused

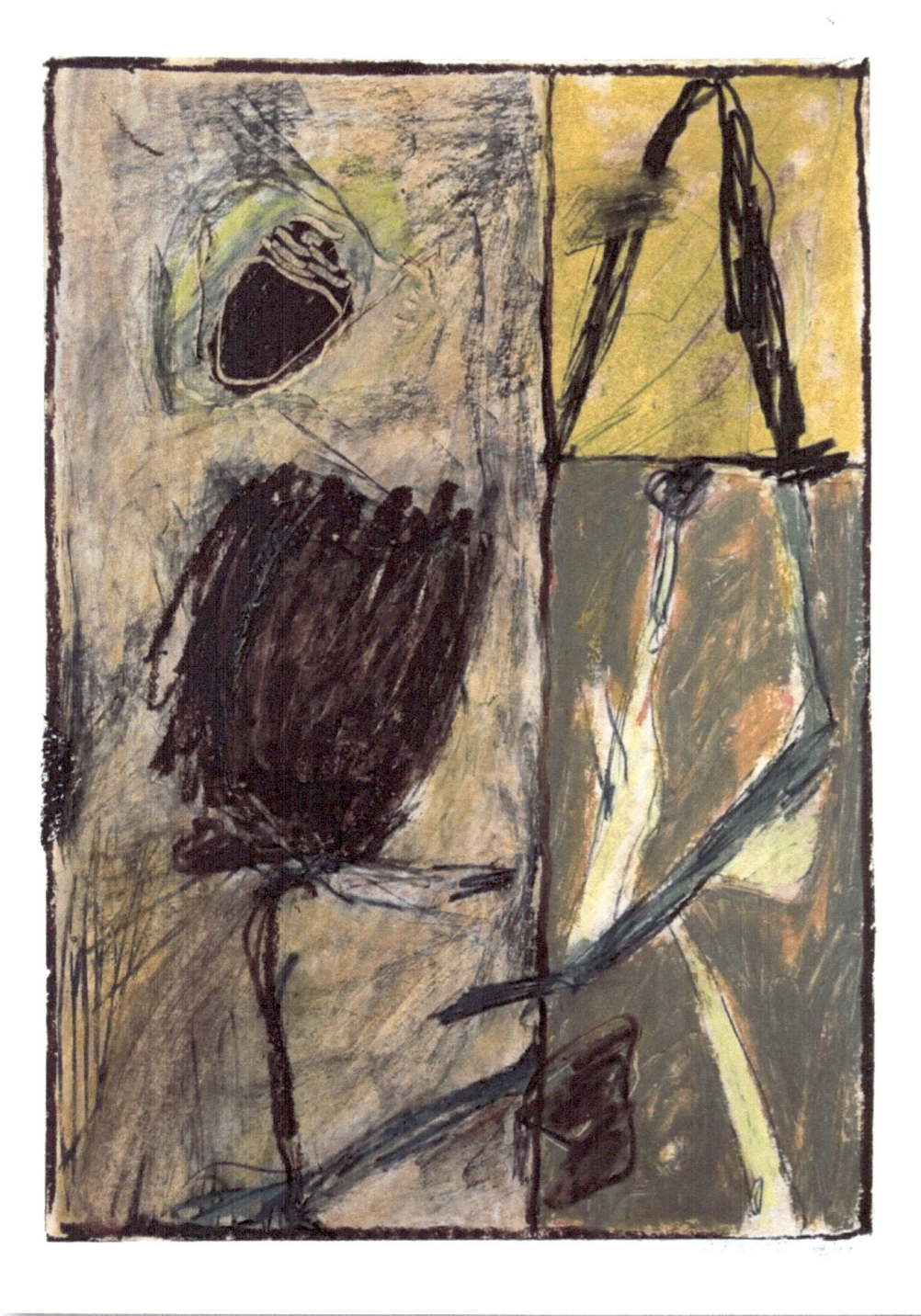

Burnt Bloom, 1998-99, 21 x 15 inches

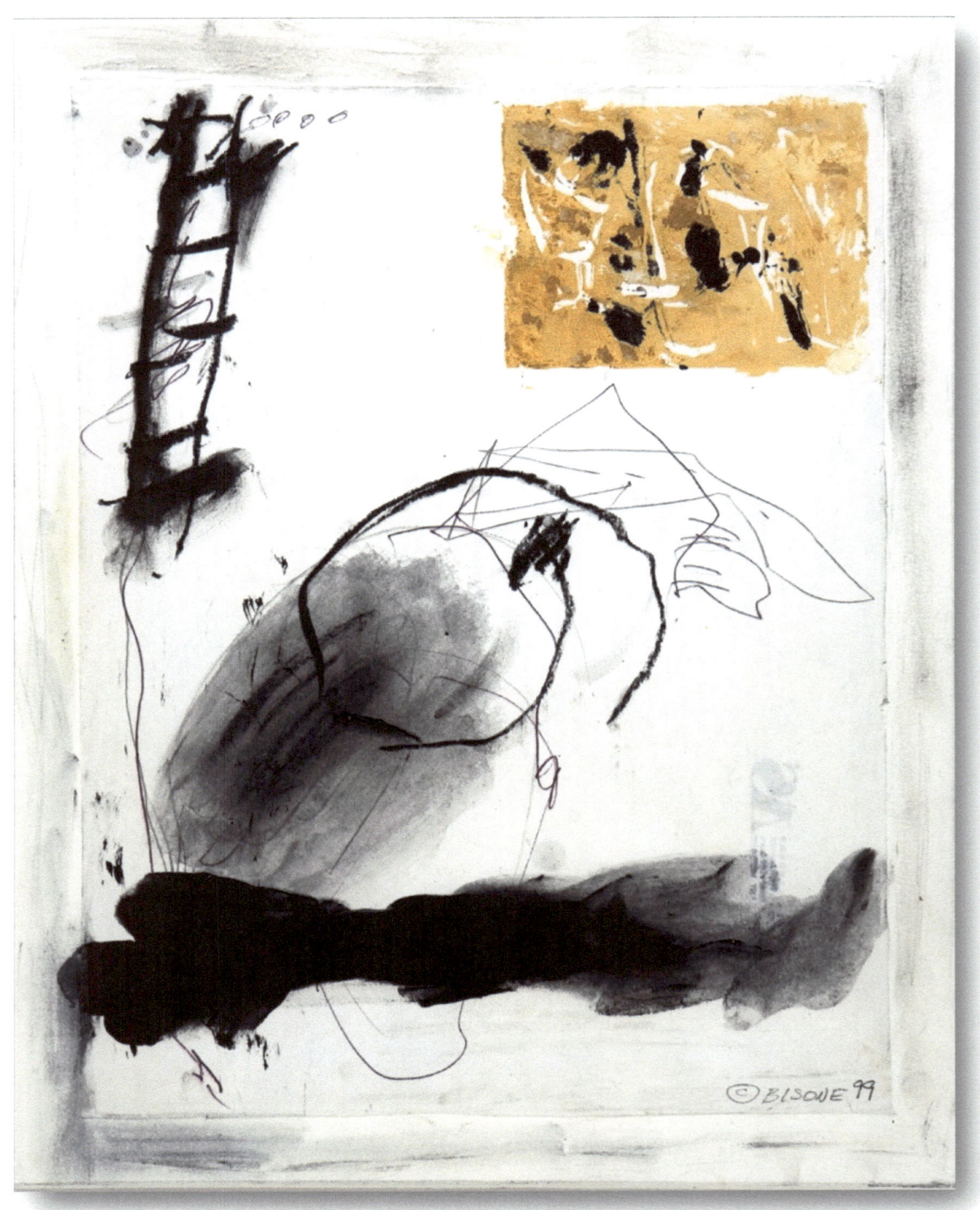

Aesthetic Echo I, 1999, 13.5 x 10.75 inches

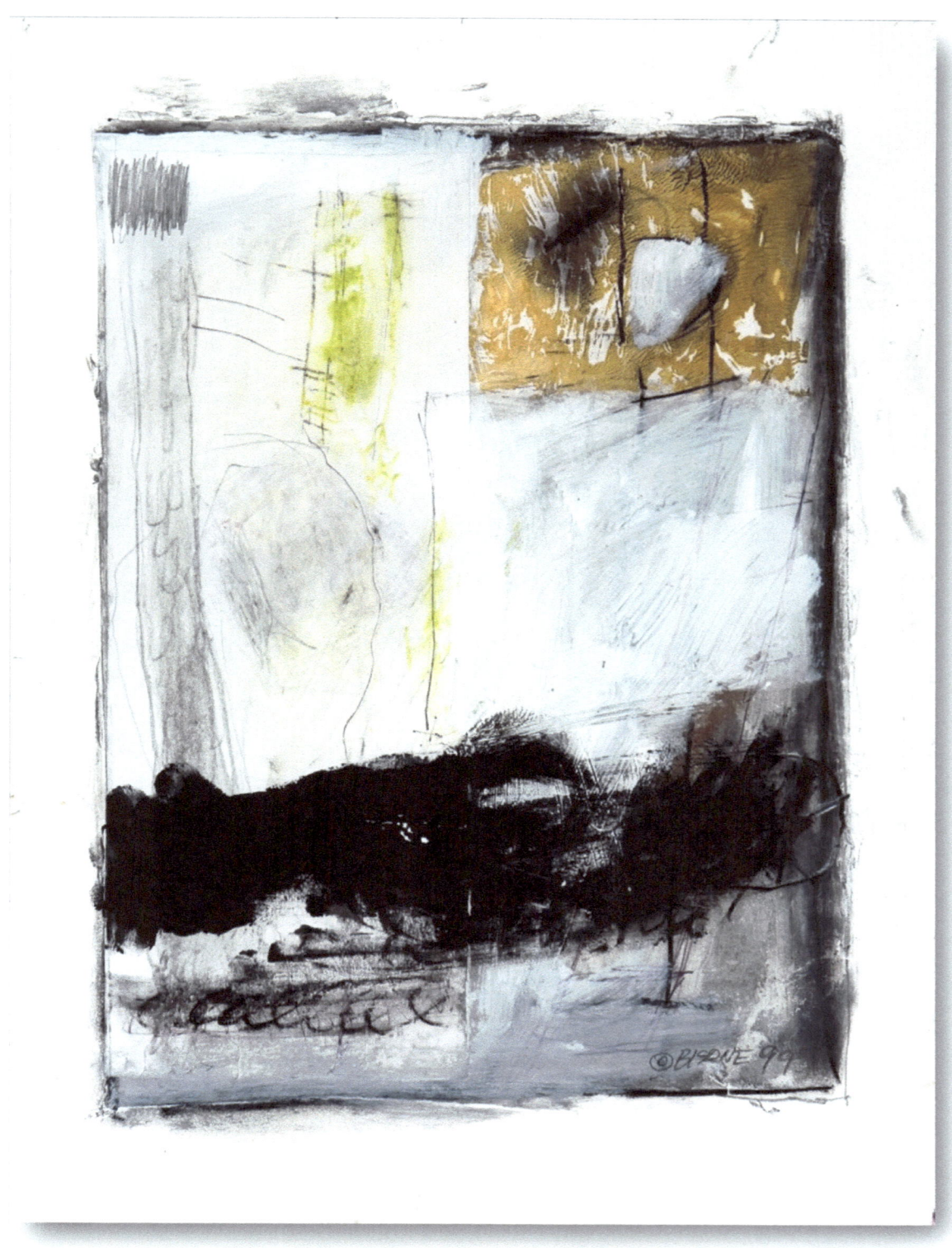

Aesthetic Echo II, 1999, 14.5 x 11 inches

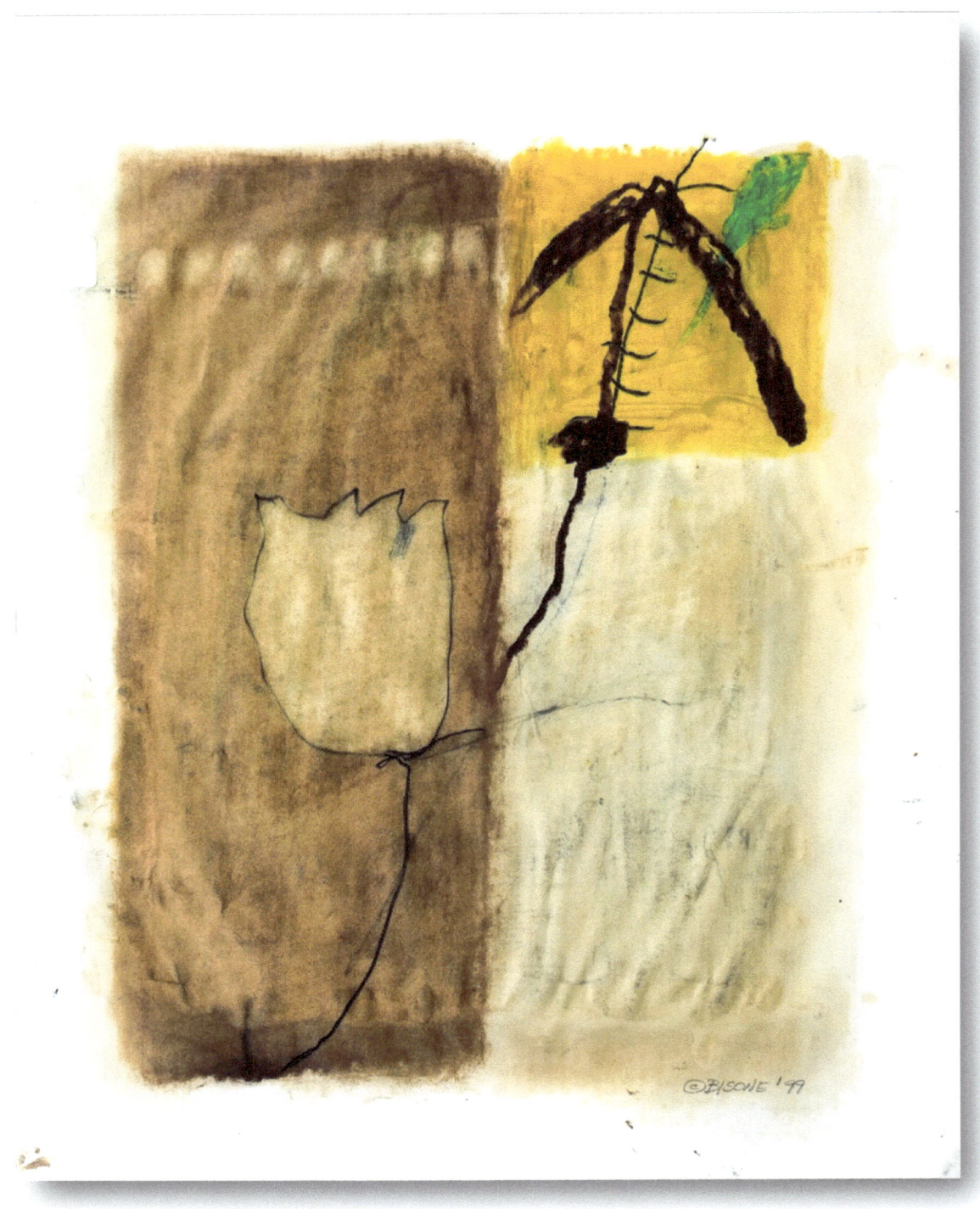

Untitled, 1999, 20 x 16 inches

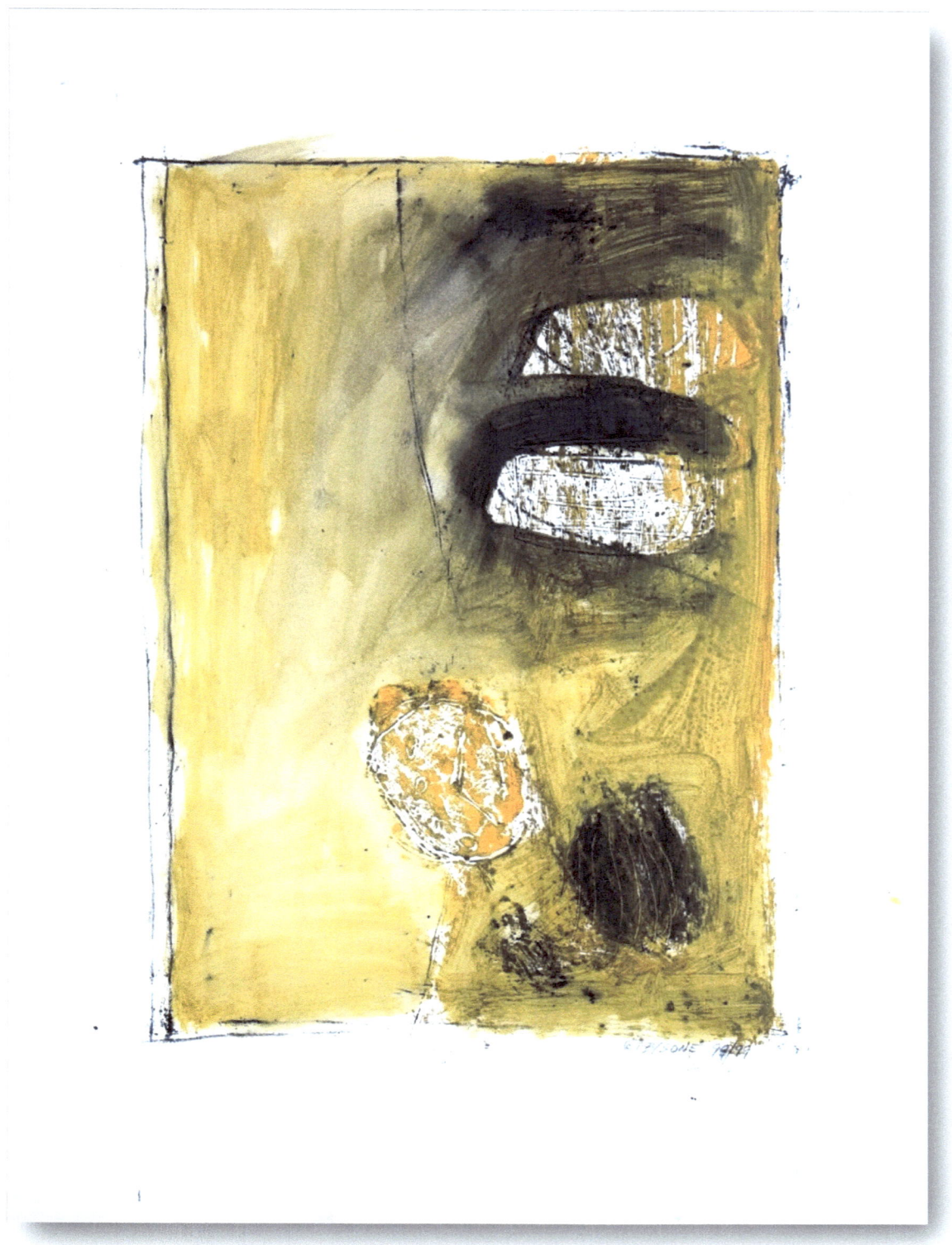

Yellows (Smoke & Haze), 1998-99, 24 x 18 inches

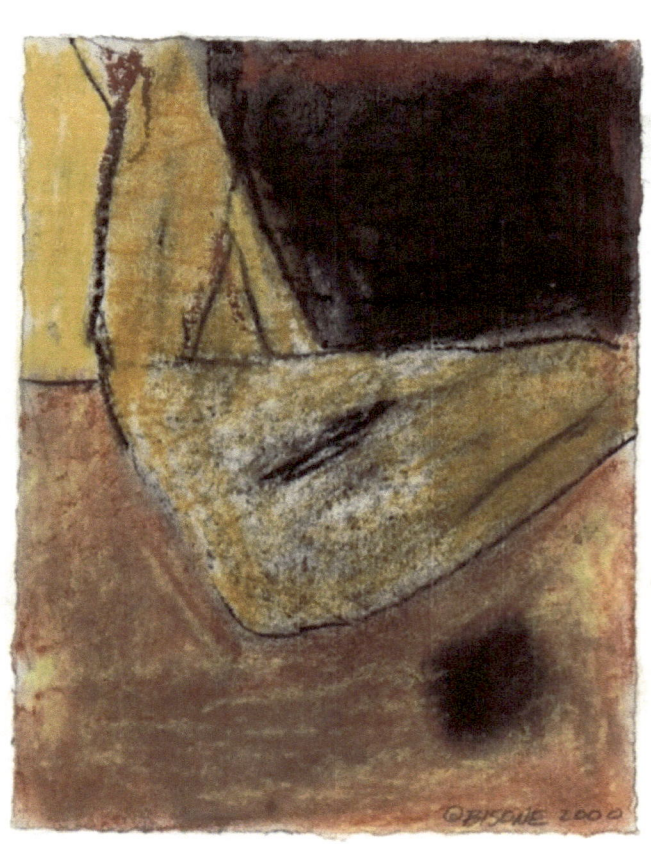

Black, Ochre, Umber, 2000, 12.25 x 9.25 inches

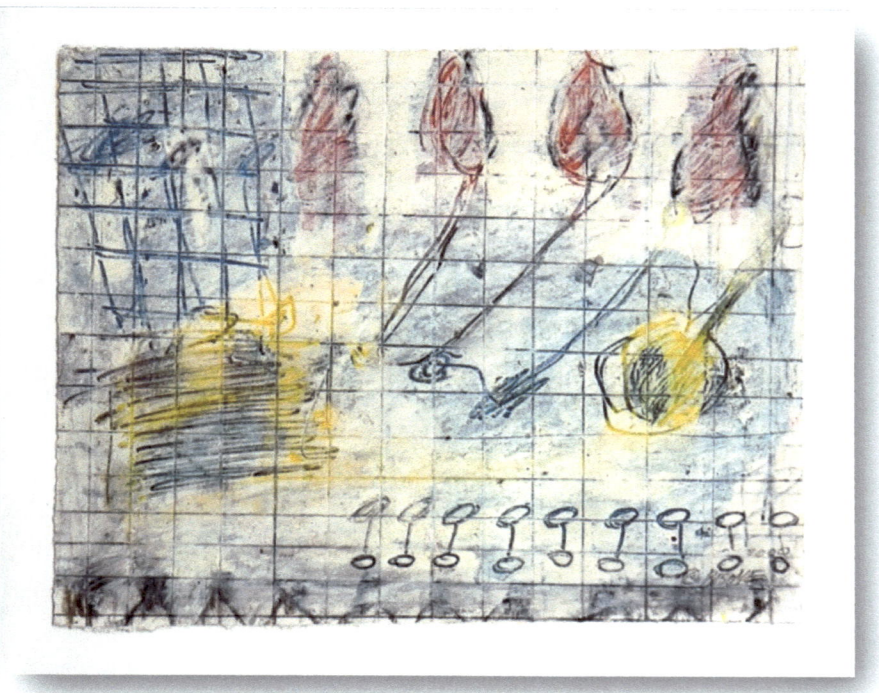

Thinking is Form III, 2000, 18 x 22 inches

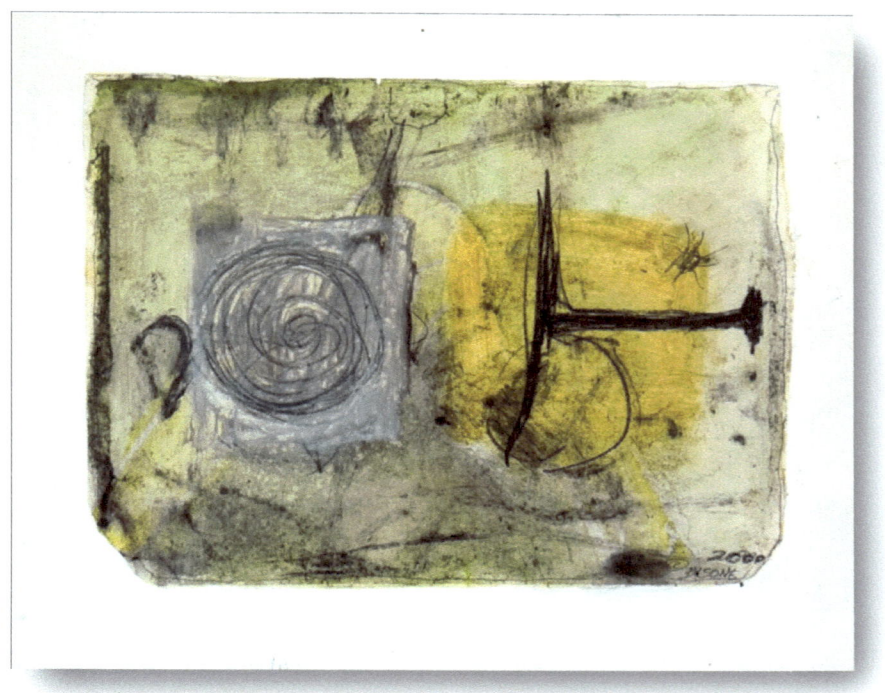

Untitled, 2000, 11 x 14 inches

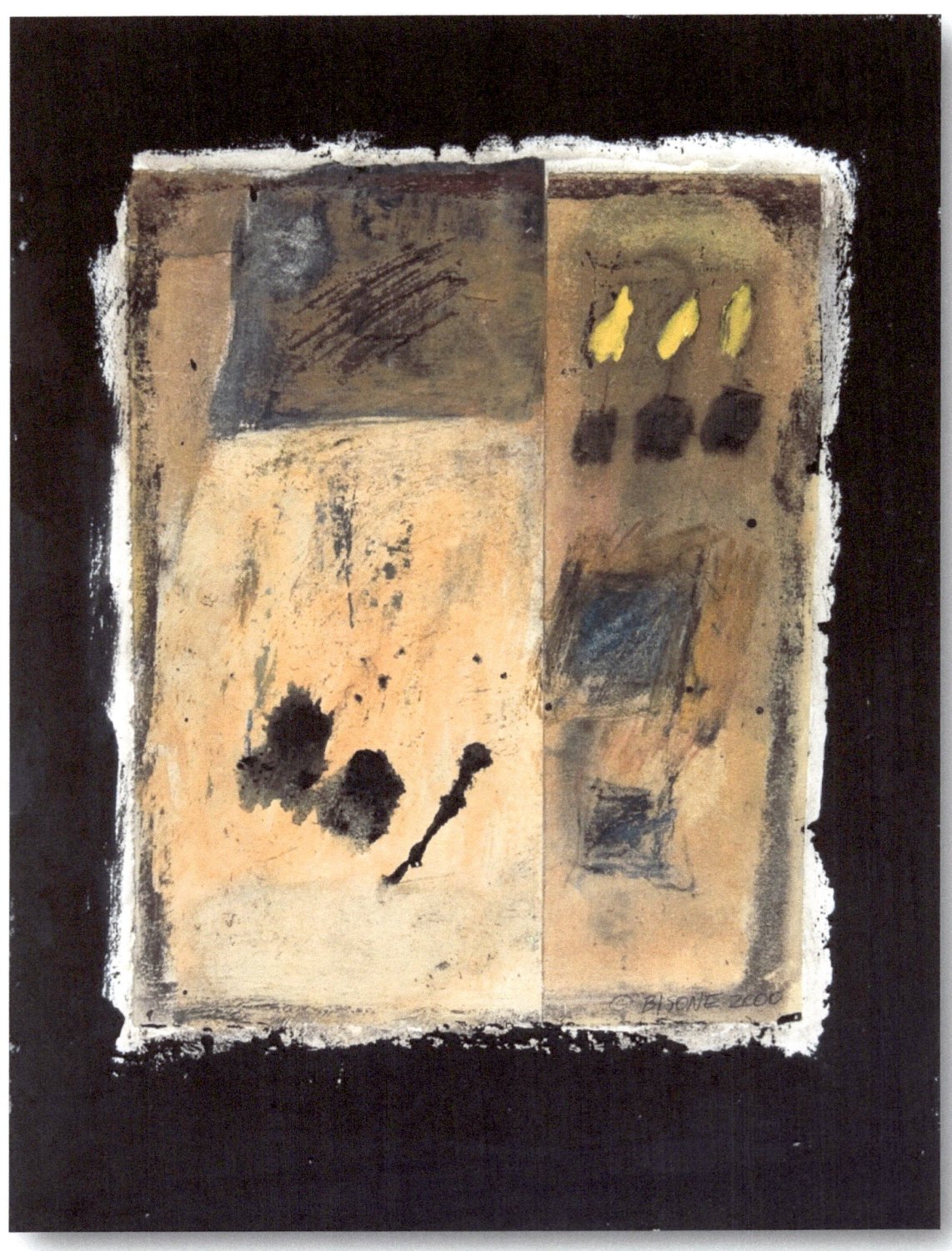

Torn Page, 2000, 12 x 9.25 inches

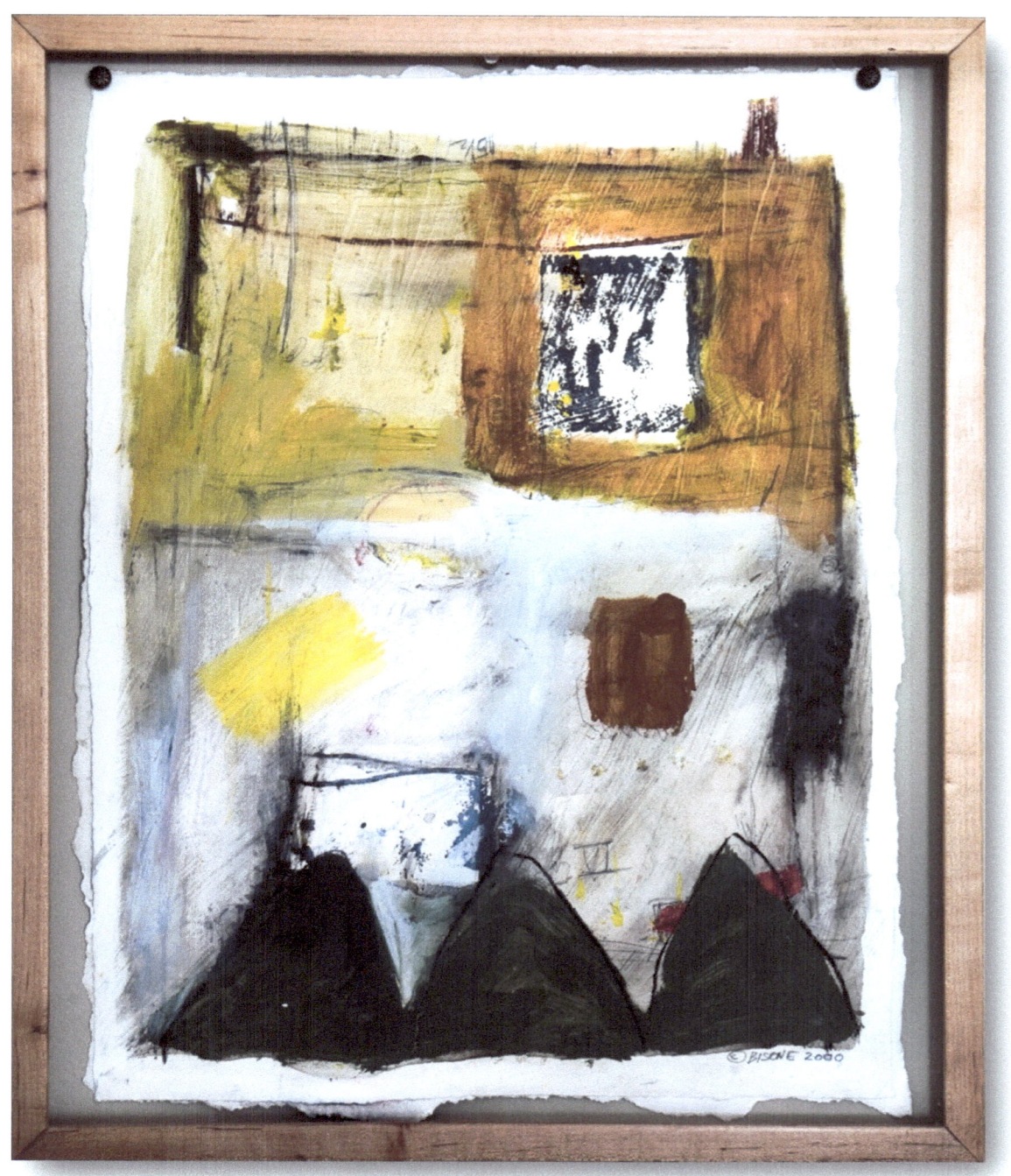

Untitled, 2000, 19 x 16 inches

first, random marks,

then, the lines connecting them

when thought takes over

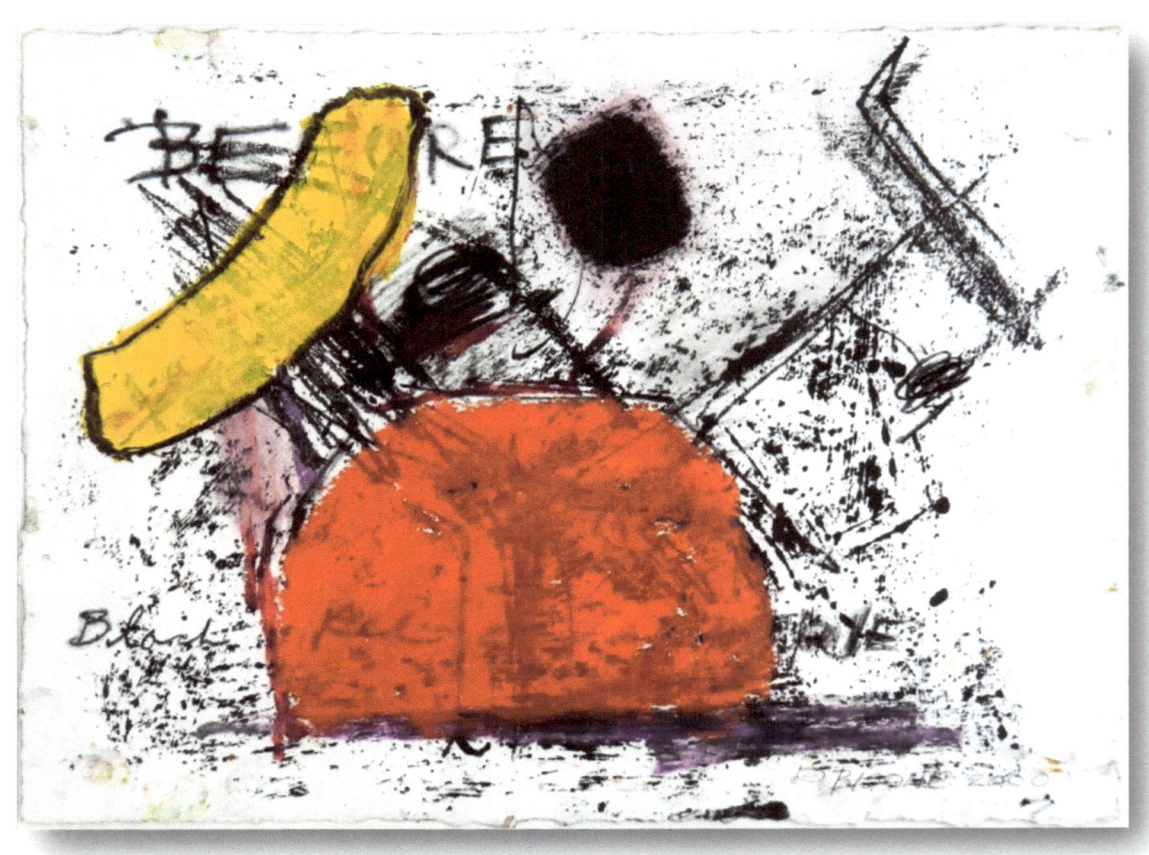

Untitled with Primary Colors, 2000, 8.75 x 12 inches

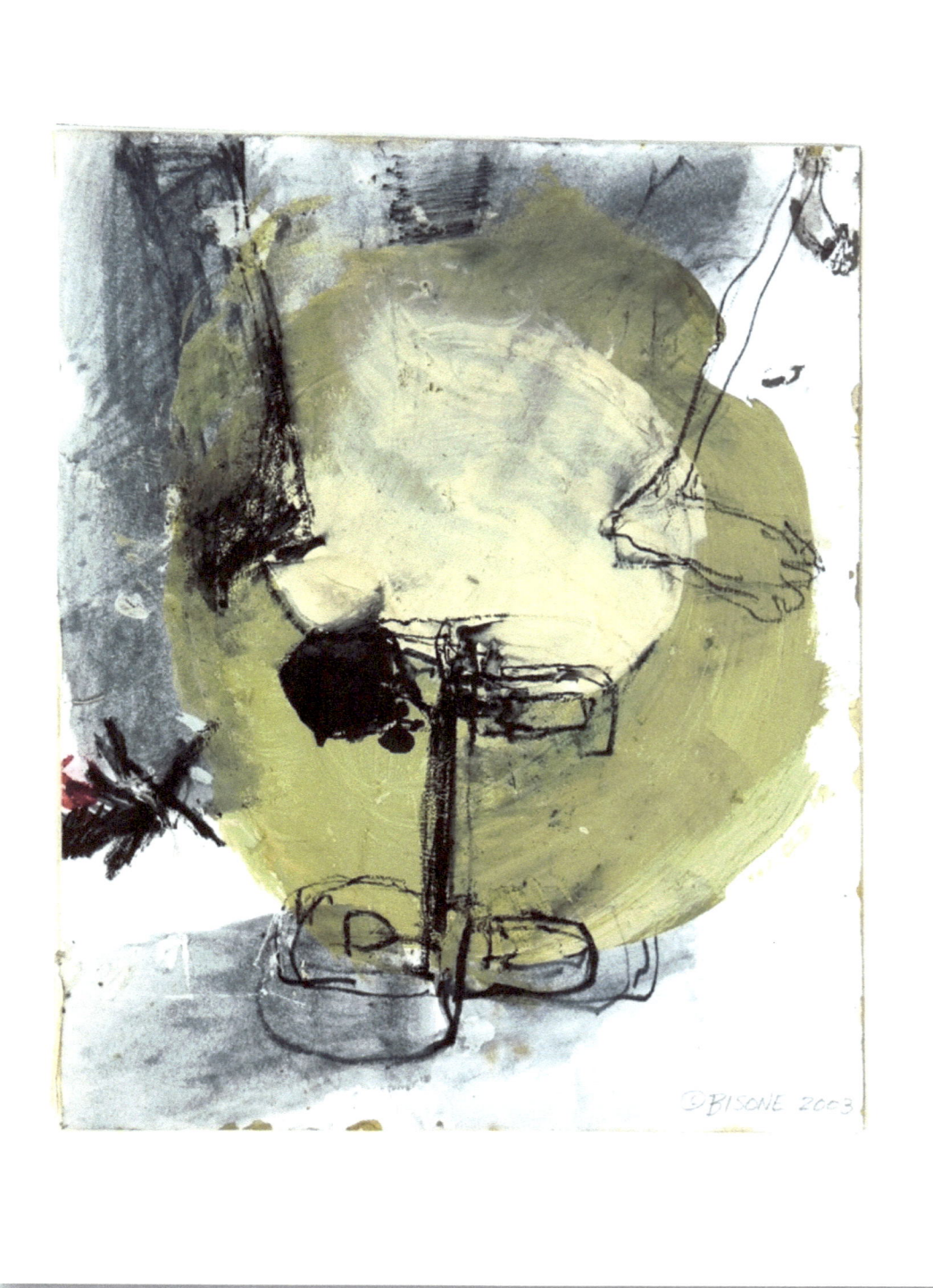

Keeping a Rendezvous, 2003, 15 x 11 inches

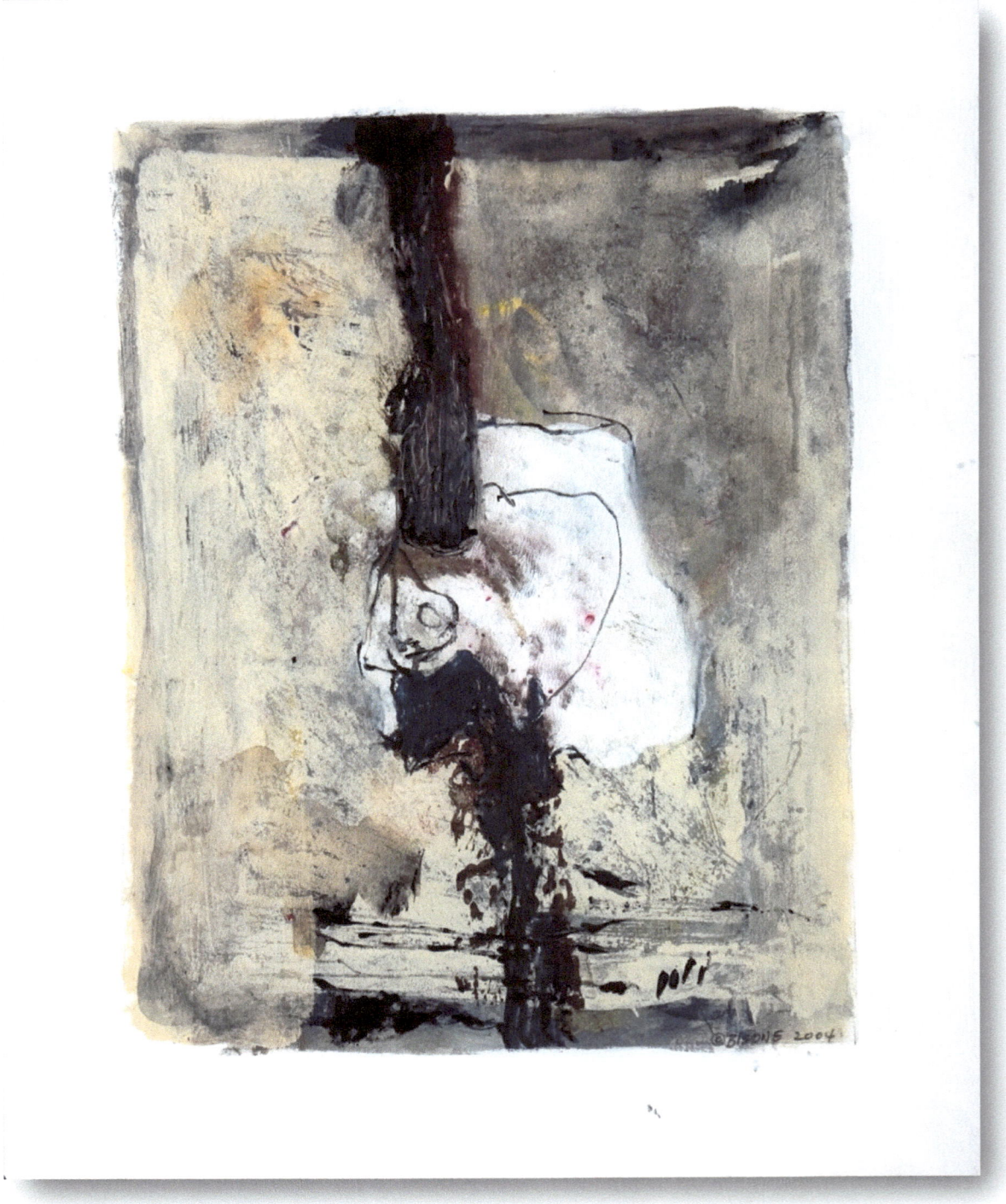

Profile, 2004, 18 x 15 inches

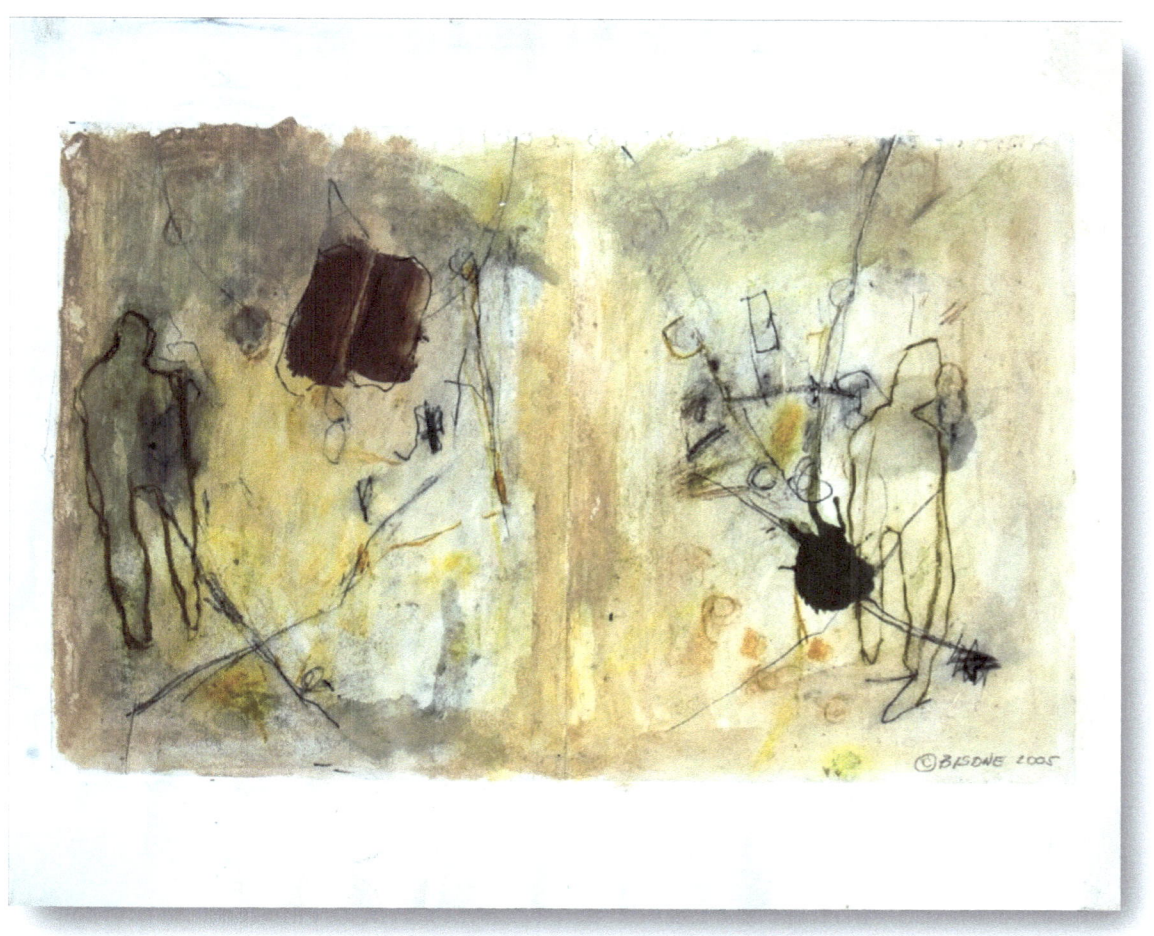

2 Travelers, 2005, 19.25 x 23.75 inches

the relationship
     between any two objects
          changes perception

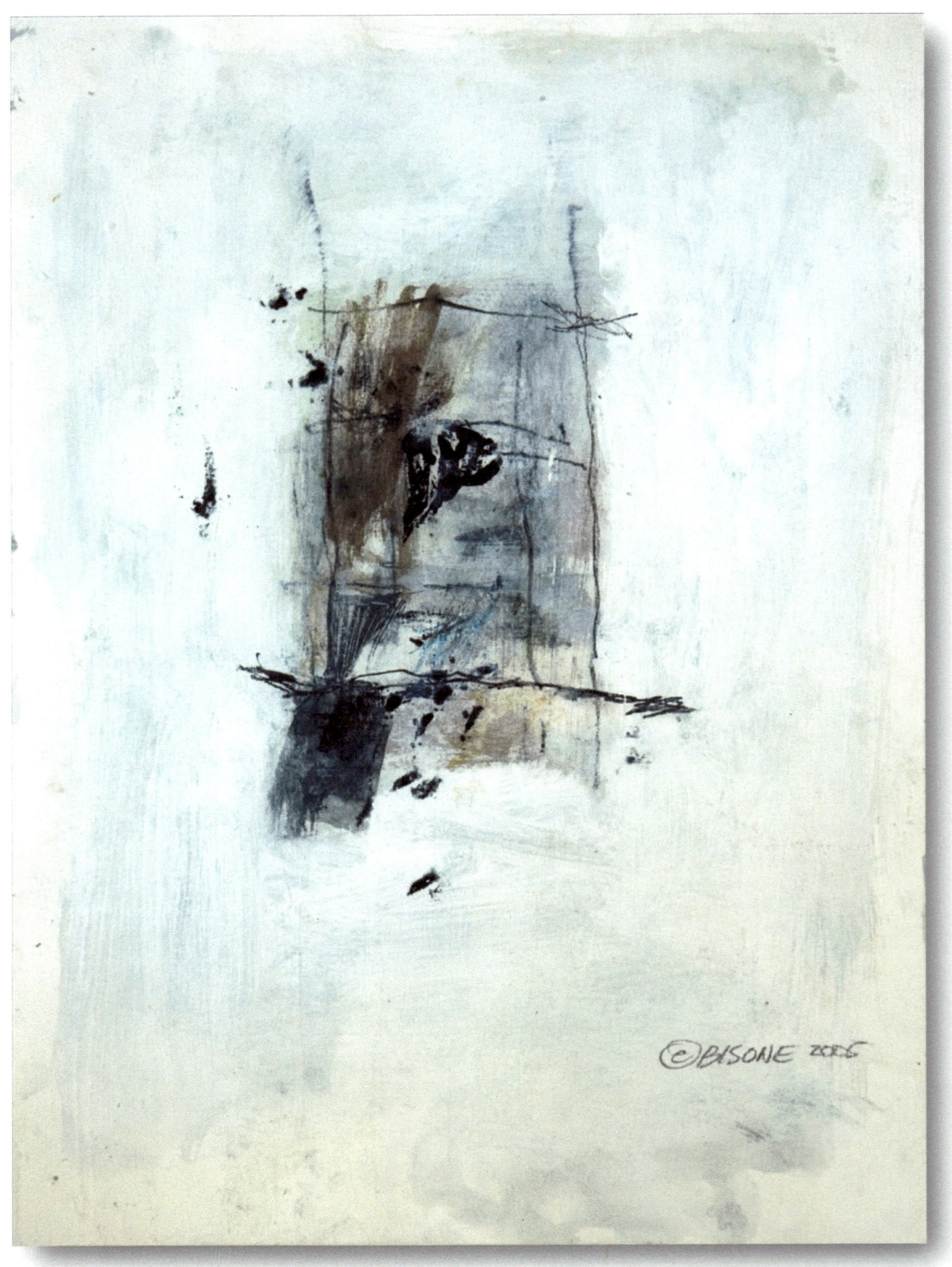

An Arrangement in Grays V, 2005, 15 x 11 inches

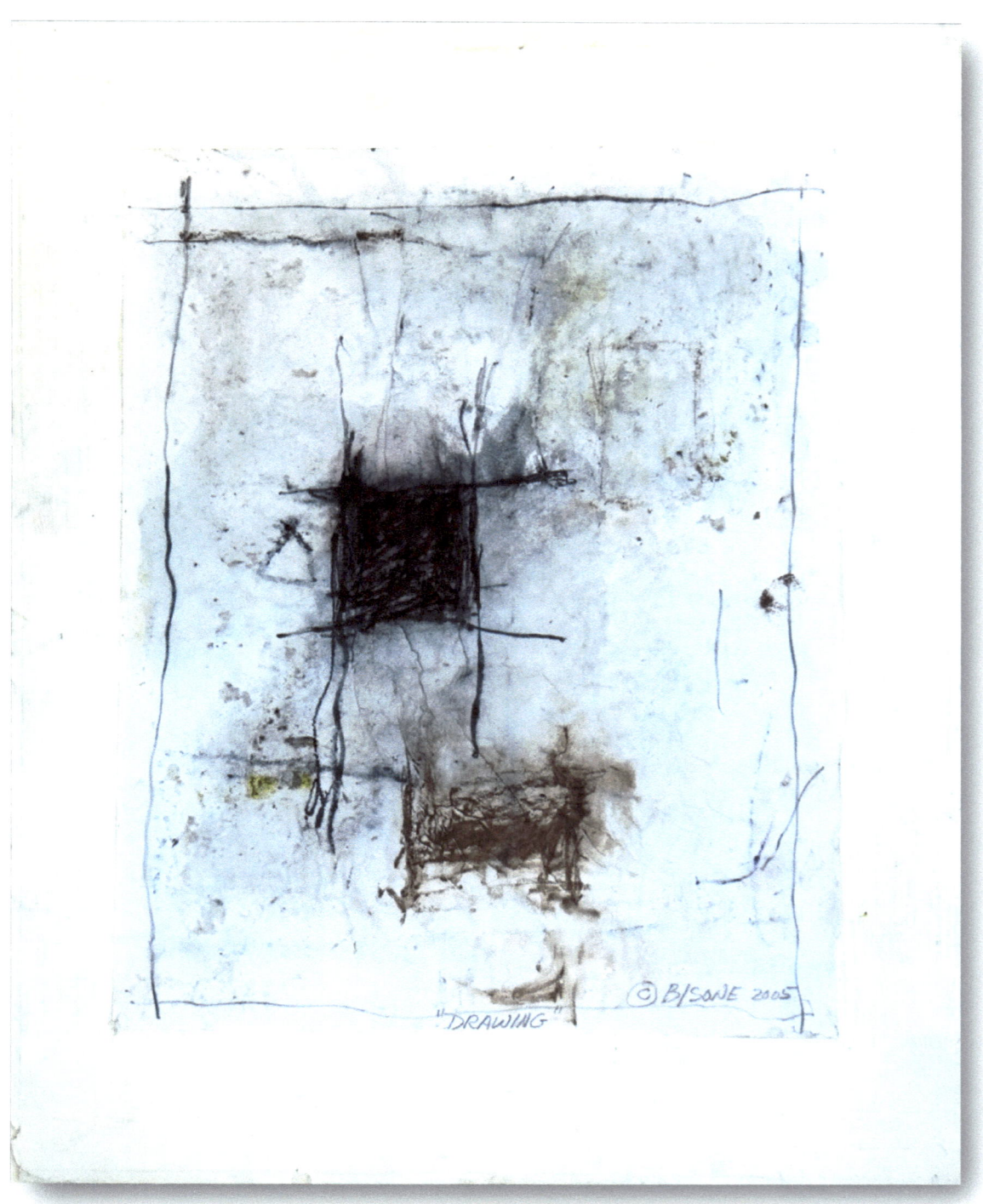

Drawing I, 2005, 14.25 x 11.5 inches

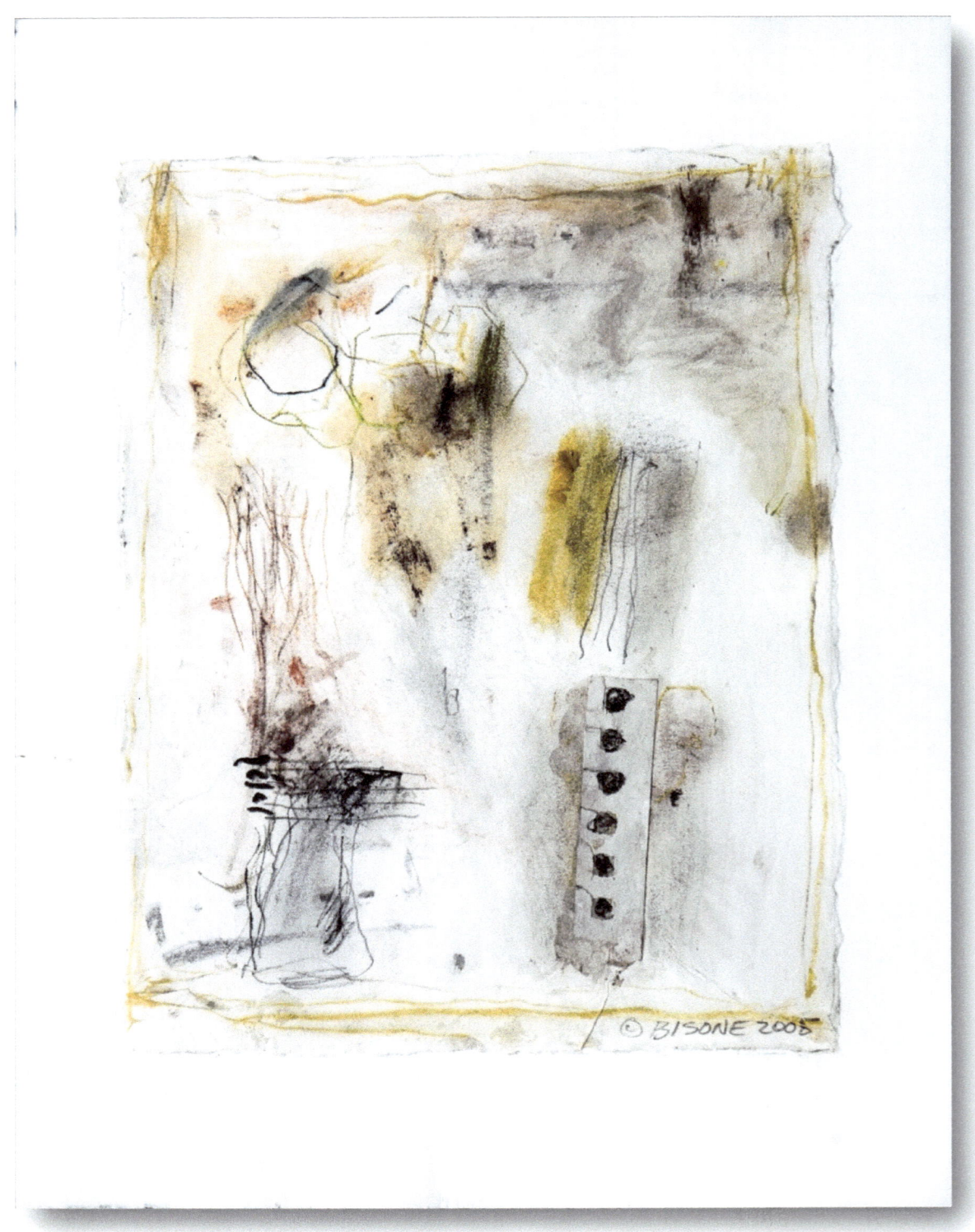

Drawing IIa, 2005, 14 x 11 inches

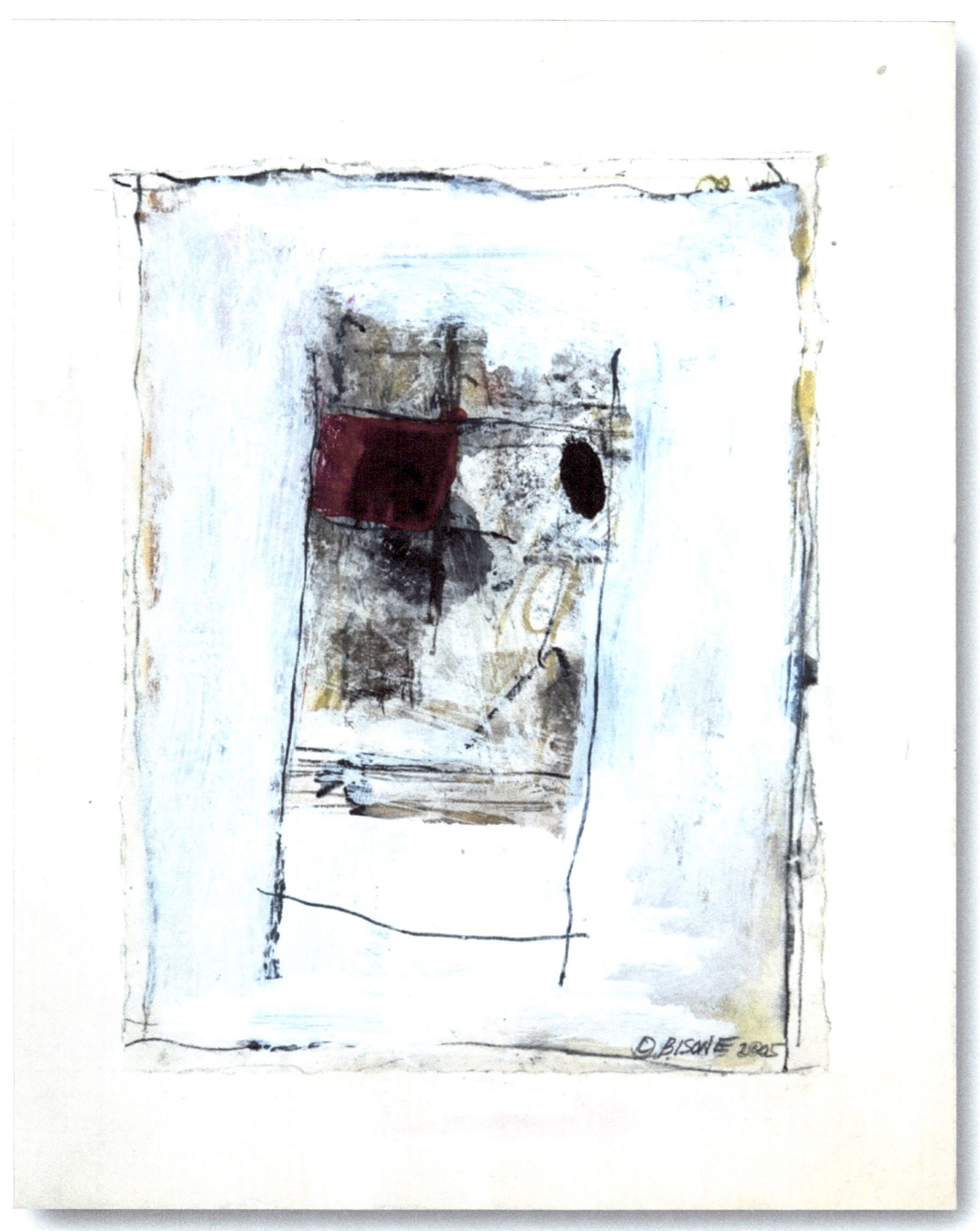

Drawing IIIa, 2005, 14 x 11 inches

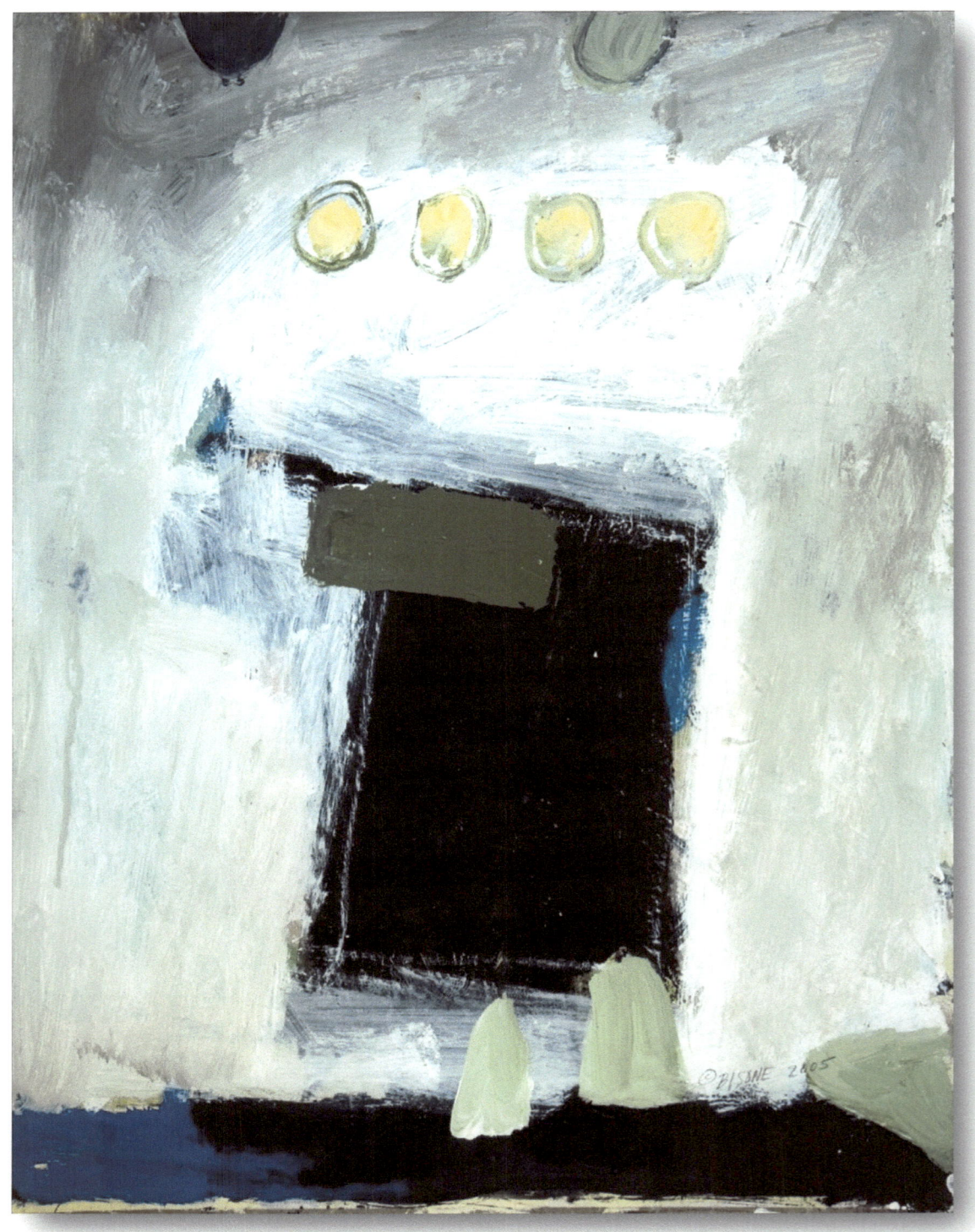

The Touch, 2005, 22 x 17 inches

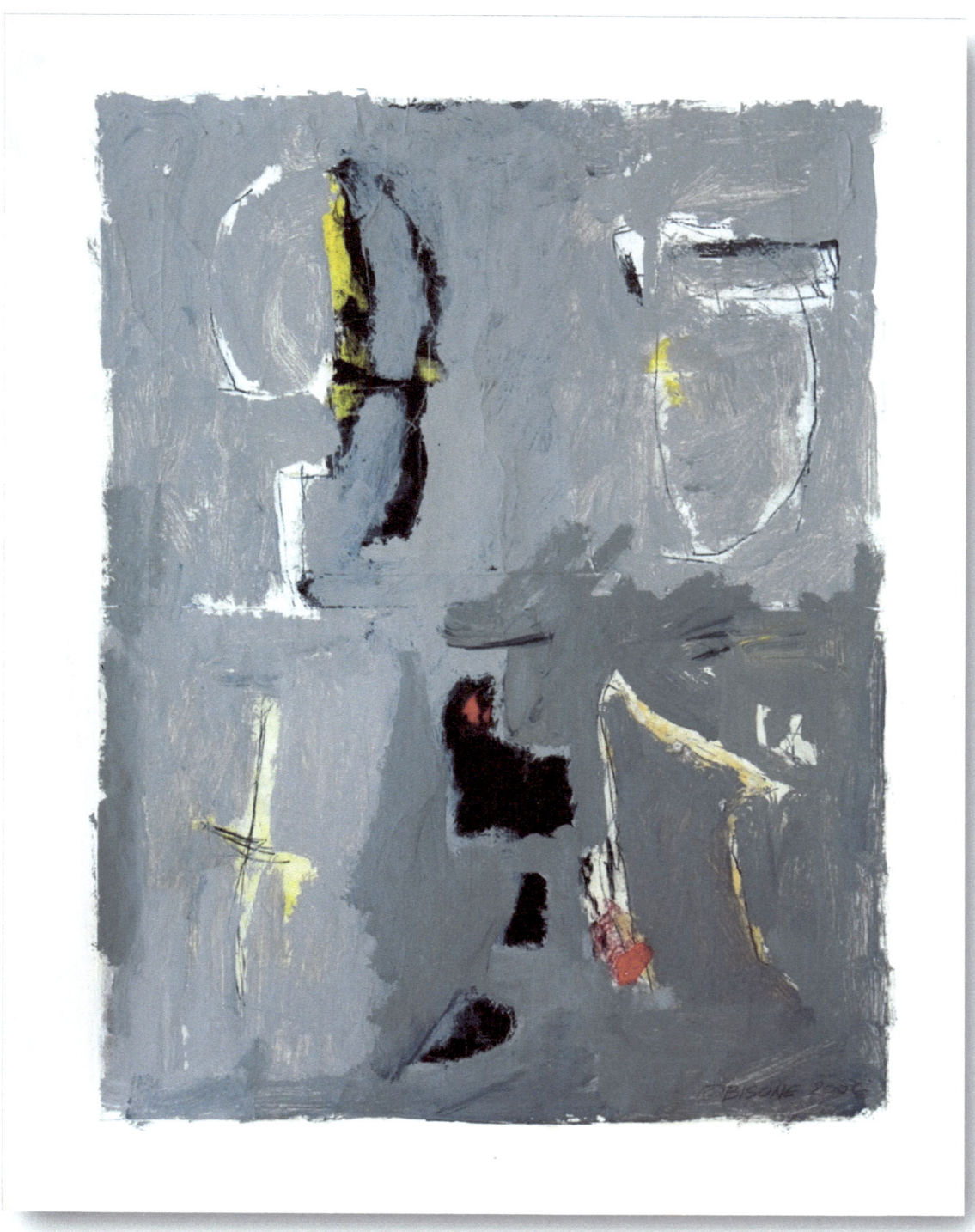

Arrangement in Shapes, Lines, and Color, 2006, 27.75 x 22 inches

line becomes language
and you read it though it's
a foreign tongue

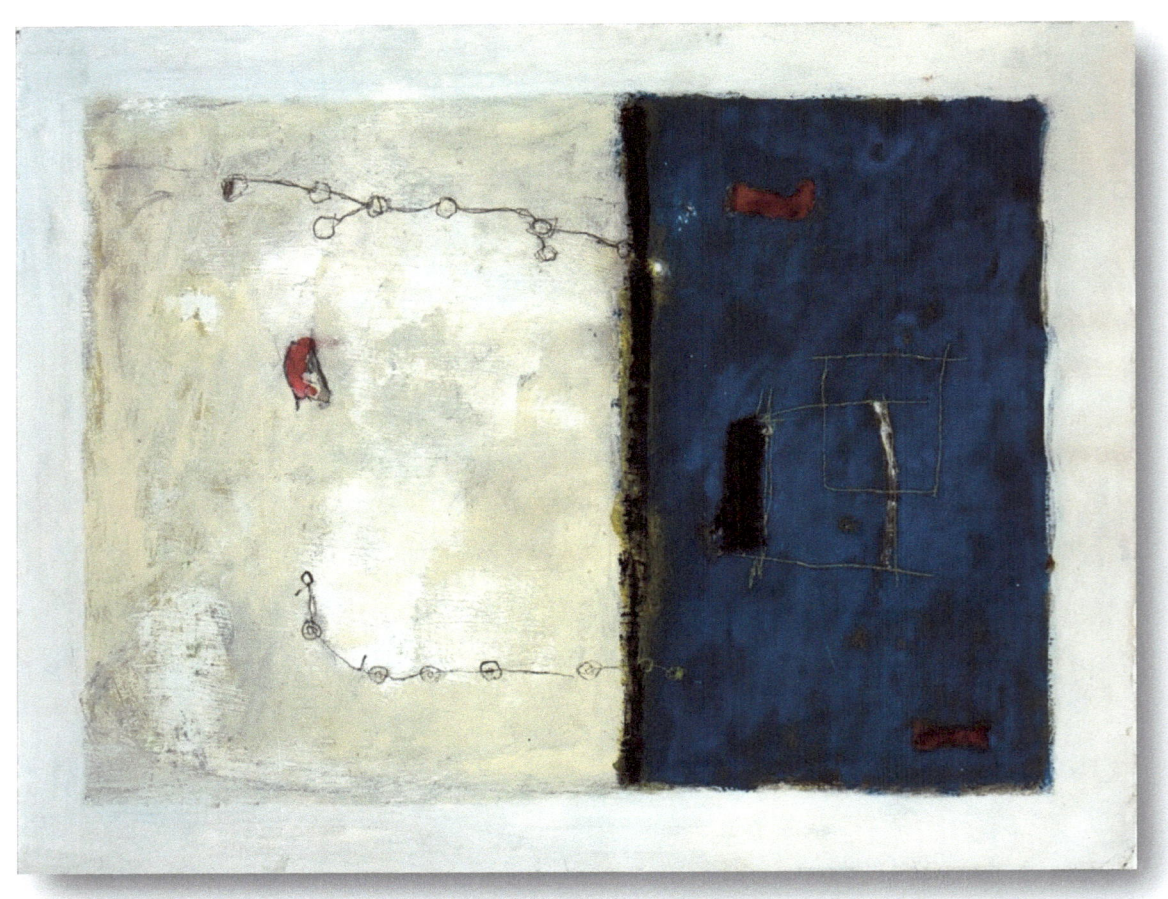

Elegy in an Urban Yard #I, 2006, 20 x 26 inches

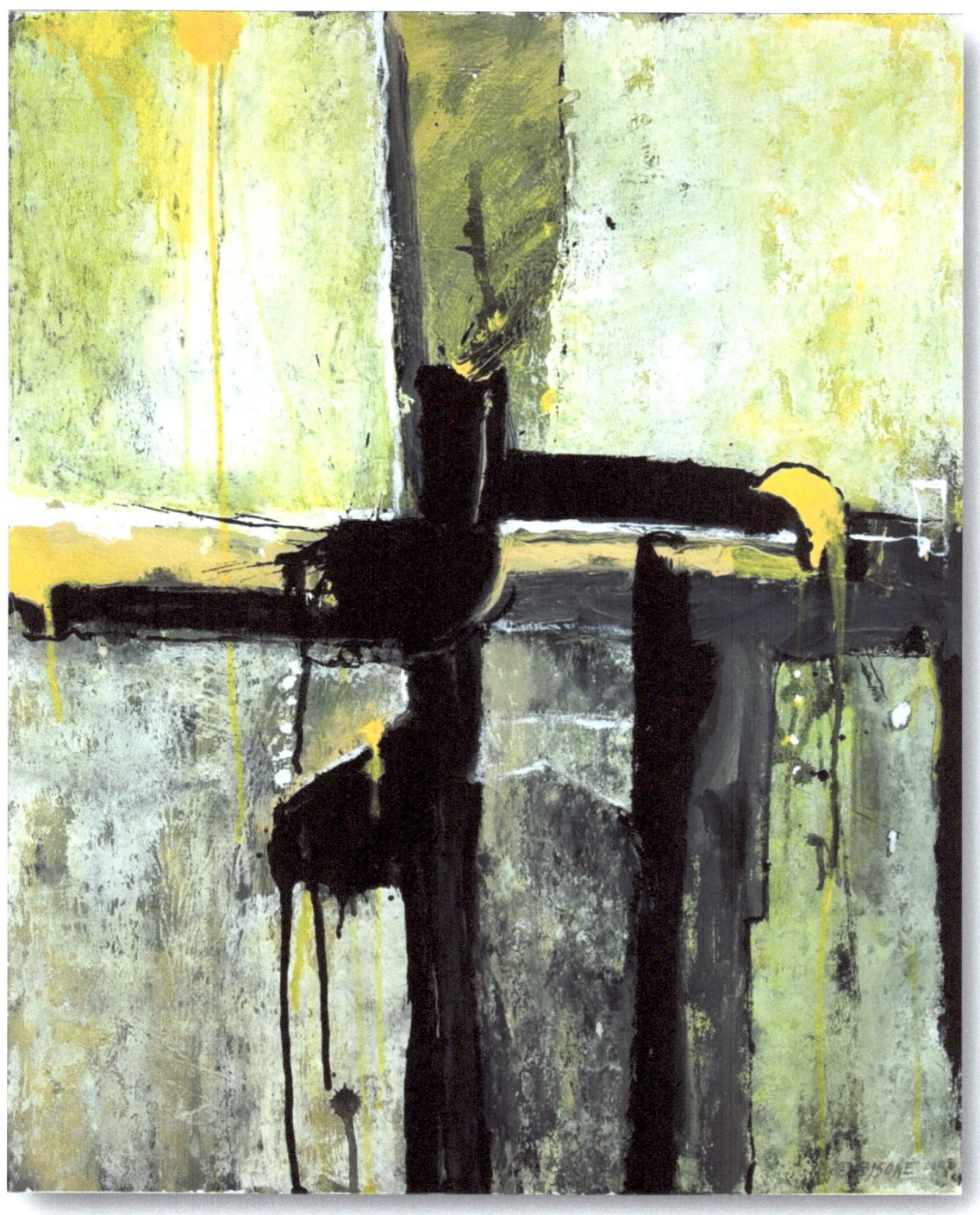

Totemic Power Monolith, 2008, 27.5 x 22 inches

11. The Unseeing

Young women seated, some with backs turned, young men behind dark glasses, winsome faith in the future. Motionless, waiting, longing for the other; bare walls, lonesome flowers, folded arms, unaware and knowing more than they can tell.

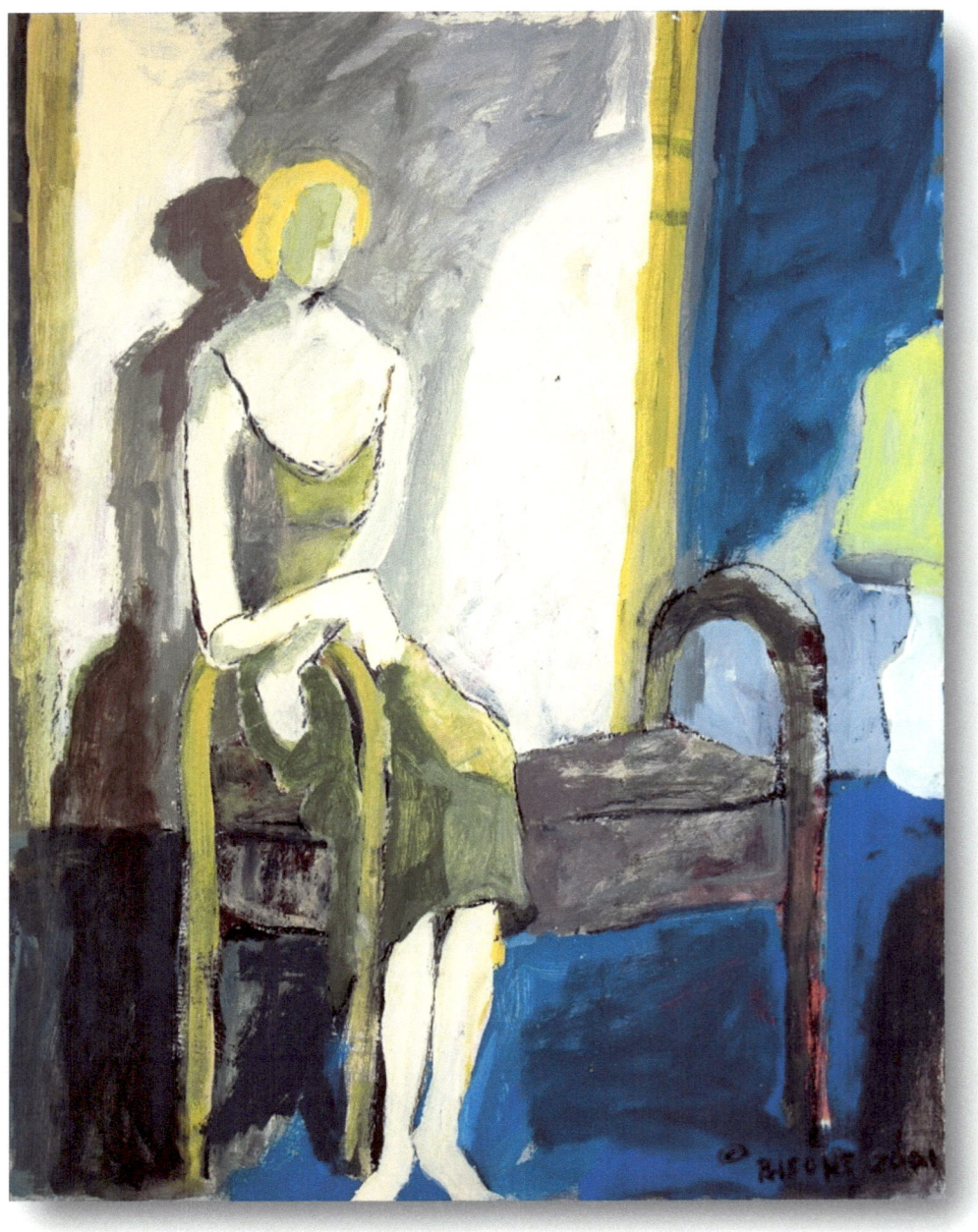

Woman in Shadows, 2001, 25.75 x 20 inches

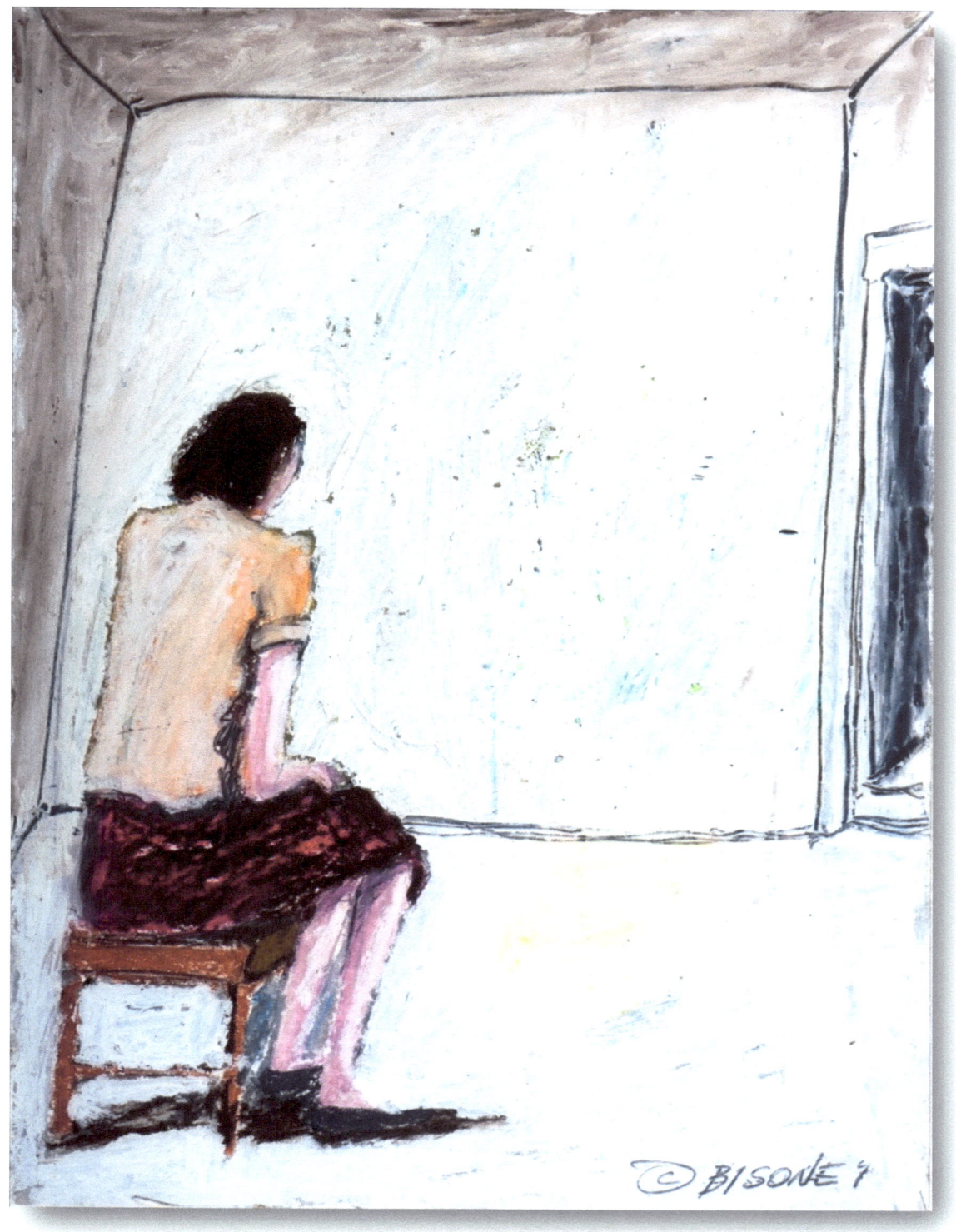

Untitled, 1995, 10.5 x 8 inches

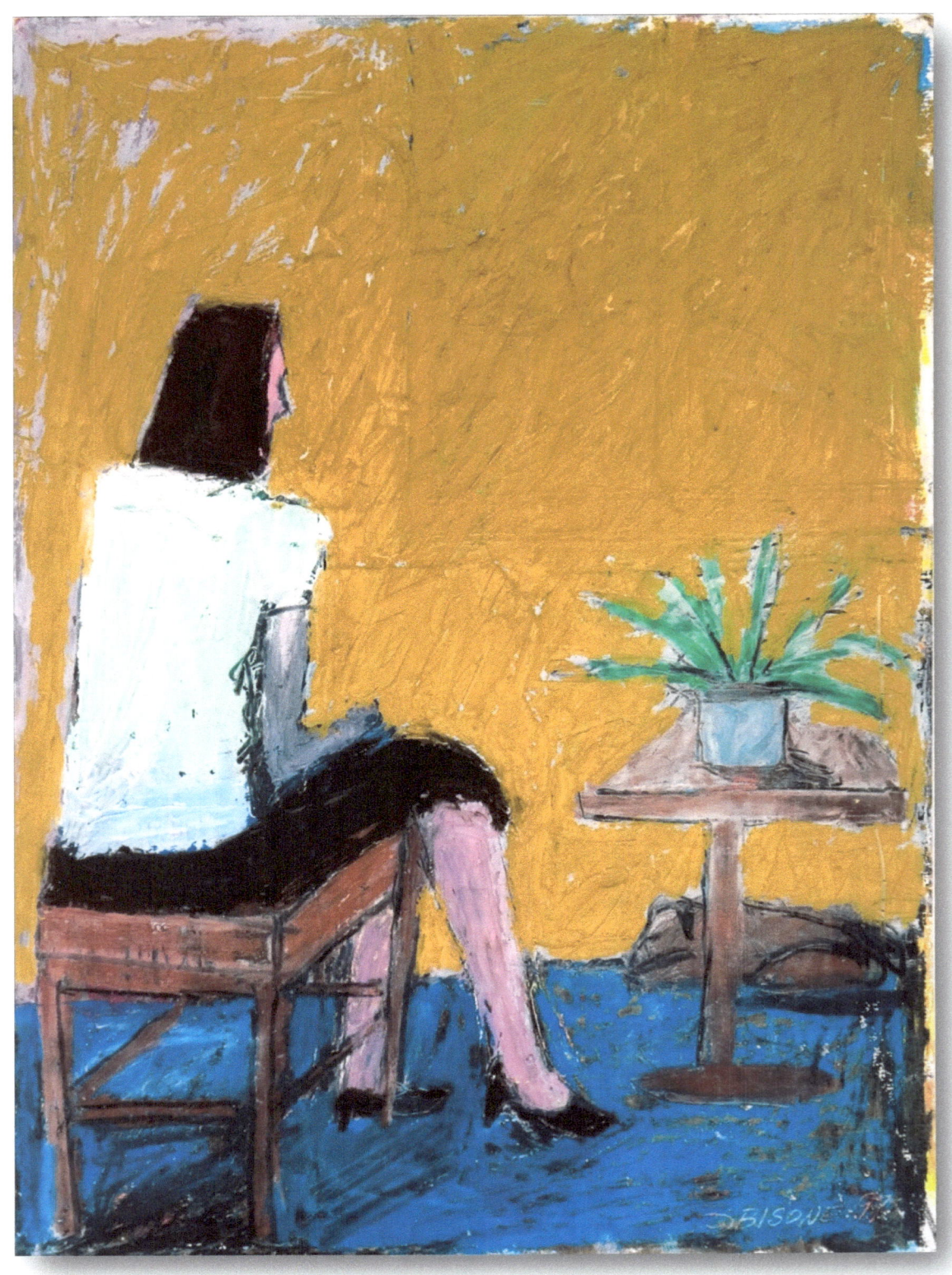

Untitled, 1997, 14 x 11 inches

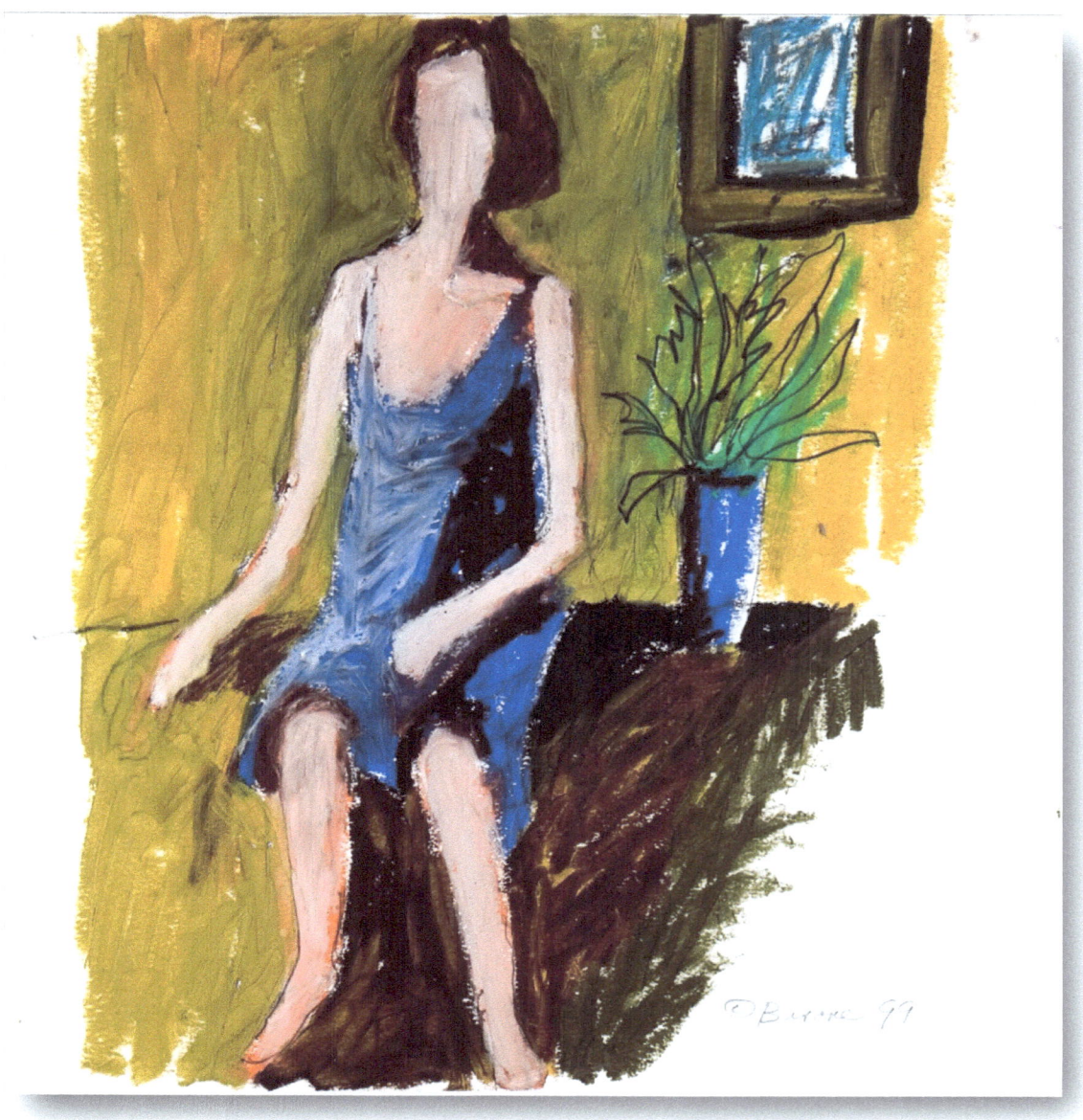

Blue Dress, 1999, 14.5 x 14 inches

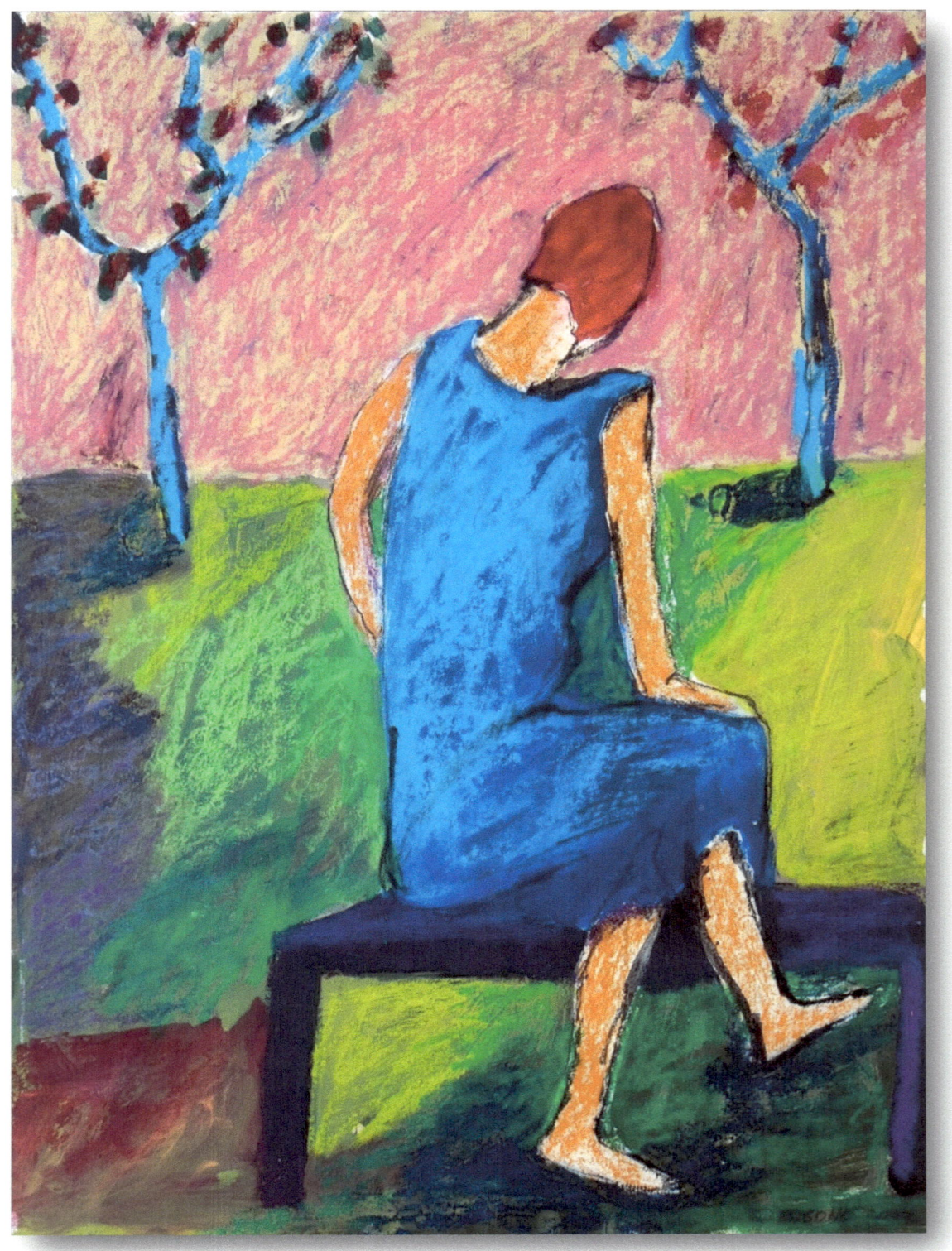

Blue Trees, 2002, 23.75 x 17.5 inches

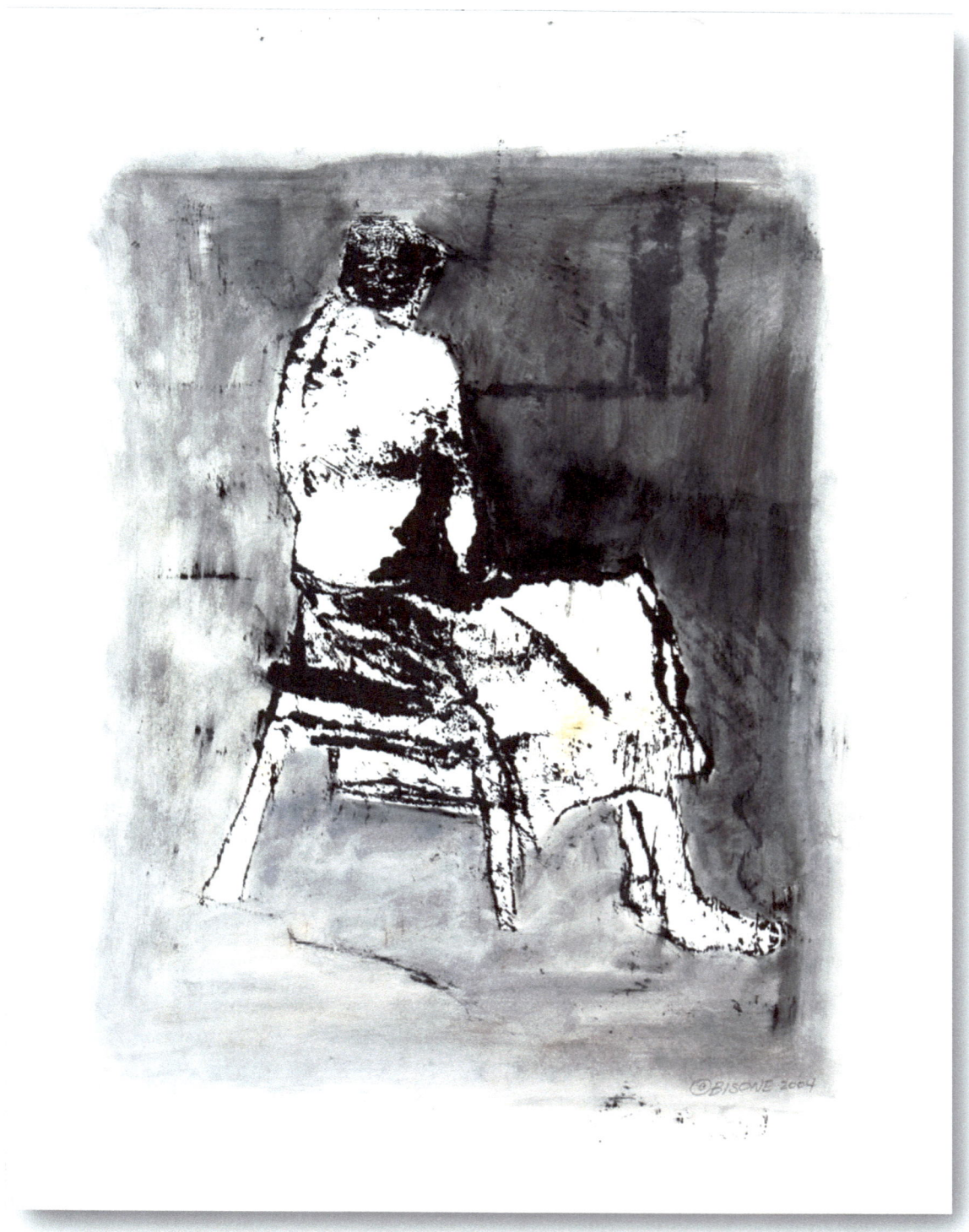

Seated Figure, 2004, 25.75 x 20 inches

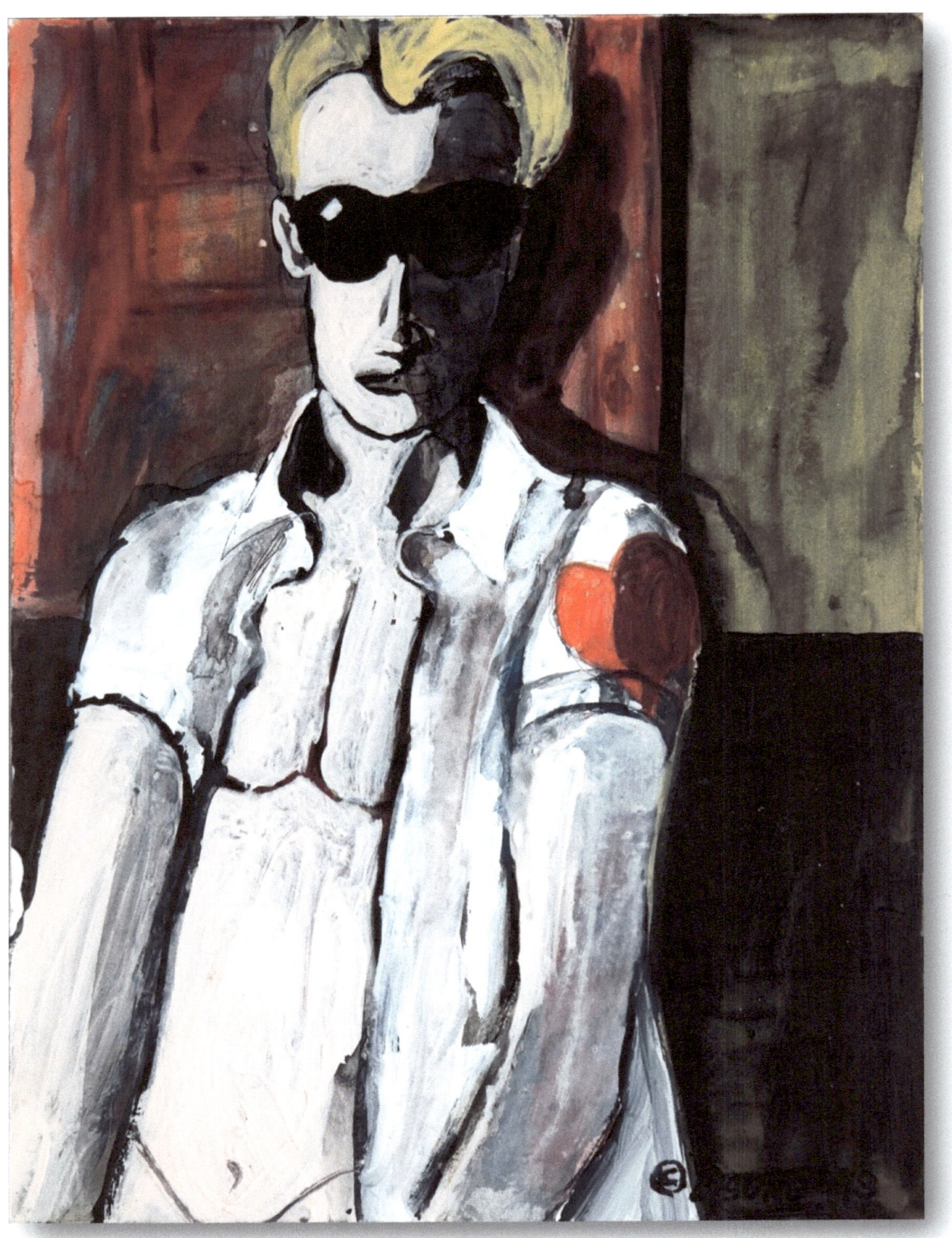

Heart on His Sleeve, 1997-98, 14 x 10.5 inches

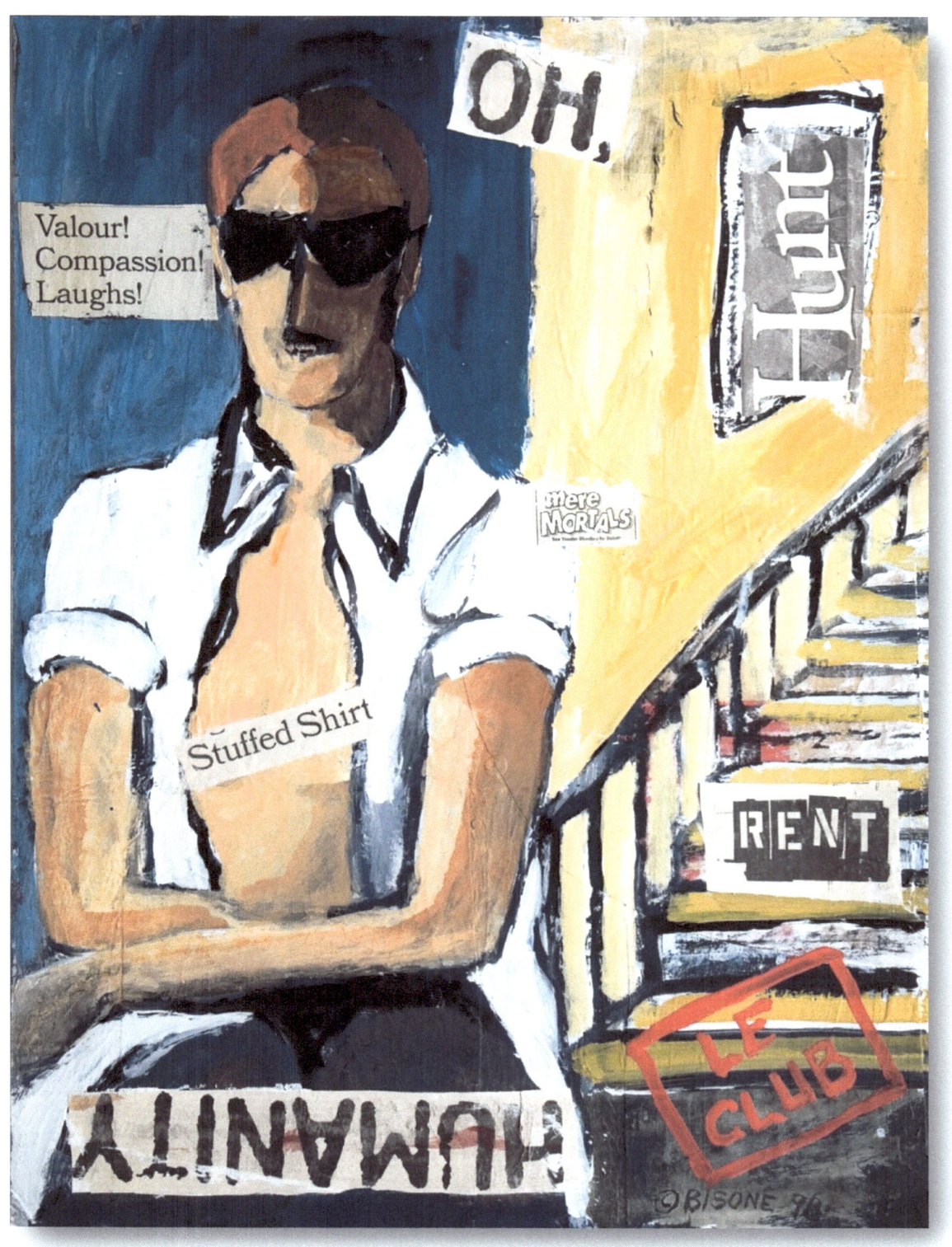

Street Youth, 1997-98, 24 x 18 inches

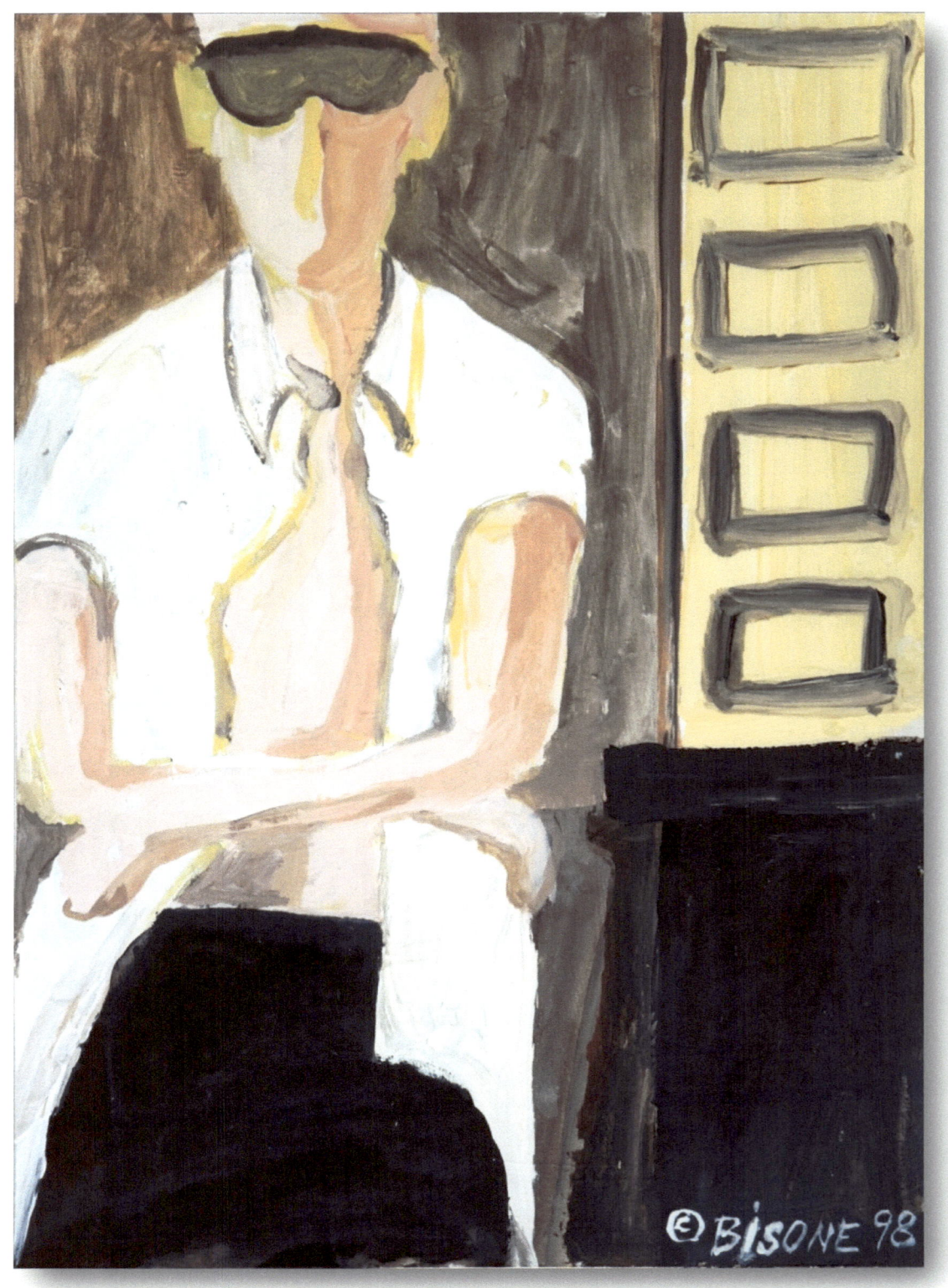

White Shirt, 1997-98, 14 x 10 inches

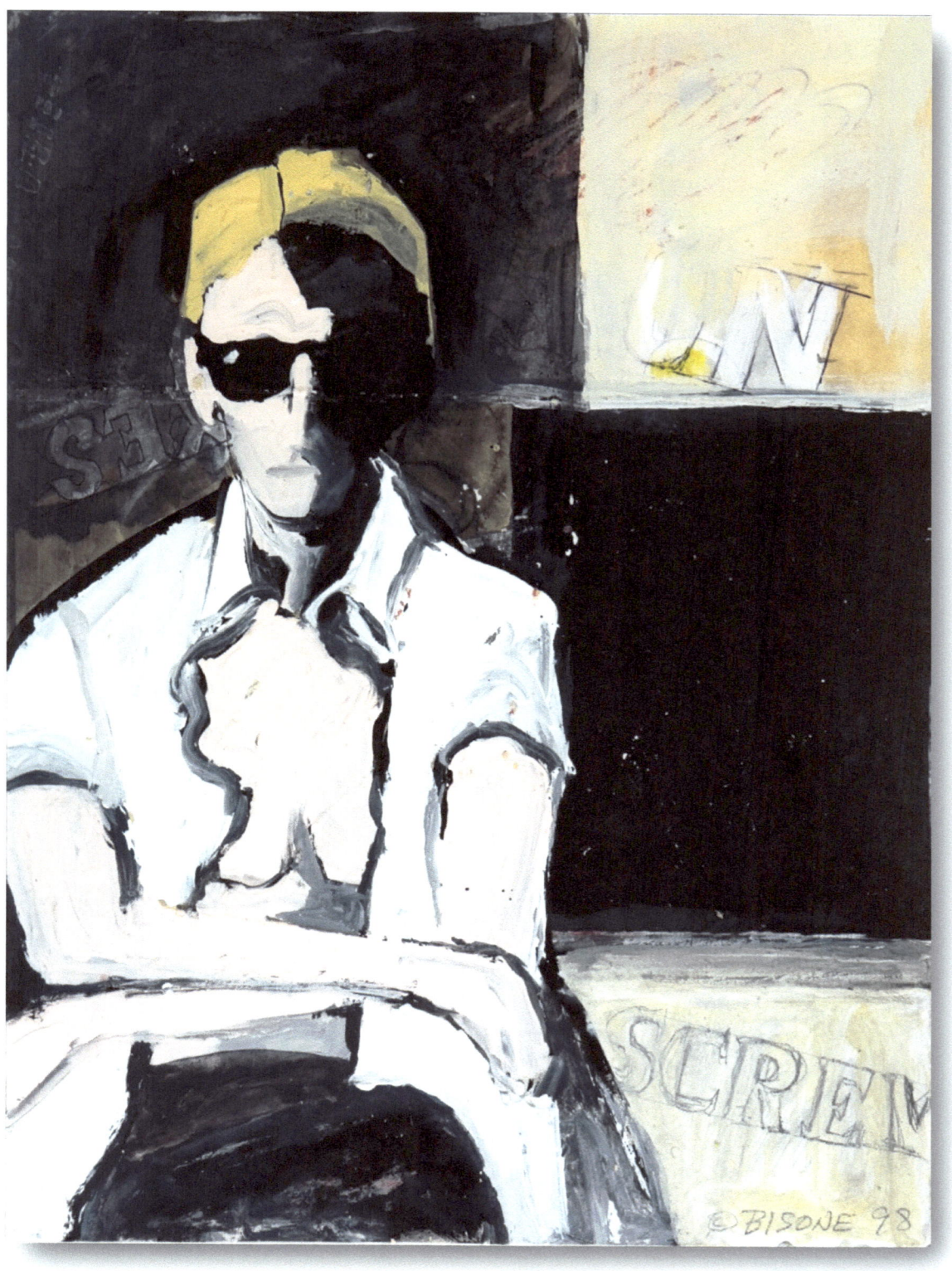

Sunglasses, 1998, 14.5 x 10.75 inches

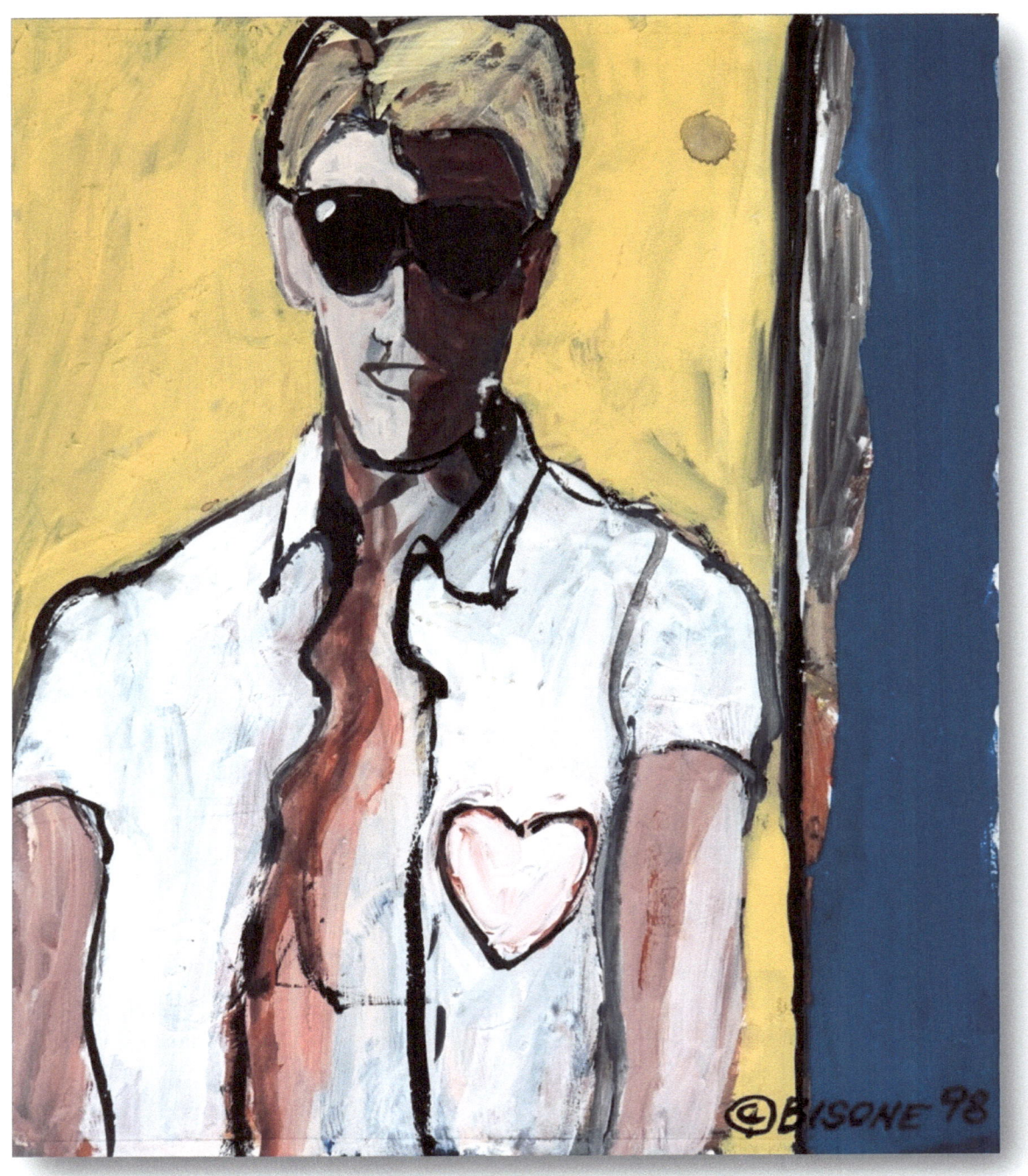

Young Man with Sunglasses, 1998, 13 x 11.25 inches

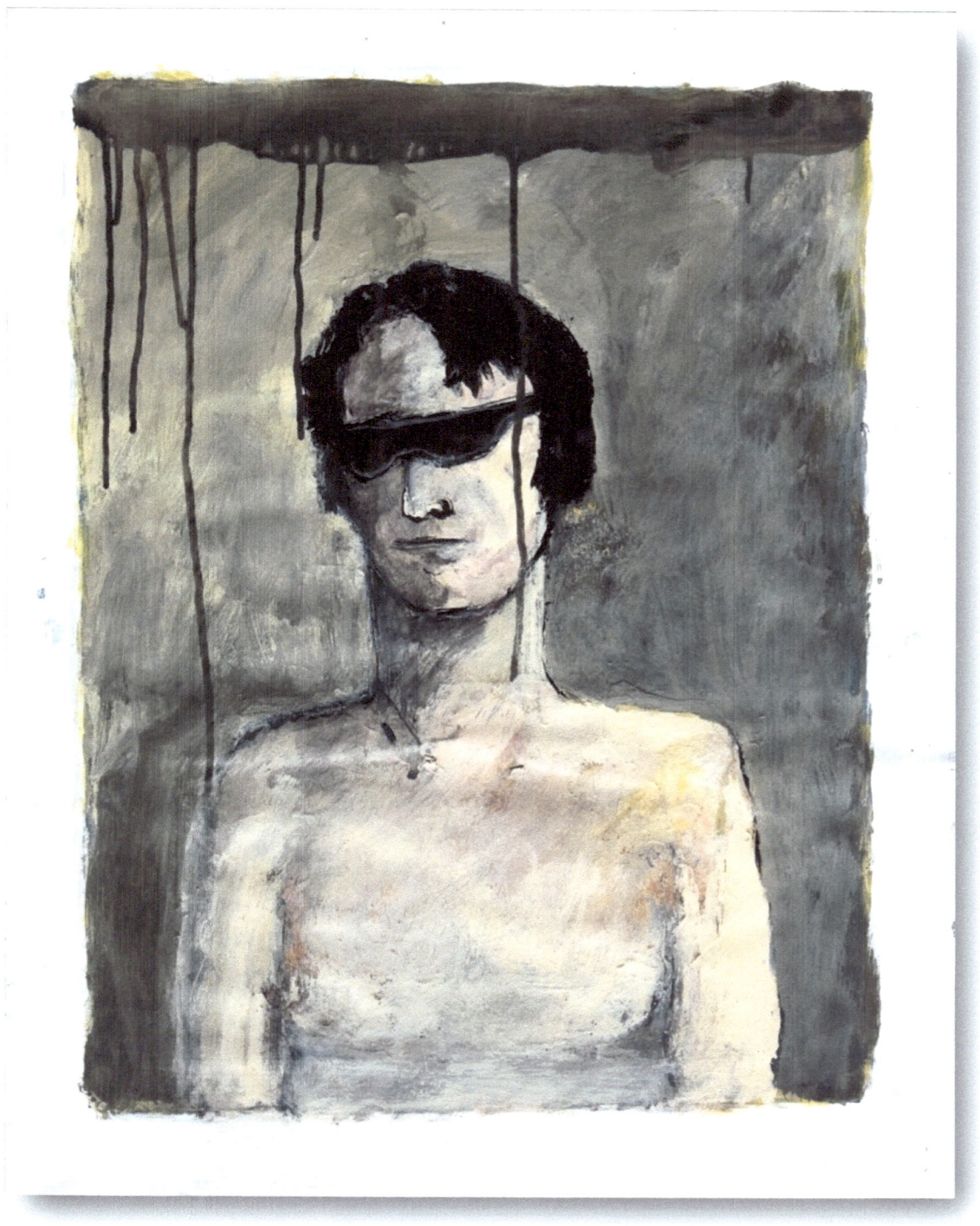

Ban Rays, 2008, 20 x 16 inches

12. Trees

All is well amidst the earthen yellows and greens and browns, but the knowledge of Good and Evil is hidden among the leaves of Bisone's trees. Lie beneath them at your peril.

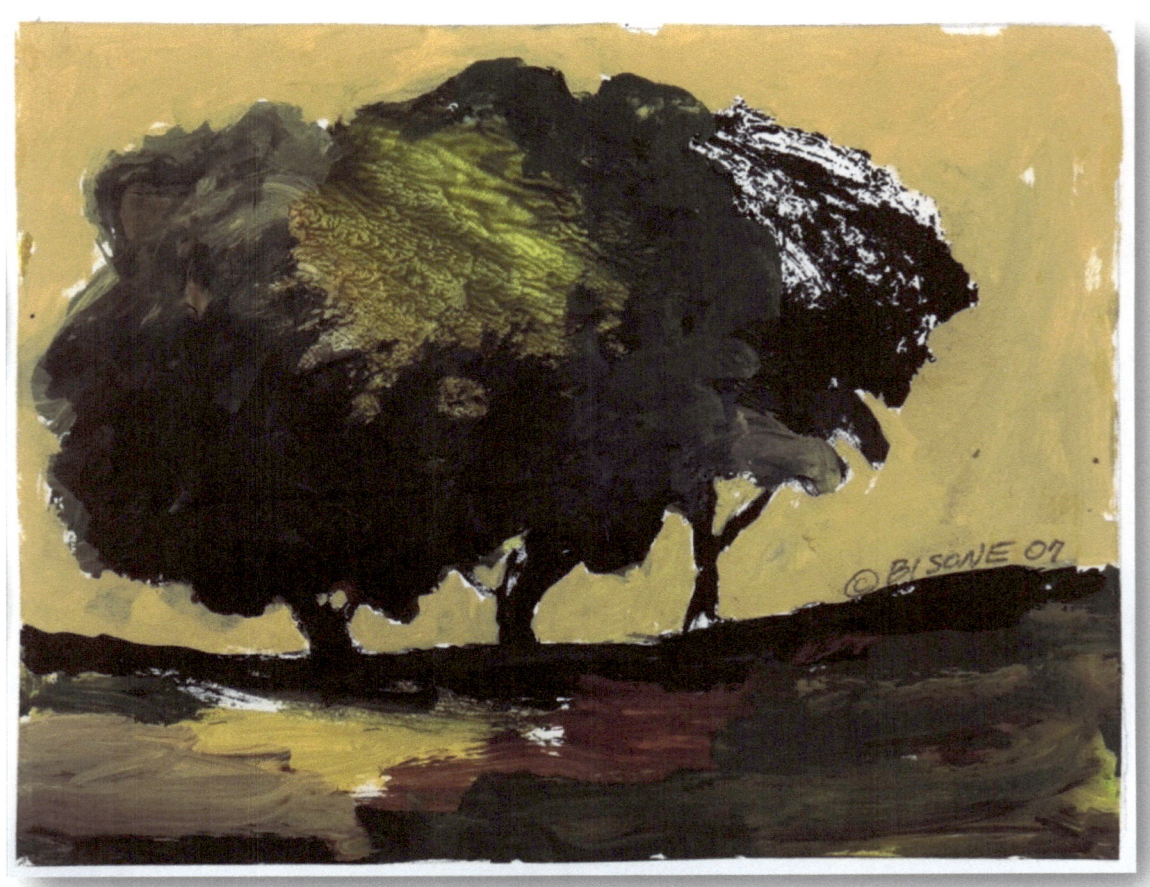

Tree, 2007, 6 x 8 inches

nature as mirror

is where many fall short;

no revelations

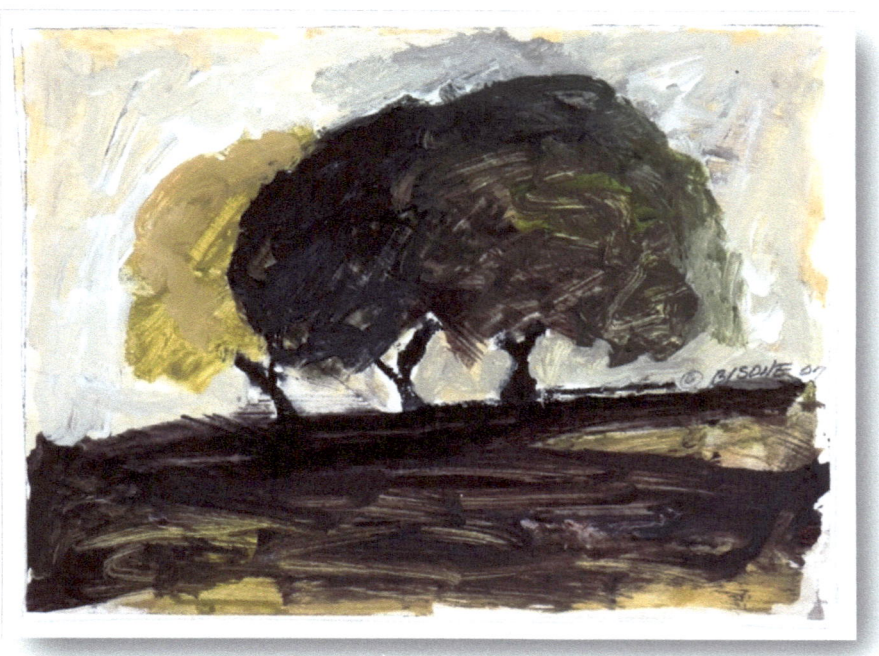

A Tree Doesn't Just Grow in Brooklyn I, 2007, 5 x 7.25 inches

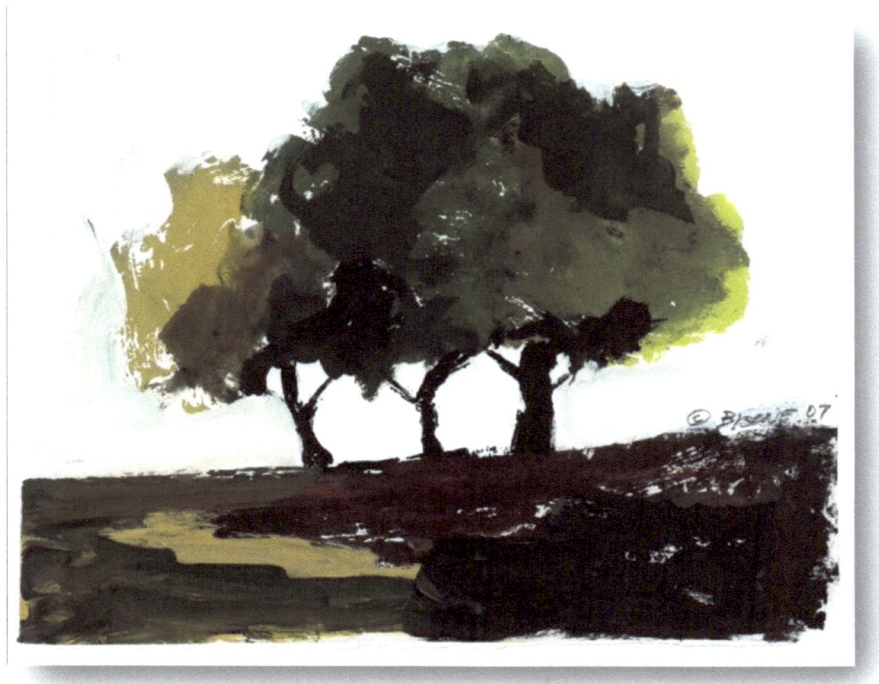

A Tree Doesn't Just Grow in Brooklyn II, 2007, 5.25 x 7.25 inches

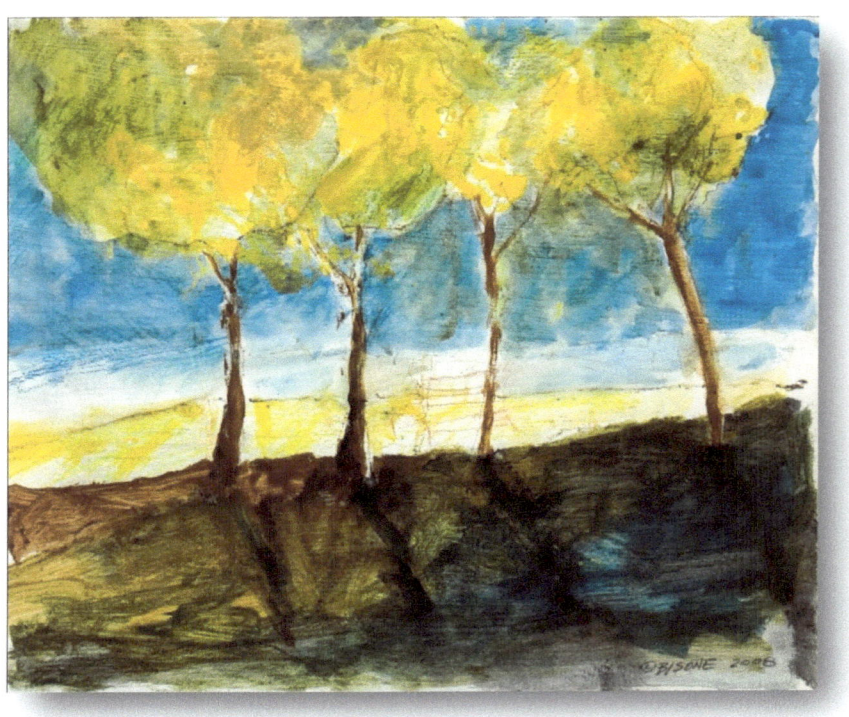

4 Trees, 2008, 14.5 x 17.25 inches

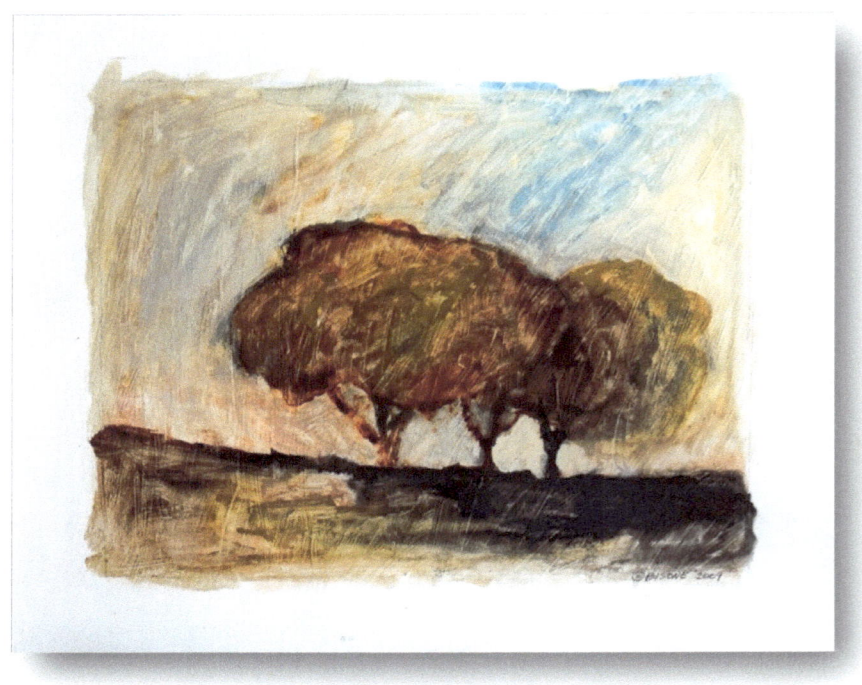

Fall Season, 2009, 15 x 18 inches

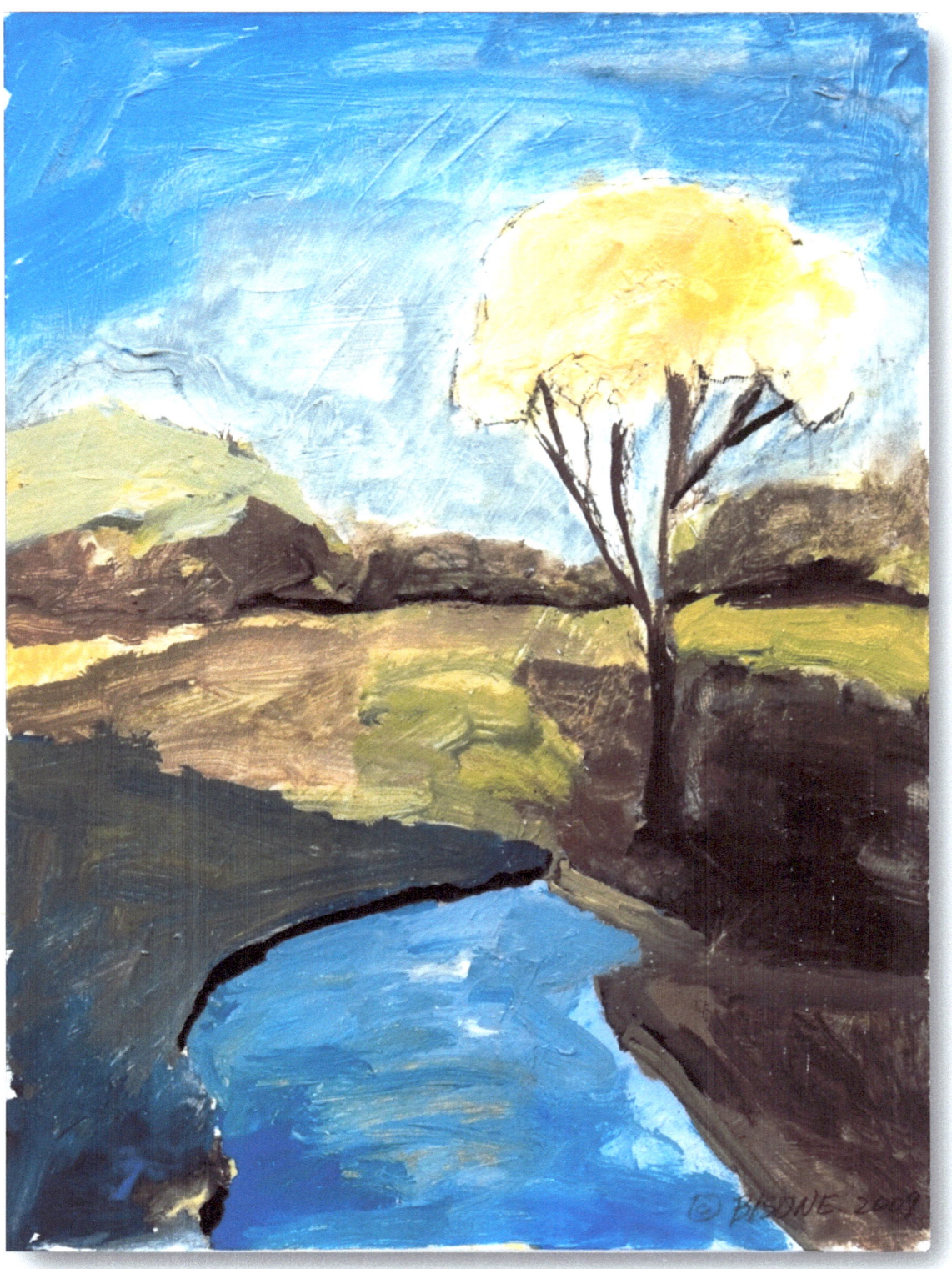

Yellow Tree, 2009, 19 x 15 inches

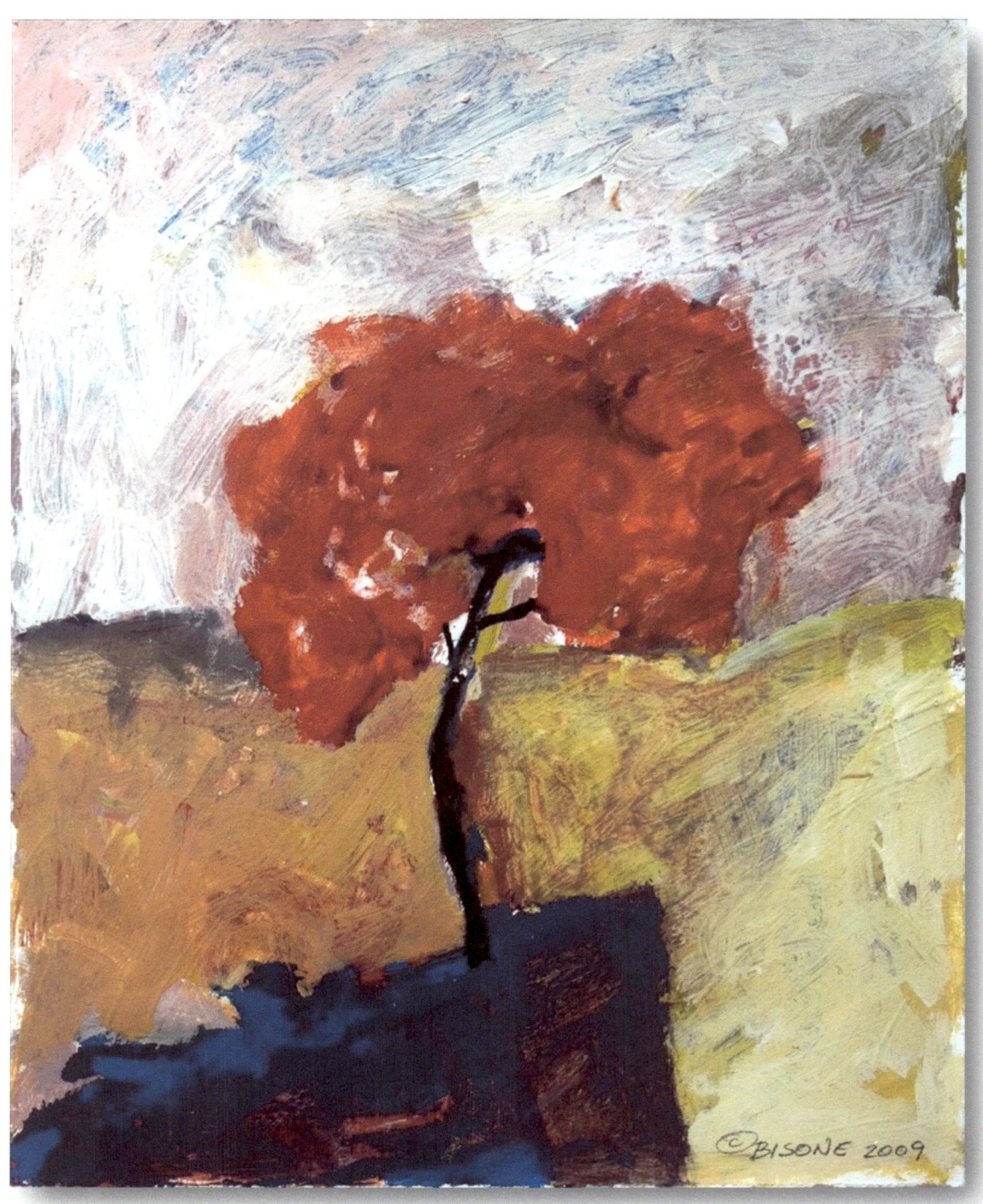

Red Tree, 2009, 14 x 11 inches

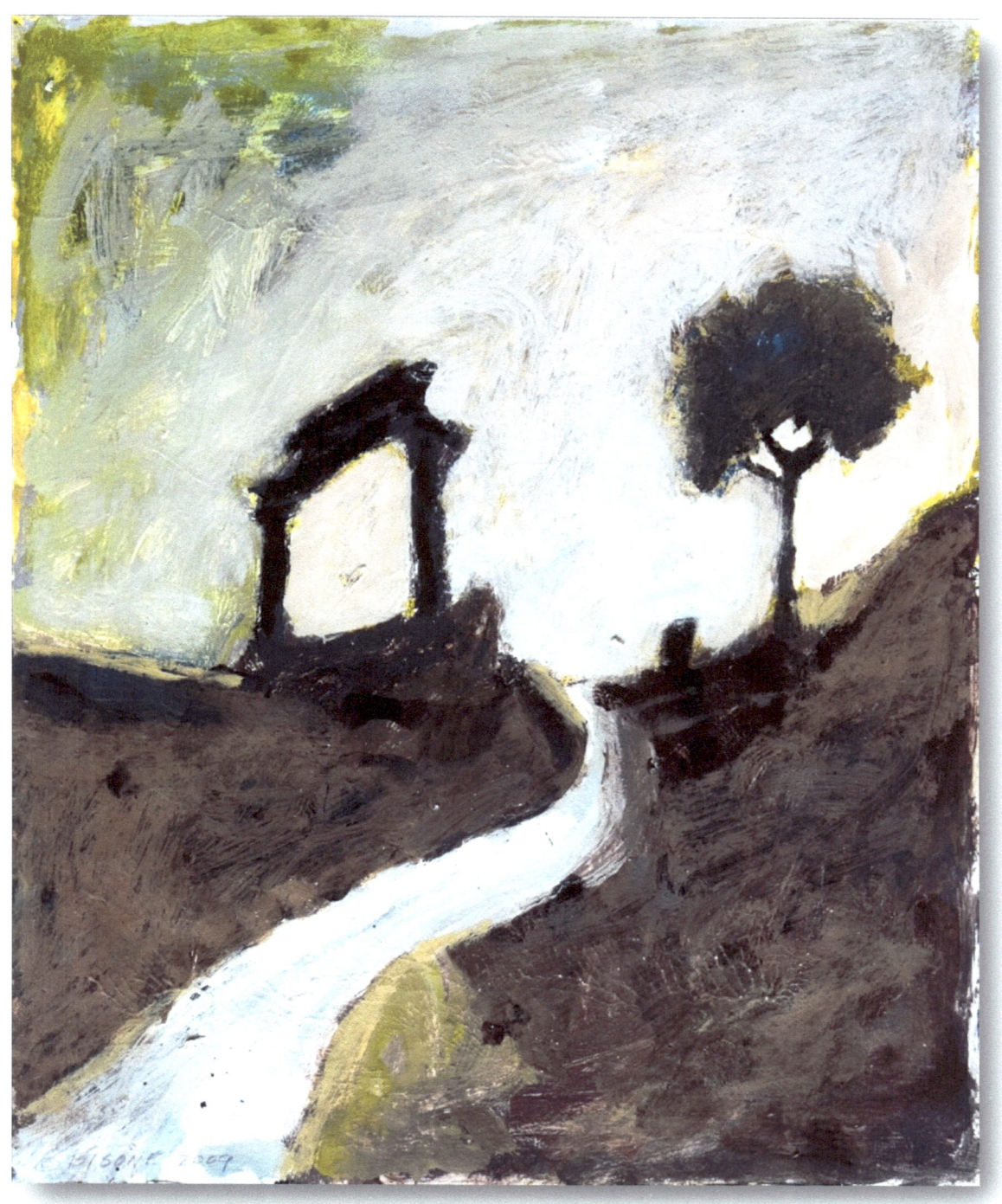

The Monument, 2009, 20 x 16 inches

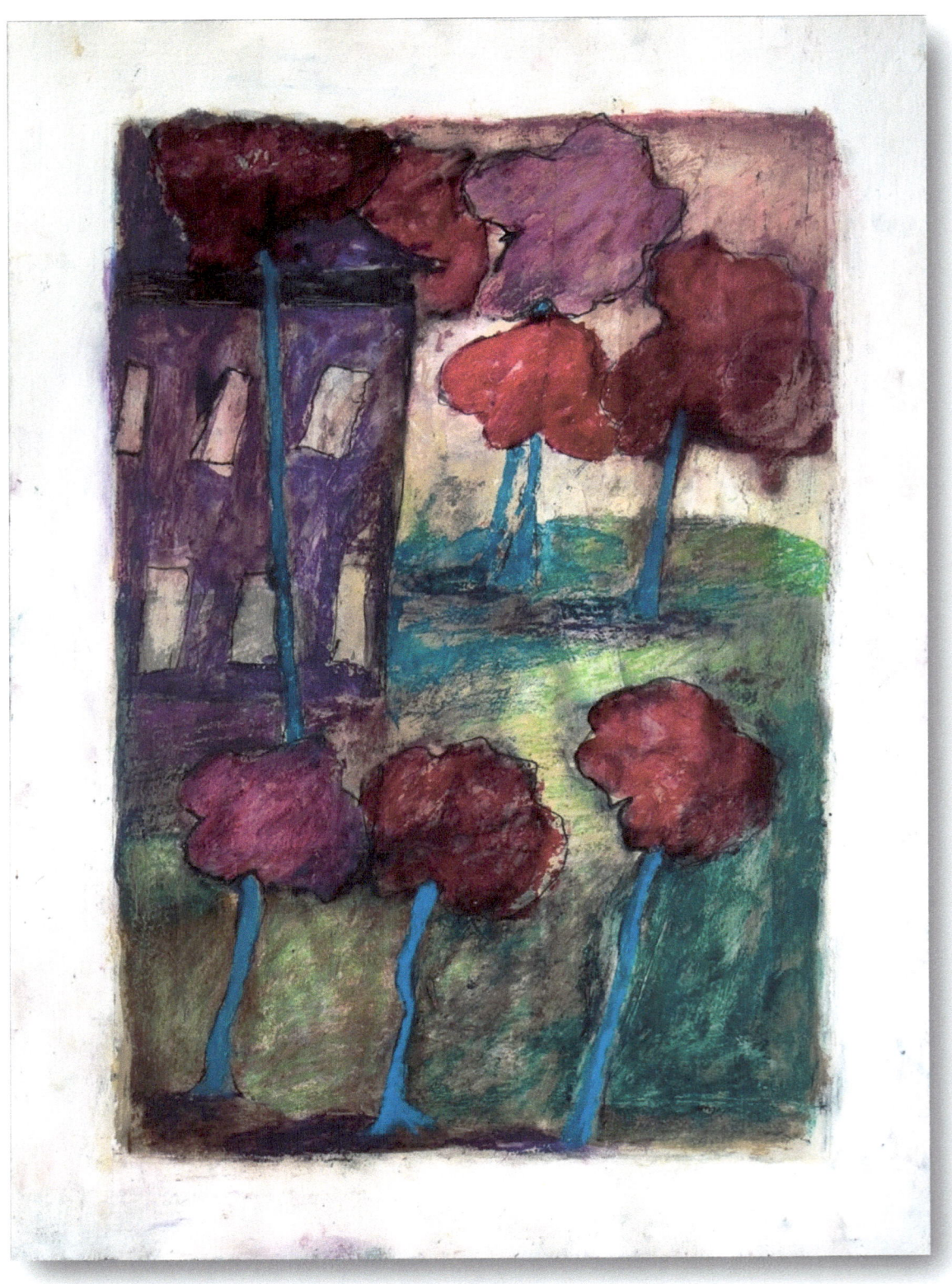

Red Trees, 2002 30 x 22 inches

13. At Play

Bisone had some obvious fun with the works depicted in this section. Yet, the existential angst is still discernable in the blank, expressionless faces.

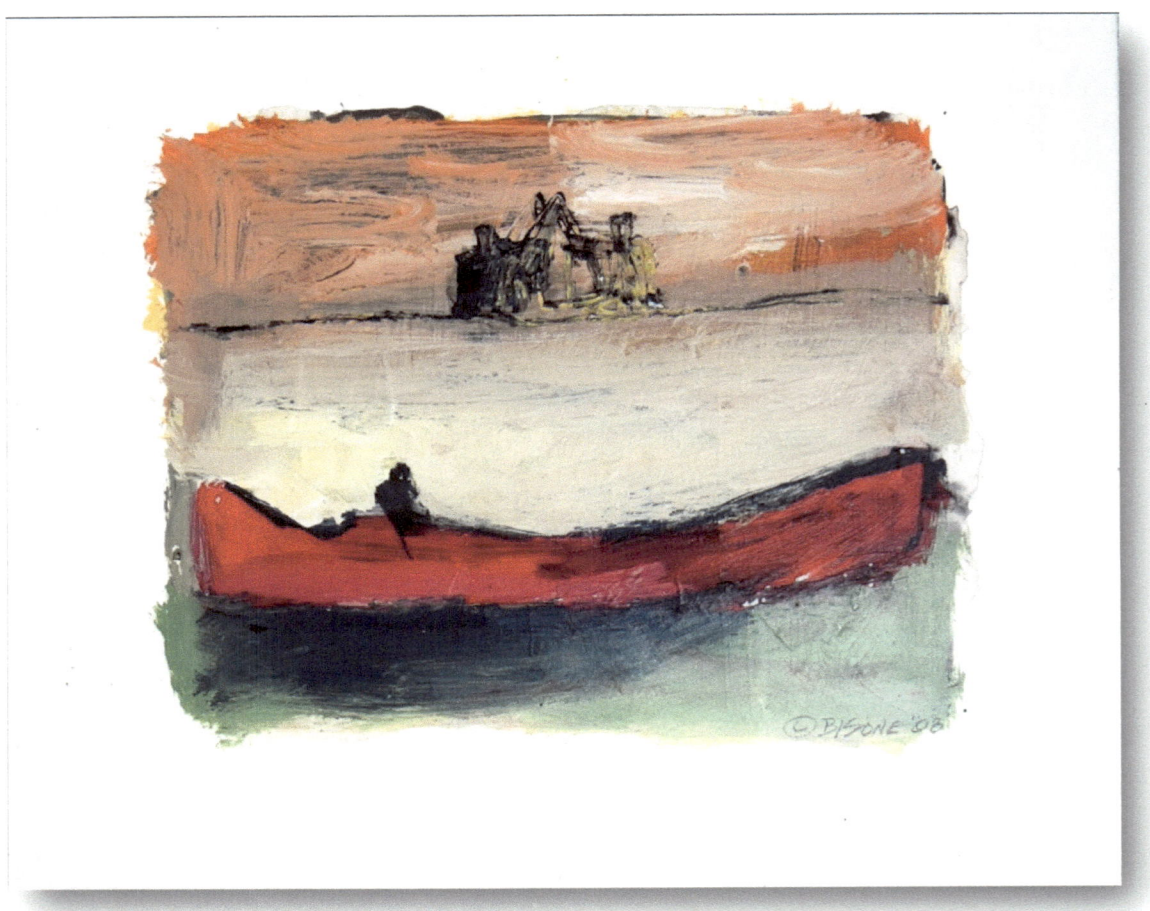

Paddle in the Water, Boys, 2008, 13 x 16.25 inches

sometimes he paints
　　　like a child plays, so caught
　　　　　up in the moment

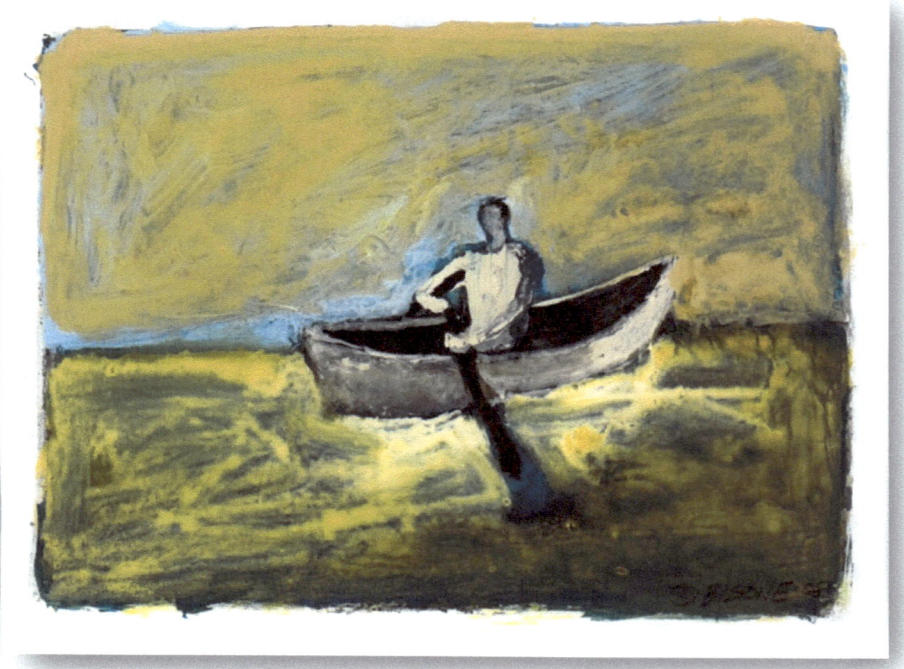

Paddle in the Water, Boys II, 2008, 8.5 x 11 inches

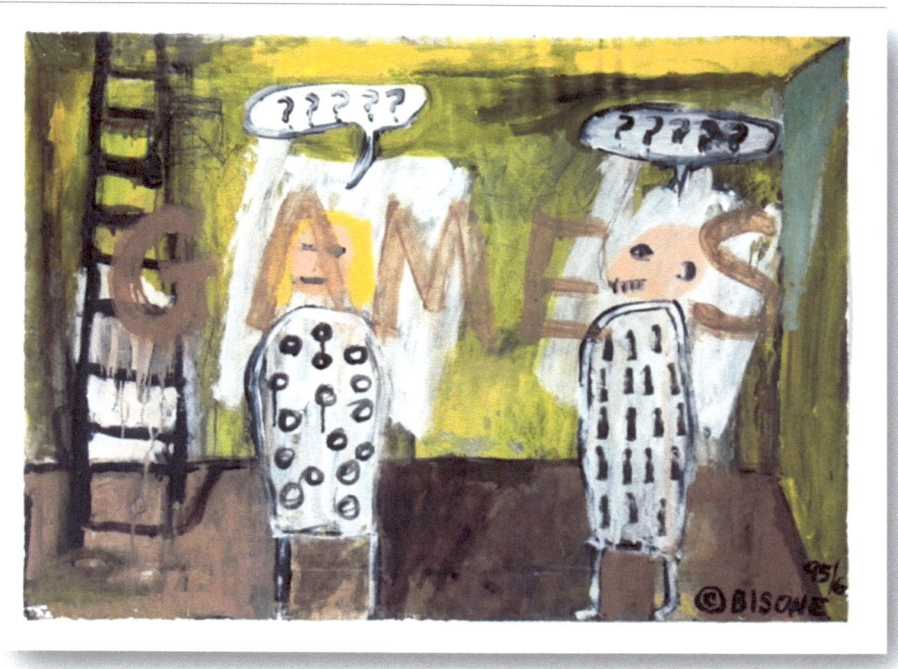

Games, 1995-96, 22 x 30 inches

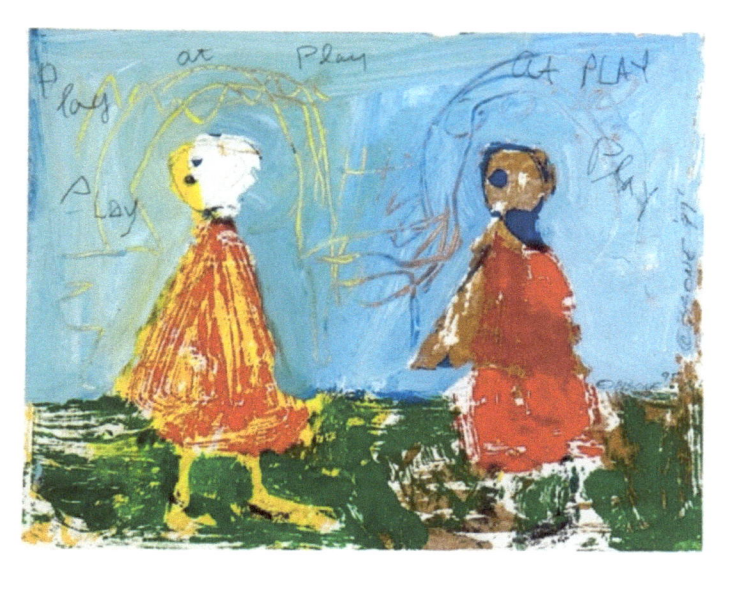

At Play, 1995, 11 x 14 inches

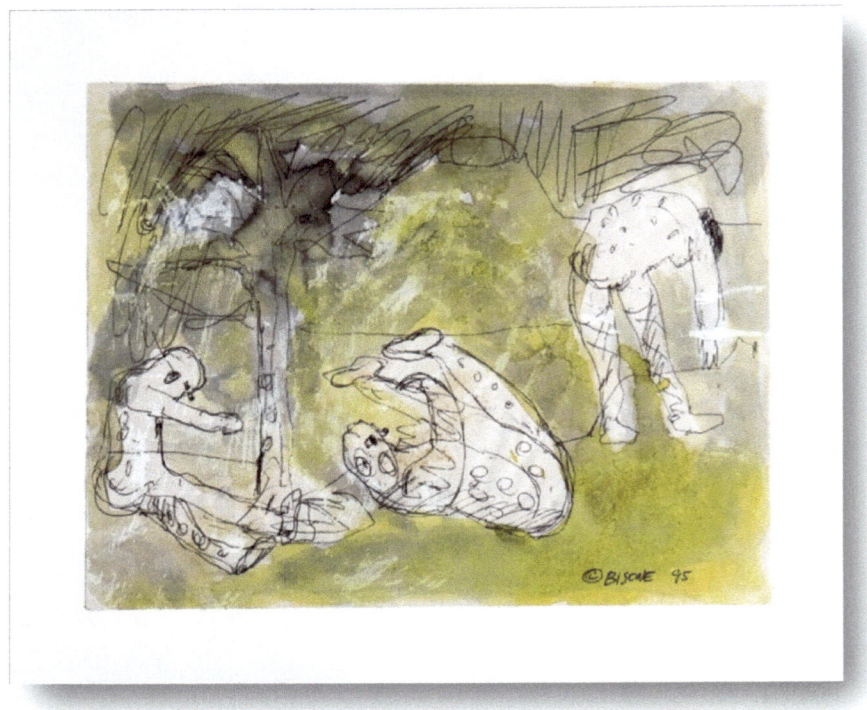

Line Drawing, 1995, 11.25 x 13.75 inches

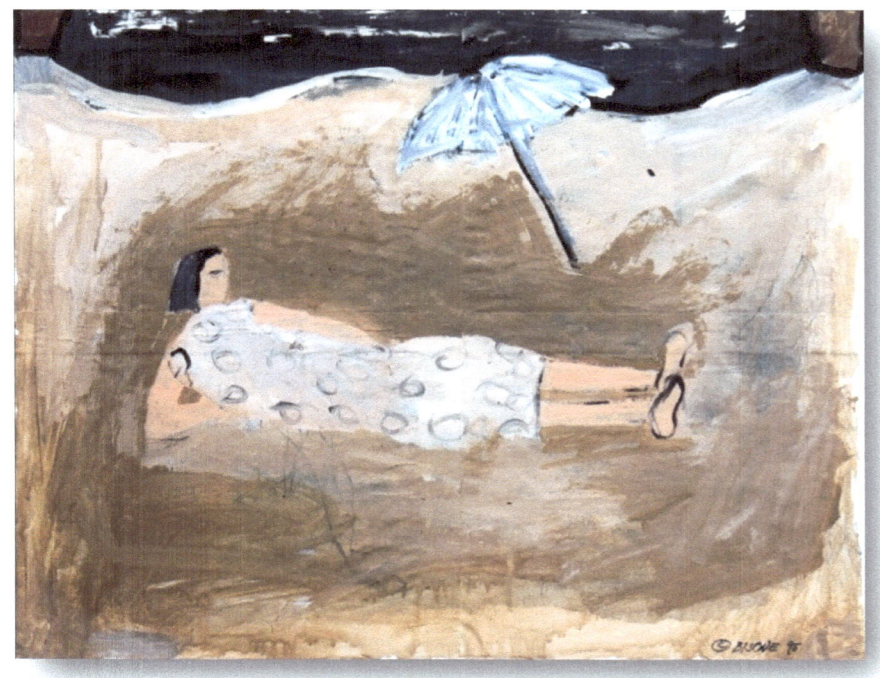

On the Beach (Homage to Milton Avery), 1995, *16* x 20.75 inches

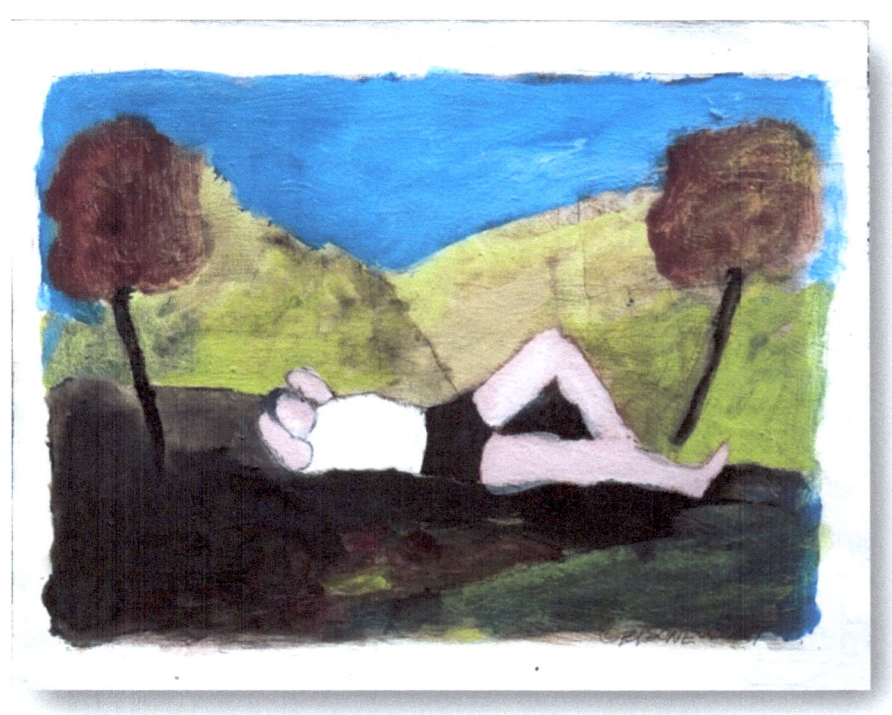

Green Hills, 2009, 15 x 19 inches

14. Vespers Series

There's a solemn, spiritual side to the artist, as exemplified by four abstracts from Bisone's Vespers Series.   Vespers are evening services within the Catholic Church (and in some Protestant churches).   More broadly, they represent time for quiet contemplation in the evening hours.

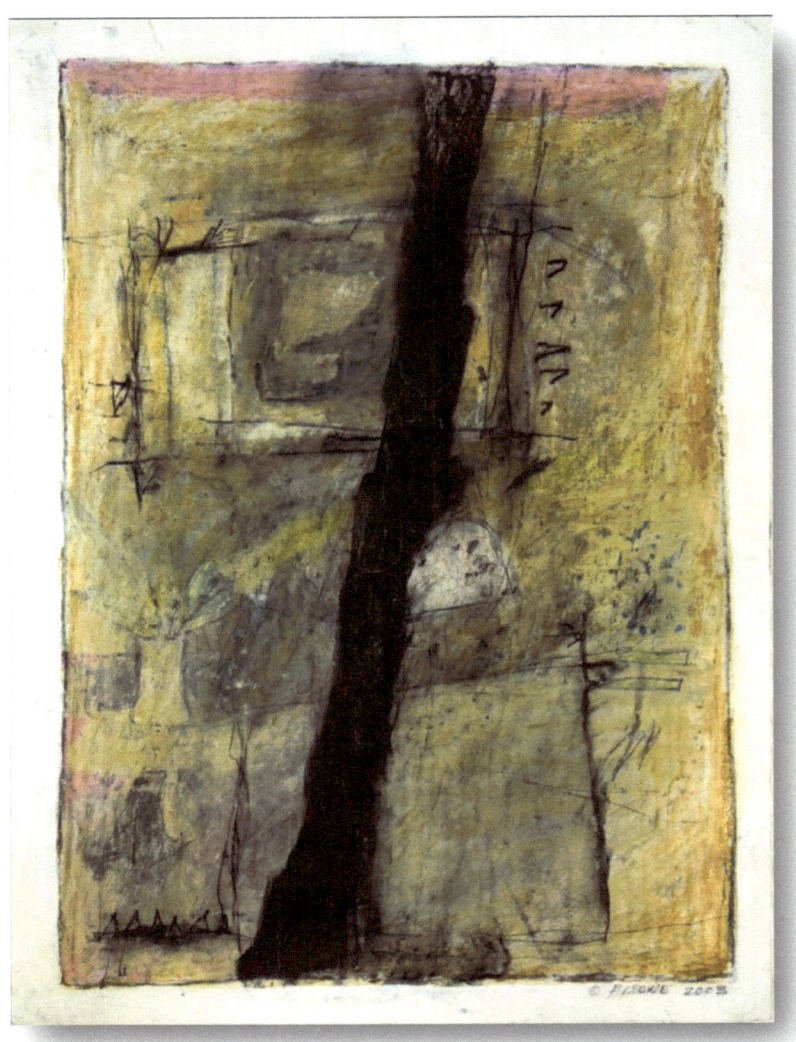

Vespers, 2003, 20.75 x 15.5 inches

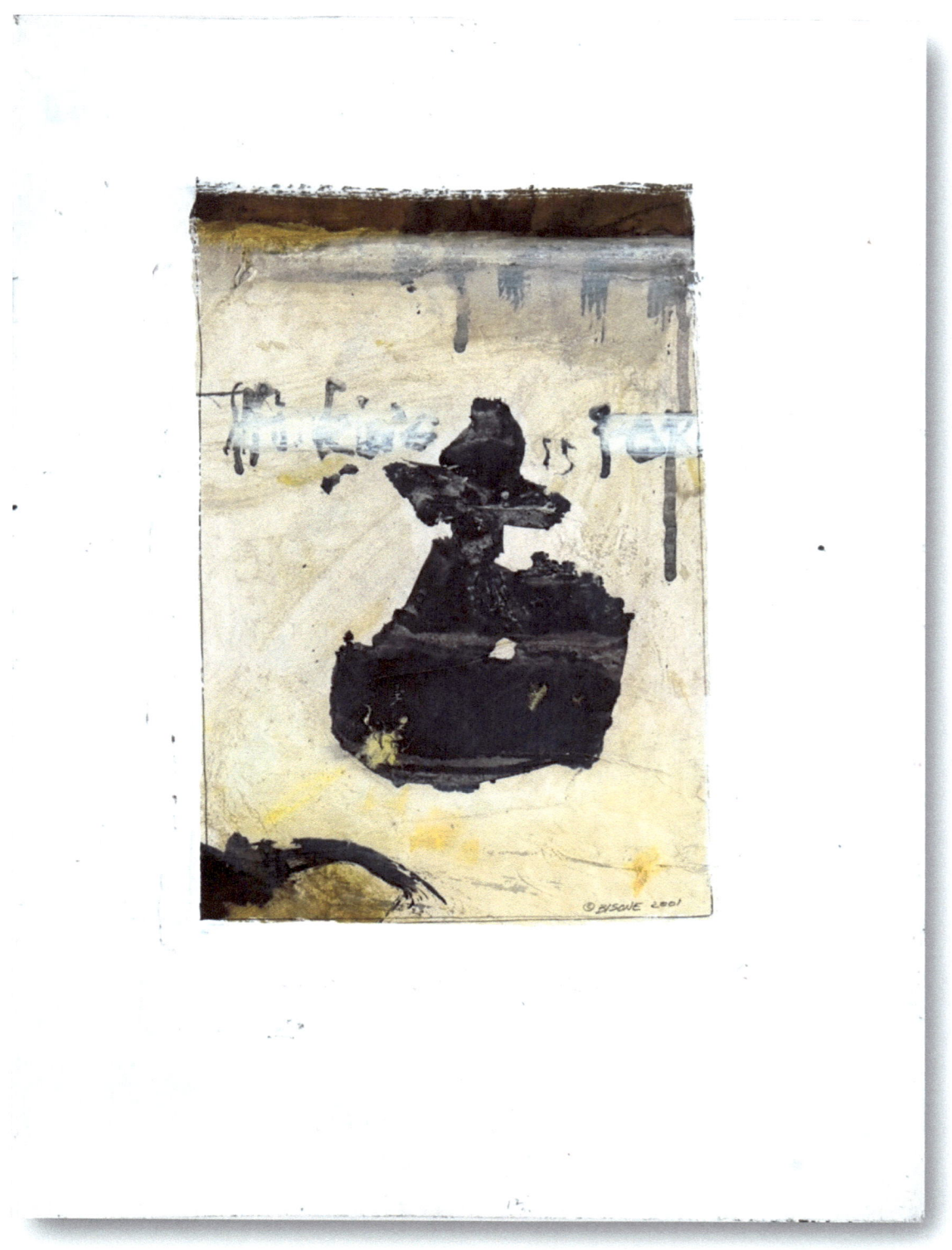

Vespers Series #1, 2001, 16 x 12 inches

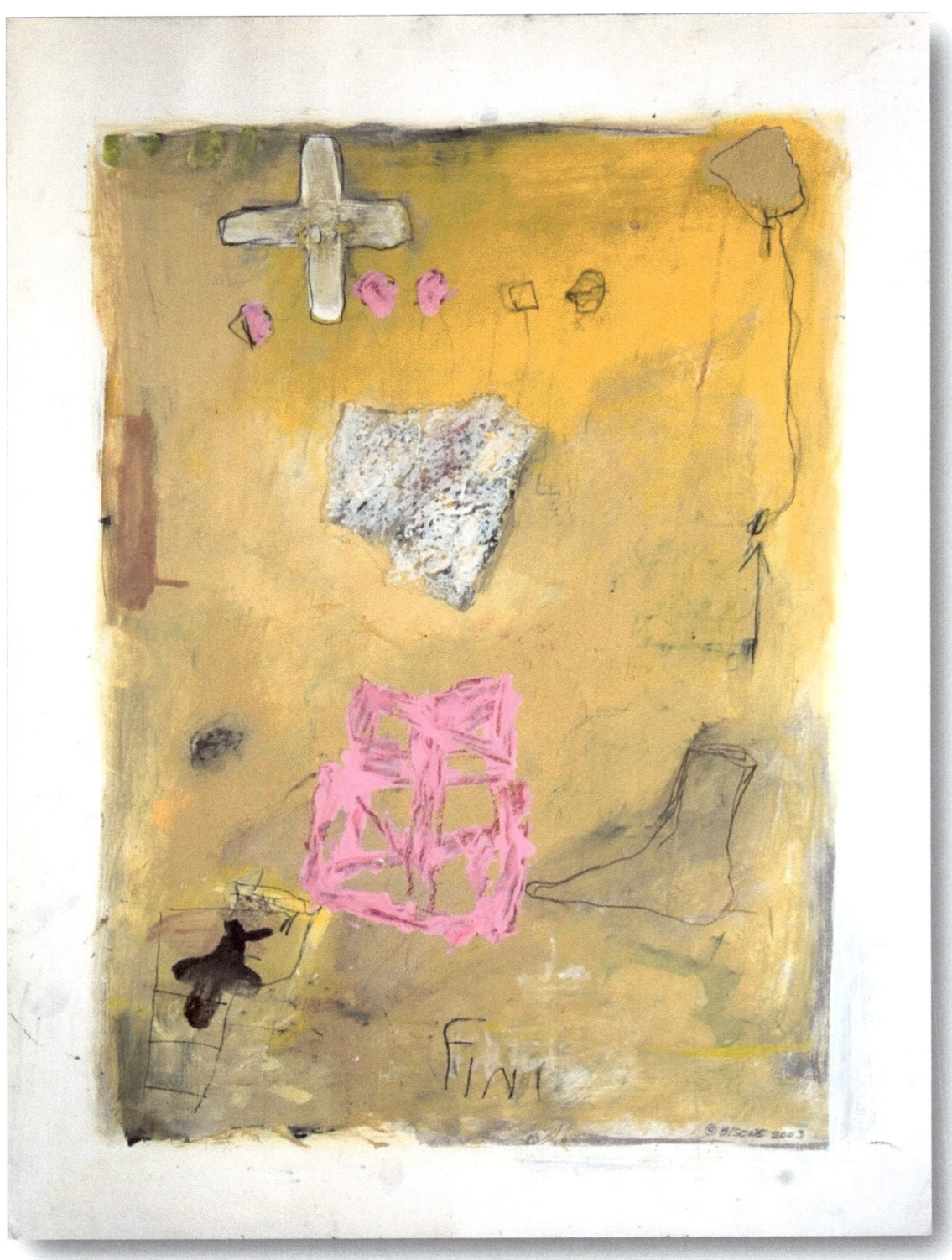

Vespers Series #VIII, 2003, 29.75 x 22.25 inches

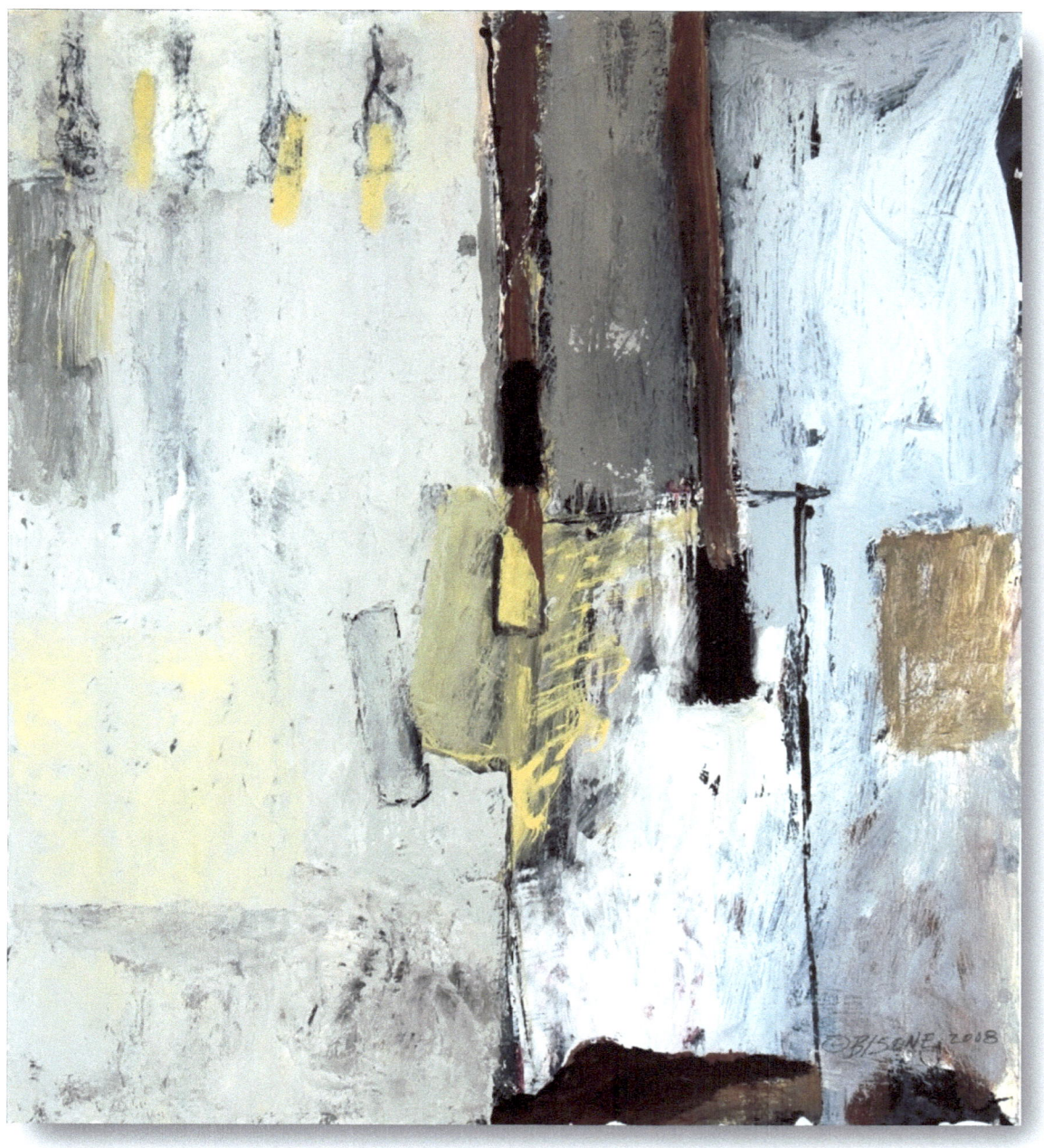

Muted Vespers, 2008, 20 x 18 inches

15. Nuggets

The works depicted in this section are a potpourri of Bisone paintings, a cross section of images that represent the artist through the styles, thoughts, and moods expressed by those paintings.

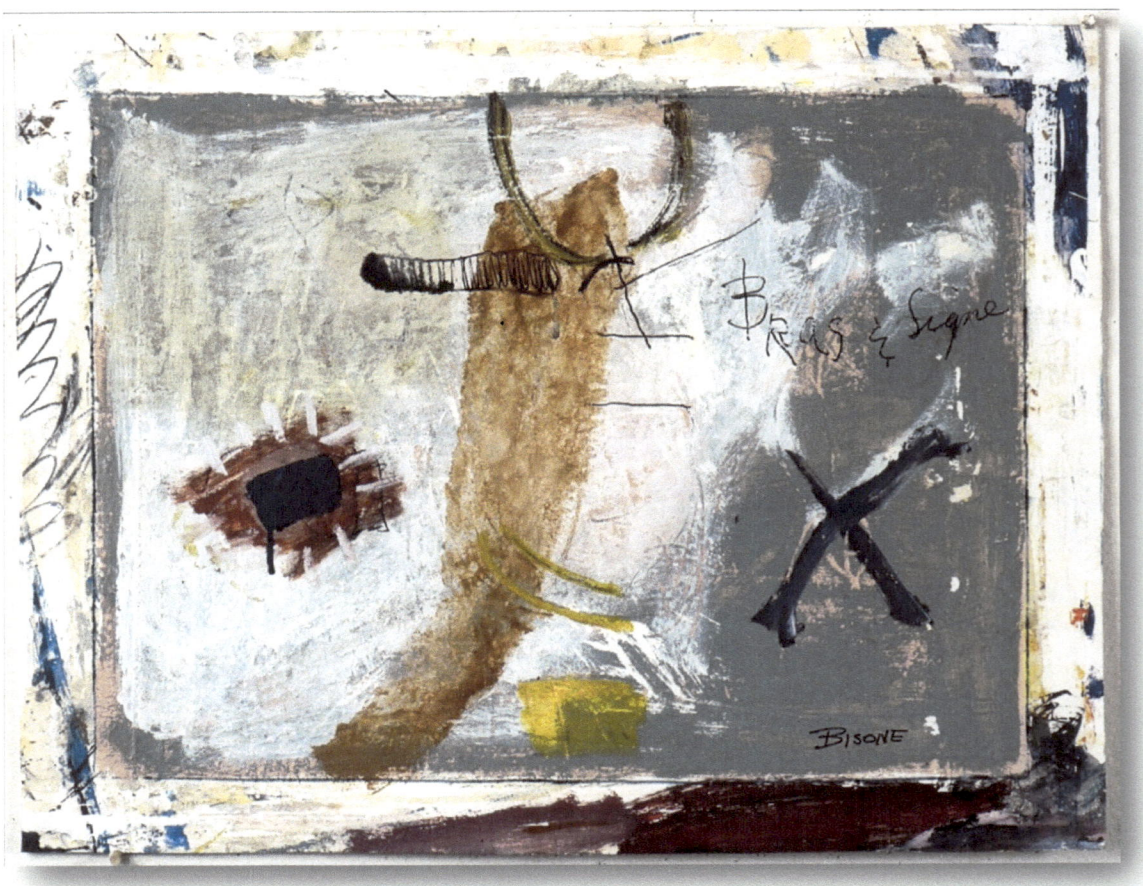

Bras & Signe, 1994, 22 x 30 inches

sometimes asking what
it isn't reveals more than
asking what it is

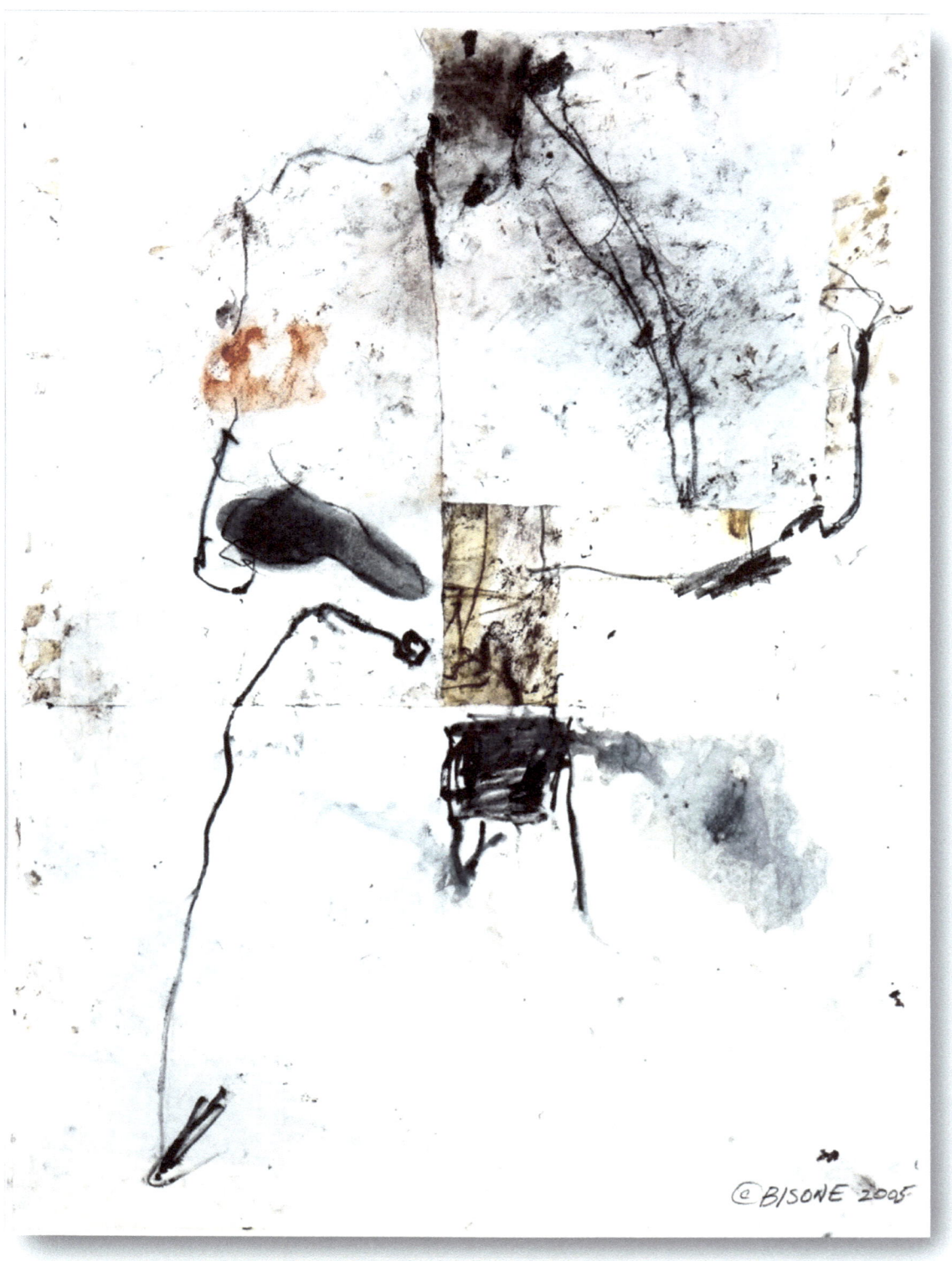

Drawing IIb, 2005, 15.75 x 11.75 inches

Bisone would often paint over works that no longer held interest for him. At other times he would simply use the reverse side of a painting. The image on the facing page was just such an instance. If you'll look very closely at the bottom of the painting (near the figure's left foot), you'll see that Bisone faintly scribbled "other side is the painting forget this side". Below is the painting the artist would prefer we remember.

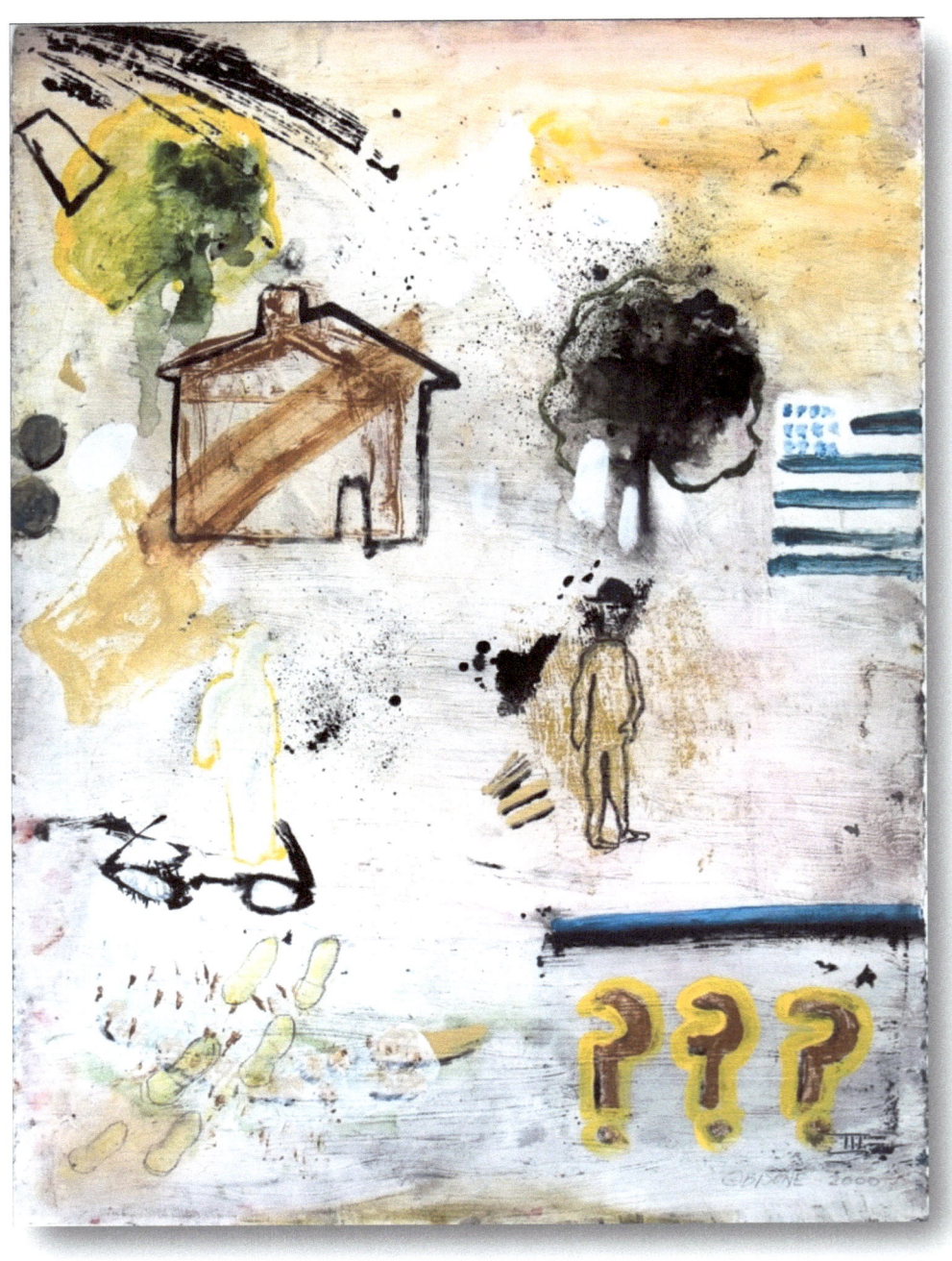

Untitled, 2000, 28 x 19 inches

first, capture it,

then, see if it's worth keeping.

if not, let it go

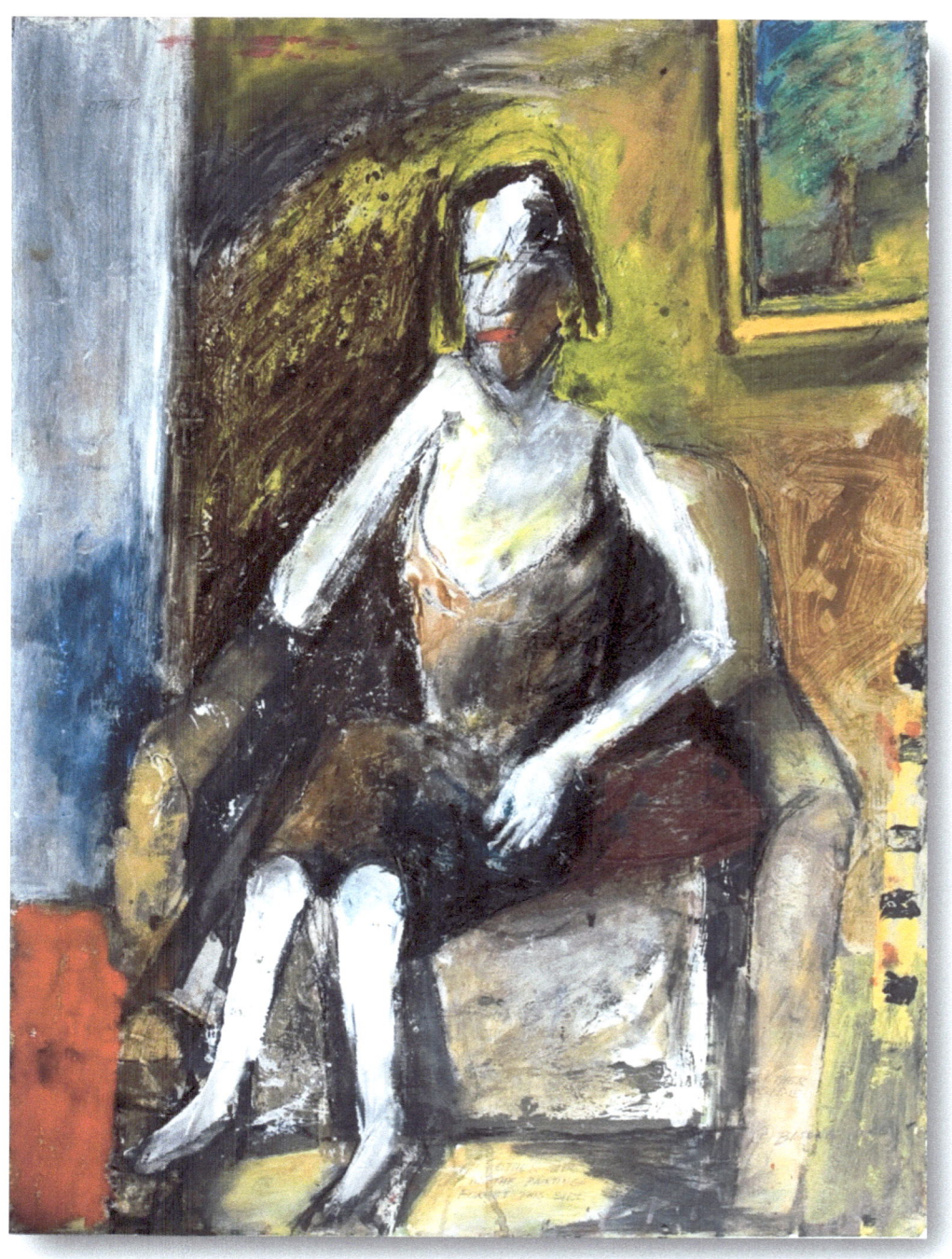

Untitled, 1997, 28 x 19 inches

to see a flower

then to present it as if

never seen before

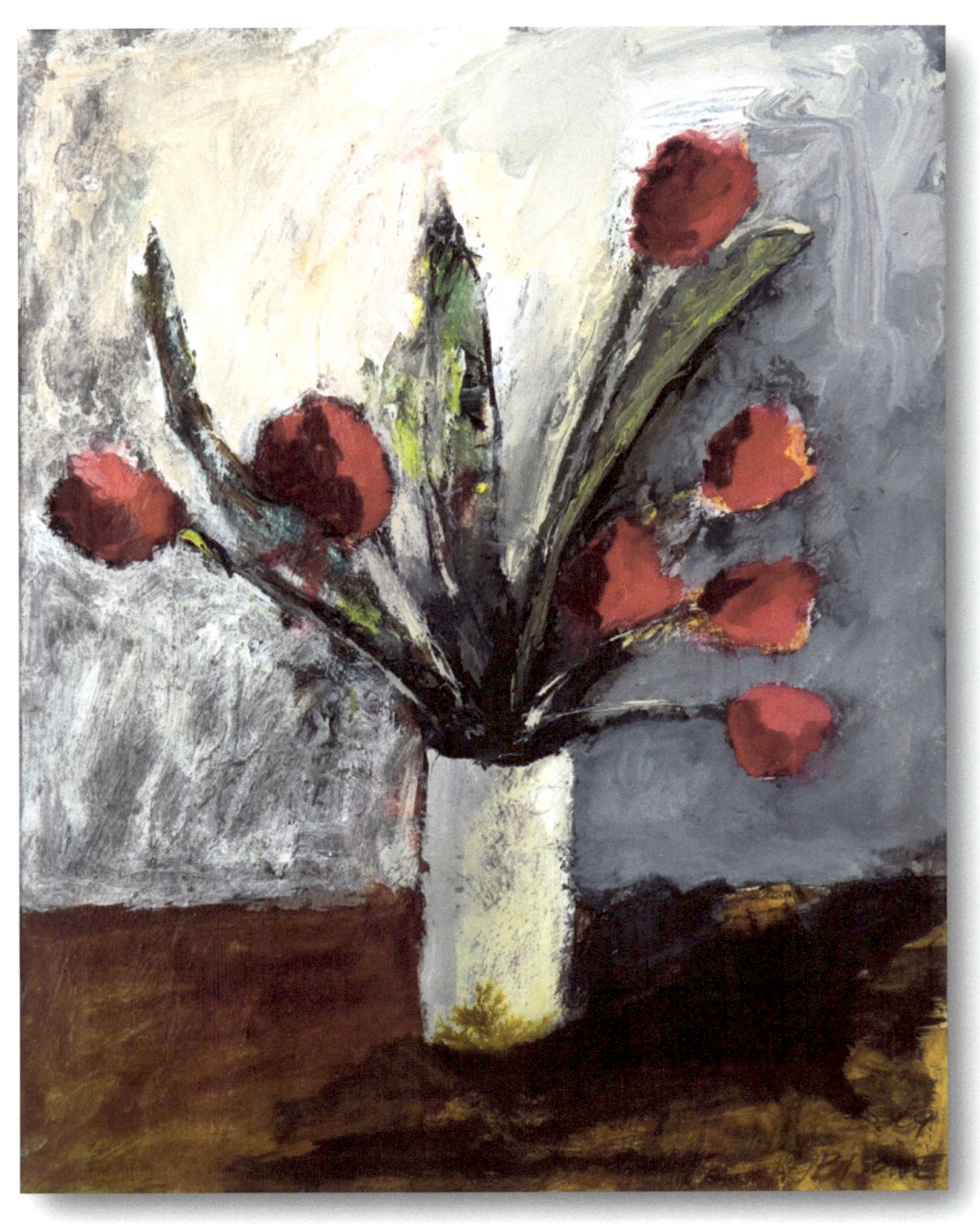

A Bouquet for the Baroness, 2009, 14 x 10.75 inches

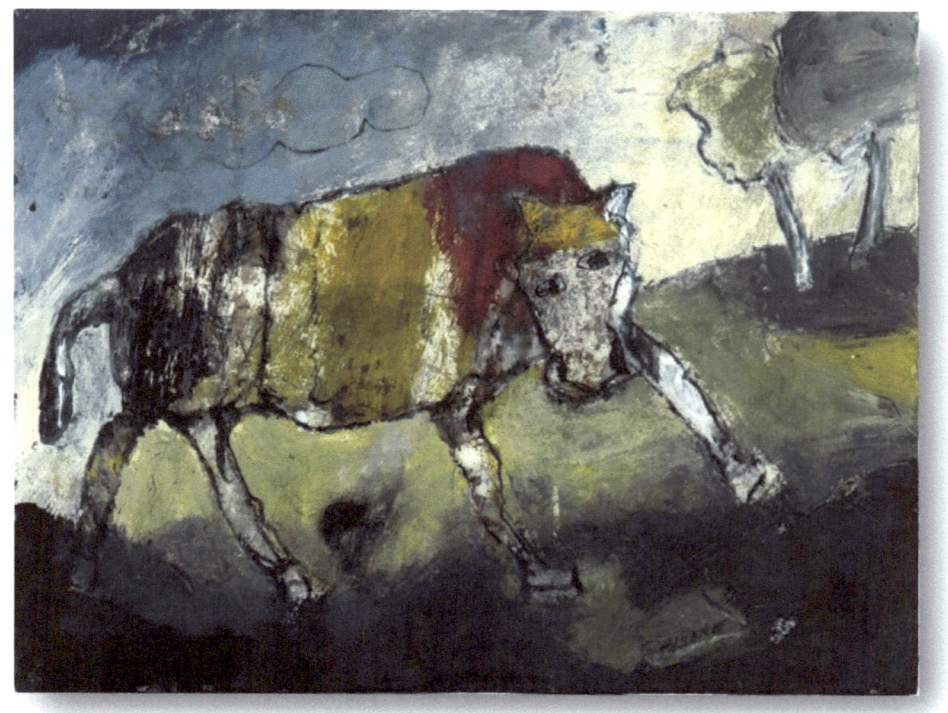

Goofy Cow, 2004, 10.5 x 13.5 inches

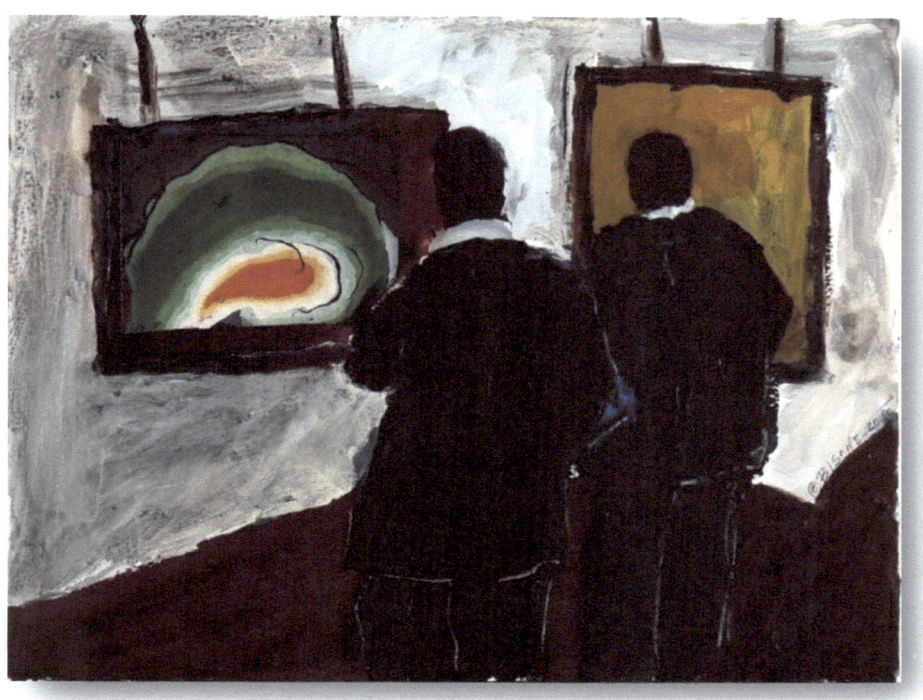

Looking at a Painting, 2010, 12 x 16 inches

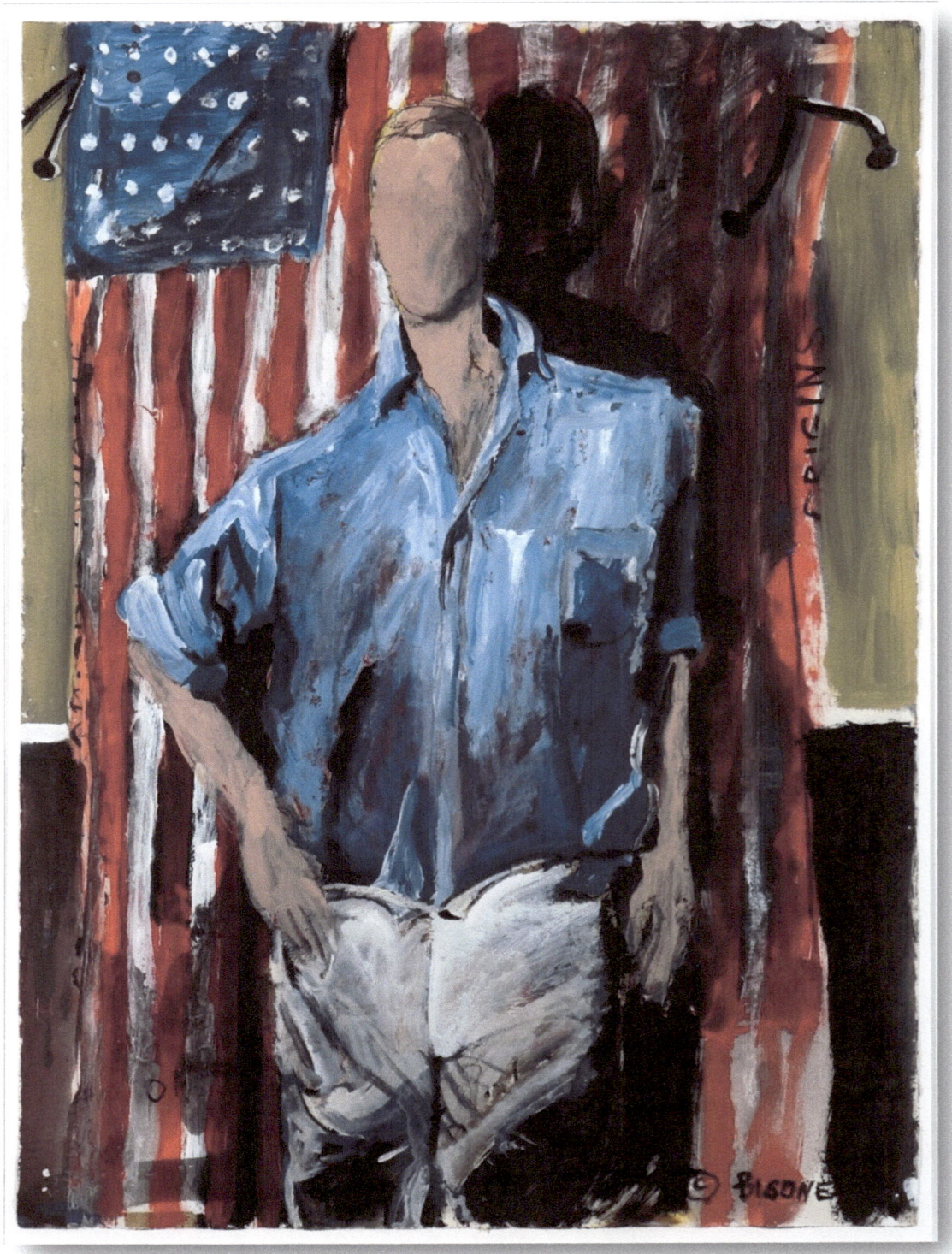

Blue Shirt, 1998, 30.5 x 22 inches

i find revolting

the depth of meaning assigned

to the meaningless

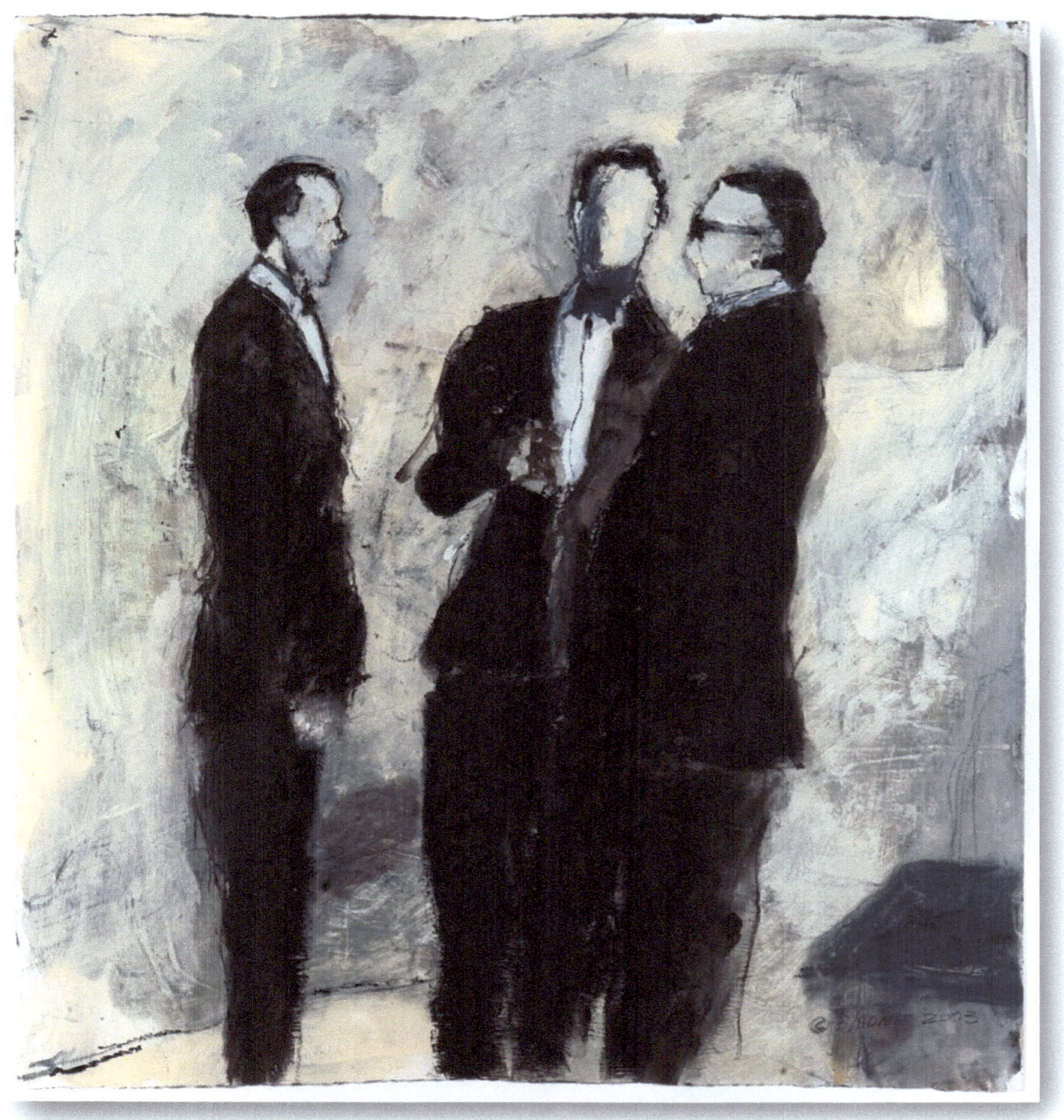

Black Tie, 2004, 23 x 21 inches

In this work, Bisone pays tribute to Marcel Duchamp, who, in 1917, submitted his *Fountain*, a urinal, to the Society of Independent Artists Exhibit in New York (under the pseudonym, R. Mutt). Although the show was not juried, and all submissions were to be displayed, the show committee decided this was not art and rejected it.

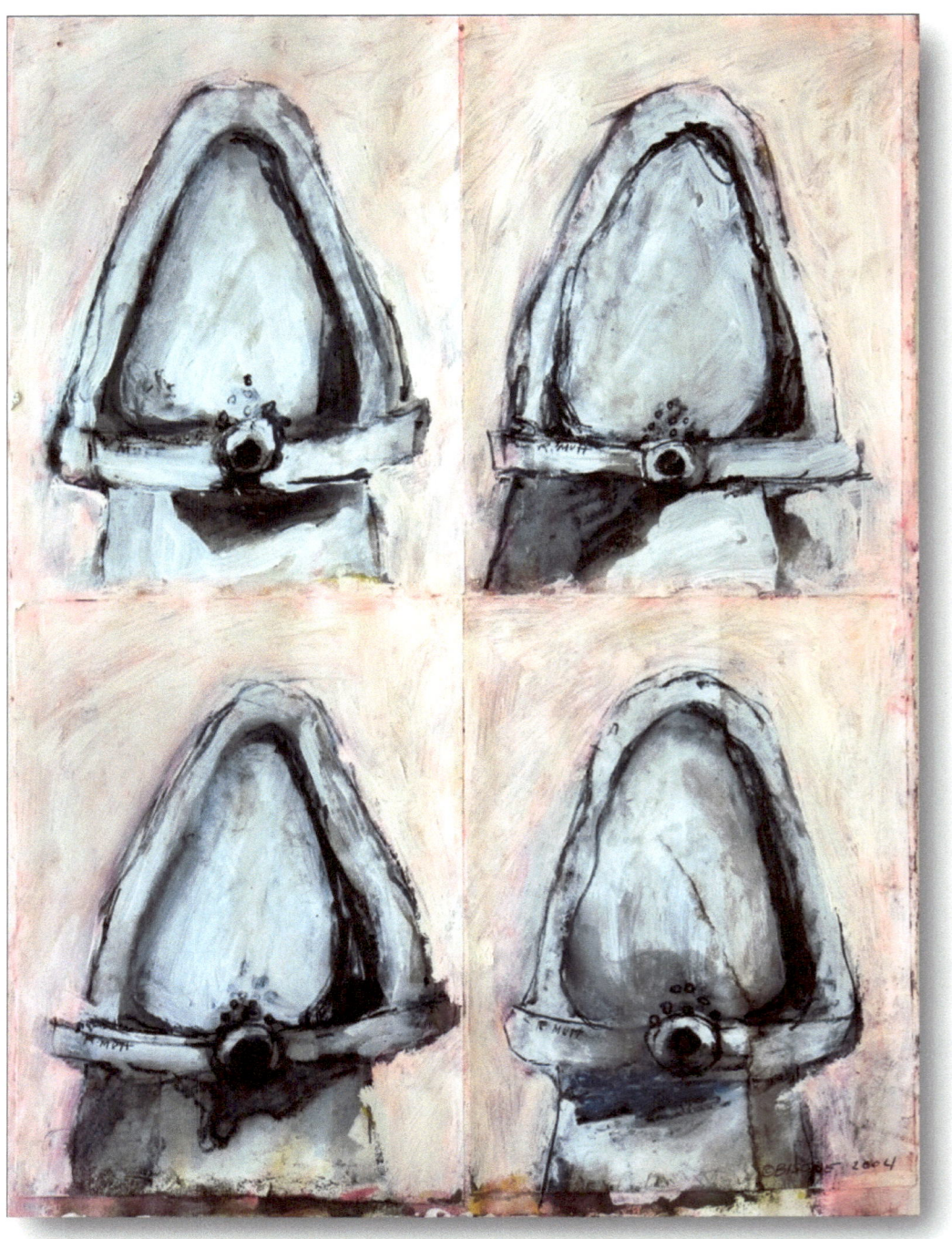

R. Mutt, 2004, 22 x 16.5 inches

if rigid, a line goes

where you want it to, always

no room for surprise

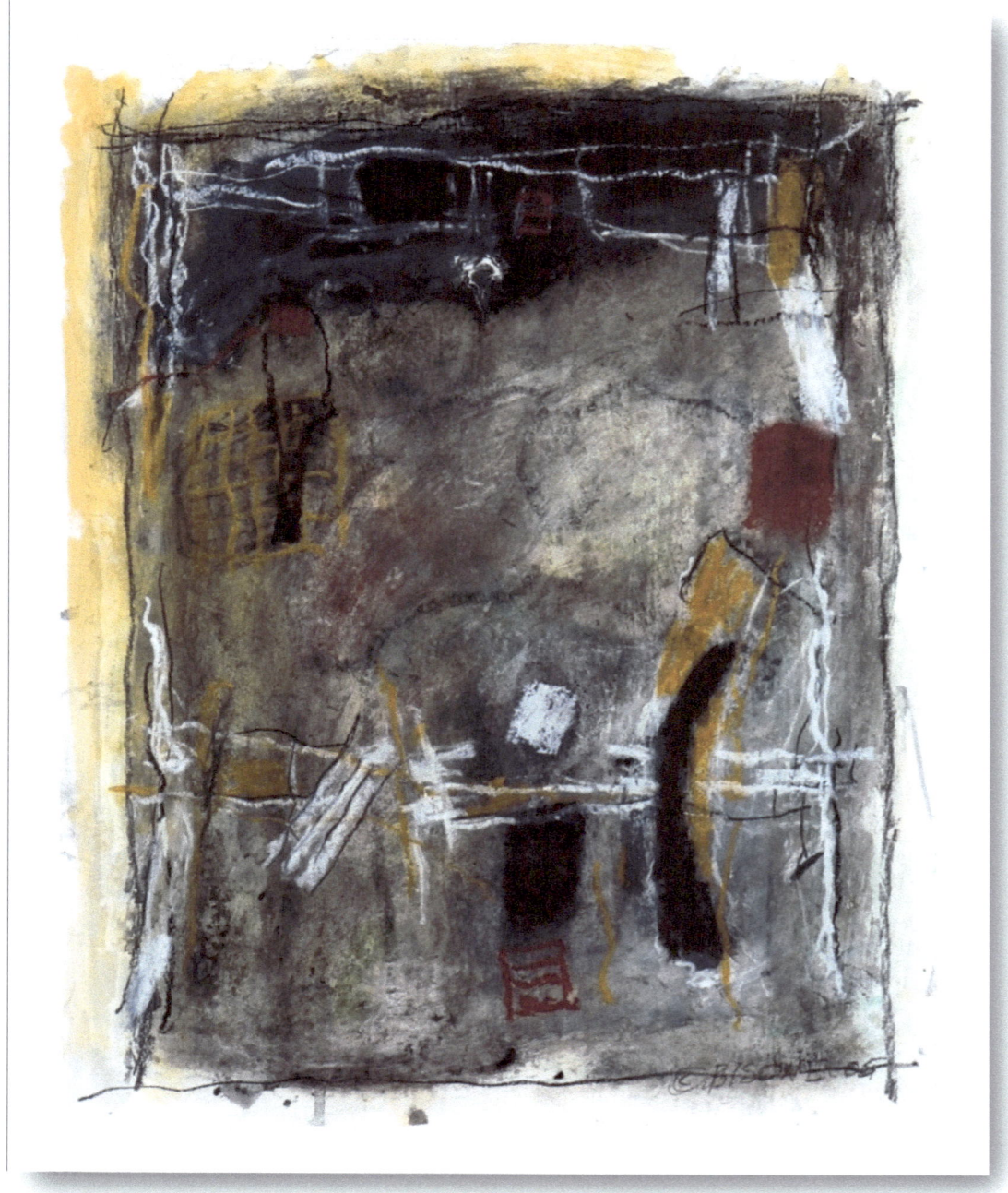

Line Painting, 2005, 23.25 x 20 inches

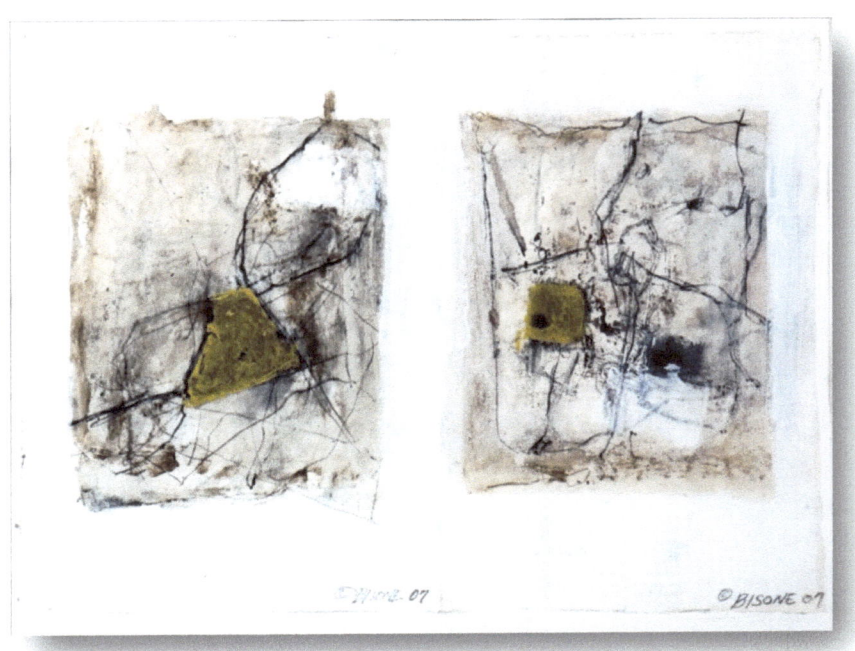

2 Sites for an Archaeological Dig, 2007, 13.5 x 17.75 inches

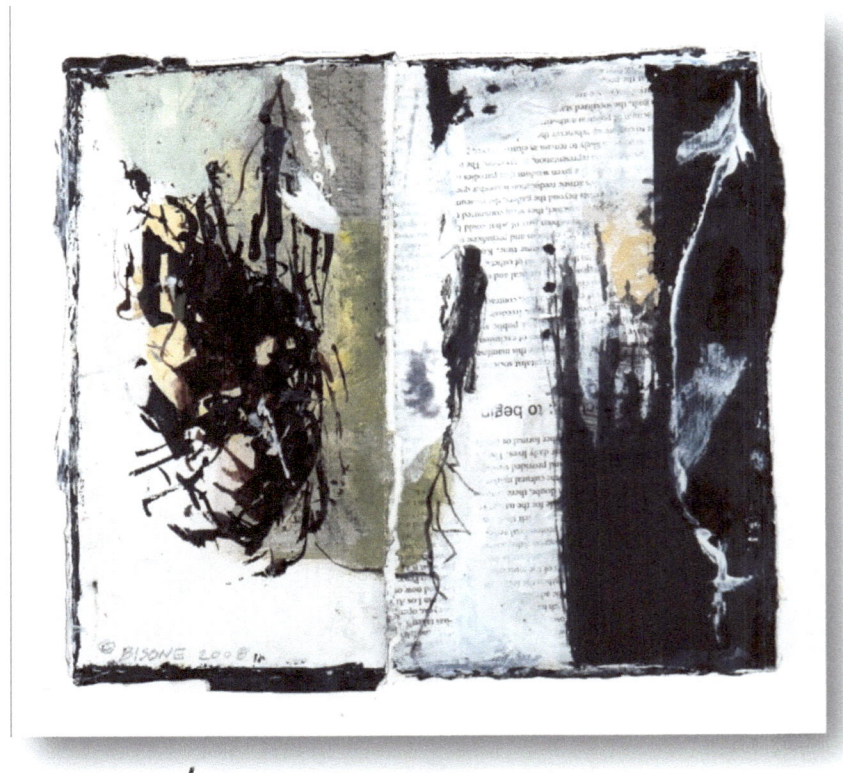

To Begin, 2008, 11 x 14 inches

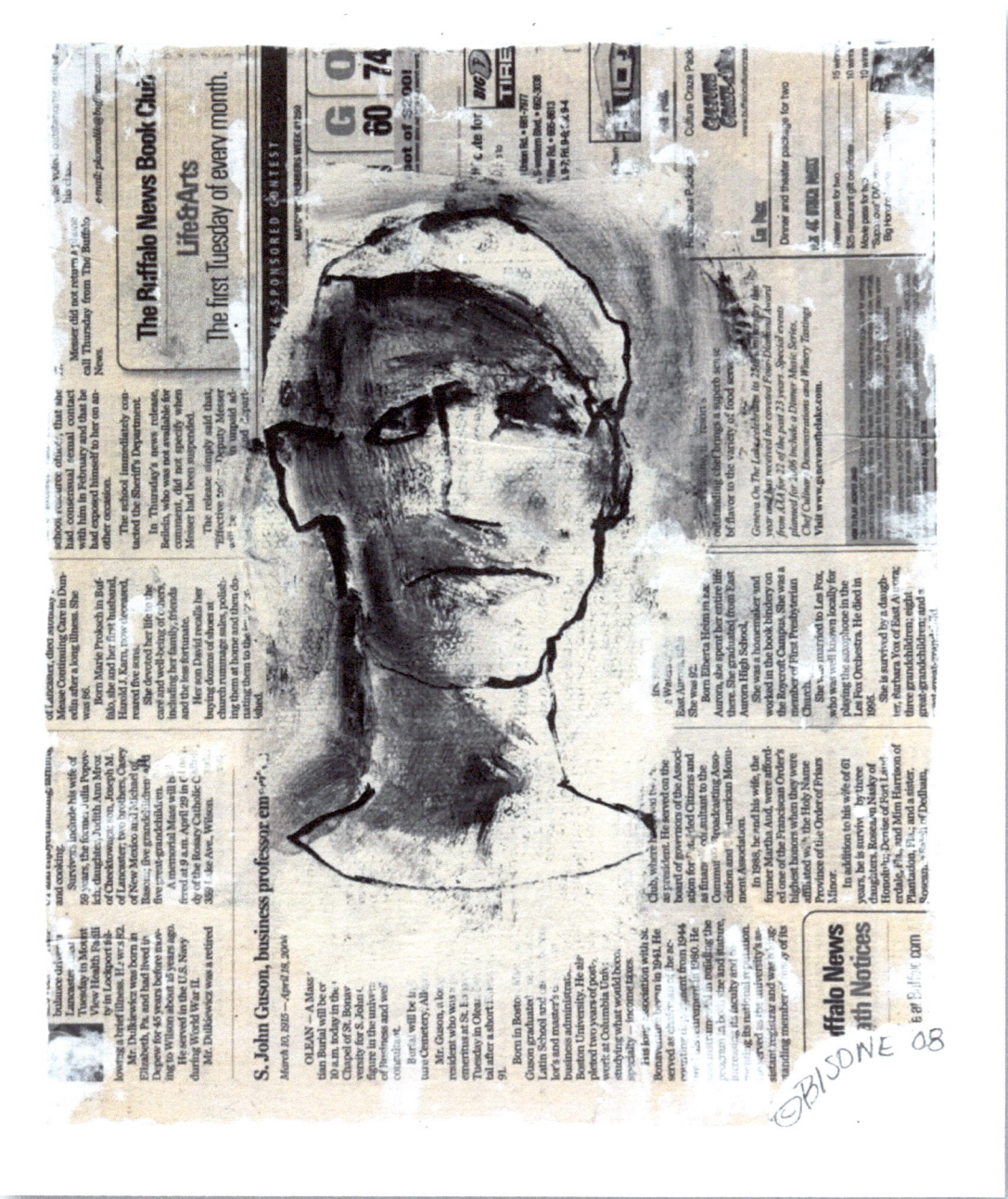

News, 2008, 22 x 18 inches

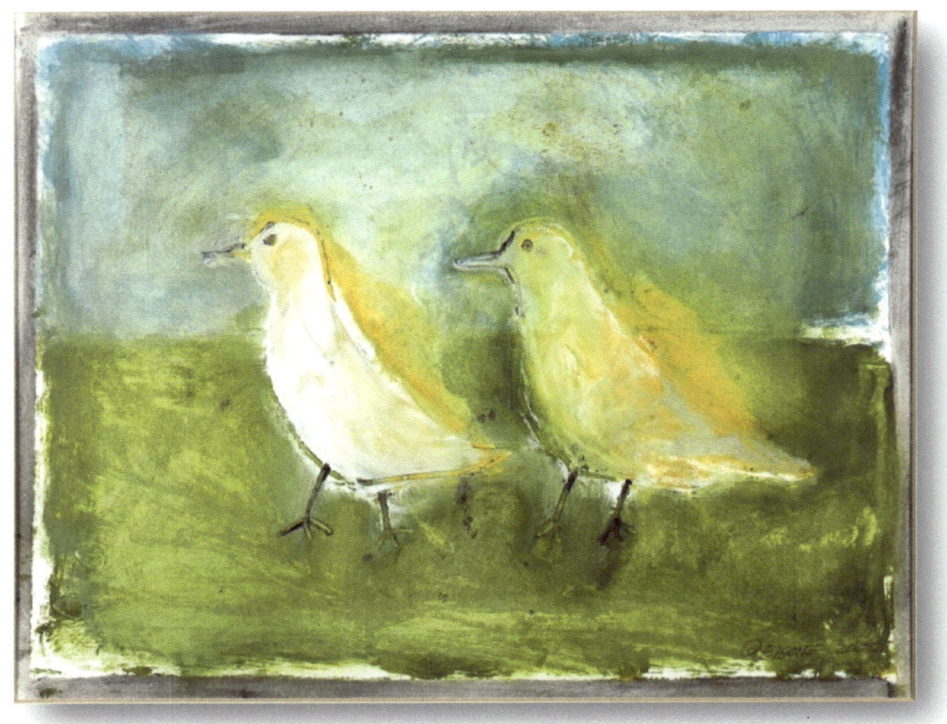

Two Birds, 2000, 10.5 x 13.5 inches

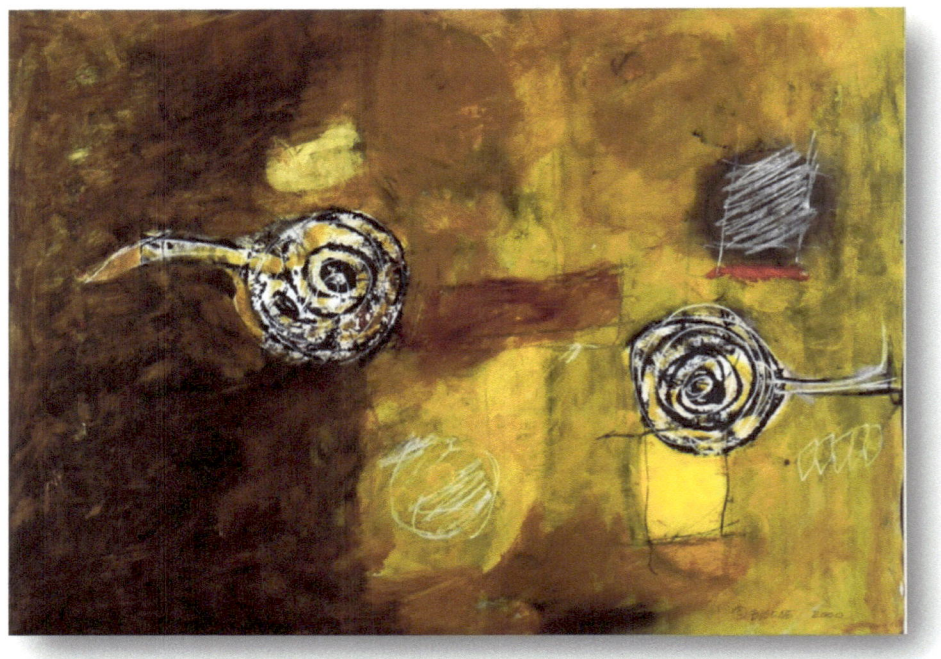

Untitled, 2000, 19.5 x 27.75 inches

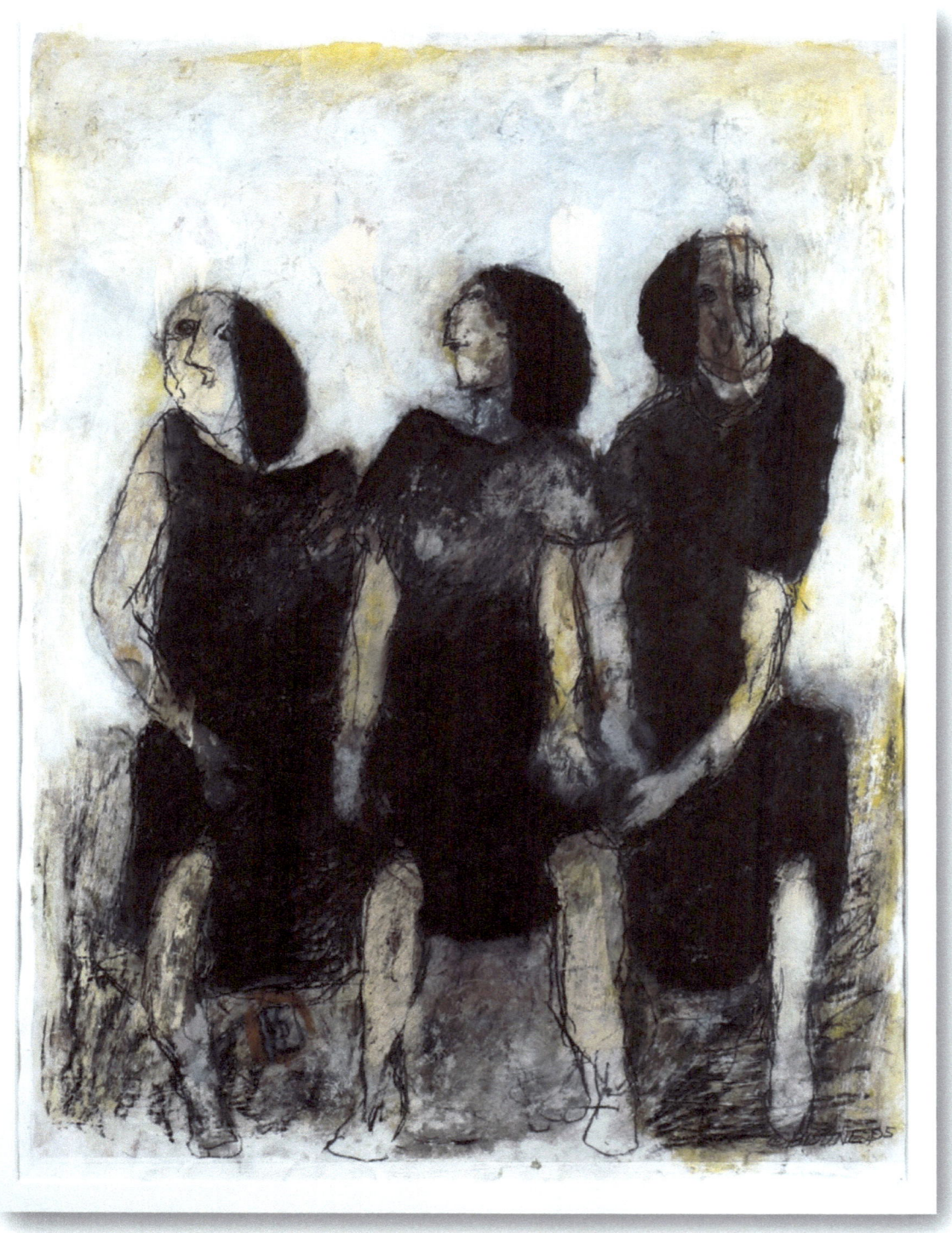

Three Hell Raisers, 2005, 25.5 x 19.125 inches

Edward G. Bisone

The painting below graced the cover of the brochure for the 2005 "TopSpin" show, one of a series of solo exhibitions featuring local and regional artists at the Castellani Art Museum at Niagara University, in Niagara Falls, NY.

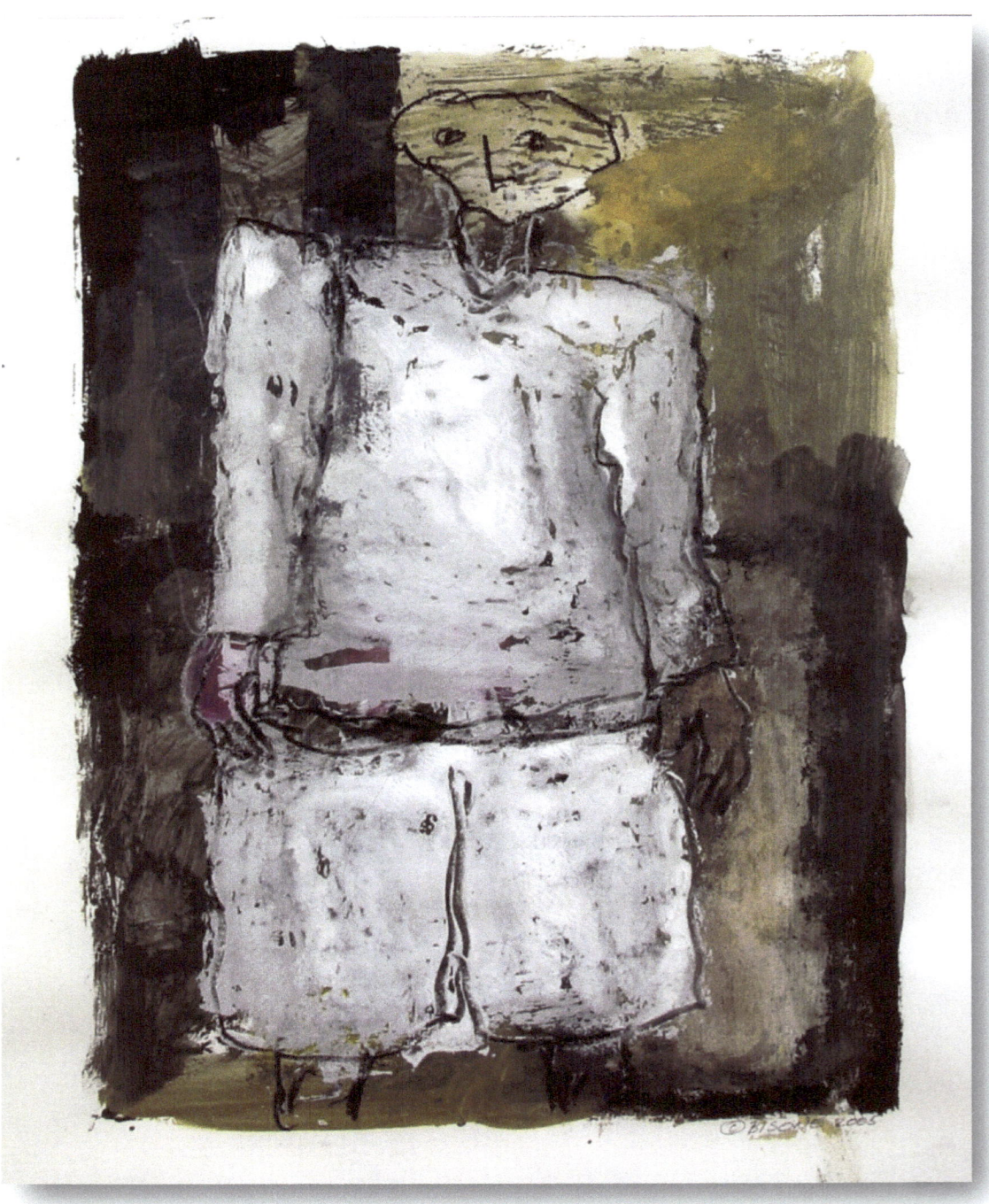

Figure in White, 2005, 24 x 19.25 inches

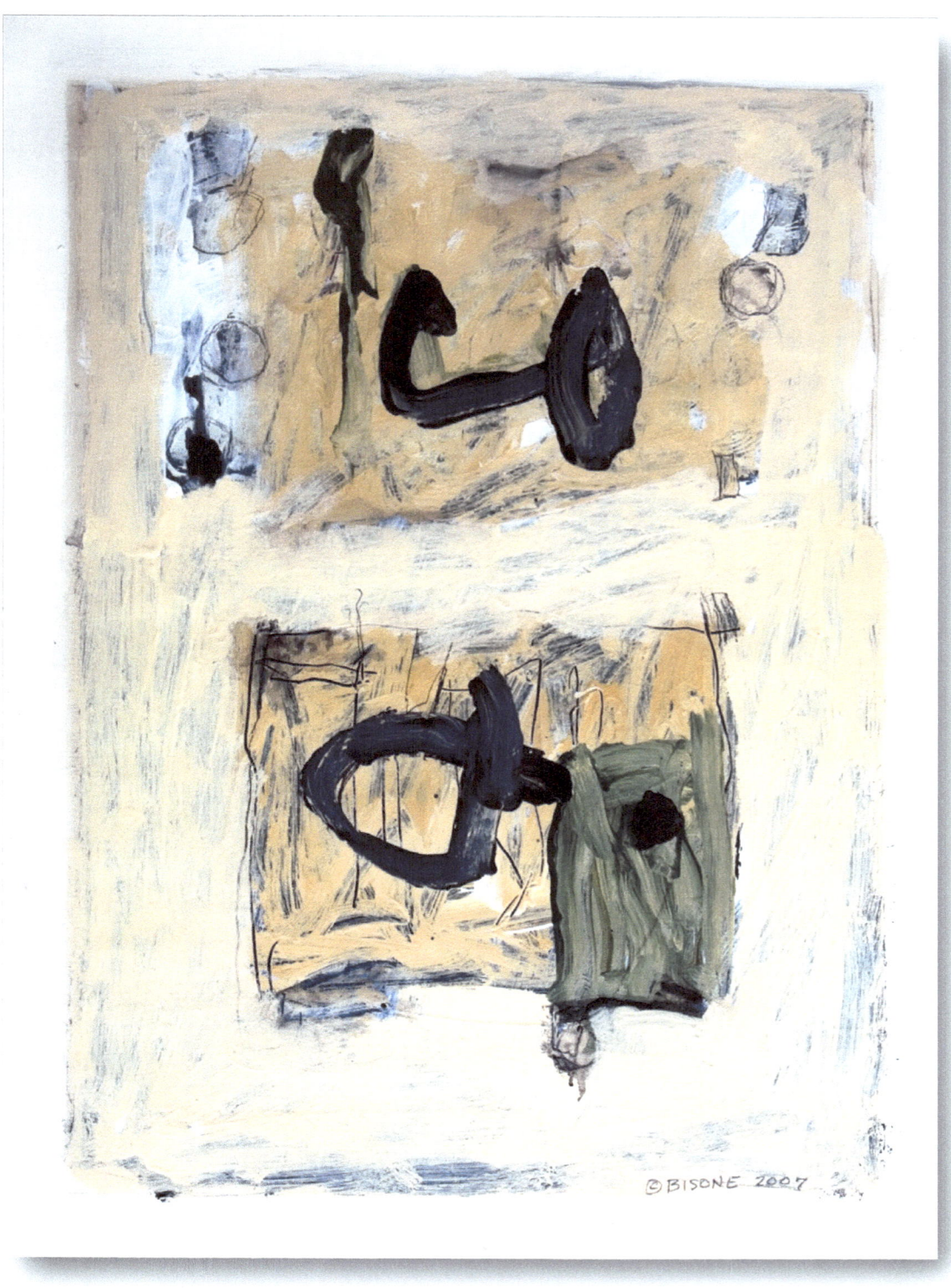

Pale Whispers and Tears Too, 2007, 24 x 18 inches

Edward G. Bisone

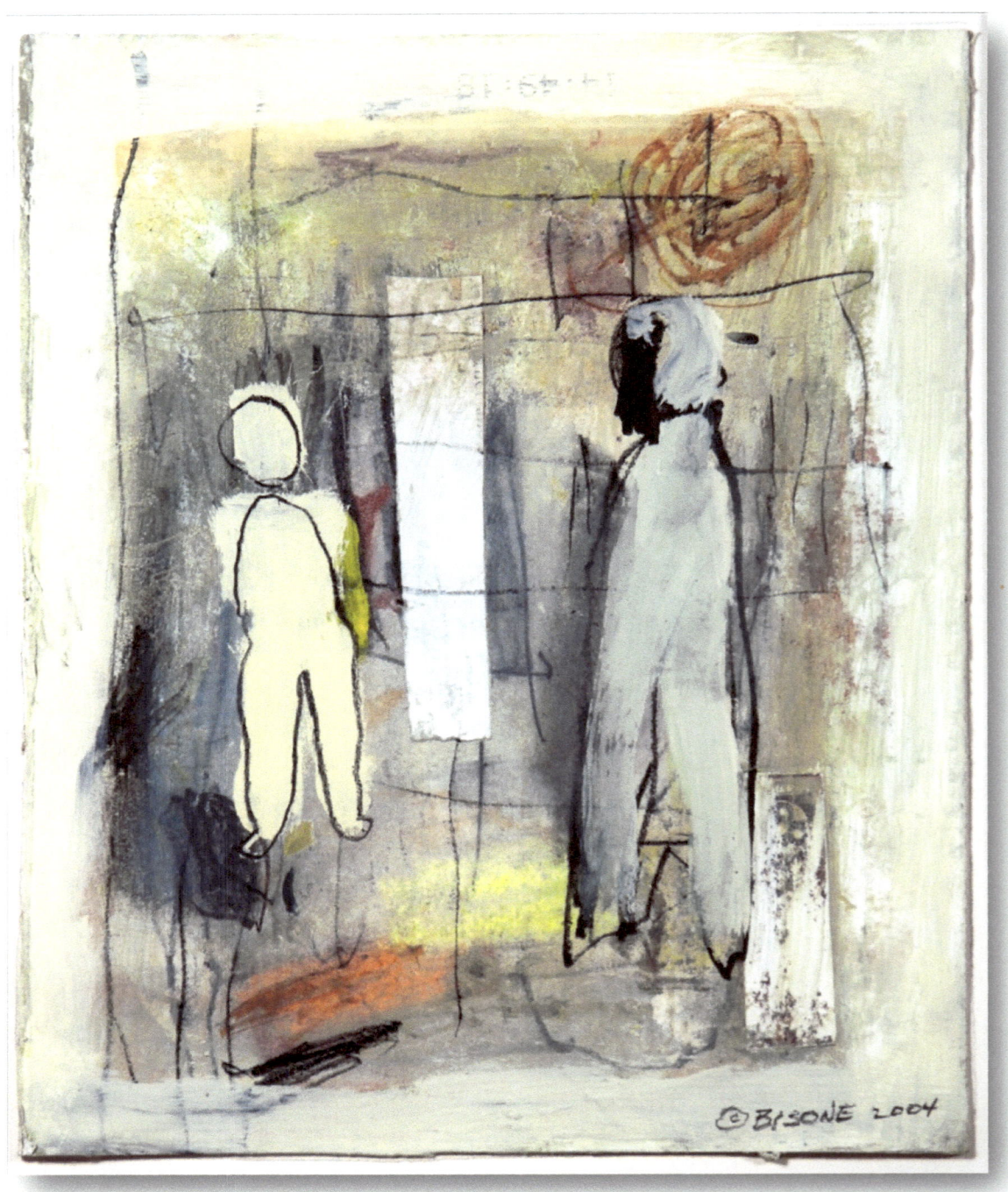

Untitled, 2004, 9.5 x 6.75 inches

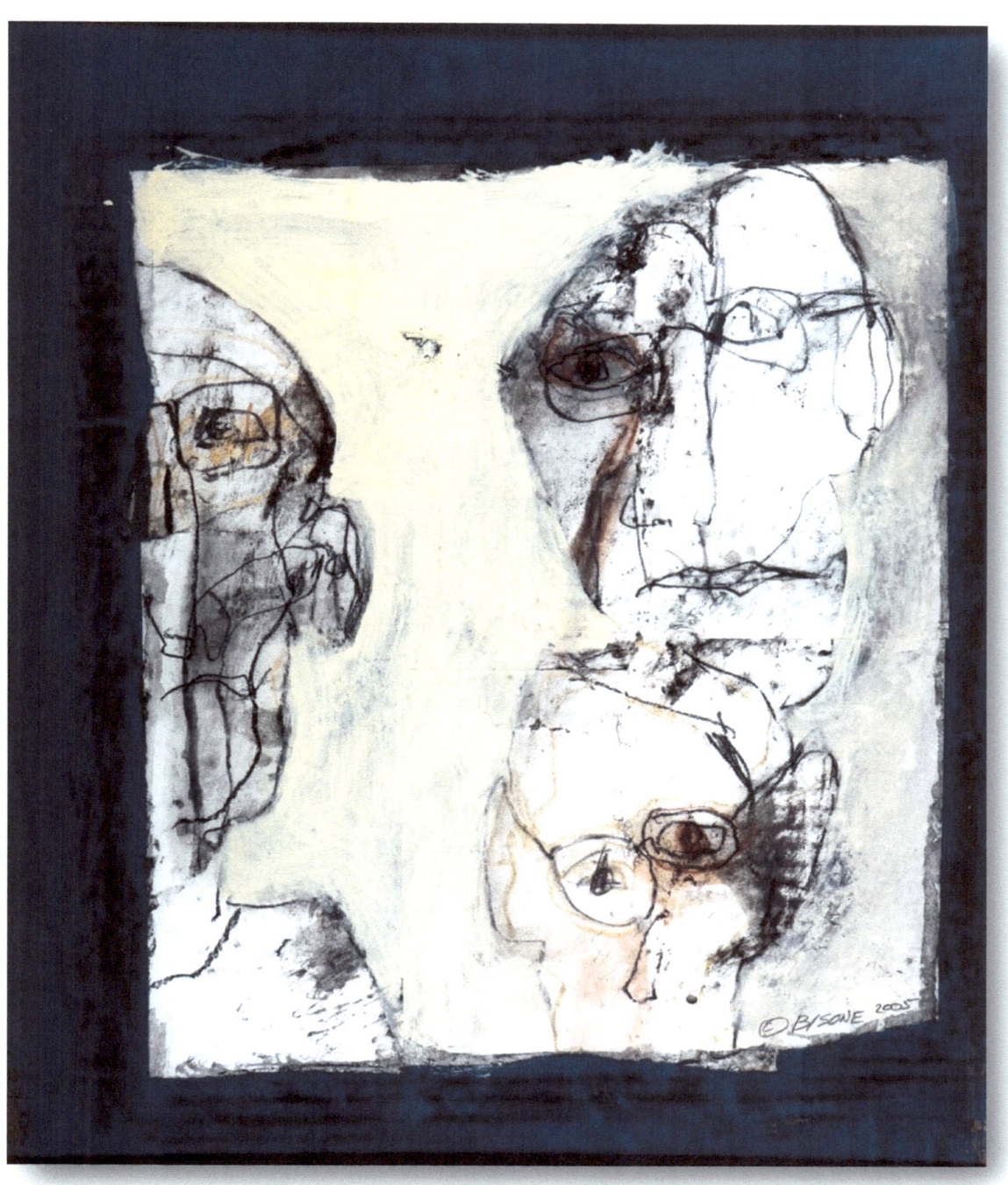

Drawing IIIb, 2005, 16 x 13.5 inches

16. Real People in the Artist's Life

Many of the "people paintings" produced by Bisone can be described as "Everyman", unnamed ordinary people with whom anyone can identify. Those depicted in this section, however, represent real people, friends of the artist. Below is Donald J. Siuta, director of the Art Dialogue Gallery, where Bisone spent much of his free time over the past 30 years.

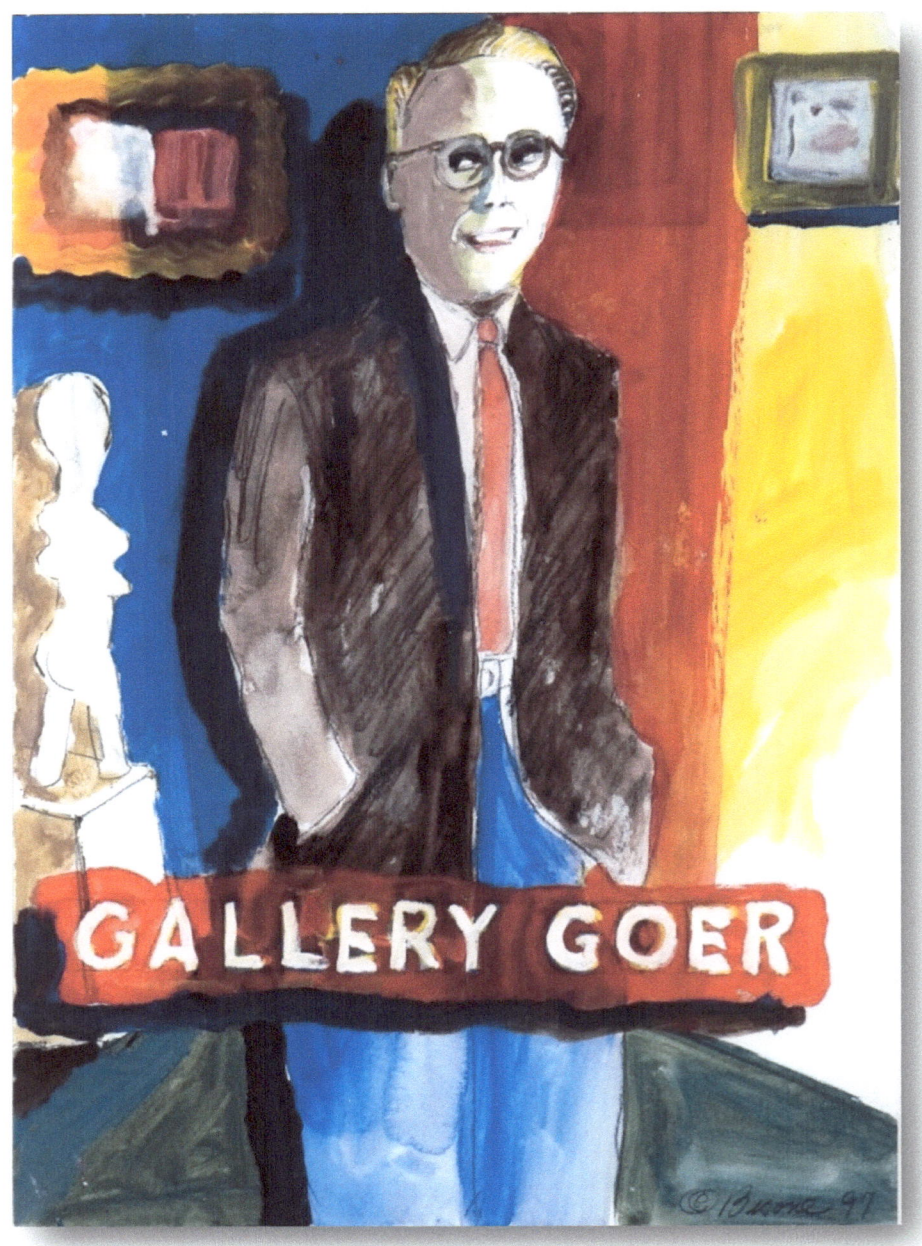

Gallery Goer, 1997, 16 x 11.5 inches

Dr. Jack Cichon is a close friend of Bisone (as well as his dentist).

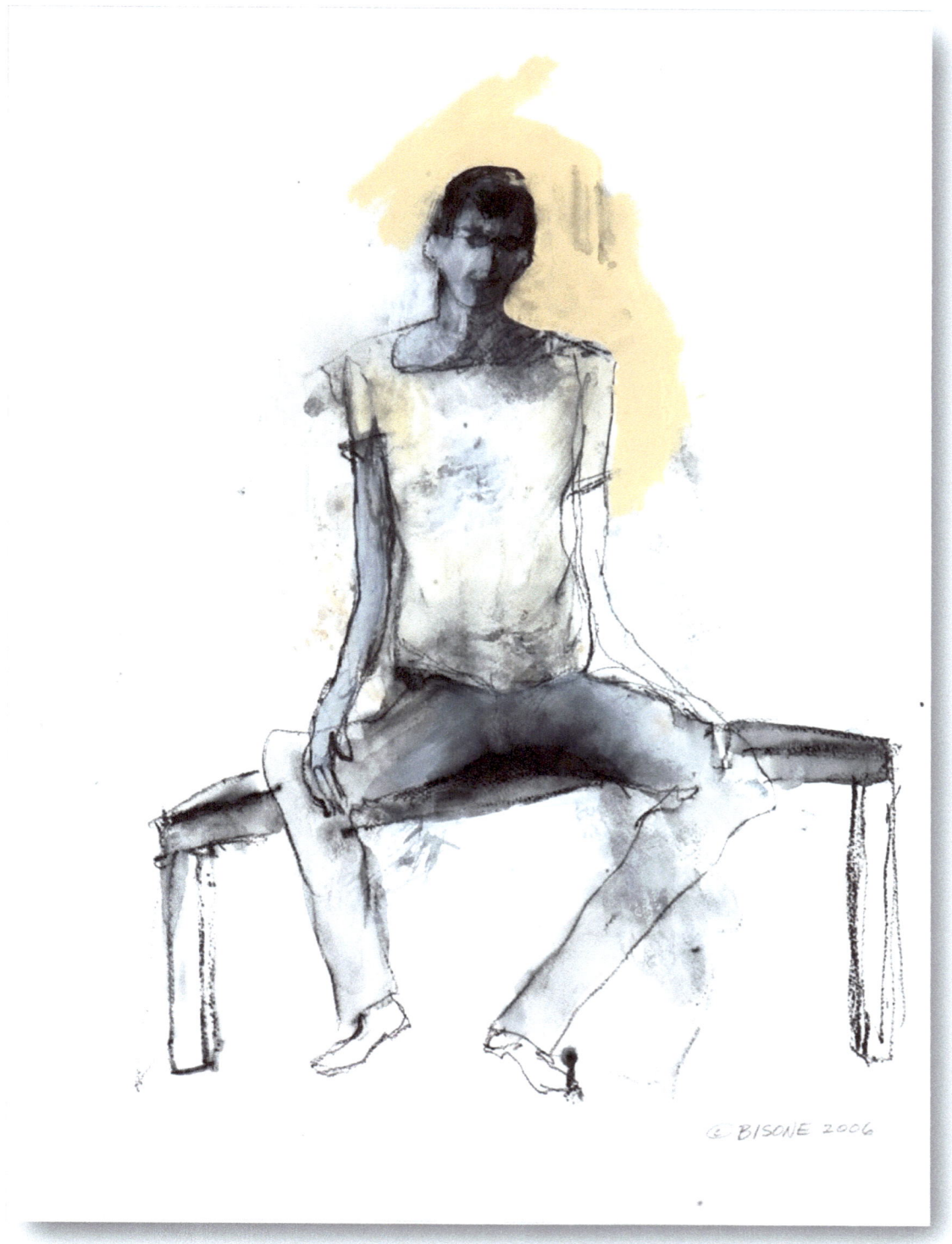

Jack, 2006, 24 x 18 inches

Edward G. Bisone

Bonnie and Donald Scheller met Eddie at Art Dialogue Gallery years ago and became part of his close circle of friends.

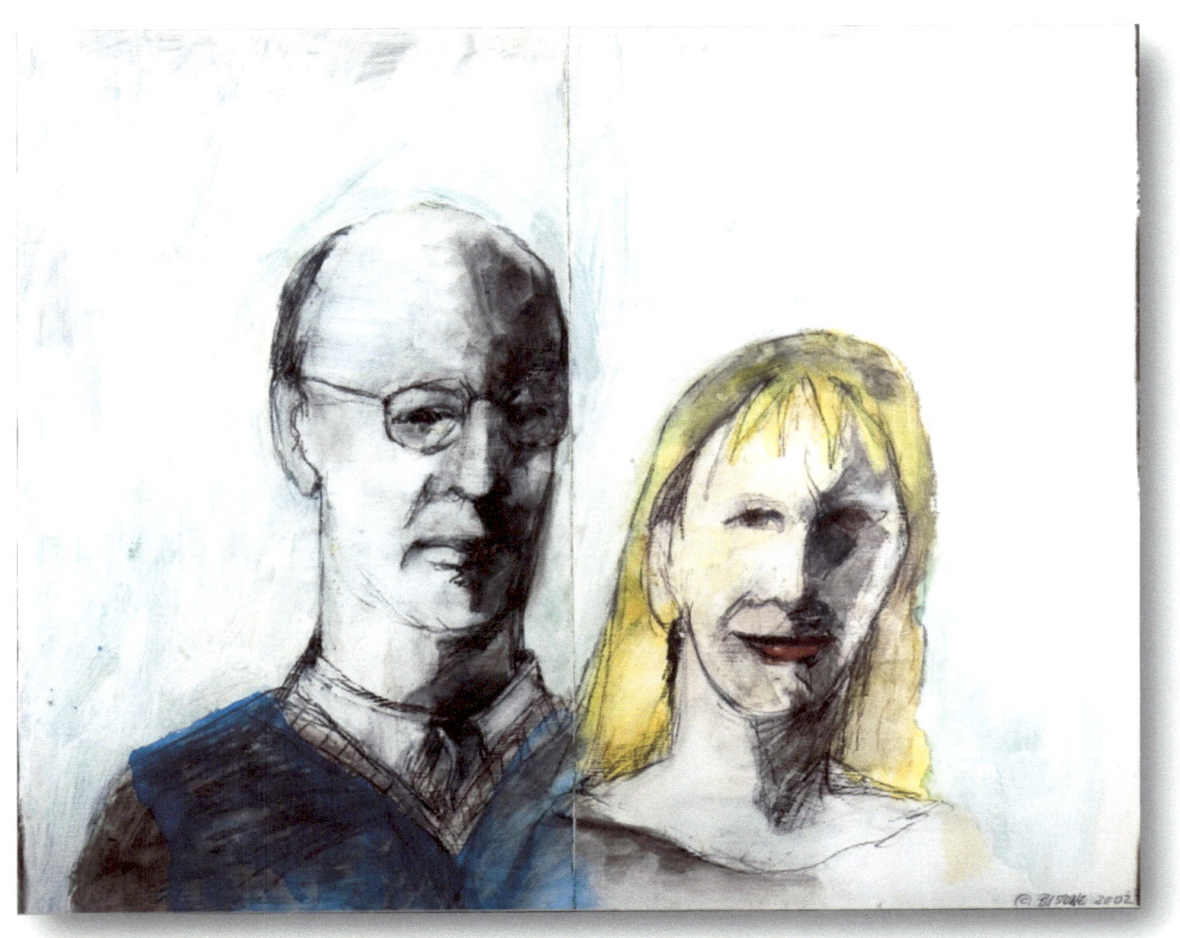

Portrait of Bonnie & Donald, 2002, 15.5 x 19.5 inches

at some point, in art
the presupposed audience
must be made real

Bob Seivert has been a friend of the artist for many years.

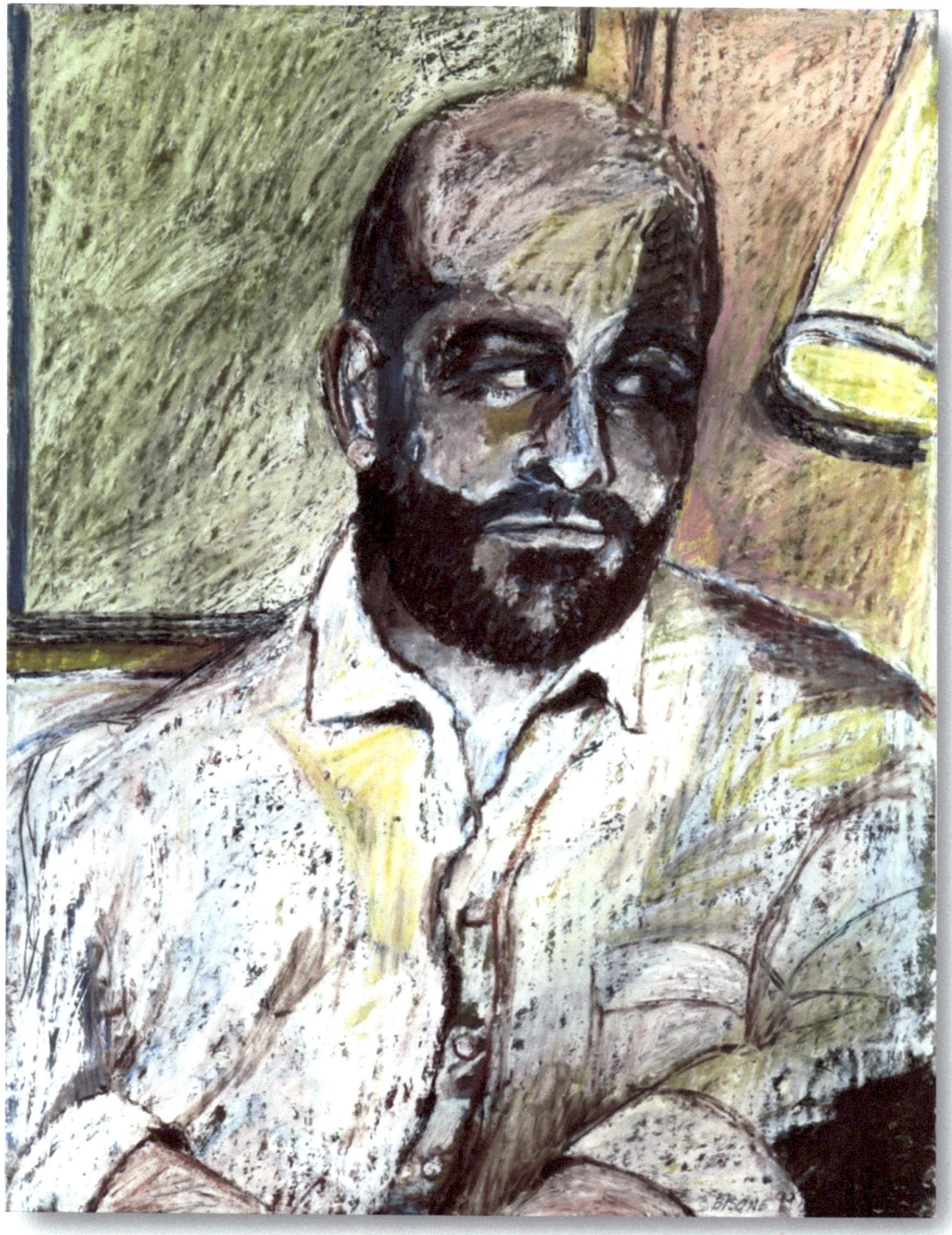

Bob Seivert I, 1999, 24 x 18 inches

While "Baroness" may not be genuine as a title, both the name and the gown befit the real Mrs. Kagelmacher, at least in the eyes of the artist (and this author).

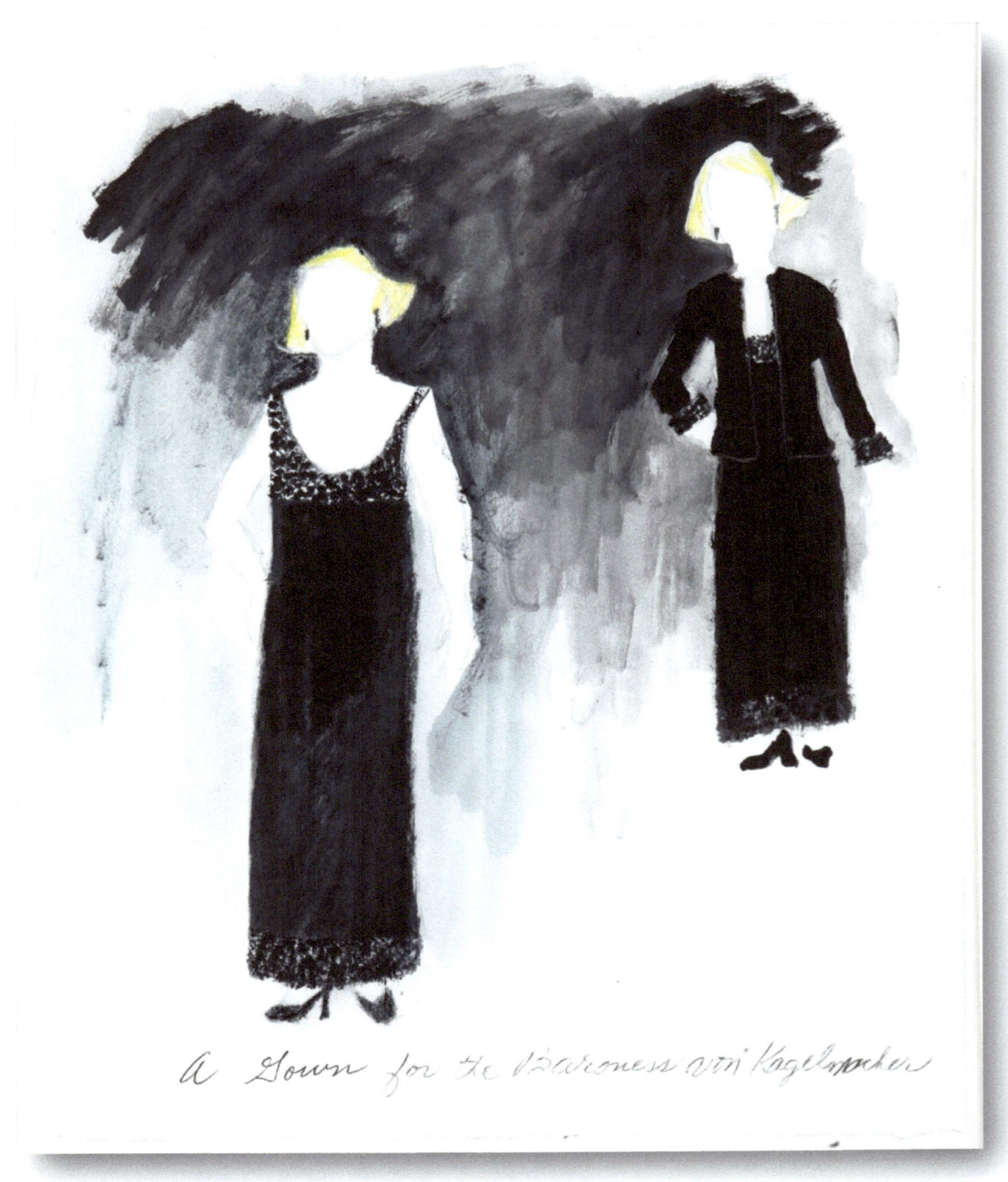

A Gown for the Baroness von Kagelmacher, 2008, 14.5 x 12 inches

17. Recent Works

Bisone makes use of whatever materials are available to him to facilitate his creative expression. The first nine paintings in this section are from the artist's recent "Envelope" series, created as though sending messages to his friends that all is well.

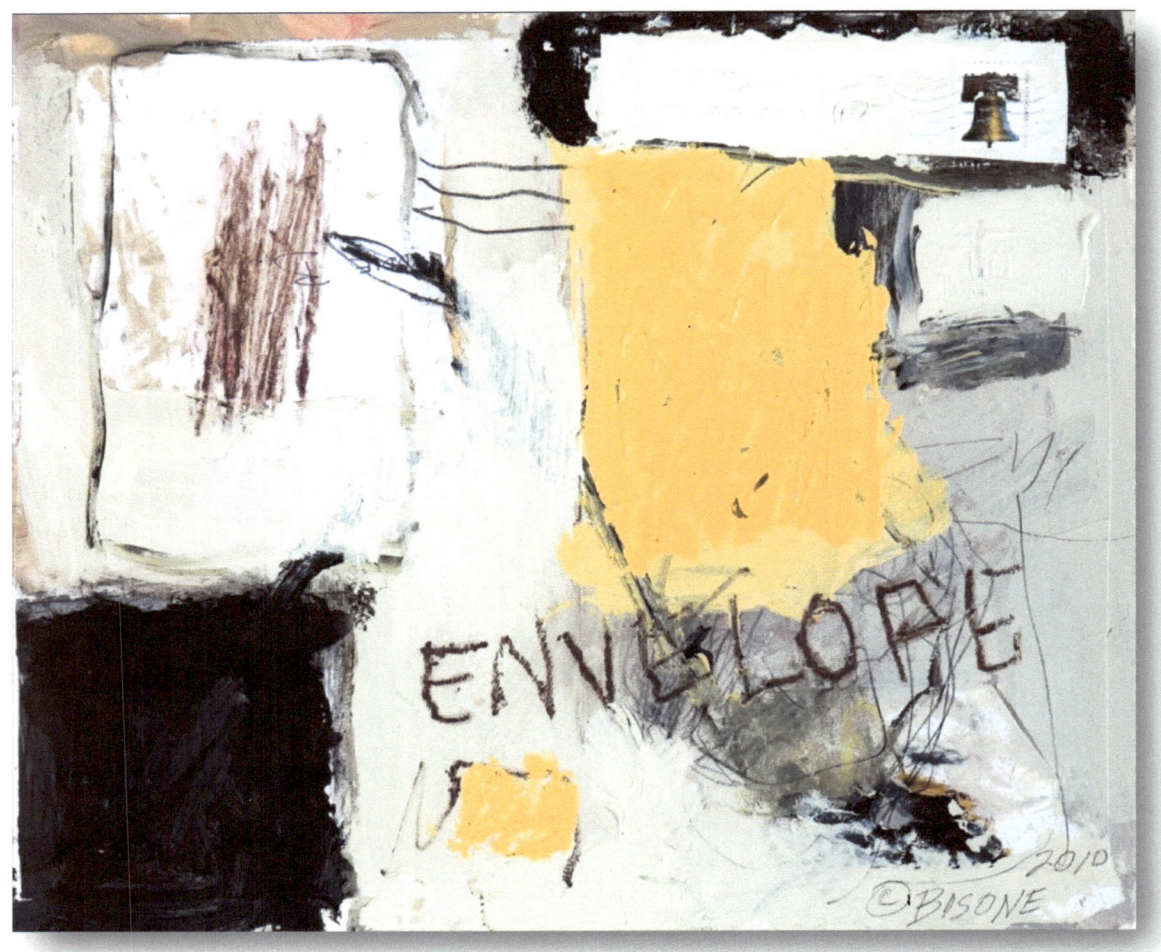

Envelope, 2010, 10 x 12 inches

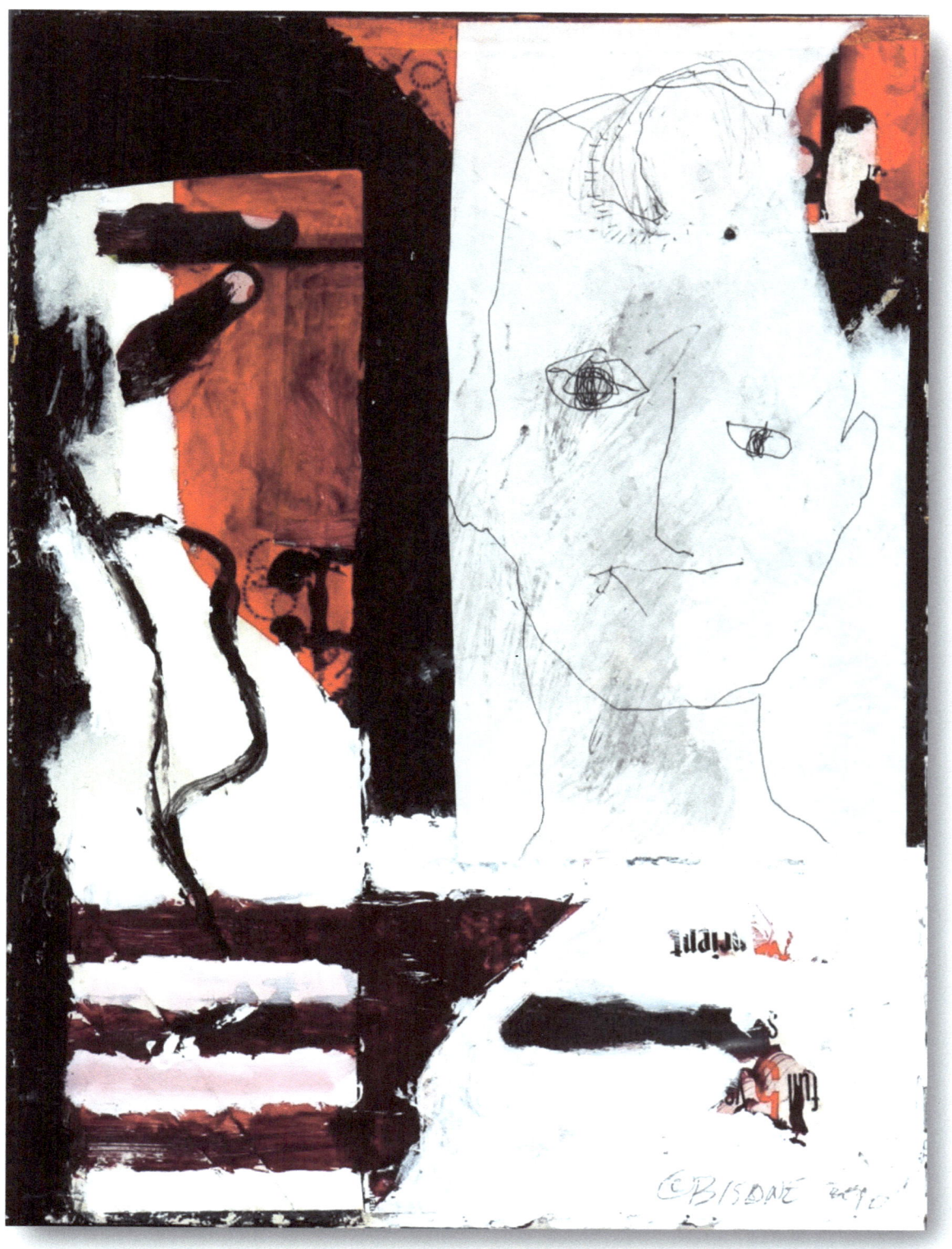

Envelope Series LX, 2010, 12 x 9 inches

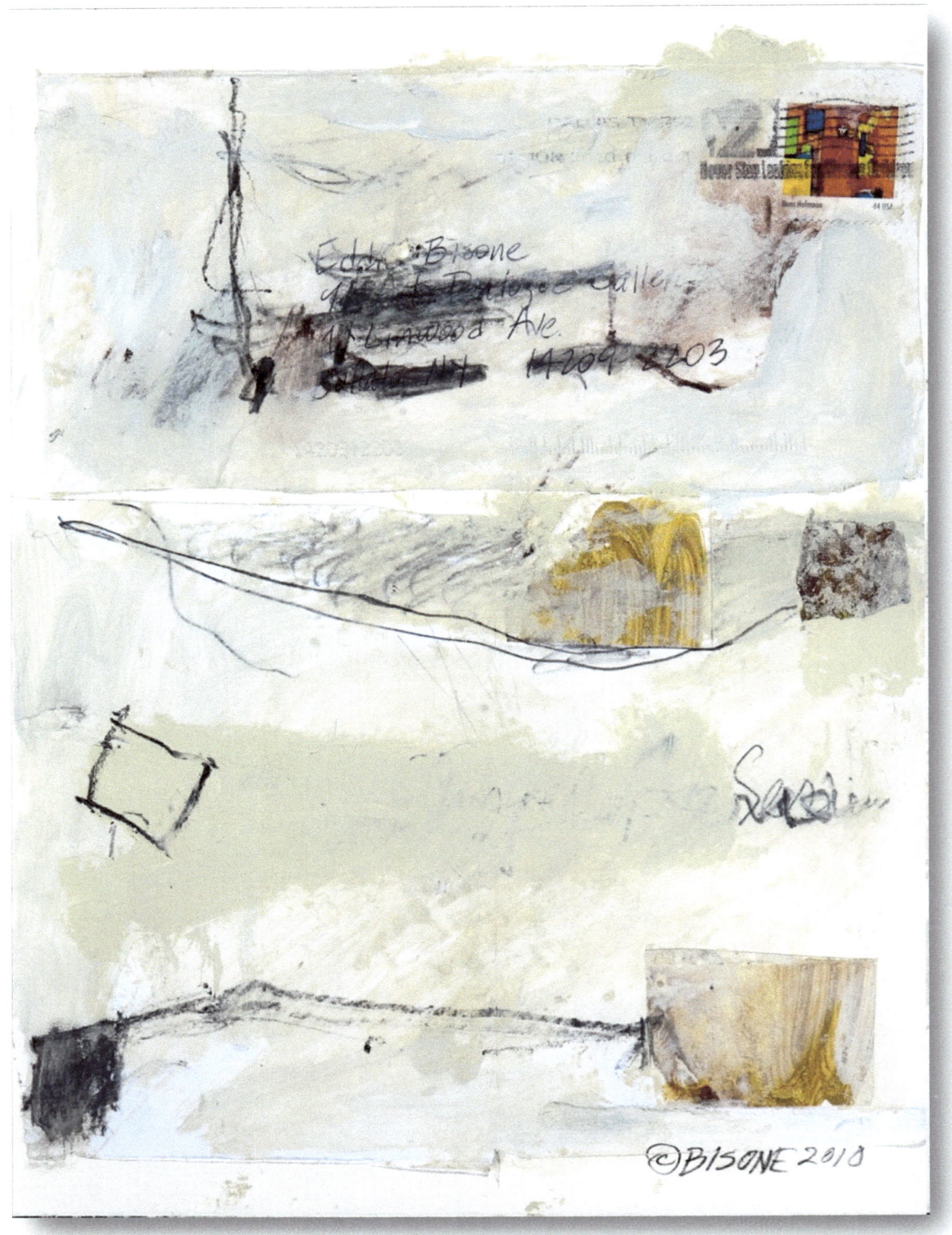

Envelope Series X, 2010, 12 x 9 inches

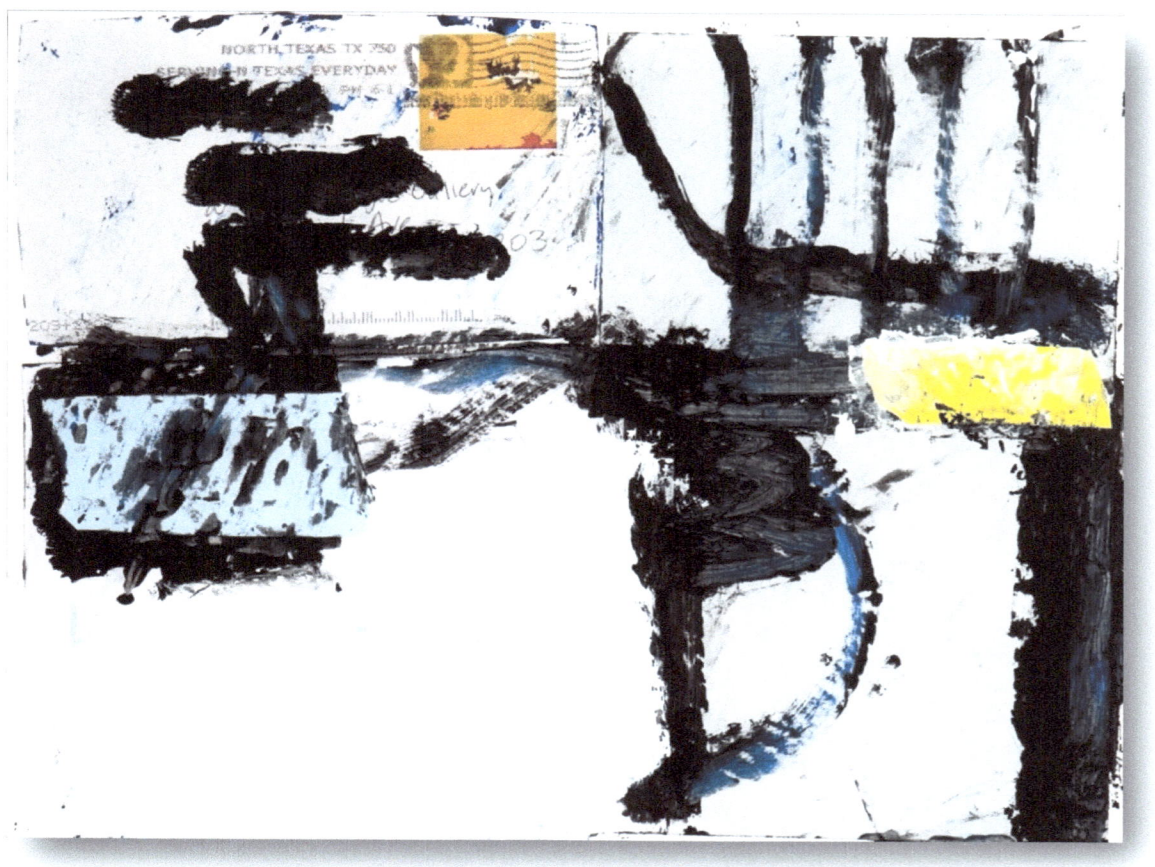

Envelope Series V, 2010, 9 x 12 inches

the fold of paper
        the crease and design of lines:
                beginning idea

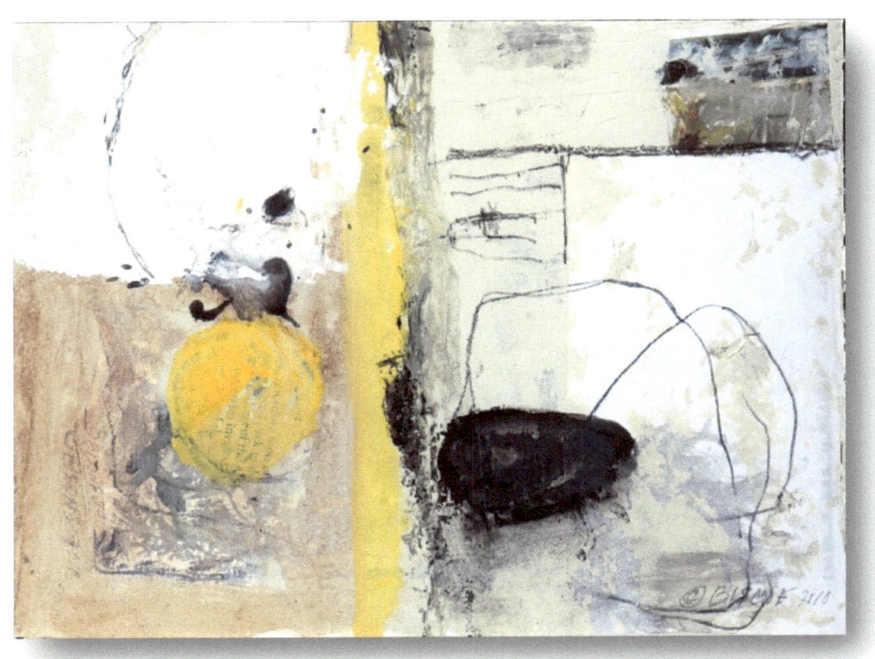

Envelope Series XI, 2010, 9 x 12 inches

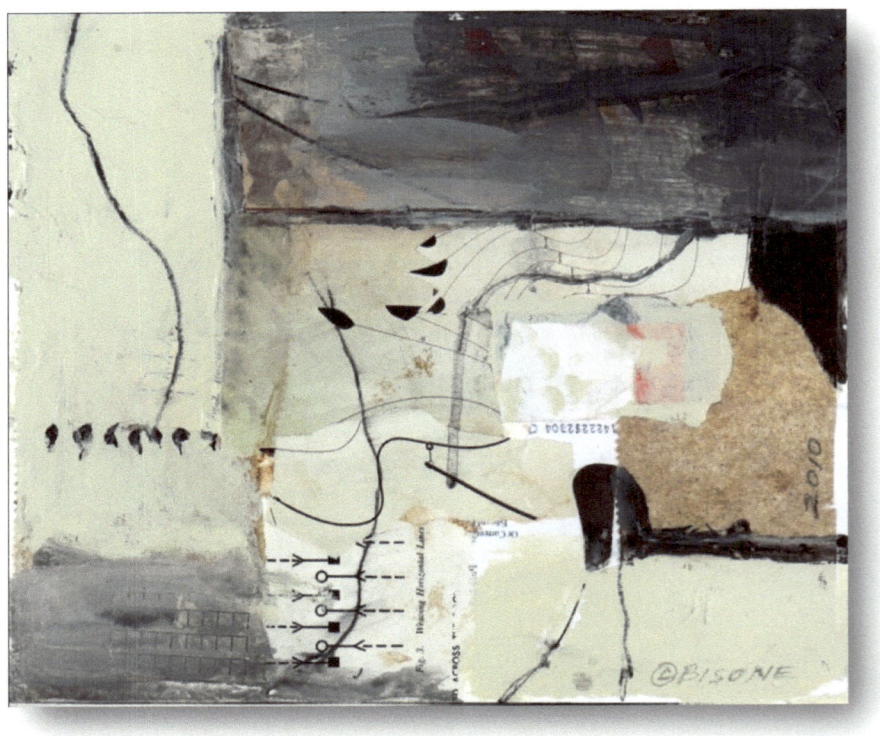

Envelope Series XV, 2010, 10 x 12 inches

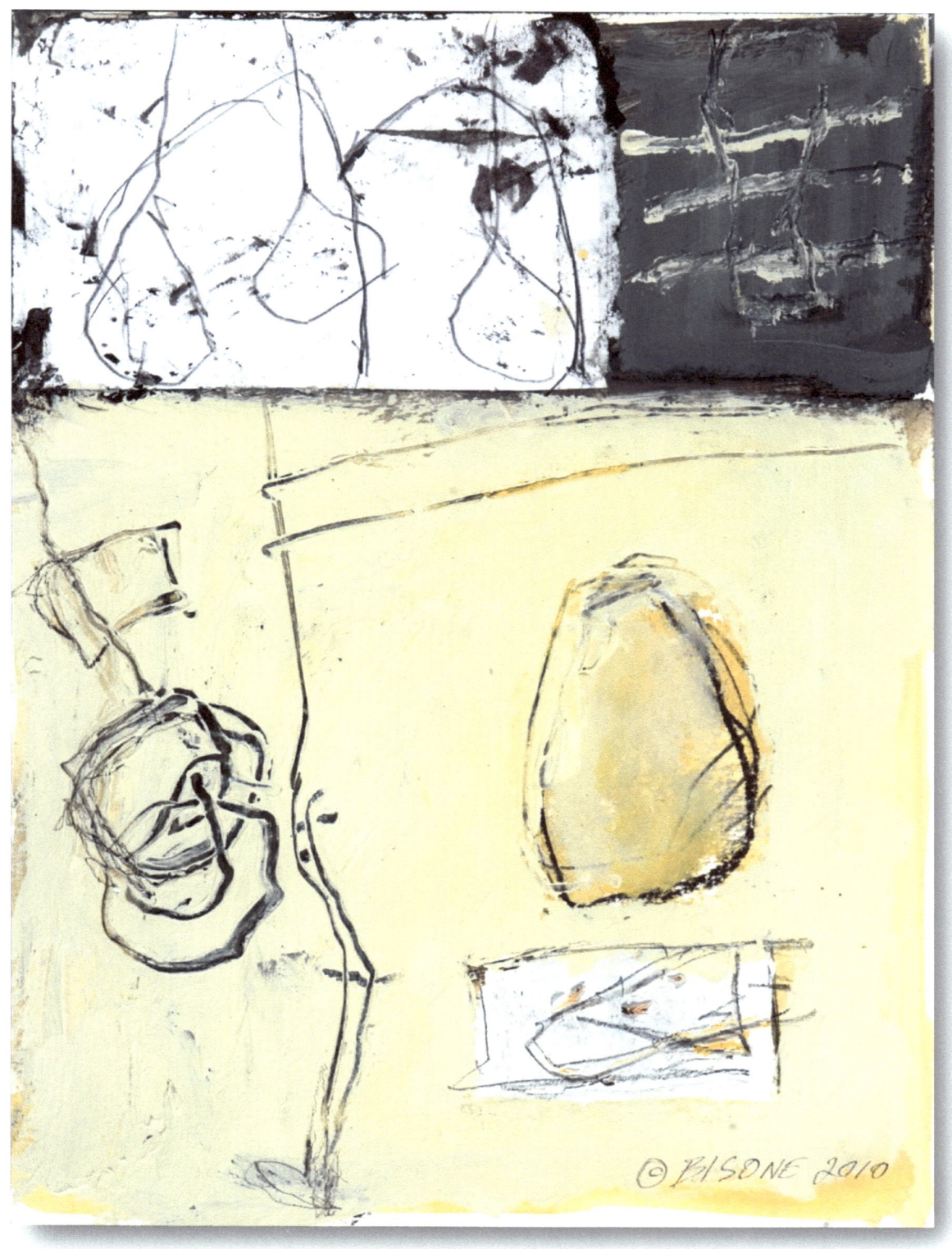

Envelope Series XX, 2010, 12 x 9 inches

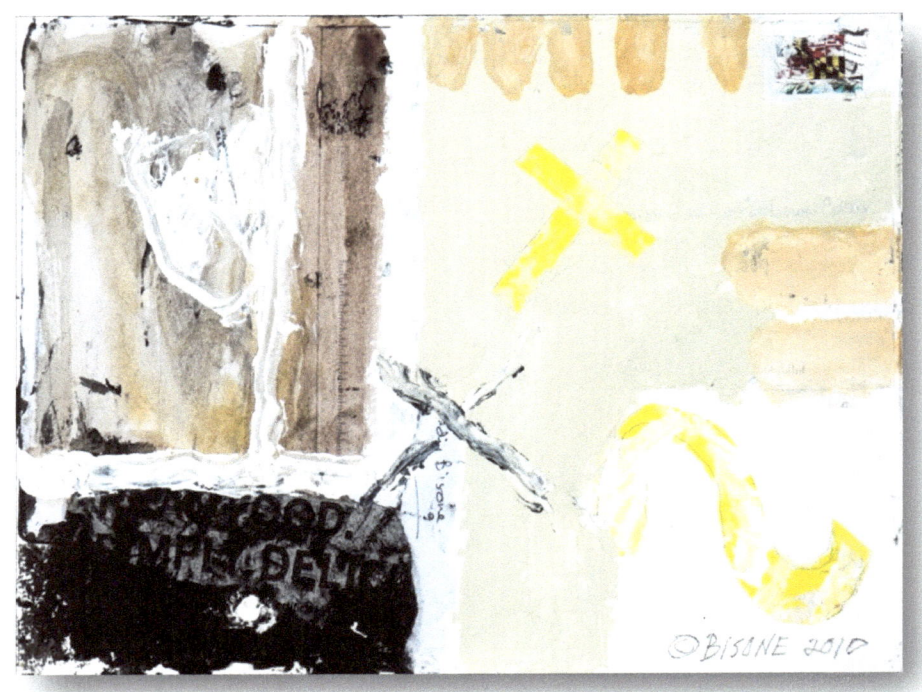

Envelope Series XXI, 2010, 9 x 12 inches

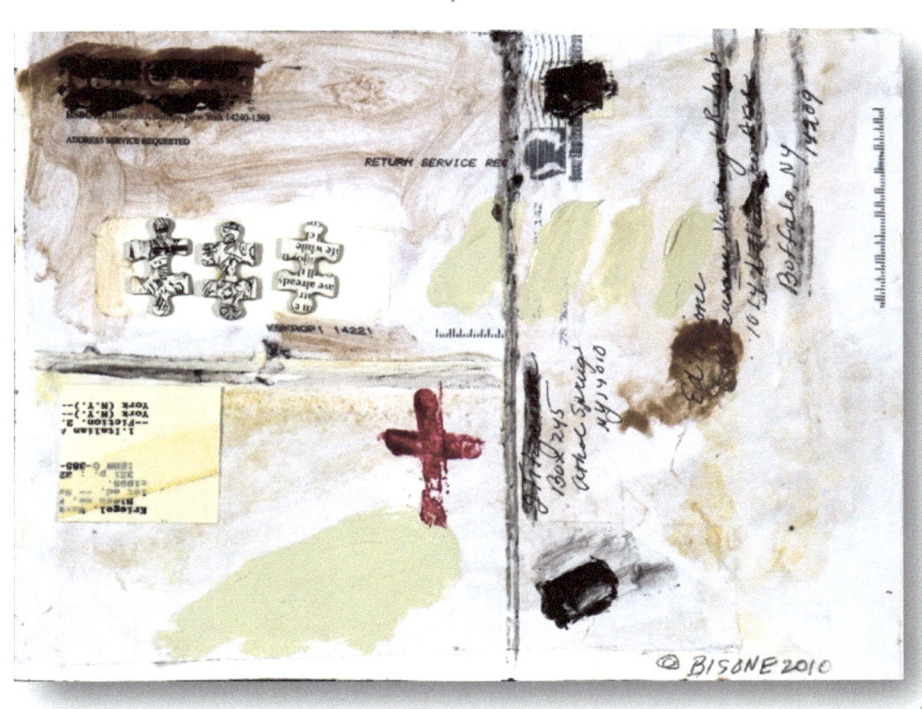

Envelope Series XXX, 2010, 9 x 12 inches

Birds have been an on again/off again subject of interest for Bisone over the years. Whether that interest is anything more than a desire to capture the form and see how it appears among the abstract shapes and colors from the artist's palette is doubtful, at least at a conscious level. For this viewer, however, Bisone's birds seem to be reaching; while they'll never have words to say what for, they appear to sense something greater than themselves.

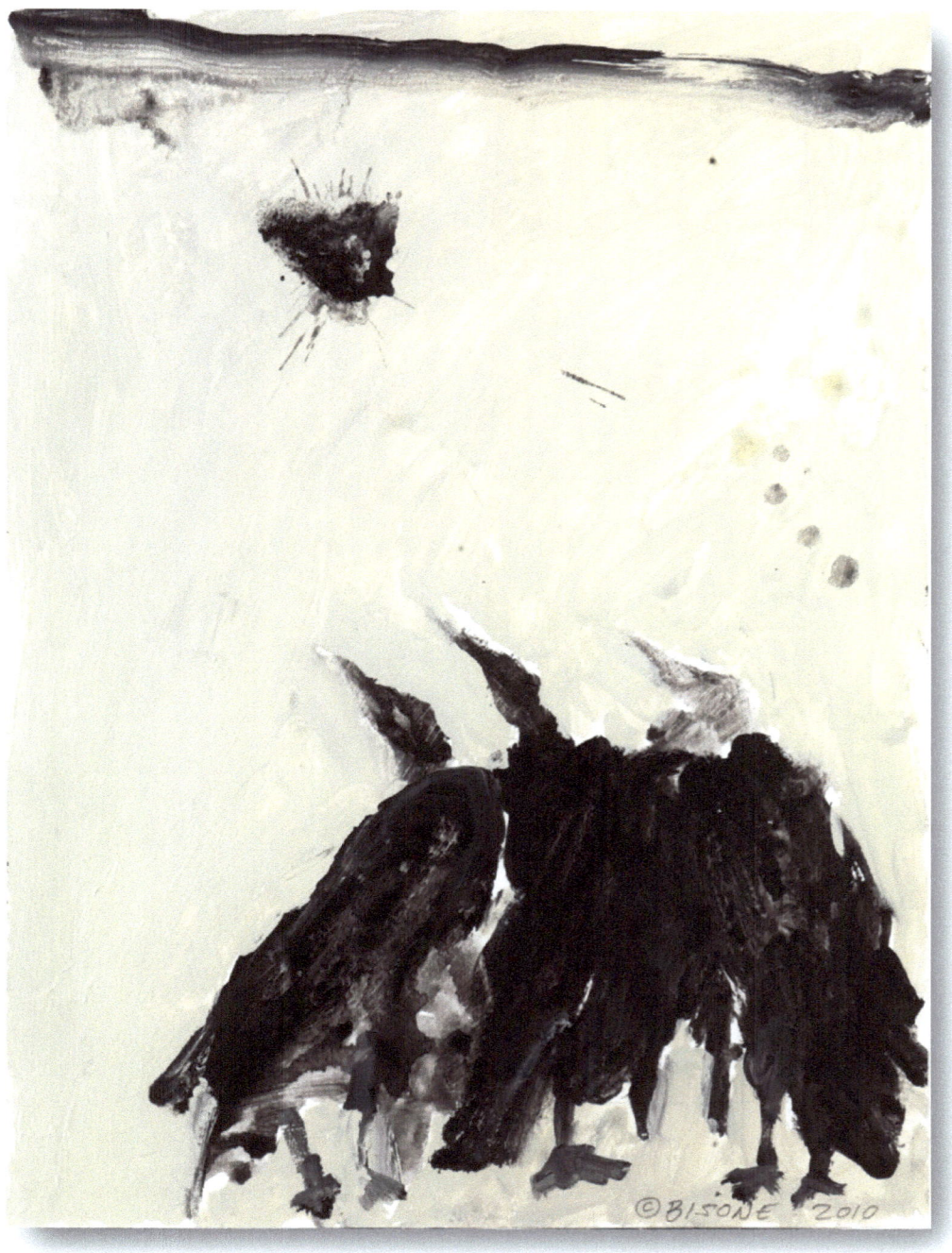

Three Curious Birds I, 2010, 16 x 12 inches

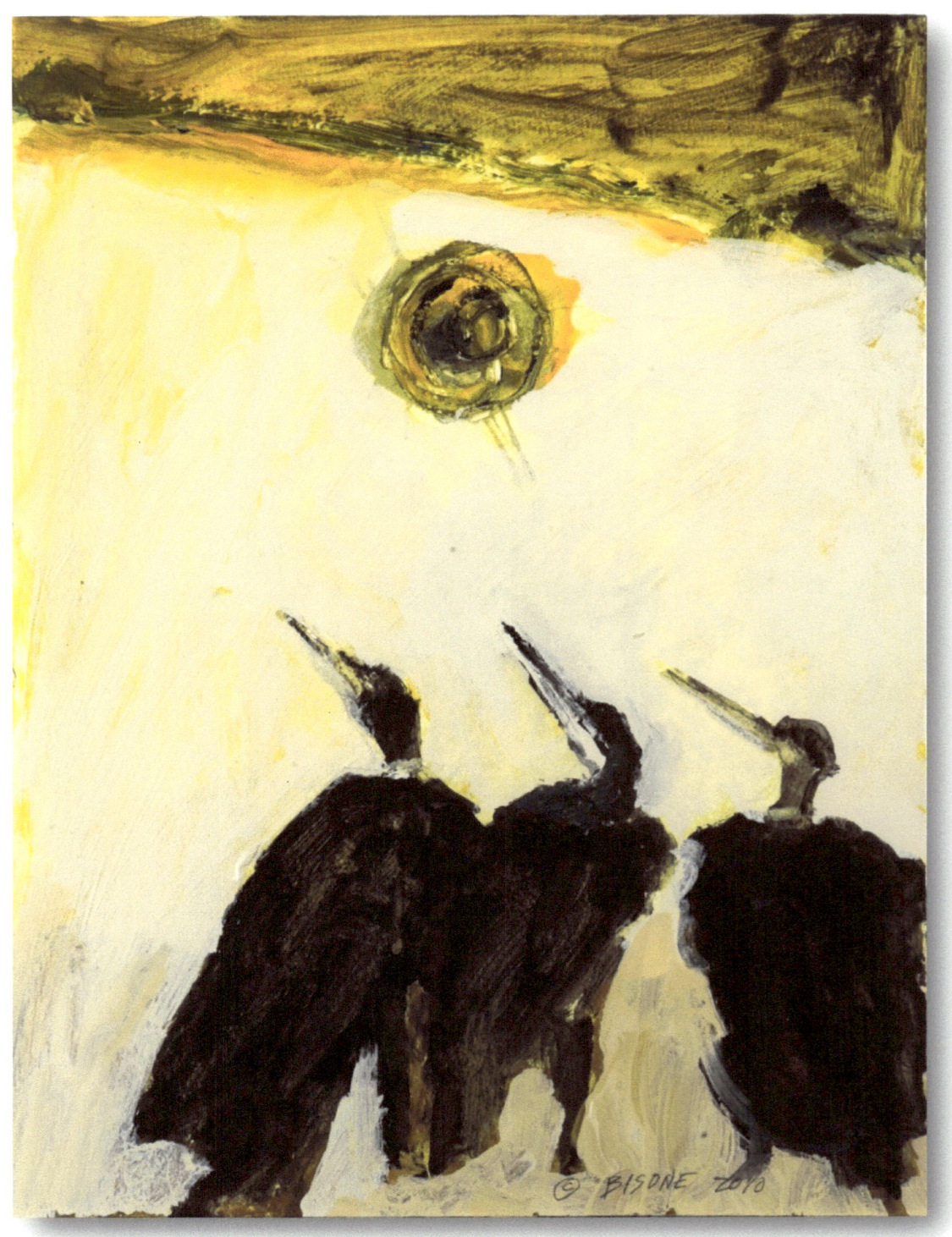

Three Curious Birds II, 2010, 16 x 12 inches

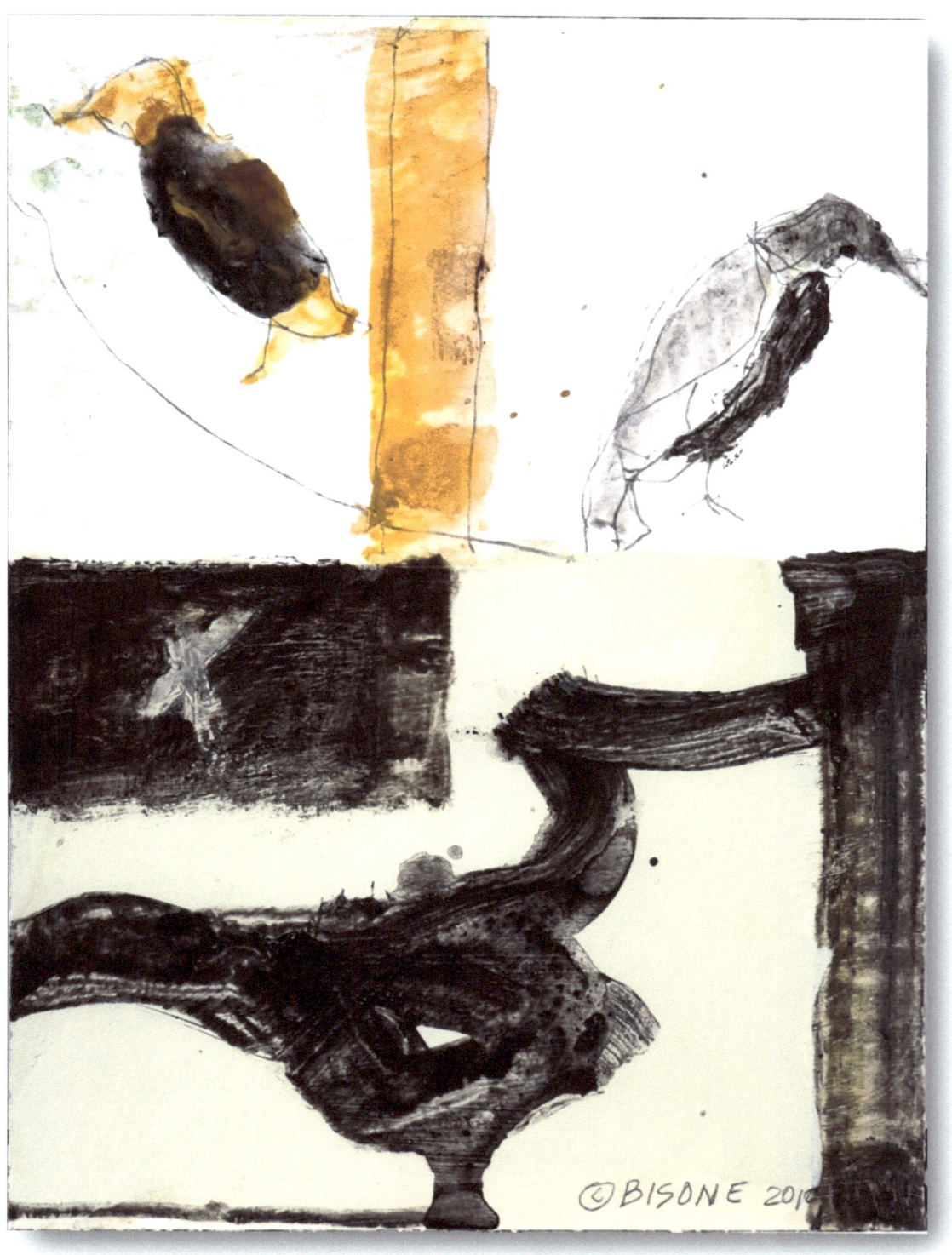

Two Birds II, 2010, 12 x 9 inches

Alphabetical Listing of Works

Chronological Listing of Works

Edward G. Bisone